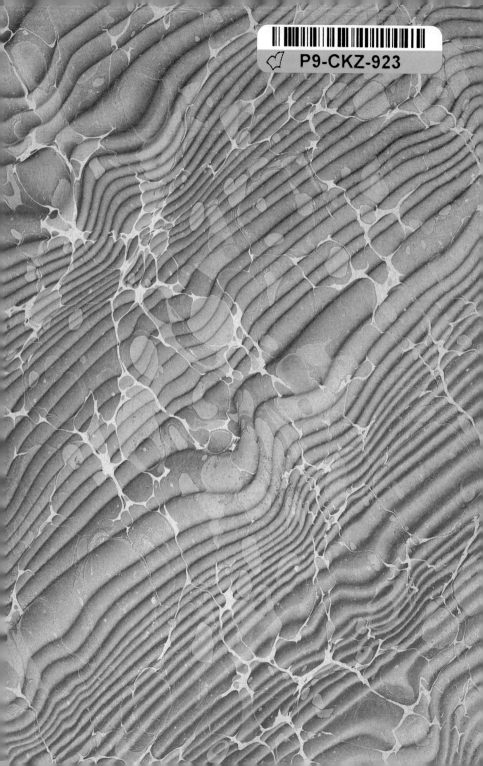

HISTORY

OF

ENGLISH LITERATURE

Eng. by H.B. Hall's Sons, New York.

Robert Burns

HISTORY

OF

ENGLISH LITERATURE

BY

H. A. TAINE, D.C.L.

TRANSLATED FROM THE FRENCH BY H. VAN LAUN

ONE OF THE MASTERS AT THE EDINBURGH ACADEMY

WITH PREFACE

BY

R. H. STODDARD

VOL. III.

NEW YORK

WORTHINGTON CO., 747 BROADWAY

1889

CONTENTS.

BOOK III.—THE CLASSIC AGE.

CHAPTER II.

Dryden.

CHAPTER III.

The Revolution.

CONTENTS.

CHAPTER V.

Swift.

CHAPTER VI.

The Novelists.

CHAPTER VII.

The Poets.

BOOK IV.—MODERN LIFE.

CHAPTER I.

Ideas and Productions.

HISTORY OF ENGLISH LITERATURE.

BOOK III.

THE CLASSIC AGE.

CHAPTER II.

Dryden.

COMEDY has led us a long way; we must return on our steps and consider other kind of writings. A higher spirit moves in the midst of the great current. In the history of this talent we shall find the history of the English classical spirit, its structure, its gaps, and its powers, its formation and its development.

I.

The subject of the following lines is a young man, Lord Hastings, who died of smallpox at the age of nineteen:

> "His body was an orb, his sublime soul
>   Did move on virtue's and on learning's pole;
>   . . . Come, learned Ptolemy, and trial make
>   If thou this hero's altitude canst take.
>   . . . Blisters with pride swell'd, which through's flesh did
>   sprout
>   Like rose-buds, stuck i' the lily skin about.

Each little pimple had a tear in it,
To wail the fault its rising did commit. . . .
Or were these gems sent to adorn his skin,
The cabinet of a richer soul within?
No comet need foretel his change drew on
Whose corpse might seem a constellation." [1]

With such a pretty morsel, Dryden, the greatest poet of the classical age, makes his *début*.

Such enormities indicate the close of a literary age. Excess of folly in poetry, as excess of injustice in political matters, lead up to and foretell revolutions. The Renaissance, unchecked and original, abandoned the minds of men to the excitement and caprice of imagination, the eccentricities, curiosities, outbreaks of a fancy which only cares to content itself, breaks out into singularities, has need of novelties, and loves audacity and extravagance, as reason loves justice and truth. After the extinction of genius folly remained; after the removal of inspiration nothing was left but absurdity. Formerly disorder and internal enthusiasm produced and excused *concetti* and wild flights; thenceforth men threw them out in cold blood, by calculation and without excuse. Formerly they expressed the state of the mind, now they belie it. So are literary revolutions accomplished. The form, no longer original or spontaneous, but imitated and passed from hand to hand, outlives the old spirit which had created it, and is in opposition to the new spirit which destroys it. This preliminary strife and progressive transformation make up the life of Dryden, and account for his impotence and his failures, his talent and his success.

[1] Dryden's *Works*, ed. Sir Walter Scott, 2d ed., 18 vols., 1821, xi. 94.

II.

Dryden's beginnings are in striking contrast with those of the poets of the Renaissance, actors, vagabonds, soldiers, who were tossed about from the first in all the contrasts and miseries of active life. He was born in 1631, of a good family; his grandfather and uncle were baronets; Sir Gilbert Pickering, his first cousin, was created a baronet by Charles the First, was a member of Parliament, chamberlain to the Protector, and one of his Peers. Dryden was brought up in an excellent school, under Dr. Busby, then in high repute; after which he passed four years at Cambridge. Having inherited by his father's death a small estate, he used his liberty and fortune only to remain in his studious life, and continued in seclusion at the University for three years more. These are the regular habits of an honourable and well-to-do family, the discipline of a connected and solid education, the taste for classical and complete studies. Such circumstances announce and prepare, not an artist, but a man of letters.

I find the same inclination and the same signs in the remainder of his life, private or public. He regularly spends his mornings in writing or reading, then dines with his family. His reading was that of a man of culture and a critical mind, who does not think of amusing or exciting himself, but who learns and judges. Virgil, Ovid, Horace, Juvenal, and Persius were his favourite authors; he translated several; their names were always on his pen; he discusses their opinions and their merits, feeding himself on that reasoning which oratorical customs had imprinted on all the works of the Roman mind. He is familiar with the new French literature, the heir of the Latin, with Corneille and Racine, Boileau, Rapin, and Bossu;[1] he reasons with them, often in their spirit, writes thoughtfully, seldom fails to arrange some good theory to justify each of his new works. He knew very well the literature of his own country, though sometimes not very accurately, gave to authors their due rank, classified the different kinds of writing, went back as far as old Chaucer, whom he translated and put into a modern dress. His mind thus filled, he would go in the afternoon to Will's coffee-house, the great literary rendezvous : young poets, students fresh from the University, literary dilettante crowded round his chair, carefully placed in summer on the balcony, in winter by the fire, thinking themselves fortunate to listen to him, or to extract a pinch of snuff respectfully from his learned snuff-box. For indeed he was the monarch of taste and the umpire of letters ; he criticised novelties—Racine's last tragedy, Blackmore's heavy epic, Swift's first poems ; slightly vain, praising his own writings, to the extent of saying that " no one had ever composed or will ever compose a finer ode " than his own Alexander's Feast ; but full of information, fond of that interchange of ideas which discussion never fails to produce, capable of enduring contradiction, and admitting his adversary to be in the right. These manners show that literature had become a matter of study rather than of inspiration, an employment for taste rather than for enthusiasm, a source of amusement rather than of emotion.

---

[1] Rapin (1621–1687), a French Jesuit, a modern Latin poet and literary critic. Bossu, or properly Lebossu (1631–1680), wrote a *Traité du Poème épique*, which had a great success in its day. Both critics are now completely forgotten.—TR.

His audience, his friendships, his actions, his quarrels, had the same tendency. He lived amongst great men and courtiers, in a society of artificial manners and measured language. , He had married the daughter of Thomas, Earl of Berkshire; he was historiographer-royal and poet-laureate. He often saw the king and the princes. He dedicated each of his works to some lord, in a laudatory, flunkeyish preface, bearing witness to his intimate acquaintance with the great. He received a purse of gold for each dedication, went to return thanks; introduces some of these Lords under pseudonyms in his *Essay on the Dramatic Art*; wrote introductions for the works of others, called them Mæcenas, Tibullus, or Pollio; discussed with them literary works and opinions. The re-establishment of the court had brought back the art of conversation, vanity, the necessity for appearing to be a man of letters and of possessing good taste, all the company-manners which are the source of classical literature, and which teach men the art of speaking well.[1] On the other hand, literature, brought under the influence of society, entered into society's interests, and first of all in petty private quarrels. Whilst men of letters learned etiquette, courtiers learned how to write. They soon became jumbled together, and naturally fell to blows. The Duke of Buckingham wrote a parody on Dryden, *The Rehearsal*, and took infinite pains to teach the chief actor Dryden's tone and gestures. Later, Rochester took up the cudgels against the poet, supported a cabal in favour of Settle against him, and hired a band

---

[1] In his *Defence of the Epilogue of the Second Part of the Conquest of Granada*, iv. 226, Dryden says : "Now, if they ask me, whence it is that our conversation is so much refined? I must freely, and without flattery, ascribe it to the court."

of ruffians to cudgel him. Besides this, Dryden had quarrels with Shadwell and a crowd of others, and finally with Blackmore and Jeremy Collier. To crown all, he entered into the strife of political parties and religious sects, fought for the Tories and Anglicans, then for the Roman Catholics; wrote *The Medal*, *Absalom and Achitophel* against the Whigs : *Religio Laici* against Dissenters and Papists ; then *The Hind and Panther* for James II., with the logic of controversy and the bitterness of party. It is a long way from this combative and argumentative existence to the reveries and seclusion of the true poet. Such circumstances teach the art of writing clearly and soundly, methodical and connected discussion, strong and exact style, banter and refutation, eloquence and satire; these gifts are necessary to make a man of letters heard or believed, and the mind enters compulsorily upon a track when it is the only one that can conduct it to its goal. Dryden entered upon it spontaneously. In his second production,[1] the abundance of well-ordered ideas, the energy and oratorical harmony, the simplicity, the gravity, the heroic and Roman spirit, announce a classic genius, the relative not of Shakspeare, but of Corneille, capable not of dramas, but of discussions.

III.

And yet, at first, he devoted himself to the drama : he wrote twenty-seven pieces, and signed an agreement with the actors of the King's Theatre to supply them with three every year. The theatre, forbidden under the Commonwealth, had just re-opened with extraordinary magnificence and success. The rich scenes made moveable, the women's parts no longer played by

[1] *Heroic stanzas to the memory of Oliver Cromwell.*

boys, but by women, the novel and splendid wax-lights, the machinery, the recent popularity of actors who had become heroes of fashion, the scandalous importance of the actresses, who were mistresses of the aristocracy and of the king, the example of the court and the imitation of France, drew spectators in crowds. The thirst for pleasure, long repressed, knew no bounds. Men indemnified themselves for the long abstinence imposed by fanatical Puritans; eyes and ear, disgusted with gloomy faces, nasal pronunciation, official ejaculations on sin and damnation, satiated themselves with sweet singing, sparkling dress, the seduction of voluptuous dances. They wished to enjoy life, and that in a new fashion; for a new world, that of the courtiers and the idle, had been formed. The abolition of feudal tenures, the vast increase of commerce and wealth, the concourse of landed proprietors, who let their lands and came to London to enjoy the pleasures of the town and to court the favours of the king, had installed on the summit of society, in England as well as in France, rank, authority, the manners and tastes of the world of fashion, of the idle, the drawing-room frequenters, lovers of pleasure, conversation, wit, and polish, occupied with the piece in vogue, less to amuse themselves than to criticise it. Thus was Dryden's drama built up; the poet, greedy of glory and pressed for money, found here both money and glory, and was half an innovator, with a large reinforcement of theories and prefaces, diverging from the old English drama, approaching the new French tragedy, attempting a compromise between classical eloquence and romantic truth, accommodating himself as well as he could to the new public, which paid and applauded him.

" The language, wit, and conversation of our age, are improved and refined above the last. . . . Let us consider in
what the refinement of a language principally consists ; that is,
' either in rejecting such old words, or phrases, which are ill-
sounding or improper ; or in admitting new, which are more
proper, more sounding, and more significant.' . . . Let any
man, who understands English, read diligently the works of
Shakspeare and Fletcher, and I dare undertake, that he will find
in every page either some solecism of speech, or some notorious
flaw in sense. . . . Many of (their plots) were made up of some
ridiculous incoherent story, which in one play many times took
up the business of an age.   I suppose I need not name *Pericles
Prince of Tyre*, nor the historical plays of Shakspeare ; besides
many of the rest, as the *Winter's Tale*, *Love's Labour Lost*,
Measure for Measure, which were either grounded on impossi-
bilities, or at least so meanly written, that the comedy neither
caused your mirth, nor the serious part your concernment. . . .
I could easily demonstrate, that our admired Fletcher neither
understood correct plotting, nor that which they call the decorum
of the stage. . . . The reader will see Philaster wounding his
mistress, and afterwards his boy, to save himself. . . . And for
his shepherd he falls twice into the former indecency of wounding women." [1]

Fletcher nowhere permits kings to retain a dignity
suited to kings.   Moreover, the action of these authors'
plays is always barbarous.   They introduce battles on
the stage ; they transport the scene in a moment to a
distance of twenty years or five hundred leagues, and a
score of times consecutively in one act ; they jumble
together three or four different actions, especially in
the historical dramas.   But they sin most in style.
Dryden says of Shakspeare :—" Many of his words,

[1] *Defence of the Epilogue of the Second Part of the Conquest of
Granad.*, iv. 213.

and more of his phrases, are scarce intelligible. And of those which we understand, some are ungrammatical, others coarse; and his whole style is so pestered with figurative expressions, that it is as affected as it is obscure."[1] Ben Jonson himself often has bad plots, redundancies, barbarisms : " Well-placing of words, for the sweetness of pronunciation, was not known till Mr. Waller introduced it "[2] All, in short, descend to quibbles, low and common expressions: " In the age wherein those poets lived, there was less of gallantry than in ours. . . . Besides the want of education and learning, they wanted the benefit of converse. . . . Gentlemen will now be entertained with the follies of each other; and, though they allow Cob and Tibb to speak properly, yet they are not much pleased with their tankard, or with their rags."[3]   For these gentlemen we must now write, and especially for " reasonable men ;" for it is not enough to have wit or to love tragedy, in order to be a good critic : we must possess sound knowledge and a lofty reason, know Aristotle, Horace, Longinus, and pronounce judgment according to their rules.[4]   These rules, based upon observation and logic, prescribe unity of action; that this action should have a beginning, middle, and end; that its parts should proceed naturally one from the other; that it should excite terror and pity, so as to instruct and improve us; that the characters should be distinct, harmonious, conformable with tradition or the design of the poet. Such, says Dryden, will be the new tragedy, closely allied, it seems, to the French, especially

[1] Preface to *Troilus and Cressida*, vi. 239.
[2] *Defence of the Epilogue of the Conquest of Granada*, iv. 219.
[3] *Ibid.* 225-228.   [4] Preface to *All for Love*, v. 306.

as he quotes Bossu and Rapin, as if he took them for instructors.

Yet it differs from it, and Dryden enumerates all that an English pit can blame on the French stage. He says :

"The beauties of the French poesy are the beauties of a statue, but not of a man, because not animated with the soul of poesy, which is imitation of humour and passions. . . . He who will look upon their plays which have been written till these last ten years, or thereabouts, will find it an hard matter to pick out two or three passable humours amongst them. Corneille himself, their arch-poet, what has he produced except the *Liar ?* and you know how it was cried up in France ; but when it came upon the English stage, though well translated, . . . the most favourable to it would not put it in competition with many of Fletcher's or Ben Jonson's. . . . Their verses are to me the coldest I have ever read, . . . their speeches being so many declamations. When the French stage came to be reformed by Cardinal Richelieu, those long harangues were introduced, to comply with the gravity of a churchman. Look upon the *Cinna* and the *Pompey ;* they are not so properly to be called plays as long discourses of reasons of state ; and *Polieucte*, in matters of religion is as solemn as the long stops upon our organs. Since that time it is grown into a custom, and their actors speak by the hour-glass, like our parsons. . . . I deny not but this may suit well enough with the French ; for as we who are a more sullen people, come to be diverted at our plays, so they, who are of an airy and gay temper, come thither to make themselves more serious." [1]

As for the tumults and combats which the French relegate behind the scenes, "nature has so formed our countrymen to fierceness, . . . they will scarcely suffer combats and other objects of horror to be taken from them." [2] Thus the French, by fettering themselves with

[1] *An Essay of Dramatic Poesy*, xv. 337-341.   [2] *Ibid.* 343.

these scruples,[1] and confining themselves in their unities
and their rules, have removed action from their stage,
and brought themselves down to unbearable monotony
and dryness. They lack originality, naturalness, variety,
fulness.

"... Contented to be thinly regular: ...
Their tongue, enfeebled, is refined too much,
And, like pure gold, it bends at every touch.
Our sturdy Teuton yet will art obey,
More fit for manly thought, and strengthened with allay."[2]

Let them laugh as much as they like at Fletcher and
Shakspeare; there is in them " a more masculine fancy
and greater spirit in the writing than there is in any of
the French."

Though exaggerated, this criticism is good; and because it is good, I mistrust the works which the writer

[1] In the preface of *All for Love*, v. 308, Dryden says : "In this
nicety of manners does the excellency of French poetry consist. Their
heroes are the most civil people breathing, but their good breeding
seldom extends to a word of sense ; all their wit is in their ceremony ;
they want the genius which animates our stage. . . . Thus, their
Hippolytus is so scrupulous in point of decency, that he will rather
expose himself to death than accuse his step-mother to his father ; and
my critics, I am sure, will commend him for it : But we of grosser
apprehensions are apt to think that this excess of generosity is not
practicable but with fools and madmen. . . . But take Hippolytus
out of his poetic fit, and I suppose he would think it a wiser part to
set the saddle on the right horse, and chuse rather to live with the
reputation of a plain-spoken honest man, than to die with the infamy
of an incestuous villain. . . . (The poet) has chosen to give him the
turn of gallantry, sent him to travel from Athens to Paris, taught him
to make love, and transformed the Hippolytus of Euripides into
Monsieur Hippolite." This criticism shows in a small compass all the
common sense and freedom of thought of Dryden ; but, at the same
time, all the coarseness of his education and of his age.

[2] Epistle xiv., to Mr. Motteux, xi. 70.

is to produce. It is dangerous for an artist to be excellent in theory; the creative spirit is hardly consonant with the criticising spirit: he who,. quietly seated on the shore, discusses and compares, is hardly capable of plunging straight and boldly into the stormy sea of invention. Moreover, Dryden holds himself too evenly poised betwixt the moods; original artists love exclusively and unjustly a certain idea and a certain world; the rest disappears from their eyes; confined to one region of art, they deny or scorn the other; it is because they are limited that they are strong. We see beforehand that Dryden, pushed one way by his English mind, will be drawn another way by his French rules; that he will alternately venture and partly restrain himself; that he will attain mediocrity, that is, platitude; that his faults will be incongruities, that is, absurdities. All original art is self-regulated, and no original art can be regulated from without: it carries its own counterpoise, and does not receive it from elsewhere; it constitutes an inviolable whole; it is an animated existence, which lives on its own blood, and which languishes or dies if deprived of some of its blood and supplied from the veins of another. Shakspeare's imagination cannot be guided by Racine's reason, nor Racine's reason be exalted by Shakspeare's imagination; each is good in itself, and excludes its rival; to unite them would be to produce a bastard, a weakling, and a monster. Disorder, violent and sudden action, harsh words, horror, depth, truth, exact imitation of reality, and the lawless outbursts of mad passions,—these features of Shakspeare become each other. Order, measure, eloquence, aristocratic refinement, worldly urbanity, exquisite painting of delicacy and virtue, all Racine's features suit each other. It would destroy the one to attenuate, the other to inflame him. Their whole being and beauty consist in the agreement of their parts: to mar this agreement would be to abolish their being and their beauty. In order to produce, we must invent a personal and harmonious conception: we must not mingle two strange and opposite ones. Dryden has left undone what he should have done, and has done what he should not have done.

He had, moreover, the worst of audiences, debauched and frivolous, void of individual taste, floundering amid confused recollections of the national literature and deformed imitations of foreign literature, expecting nothing from the stage but the pleasure of the senses or the gratification of curiosity. In reality, the drama, like every work of art, only gives life and truth to a profound ideal of man and of existence; there is a hidden philosophy under its circumvolutions and violences, and the public ought to be capable of comprehending it, as the poet is of conceiving it. The audience must have reflected or felt with energy or refinement, in order to take in energetic or refined thoughts; Hamlet and Iphigénie will never move a vulgar roisterer or a lover of money. The character who weeps on the stage only rehearses our own tears; our interest is but sympathy; and the drama is like an external conscience, which shows us what we are, what we love, what we have felt. What could the drama teach to gamesters like St. Albans, drunkards like Rochester, prostitutes like Castlemaine, old boys like Charles II.? What spectators were those coarse epicureans, incapable even of an assumed decency, lovers of brutal pleasures, barbarians in their sports obscene in words, void of honour, humanity, politeness, who made the court a house of ill fame! The splendid decorations, change of scenes, the patter of long verse and forced sentiments, the observance of a few rules imported from Paris,—such was the natural food of their vanity and folly, and such the theatre of the English Restoration

I take one of Dryden's tragedies, very celebrated in time past, *Tyrannic Love, or the Royal Martyr*;—a fine title, and fit to make a stir. The royal martyr is St. Catharine, a princess of royal blood as it appears, who is brought before the tyrant Maximin. She confesses her faith, and a pagan philosopher Apollonius is set loose against her, to refute her. Maximin says:

> "War is my province!—Priest; why stand you mute?
> You gain by heaven, and, therefore, should dispute."

Thus encouraged, the priest argues; but St. Catharine replies in the following words:

> ". . . Reason with your fond religion fights,
> For many gods are many infinites;
> This to the first philosophers was known,
> Who, under various names, ador'd but one." [1]

Apollonius scratches his ear a little, and then answers that there are great truths and good moral rules in paganism. The pious logician immediately replies:

> "Then let the whole dispute concluded be
> Betwixt these rules, and Christianity." [2]

Being nonplussed, Apollonius is converted on the spot, insults the prince, who, finding St. Catharine very

---

[1] *Tyrannic Love*, iii. 2. 1.   [2] *Ibid.*

beautiful, becomes suddenly enamoured, and makes jokes:

> " Absent, I may her martyrdom decree,
> But one look more will make that martyr me." [1]

In this dilemma he sends Placidius, " a great officer," to St. Catharine; the great officer quotes and praises the gods of Epicurus; forthwith the lady propounds the doctrine of final causes, which upsets that of atoms. Maximin comes himself, and says:

> " Since you neglect to answer my desires,
> Know, princess, you shall burn in other fires." [2]

Thereupon she beards and defies him, calls him a slave, and walks off. Touched by these delicate manners, he wishes to marry her lawfully, and to repudiate his wife. Still, to omit no expedient, he employs a magician, who utters invocations (on the stage), summons the infernal spirits, and brings up a troop of Spirits; these dance and sing voluptuous songs about the bed of St. Catharine. Her guardian-angel comes and drives them away. As a last resource, Maximin has a wheel brought on the stage, on which to expose St. Catharine and her mother. Whilst the executioners are going to strip the saint, a modest angel descends in the nick of time, and breaks the wheel; after which the ladies are carried off, and their throats are cut behind the wings. Add to these

---

[1] *Tyrannic Love*, iii. 2. 1.

[2] *Ibid.* 3. 1. This Maximin has a turn for jokes. Porphyrius, to whom he offers his daughter in marriage, says that " the distance was so vast;" whereupon Maximin replies : " Yet heaven and earth, which so remote appear, are by the air, which flows betwixt them, near " (2. 1).

pretty inventions a twofold intrigue, the love of Maximin's daughter, Valeria, for Porphyrius, captain of the Prætorian bands, and that of Porphyrius for Berenice, Maximin's wife; then a sudden catastrophe, three deaths, and the triumph of the good people, who get married and interchange polite phrases. Such is this tragedy, which is called French-like; and most of the others are like it. In *Secret Love*, in *Marriage à la Mode*, in *Aureng-Zebe*, in the *Indian Emperor*, and especially in the *Conquest of Granada*, everything is extravagant. People cut one another to pieces, take towns, stab each other, shout lustily. These dramas have just the truth and naturalness of the libretto of an opera. Incantations abound; a spirit appears in the *Indian Emperor*, and declares that the Indian gods " are driven to exile from their native lands." Ballets are also there; Vasquez and Pizarro, seated in " a pleasant grotto," watch like conquerors the dances of the Indian girls, who gambol voluptuously about them. Scenes worthy of Lulli [1] are not wanting; Almeria, like Armide, comes to slay Cortez in his sleep, and suddenly falls in love with him. Yet the libretti of the opera have no incongruities; they avoid all which might shock the imagination or the eyes; they are written for men of taste, who shun ugliness and heaviness of any sort. Would you believe it? In the *Indian Emperor*, Montezuma is tortured on the stage, and to cap all, a priest tries to convert him in the meanwhile.[2]

---

[1] Lulli (1633-1687), a renowned Italian composer. *Armide* is one of his chief works.—Tr.

[2] *Christian Priest.* But we by martyrdom our faith avow.
Montezuma. You do no more than I for ours do now.
To prove religion true,
If either wit or sufferings would suffice,

I recognise in this frightful pedantry the handsome cavaliers of the time, logicians and hangmen, who fed on controversy, and for the sake of amusement went to look at the tortures of the Puritans. I recognise behind these heaps of improbabilities and adventures the puerile and worn-out courtiers, who, sodden with wine, were past seeing incongruities, and whose nerves were only stirred by startling surprises and barbarous events.

Let us go still further. Dryden would set up on his stage the beauties of French tragedy, and in the first place its nobility of sentiment. Is it enough to copy, as he does, phrases of chivalry? He would need a whole world, for a whole world is necessary to form noble souls. Virtue, in the French tragic poets, is based on reason, religion, education, philosophy. Their characters have that uprightness of mind, that clearness of logic, that lofty judgment, which plant in a man settled maxims and self-government. We perceive in their company the doctrines of Bossuet and Descartes; with them, reflection aids conscience; the habits of society add tact and *finesse*. The avoidance of violent actions and physical horrors, the mood and order of the fable, the art of disguising or shunning coarse or low persons, the continuous perfection of the most measured and noble style, everything contributes

All faiths afford the constant and the wise,
And yet even they, by education sway'd,
In age defend what infancy obeyed.
　Christian Priest. Since age by erring childhood is misled,
Refer yourself to our unerring head.
　Montezuma. Man, and not err! what reason can you give?
　Christian Priest. Renounce that carnal reason, and believe. . . .
　Pizarro. Increase their pains, the cords are yet too slack.
　　　　　　　　　　—The Indian Emperor, v. 2.

to raise the stage to a sublime region, and we believe
in higher souls by seeing them in a purer air. Can
we believe in them in Dryden? Frightful or infamous
characters every instant drag us down by their coarse
expressions in their own mire. Maximin, having stabbed
Placidius, sits on his body, stabs him twice more, and
says to the guards:

> " Bring me Porphyrius and my empress dead :—
> I would brave heaven, in my each hand a head."[1]

Nourmahal, repulsed by her husband's son, insists four
times, using such indecent and pedantic words as the
following:

> " And why this niceness to that pleasure shown,
> Where nature sums up all her joys in one. . . .
> Promiscuous love is nature's general law ;
> For whosoever the first lovers were,
> Brother and sister made the second pair,
> And doubled by their love their piety. . . .
> You must be mine, that you may learn to live."[2]

[1] *Tyrannic Love*, iii. 5. 1. When dying Maximin says : " And
shoving back this earth on which I sit, I'll mount, and scatter all the
Gods I hit."

[2] *Aureng-Zebe*, v. 4. 1. Dryden thought he was imitating Racine,
when six lines further on he makes Nourmahal say :
> " I am not changed, I love my husband still ;
> But love him as he was, when youthful grace
> And the first down began to shade his face :
> That image does my virgin-flames renew,
> And all your father shines more bright in you."

Racine's Phèdre (2. 5) thinks her husband Theseus dead, and says to
her stepson Hippolytus ;.
> " Oui, prince, je languis, je brûle pour Thésée :
> Je l'aime . . .
> Mais fidèle, mais fier, et même un peu farouche,
> Charmant, jeune, traînant tous les cœurs après soi,
> Tel qu'on dépeint nos dieux, ou tel que je vous voi.

Illusion vanishes at once; instead of being in a room with noble characters, we meet with a mad prostitute and a drunken savage. When we lift the masks the others are little better. Almeria, to whom a crown is offered, says insolently:

> "I take this garland, not as given by you,
> But as my merit, and my beauty's due."[1]

Indamora, to whom an old courtier makes love, settles him with the boastfulness of an upstart and the coarseness of a kitchen-maid:

> "Were I no queen, did you my beauty weigh,
> My youth in bloom, your age in its decay."[2]

None of these heroines know how to conduct themselves; they look on impertinence as dignity, sensuality as tenderness; they have the recklessness of the courtesan, the jealousies of the grisette, the pettiness of a chapman's wife, the billingsgate of a fishwoman. The heroes are the most unpleasant of swashbucklers. Leonidas, first recognised as hereditary prince, then suddenly forsaken, consoles himself with this modest reflection:

> "'Tis true I am alone.
> So was the godhead, ere he made the world,
> And better served himself than served by nature.
> . . . I have scene enough within
> To exercise my virtue."[3]

Shall I speak of that great trumpet-blower Almanzor,

> Il avait votre port, vos yeux, votre langage ;
> Cette noble pudeur colorait son visage."

According to a note in Sir Walter Scott's edition of Dryden's works, Langbaine traces this speech also to Seneca's Hippolytus.—Tr.

[1] *The Indian Emperor*, i. 2.   [2] *Aureng-Zebe*, v. 2, 1.
[3] *Marriage à la Mode*, iv. 3. 1.

painted, as Dryden confesses, after Artaban,[1] a redresser
of wrongs, a battalion-smiter, a destroyer of kingdoms ? [2]
We find nothing but overcharged sentiments, sudden
devotedness, exaggerated generosities, high - sounding
bathos of a clumsy chivalry; at bottom the characters
are clods and barbarians, who have tried to deck themselves in French honour and fashionable politeness.
And such, in fact, was the English court : it imitated
that of Louis XIV. as a sign-painter imitates an artist.
It had neither taste nor refinement, and wished to appear
as if it possessed them.   Panders and licentious women,
ruffianly or butchering courtiers, who went to see Harrison
drawn, or to mutilate Coventry, maids of honour who
have awkward accidents at a ball,[3] or sell to the planters
the convicts presented to them, a palace full of baying
dogs and bawling gamesters, a king who would bandy
obscenities in public with his half-naked mistresses,[4]—
such was this illustrious society; from French modes
they took but dress, from French noble sentiments but
high-sounding words.

---

[1] The first image I had of him was from the Achilles of Homer,
the next from Tasso's Rinaldo, and the third from the Artaban of
Monsieur Calpranède."—Preface to *Almanzor*.

[2] " The Moors have heaven, and me, to assist their cause " (i. 1).
    " I'll whistle thy tame fortune after me " (3. 1).
He falls in love, and speaks thus
            " 'Tis he ; I feel him now in every part ;
            Like a new lord he vaunts about my heart,
            Surveys in state each corner of my breast,
            While poor fierce I, that was, am dispossess'd " (3. 1).

[3] See vol. ii. 341.

[4] Compare the song of the Zambra dance in the first part of *Almanzor and Almahide*, 3. 1.

IV.

The second point worthy of imitation in classical tragedy is the style. Dryden, in fact, purifies his own, and renders it more clear, by introducing close reasoning and precise words. He has oratorical discussions like Corneille, well-delivered retorts, symmetrical, like carefully parried arguments. He has maxims vigorously enclosed in the compass of a single line, distinctions, developments, and the whole art of special pleading. He has happy antitheses, ornamental epithets, finely-wrought comparisons, and all the artifices of the literary mind. What is most striking is, that he abandons that kind of verse specially appropriated to the English drama which is without rhyme, and the mixture of prose and verse common to the old authors, for a rhymed tragedy like the French, fancying that he is thus inventing a new species, which he calls heroic play. But in this transformation the good perished, the bad remains. For rhyme differs in different races. To an Englishman it resembles a song, and transports him at once to an ideal and fairy world. To a Frenchman it is only a conventionalism or an expediency, and transports him at once to an ante-chamber or a drawing-room; to him it is an ornamental dress and nothing more; if it mars prose, it ennobles it; it imposes respect, not enthusiasm, and changes a vulgar into a high-bred style. Moreover, in French aristocratic verse everything is connected; pedantry, logical machinery of every kind, is excluded from it; there is nothing more disagreeable to well-bred and refined persons than the scholastic rust. Images are rare, but always well kept up; bold poesy, real fantasy, have no place in it; their brilliancy and divergencies would derange the politeness and regular flow of

the social world. The right word, the prominence of
free expressions, are not to be met with in it; general
terms, always rather threadbare, suit best the caution
and niceties of select society. Dryden sins heavily
against all these rules. His rhymes, to an Englishman's
ear, scatter at once the whole illusion of the stage; they
see that the characters who speak thus are but squeaking
puppets; he himself admits that his heroic tragedy is
only fit to represent on the stage chivalric poems like
those of Ariosto and Spenser.

Poetic dash gives the finishing stroke to all likelihood.
Would we recognise the dramatic accent in this epic
comparison?

> " As some fair tulip, by a storm oppress'd
> Shrinks up, and folds its silken arms to rest;
> And, bending to the blast, all pale and dead,
> Hears, from within, the wind sing round its head,—
> So, shrouded up, your beauty disappears:
> Unveil, my love, and lay aside your fears,
> The storm, that caused your fright, is pass'd and done." [1]

What a singular triumphal song are these *concetti* of
Cortez as he lands:

> " On what new happy climate are we thrown,
> So long kept secret, and so lately known?
> As if our old world modestly withdrew,
> And here in private had brought forth a new." [2]

Think how these patches of colour would contrast with
the sober design of French dissertation. Here lovers
vie with each other in metaphors; there a wooer, in
order to magnify the beauties of his mistress, says that

---

[1] The first part of *Almanzor and Almahide*, iv. 5. 2.
[2] *The Indian Emperor*, ii. 1. 1.

"bloody hearts lie panting in her hand." In every page harsh or vulgar words spoil the regularity of a noble style. Ponderous logic is broadly displayed in the speeches of princesses. "Two ifs," says Lyndaraxa, "scarce make one possibility."[1] Dryden sets his college cap on the heads of these poor women. Neither he nor his characters are well brought up; they have taken from the French but the outer garb of the bar and the schools; they have left behind symmetrical eloquence, measured diction, elegance and delicacy. A while before, the licentious coarseness of the Restoration pierced the mask of the fine sentiments with which it was covered; now the rude English imagination breaks the oratorical mould in which it tried to enclose itself.

Let us look at the other side of the picture. Dryden would keep the foundation of the old English drama, and retains the abundance of events, the variety of plot, the unforeseen accidents, and the physical representation of bloody or violent action. He kills as many people as Shakspeare. Unfortunately, all poets are not justified in killing. When they take their spectators among murders and sudden accidents, they ought to have a hundred hidden preparations. Fancy a sort of rapture and romantic folly, a most daring style, eccentric and poetical, songs, pictures, reveries spoken aloud, frank scorn of all verisimilitude, a mixture of tenderness, philosophy, and mockery, all the retiring charms of varied feelings, all the whims of nimble fancy; the truth of events matters little. No one who ever saw *Cymbeline*

---

[1] The first part of *Almanzor and Almahide*, iv. 2. 1. This same Lyndaraxa says also to Abdalla (4. 2), "Poor women's thoughts are all *extempore.*" These logical ladies can be very coarse; for example, this same damsel says in act 2. 1, to the same lover, who entreats her to make him "happy," "If I make you so, you shall pay my price."

or *As you Like it* looked at these plays with the eyes of a politician or a historian; no one took these military processions, these accessions of princes, seriously; the spectators were present at dissolving views. They did not demand that things should proceed after the laws of nature; on the contrary, they willingly did require that they should proceed against the laws of nature. The irrationality is the charm. That new world must be all imagination; if it was only so by halves, no one would care to rise to it. This is why we do not rise to Dryden's. A queen dethroned, then suddenly set up again; a tyrant who finds his lost son, is deceived, adopts a girl in his place; a young prince led to punishment, who snatches the sword of a guard, and recovers his crown: such are the romances which constitute the *Maiden Queen* and the *Marriage à la Mode.* We can imagine what a display classical dissertations make in this medley; solid reason beats down imagination, stroke after stroke, to the ground. We cannot tell if the matter be a true portrait or a fancy painting; we remain suspended between truth and fancy; we should like either to get up to heaven or down to earth, and we jump down as quick as possible from the clumsy scaffolding where the poet would perch us.

On the other hand, when Shakspeare wishes to impress a doctrine, not raise a dream, he attunes us to it beforehand, but after another fashion. We naturally remain in doubt before a cruel action: we divine that the red irons which are about to put out the eyes of little Arthur are painted sticks, and that the six rascals who besiege Rome, are supernumeraries hired at a shilling a night. To conquer this mistrust we must employ the most natural style, circumstantial and rude imitation of the manners of the guardroom and of the alehouse; I can only believe in Jack Cade's sedition on hearing the dirty words of bestial lewdness and mobbish stupidity. You must let me have the jests, the coarse laughter, drunkenness, the manners of butchers and tanners, to make me imagine a mob or an election. So in murders, let me feel the fire of bubbling passion, the accumulation of despair or hate which have unchained the will and nerved the hand. When the unchecked words, the fits of rage, the convulsive ejaculations of exasperated desire, have brought me in contact with all the links of the inward necessity which has moulded the man and guided the crime, I no longer think whether the knife is bloody, because I feel with inner trembling the passion which has handled it. Have I to see if Shakspeare's Cleopatra be really dead? The strange laugh that bursts from her when the basket of asps is brought, the sudden tension of nerves, the flow of feverish words, the fitful gaiety, the coarse language, the torrent of ideas with which she overflows, have already made me sound all the depths of suicide,[1]

> "He words me, girls; he words me, that I should not
> Be noble to myself; but hark thee Charmian. . . .
>   Now, Iras, what think'st thou?
> Thou, an Egyptian puppet shalt be shown
> In Rome, as well as I : mechanic slaves,
> With greasy aprons, rules and hammers, shall
> Uplift us to the view. . . .
>   Saucy lictors
> Will catch at us, like strumpets ; and scald rhymers
> Ballad us out o' tune ; the quick comedians
> Extemporally will stage us, and present
> Our Alexandrian revels ; Antony
> Shall be brought drunken forth, and I shall see
> Some squeaking Cleopatra boy my greatness
> I' the posture of a whore. . . .

and I have foreseen it as soon as she came on the stage.
This madness of the imagination, incited by climate
and despotic power ; these woman's, queen's, prostitute's
nerves ; this marvellous self-abandonment to all the fire
of invention and desire—these cries, tears, foam on the
lips, tempest of insults, actions, emotions ; this prompti-
tude to murder, announce the rage with which she
would rush against the least obstacle and be dashed to
pieces. What does Dryden effect in this matter with
his written phrases ? What of the maid speaking, in
the author's words, who bids her half-mad mistress
" call reason to assist you ? "[1] What of such a Cleopatra
as his, designed after Lady Castlemaine,[2] skilled in

> Husband, I come :
> Now to that name my courage prove my title!
> I am fire and air ; my other elements
> I give to baser life. So ; have you done ?
> Come, then, and take the last warmth of my lips.
> Farewell, kind Charmian ; Iras, long farewell. . . .
>   Dost thou not see my baby at my breast,
> That sucks the nurse asleep ?"
>   Shakspeare's *Antony and Cleopatra*, 5. 2.

These two last lines, referring to the asp, are sublime as the bitter joke
of a courtesan and an artist.

[1] " *Iras.* Call reason to assist you.
  Cleopatra. I have none,
And none would have : My love's a noble madness
Which shews the cause deserved it : Modest sorrow
Fits vulgar love, and for a vulgar man ;
But I have loved with such transcendant passion,
I soared, at first, quite out of reason's view,
And now am lost above it." —*All for Love*, v. 2. 1.

[2] " *Cleop.* Come to me, come, my soldier, to my arms !
You've been too long away from my embraces ;
But, when I have you fast, and all my own,
With broken murmurs, and with amorous sighs,
I'll say, you were unkind, and punish you,
And mark you red with many an eager kiss. "—
      All for Love, v. 3. 1.

artifices and whimpering, voluptuous and a coquette,
with neither the nobleness of virtue, nor the greatness
of crime :

> " Nature meant me
> A wife ; a silly, harmless household dove,
> Fond without art, and kind without deceit." [1]

Nay, Nature meant nothing of the kind, or otherwise this
turtle-dove would not have tamed or kept an Antony ;
a woman without any prejudices alone could do it, by the
superiority of boldness and the fire of genius.   I can see
already from the title of the piece why Dryden has
softened Shakspeare : *All for Love ; or, the World well
Lost.*   What a wretchedness, to reduce such events to a
pastoral, to excuse Antony, to praise Charles II. indi-
rectly, to bleat as in a sheepfold ! And such was the taste
of his contemporaries.   When Dryden wrote the *Tempest*
after Shakspeare, and the *State of Innocence* after Milton,
he again spoiled the ideas of his masters ; he turned
Eve and Miranda into courtesans ;[2] he extinguished
everywhere, under conventionalism and indecencies,
the frankness, severity, delicacy, and charm of the
original invention.   By his side, Settle, Shadwell, Sir
Robert Howard did worse.   *The Empress of Morocco,*
by Settle, was so admired, that the gentlemen and
ladies of the court learned it by heart, to play at
Whitehall before the king.   And this was not a passing
fancy ; although modified, the taste was to endure.   In

---

[1] *All for Love,* 4. 1.

[2] Dryden's Miranda, says, in the *Tempest* (2. 2) : "And if I can
but escape with life, I had. rather be in pain nine months, as my
father threatened, than lose my longing." Miranda has a sister ; they
quarrel, are jealous of each other, and so on.   See also in *The State of
Innocence,* 3. 1, the description which Eve gives of her happiness, and
the ideas which her confidences suggest to Satan.

vain poets rejected a part of the French alloy wherewith they had mixed their native metal; in vain they
returned to the old unrhymed verses of Jonson and
Shakspeare; in vain Dryden, in the parts of Antony,
Ventidius, Octavia, Don Sebastian, and Dorax, recovered
a portion of the old naturalness and energy; in vain
Otway, who had real dramatic talent, Lee and Southern,
attained a true or touching accent, so that once, in *Venice
Preserved*, it was thought that the drama would be
regenerated. The drama was dead, and tragedy could
not replace it; or rather each one died by the other;
and their union, which robbed them of strength in
Dryden's time, enervated them also in the time of his
successors. Literary style blunted dramatic truth;
dramatic truth marred literary style; the work was
neither sufficiently vivid nor sufficiently well written;
the author was too little of a poet or of an orator; he
had neither Shakspeare's fire of imagination nor Racine's
polish and art.[1] He strayed on the boundaries of two
dramas, and suited neither the half-barbarous men of
art nor the well-polished men of the court. Such indeed
was the audience, hesitating between two forms of
thought, fed by two opposite civilisations. They had
no longer the freshness of feelings, the depth of impression, the bold originality and poetic folly of the cavaliers and adventurers of the Renaissance; nor will they
ever acquire the aptness of speech, gentleness of
manners, courtly habits, and cultivation of sentiment
and thought which adorned the court of Louis XIV.
They are quitting the age of solitary imagination and
invention, which suits their race, for the age of reasoning
and worldly conversation, which does not suit their race;

---

[1] This impotence reminds one of Casimir Delavigne.

they lose their own merits, and do not acquire the merits of others. They were meagre poets and ill-bred courtiers, having lost the art of imagination and having not yet acquired good manners, at times dull or brutal, at times emphatic or stiff. For the production of fine poetry, race and age must concur. This race, diverging from its own age, and fettered at the outset by foreign imitation, formed its classical literature but slowly; it will only attain it after transforming its religious and political condition: the age will be that of English reason. Dryden inaugurates it by his other works, and the writers who appear in the reign of Queen Anne will give it its completion, its authority, and its splendour.

V.

But let us pause a moment longer to inquire whether, amid so many abortive and distorted branches, the old theatrical stock, abandoned by chance to itself, will not produce at some point a sound and living shoot. When a man like Dryden, so gifted, so well informed and experienced, works with a will, there is hope that he will some time succeed; and once, in part at least, Dryden did succeed. It would be treating him unjustly to be always comparing him with Shakspeare; but even on Shakspeare's ground, with the same materials, it is possible to create a fine work; only the reader must forget for a while the great inventor, the inexhaustible creator of vehement and original souls, and to consider the imitator on his own merits, without forcing an overwhelming comparison.

There is vigour and art in this tragedy of Dryden, *All for Love.* "He has informed us, that this was the

only play written to please himself." [1]   And he had
really composed it learnedly, according to history and
logic.   And what is better still, he wrote it in a manly
style.   In the preface he says : " The fabric of the play
is regular enough, as to the inferior parts of it ; and the
unities of time, place, and action, more exactly observed,
than perhaps the English theatre requires.   Particularly,
the action is so much one, that it is the only of the
kind without episode, or underplot ; every scene in the
tragedy conducing to the main design, and every act
concluding with a turn of it. [2]   He did more ; he abandoned the French ornaments, and returned to national
tradition : " In my style I have professed to imitate the
divine Shakspeare ; which that I might perform more
freely, I have disincumbered myself from rhyme. . . .
Yet, I hope, I may affirm, and without vanity, that by
imitating him, I have excelled myself throughout the
play ; and particularly, that I prefer the scene betwixt
Antony and Ventidius in the first act, to anything which
I have written in this kind. " [3]   Dryden was right ; if
Cleopatra is weak, if this feebleness of conception takes
away the interest and mars the general effect, if the
new rhetoric and the old emphasis at times suspend the
emotion and destroy the likelihood, yet on the whole
the drama stands erect, and what is more, moves on.
The poet is skilful ; he has planned, he knows how to
construct a scene, to represent the internal struggle by
which two passions contend for a human heart.   We
perceive the tragical vicissitude of the strife, the progress
of a sentiment, the overthrow of obstacles, the slow
growth of desire or wrath, to the very instant when the

[1] See the introductory notice, by Sir Walter Scott, of *All for Love*,
v. 290.   [2] *Ibid.* v. 307.   [3] *Ibid.* v. 319.

resolution, rising up of itself or seduced from without, rushes suddenly in one groove. There are natural words; the poet thinks and writes too genuinely not to discover them at need. There are manly characters : he himself is a man ; and beneath his courtier's pliability, his affectations as a fashionable poet, he has retained his stern and energetic character. Except for one scene of recrimination, his Octavia is a Roman matron ; and when, even in Alexandria, in Cleopatra's palace, she comes to look for Antony, she does it with a simplicity and nobility, not to be surpassed. " Cæsar's sister," cries out Antony, accosting her. Octavia answers ;

> " That's unkind.
> Had I been nothing more than Cæsar's sister,
> Know, I had still remain'd in Cæsar's camp :
> But your Octavia, your much injured wife,
> Though banish'd from your bed, driven from your house,
> In spite of Cæsar's sister, still is yours.
> 'Tis true, I have a heart disdains your coldness,
> And prompts me not to seek what you should offer ;
> But a wife's virtue still surmounts that pride.
> I come to claim you as my own ; to show
> My duty first, to ask, nay beg, your kindness :
> Your hand, my lord ; 'tis mine, and I will have it." [1]

Antony humiliated, refuses the pardon Octavia has brought him, and tells her :

> " I fear, Octavia, you have begg'd my life, . . .
> Poorly and basely begg'd it of your brother.
>   *Octavia.* Poorly and basely I could never beg,
> Nor could my brother grant. . . .
>   My hard fortune
> Subjects me still to your unkind mistakes.

[1] *All for Love*, v. 3. 1.

But the conditions I have brought are such,
You need not blush to take : I love your honour,
Because 'tis mine ; it never shall be said
Octavia's husband was her brother's slave.
Sir, you are free ; free, even from her you loath ;
For, though my brother bargains for your love,
Makes me the price and cement of your peace,
I have a soul like yours ; I cannot take
Your love as alms, nor beg what I deserve.
I'll tell my brother we are reconciled ;
He shall draw back his troops, and you shall march
To rule the East : I may be dropt at Athens ;
No matter where.   I never will complain,
But only keep the barren name of wife,
And rid you of the trouble."[1]

This is lofty ; this woman has a proud heart, and also a
wife's heart : she knows how to give and how to bear ;
and better, she knows how to sacrifice herself without
self-assertion, and calmly ; no vulgar mind conceived
such a soul as this.   And Ventidius, the old general,
who with her and previous to her, comes to rescue
Antony from his illusion and servitude, is worthy to
speak in behalf of honour, as she had spoken for duty.
Doubtless he was a plebeian, a rude and plain-speaking
soldier, with the frankness and jests of his profession,
sometimes clumsy, such as a clever eunuch can dupe, " a
thick-skulled hero," who, out of simplicity of soul, from
the coarseness of his training, unsuspectingly brings
Antony back to the meshes, which he seemed to be
breaking through.   Falling into a trap, he tells Antony
that he has seen Cleopatra unfaithful with Dolabella :

[1] *All for Love*, v. 3. 1.

" *Antony.* My Cleopatra?
　Ventidius. Your Cleopatra.
Dolabella's Cleopatra.
Every man's Cleopatra.
　Antony. Thou liest.
　Ventidius. I do not lie, my lord.
Is this so strange? Should mistresses be left,
And not provide against a time of change?
You know she's not much used to lonely nights." [1]

It was just the way to make Antony jealous and bring
him back furious to Cleopatra. But what a noble heart
has this Ventidius, and how we catch, when he is alone
with Antony, the manly voice, the deep tones which
had been heard on the battlefield! He loves his
general like a good and honest dog, and asks no better
than to die, so it be at his master's feet. He growls
stealthily on seeing him cast down, crouches round him,
and suddenly weeps:

" *Ventidius.* Look, emperor, this is no common dew. [*Weeping.*
I have not wept this forty years; but now
My mother comes afresh into my eyes,
I cannot help her softness.
　Antony. By Heaven, he weeps! poor, good old man, he weeps!
The big round drops course one another down
The furrows of his cheeks.—Stop them, Ventidius,
Or I shall blush to death: they set my shame,
That caused them full before me.
　Ventidius. I'll do my best.
　Antony. Sure there's contagion in the tears of friends:
See, I have caught it too. Believe me, 'tis not
For my own grief, but thine. Nay, Father!" [2]

---

[1] *All for Love,* 4. 1.　　　　[2] *Ibid.* 1. 1.

As we hear these terrible sobs, we think of Tacitus'
veterans, who escaping from the marshes of Germany,
with scarred breasts, white heads, limbs stiff with service, kissed the hands of Drusus, carried his fingers to
their gums, that he might feel their worn and loosened
teeth, incapable to bite the wretched bread which was
given to them:

> " No ; 'tis you dream ; you sleep away your hours
> In desperate sloth, miscall'd philosophy.
> Up, up, for honour's sake ; twelve legions wait you,
> And long to call you chief : By painful journies,
> I led them, patient both of heat and hunger,
> Down from the Parthian marshes to the Nile.
> 'Twill do you good to see their sun-burnt faces,
> Their scarred cheeks, and chopt hands ; there's virtue in them.
> They'll sell those mangled limbs at dearer rates
> Than yon trim bands can buy." [1]

And when all is lost, when the Egyptians have turned
traitors, and there is nothing left but to die well, Ventidius says ;

> " There yet remain
> Three legions in the town.   The last assault
> Lopt off the rest : if death be your design,—
> As I must wish it now,—these are sufficient
> To make a heap about us of dead foes,
> An honest pile for burial. . . . Chuse your death ;
> For, I have seen him in such various shapes,
> I care not which I take : I'm only troubled.
> The life I bear is worn to such a rag,
> 'Tis scarce worth giving.   I could wish, indeed,
> We threw it from us with a better grace ;

[1] *All for Love*, 1. 1.

That, like two lions taken in the toils,
We might at least thrust out our paws, and wound
The hunters that inclose us." [1] . . .

Antony begs him to go, but he refuses ; and then he
entreats Ventidius to kill him :

" *Antony.* Do not deny me twice.
Ventidius. By Heaven I will not.
Let it not be to outlive you.
Antony. Kill me first,
And then die thou ; for 'tis but just thou serve
Thy friend, before thyself.
Ventidius. Give me your hand.
We soon shall meet again. Now, farewell, emperor !
[*Embrace.*
. . . I will not make a business of a trifle :
And yet I cannot look on you, and kill you.
Pray, turn your face.
Antony. I do : strike home, be sure.
Ventidius. Home, as my sword will reach." [2]

And with one blow he kills himself.   These are the
tragic, stoical manners of a military monarchy, the great
profusion of murders and sacrifices wherewith the men
of this overturned and shattered society killed and died.
This Antony, for whom so much has been done, is not
undeserving of their love : he has been one of Cæsar's
heroes, the first soldier of the van ; kindness and generosity breathe from him to the last ; if he is weak
against a woman, he is strong against men ; he has the
muscles and heart, the wrath and passions of a soldier ;
it is this feverheat of blood, this too quick sentiment of
honour, which has caused his ruin ; he cannot forgive
his own crime ; he possesses not that lofty genius which,

[1] *All for Love*, 5. 1.   [2] *Ibid.*

dwelling in a region superior to ordinary rules, emancipates a man from hesitation, from discouragement and remorse; he is only a soldier, he cannot forget that he has not executed the orders given to him:

> " *Ventidius.* Emperor!
>
> *Antony.* Emperor? Why, that's the style of victory;
> The conquering soldier, red with unfelt wounds,
> Salutes his general so; but never more
> Shall that sound reach my ears.
>
> *Ventidius.* I warrant you.
>
> *Antony.* Actium, Actium! Oh——
>
> *Ventidius.* It sits too near you.
>
> *Antony.* Here, here it lies; a lump of lead by day;
> And in my short, distracted, nightly slumbers,
> The hag that rides my dreams. . . .
>
> *Ventidius.* That's my royal master;
> And, shall we fight?
>
> *Antony.* I warrant thee, old soldier.
> Thou shalt behold me once again in iron;
> And at the head of our old troops, that beat
> The Parthians, cry aloud, 'Come, follow me.' " [1]

He fancies himself on the battlefield, and already his impetuosity carries him away. Such a man is not fit to govern men; we cannot master fortune until we have mastered ourselves; this man is only made to belie and destroy himself, and to be veered round alternately by every passion. As soon as he believes Cleopatra faithful, honour, reputation, empire, everything vanishes:

> " *Ventidius.* And what's this toy,
> In balance with your fortune, honour, fame?

[1] *All for Love,* 1. 1.

> *Antony.* What is't, Ventidius ? it outweighs them all.
> Why, we have more than conquer'd Cæsar now.
> My queen's not only innocent, but loves me. . . .
> Down on thy knees, blasphemer as thou art,
> And ask forgiveness of wrong'd innocence !
> > *Ventidius.* I'll rather die than take it. Will you go ?
> > *Antony.* Go ! Whither ? Go from all that's excellent !
> . . . Give, you gods,
> Give to your boy, your Cæsar,
> This rattle of a globe to play withal,
> This gewgaw world ; and put him cheaply off :
> I'll not be pleased with less than Cleopatra." [1]

Dejection follows excess ; these souls are only tempered against fear ; their courage is but that of the bull and the lion ; to be fully themselves, they need bodily action, visible danger ; their temperament sustains them ; before great moral sufferings they give way. When Antony thinks himself deceived, he despairs. and has nothing left but to die :

> " Let him (Cæsar) walk
> Alone upon't. I'm weary of my part.
> My torch is out ; and the world stands before me,
> Like a black desert at the approach of night ;
> I'll lay me down, and stray no farther on." [2]

Such verses remind us of Othello's gloomy dreams, of Macbeth's, of Hamlet's even ; beyond the pile of swelling tirades and characters of painted cardboard, it is as though the poet had touched the ancient drama, and brought its emotion away with him.

By his side another also has felt it, a young man, a

---

[1] *All for Love*, 2. 1, end.   [2] *Ibid.* 5. 1.

poor adventurer, by turns a student, actor, officer, always wild and always poor, who lived madly and sadly in excess and misery, like the old dramatists, with their inspiration, their fire, and who died at the age of thirty-four, according to some of a fever caused by fatigue, according to others of a prolonged fast, at the end of which he swallowed too quickly a morsel of bread bestowed on him in charity. Through the pompous cloak of the new rhetoric, Thomas Otway now and then reached the passions of the other age. It is plain that the times he lived in marred him, that he blunted himself the harshness and truth of the emotion he felt, that he no longer mastered the bold words he needed, that the oratorical style, the literary phrases, the classical declamation, the well-poised antitheses, buzzed about him, and drowned his note in their sustained and monotonous hum. Had he but been born a hundred years earlier! In his *Orphan* and *Venice Preserved* we encounter the sombre imaginations of Webster, Ford, and Shakspeare, their gloomy idea of life, their atrocities, murders, pictures of irresistible passions, which riot blindly like a herd of savage beasts, and make a chaos of the battle-field, with their yells and tumult, leaving behind them but devastation and heaps of dead. Like Shakspeare, he represents on the stage human transports and rages —a brother violating his brother's wife, a husband perjuring himself for his wife; Polydore, Chamont, Jaffier, weak and violent souls, the sport of chance, the prey of temptation, with whom transport or crime, like poison poured into the veins, gradually ascends, envenoms the whole man, is communicated to all whom he touches, and contorts and casts them down together in a convulsive delirium. Like Shakspeare, he has found poignant and living words,[1] which lay bare the depths of humanity, the strange creaking of a machine which is getting out of order, the tension of the will stretched to breaking-point,[2] the simplicity of real sacrifice, the humility of exasperated and craving passion, which begs to the end, and against all hope, for its fuel and its gratification.[3] Like Shakspeare, he has conceived genuine women,[4]—Monimia, above all Belvidera, who, like Imogen, has given herself wholly, and is lost as in an abyss of adoration for him whom she has chosen, who can but love, obey, weep, suffer, and who dies like a flower plucked from the stalk, when her arms are torn from the neck around which she has locked them. Like Shakspeare again, he has found, at least once, the grand bitter buffoonery, the harsh sentiment of human baseness ; and he has introduced into his most painful tragedy, an impure caricature, an old senator, who unbends from his official gravity in order to play at his mistress' house the clown or the valet. How bitter !

[1] Monimia says, in the *Orphan* (5, end), when dying, " How my head swims ! 'Tis very dark ; good night."

[2] See the death of Pierre and Jaffier in *Venice Preserved* (5, last scene). Pierre, stabbed once, bursts into a laugh.

[3] " *Jaffier.* Oh, that my arms were rivetted
Thus round thee ever ! But my friends, my oath !
This, and no more. (*Kisses her*).
 Belvidera. Another, sure another
For that poor little one you've ta'en such care of ;
I'll giv't him truly."—*Venice Preserved*, 5. 1.
There is jealousy in this last word.

[4] " Oh, thou art tender all,
Gentle and kind, as sympathizing nature,
Dove-like, soft and kind. . . .
I'll ever live your most obedient wife,
Nor ever any privilege pretend
Beyond your will."—*Orphan*, 4. 1.

how true was his conception, in making the busy man eager to leave his robes and his ceremonies ! how ready the man is to abase himself, when, escaped from his part, he comes to his real self! how the ape and the dog crop up in him! The senator Antonio comes to his Aquilina, who insults him; he is amused; hard words are a relief to compliments; he speaks in a shrill voice, runs into a falsetto like a zany at a country fair :

"*Antonio.* Nacky, Nacky, Nacky,—how dost do, Nacky ? Hurry, durry. I am come, little Nacky. Past eleven o'clock, a late hour ; time in all conscience to go to bed, Nacky.—Nacky did I say ? Ay, Nacky, Aquilina, lina, lina, quilina ; Aquilina, Naquilina, Acky, Nacky, queen Nacky.—Come, let's to bed.— You fubbs, you pug you—You little puss.—Purree tuzzy—I am a senator.

Aquilina. You are a fool I am sure.

Antonio. May be so too, sweet-heart. Never the worse senator for all that. Come, Nacky, Nacky ; let's have a game at romp, Nacky ! . . . You won't sit down ? Then look you now ; suppose me a bull, a Basan-bull, the bull of bulls, or any bull. Thus up I get, and with my brows thus bent—I broo ; I say I broo, I broo, I broo. You won't sit down, will you—I broo. . . . Now, I'll be a senator again, and thy lover, little Nicky, Nacky. Ah, toad, toad, toad, toad, spit in my face a little, Nacky ; spit in my face, pry'thee, spit in my face, never so little ; spit but a little bit,—spit, spit, spit, spit when you are bid, I say ; do pry'thee, spit.—Now, now spit. What, you won't spit, will you ? Then I'll be a dog.

Aquilina. A dog, my lord !

Antonio. Ay a dog, and I'll give thee this t'other purse to let me be a dog—and to use me like a dog a little. Hurry durry, I will—here 'tis. (*Gives the purse.*) . . . Now bough waugh waugh, bough, waugh.

Aquilina. Hold, hold, sir. If curs bite, they must be kicked, sir. Do you see, kicked thus ?

Antonio. Ay, with all my heart. Do, kick, kick on, now I am under the table, kick again,—kick harder—harder yet—bough, waugh, waugh, bough.—Odd, Ill have a snap at thy shins.—Bough, waugh, waugh, waugh, bough—odd, she kicks bravely." [1]

At last she takes a whip, thrashes him soundly, and turns him out of the house. He will return, we may be sure of that ; he has spent a pleasant evening ; he rubs his back, but he was amused. In short, he was but a clown who had missed his vocation, whom chance has given an embroidered silk gown, and who turns out at so much an hour political harlequinades. He feels more natural, more at his ease, playing Punch than aping a statesman.

These are but gleams : for the most part Otway is a poet of his time, dull and forced in colour ; buried, like the rest, in the heavy, grey, clouded atmosphere, half English and half French, in which the bright lights brought over from France, are snuffed out by the insular fogs. He is a man of his time ; like the rest, he writes obscene comedies, *The Soldier's Fortune, The Atheist, Friendship in Fashion.* He depicts coarse and vicious cavaliers, rogues on principle, as harsh and corrupt as those of Wycherley, Beaugard, who vaunts and practises the maxims of Hobbes ; the father, an old, corrupt rascal, who brags of his morality, and whom his son coldly sends to the dogs with a bag of crowns : Sir Jolly Jumble, a kind of base

---

[1] *Venice Preserved*, 3. 1. Antonio is meant as a copy of the " celebrated Earl of Shaftesbury, the lewdness of whose latter years," says Mr. Thornton in his edition of Otway's Works, 3 vols. 1815, " was a subject of general notoriety."—Tr.

Falstaff, a pander by profession, whom the courtesans call "papa, daddy," who, "if he sits but at the table with one, he'll be making nasty figures in the napkins :"[1] Sir Davy Dunce, a disgusting animal, "who has such a breath, one kiss of him were enough to cure the fits of the mother; 'tis worse than assafœtida. Clean linen, he says, is unwholesome . . . ; he is continually eating of garlic, and chewing tobacco ;"[2] Polydore, who, enamoured of his father's ward, tries to force her in the first scene, envies the brutes, and makes up his mind to imitate them on the next occasion.[3] Otway defiles even his heroines.[4] Truly this society sickens us. They thought to cover all their filth with fine correct meta-

---

[1] *The Soldier's Fortune*, 1. 1.   *Ibid.*

[3] "Who'd be that sordid foolish thing called man,
   To cringe thus, fawn, and flatter for a pleasure,
   Which beasts enjoy so very much above him ?
   The lusty bull ranges thro' all the field,
   And from the herd singling his female out,
   Enjoys her, and abandons her at will.
   It shall be so, I'll yet possess my love,
   Wait on, and watch her loose unguarded hours :
   Then, when her roving thoughts have been abroad,
   And brought in wanton wishes to her heart ;
   I' th' very minute when her virtue nods,
   I'll rush upon her in a storm of love,
   Beat down her guard of honour all before me,
   Surfeit on joys, till ev'n desire grew sick ;
   Then by long absence liberty regain,
   And quite forget the pleasure and the pain."—*The Orphan*, 1. 1.
It is impossible to see together more moral roguery and literary correctness.

[4] "*Page* (to Monimia). In the morning when you call me to you,
   And by your bed I stand and tell you stories,
   I am ashamed to see your swelling breasts ;
   It makes me blush, they are so very white.
   Monimia. Oh men, for flatt'ry and deceit renown'd !"
                                   —*The Orphan*, 1. 1.

phors, neatly ended poetical periods, a garment of harmonious phrases and noble expressions. They thought to equal Racine by counterfeiting his style. They did not know that in this style the outward elegance conceals an admirable propriety of thought; that if it is a masterpiece of art, it is also a picture of manners; that the most refined and accomplished in society alone could speak and understand it; that it paints a civilisation, as Shakspeare's does; that each of these lines, which appear so stiff, has its inflection and artifice; that all passions, and every shade of passion, are expressed in them,—not, it is true, wild and entire, as in Shakspeare, but pared down and refined by courtly life; that this is a spectacle as unique as the other; that nature perfectly polished is as complex and as difficult to understand as nature perfectly intact; that as for the dramatists we speak of, they were as far below the one as below the other; and that, in short, their characters are as much like Racine's as the porter of Mons. de Beauvilliers or the cook of Madame de Sévigné were like Madame de Sévigné or Mons. de Beauvilliers.[1]

VI.

Let us then leave this drama in the obscurity which it deserves, and seek elsewhere, in studied writings, for a happier employment of a fuller talent.

Pamphlets and dissertations in verse, letters, satires

---

[1] Burns said, after his arrival in Edinburgh, "Between the man of rustic life and the polite world, I observed little difference. . . . But a refined and accomplished woman was a being altogether new to me, and of which I had formed but a very inadequate idea."—(*Burns' Works*, ed. Cunningham, 1832, 8 vols, i. 207.)

translations and imitations ; here was the true domain of Dryden and of classical reason ; this the field on which logical faculties and the art of writing find their best occupation.[1] Before descending into it, and observing their work, it will be as well to study more closely the man who so wielded them.

His was a singularly solid and judicious mind, an excellent reasoner, accustomed to mature his ideas, armed with good long-meditated proofs, strong in discussion, asserting principles, establishing his subdivisions, citing authorities, drawing inferences ; so that, if we read his prefaces without reading his dramas, we might take him for one of the masters of the dramatic art. He naturally attains a prose style, definite and precise ; his ideas are unfolded with breadth and clearness ; his style is well moulded, exact and simple, free from the affectations and ornaments with which Pope's was burdened afterwards ; his expression is, like that of Corneille, ample and full ; the cause of it is simply to be found in the inner arguments which unfold and sustain it. We can see that he thinks, and that on his own behalf ; that he combines and verifies his thoughts ; that besides all this, he naturally has a just perception, and that with his method he has good sense. He has the tastes and the weaknesses which suit his cast of intellect. He holds in the highest estimation " the admirable Boileau, whose numbers are excellent, whose expressions are noble, whose thoughts are just, whose language is pure, whose satire is pointed, and whose sense is close. What he borrows from the ancients, he repays with usury of his own, in coin as good, and almost as uni-

---

[1] Dryden says, in his *Essay on Satire*, xiii. 30, " the stage to which my genius never much inclined me."

versally valuable." [1] He has the stiffness of the logician
poets, too strict and argumentative, blaming Ariosto
" who neither designed justly, nor observed any unity
of action, or compass of time, or moderation in the
vastness of his draught; his style is luxurious, without
majesty or decency, and his adventures without the
compass of nature and possibility." [2] He understands
delicacy no better than fancy. Speaking of Horace, he
finds that " his wit is faint and his salt almost insipid.
Juvenal is of a more vigorous and masculine wit; he
gives me as much pleasure as I can bear." [3] For the
same reason he depreciates the French style : " Their
language is not strung with sinews, like our English;
it has the nimbleness of a greyhound, but not the bulk
and body of a mastiff. . . . They have set up purity for
the standard of their language; and a masculine vigour
is that of ours." [4] Two or three such words depict a
man ; Dryden has just shown, unwittingly the measure
and quality of his mind.

This mind, as we may imagine, is heavy, and especially so in flattery. Flattery is the chief art in a
monarchical age. Dryden is hardly skilful in it, any
more than his contemporaries. Across the Channel, at
the same epoch, they praised just as much, but without
cringing too low, because praise was decked out ; now
disguised or relieved by charm of style ; now looking
as if men took to it as to a fashion. Thus delicately
tempered, people are able to digest it. But here, far
from the fine aristocratic kitchen, it weighs like an
undigested mass upon the stomach. I have related how
Lord Clarendon, hearing that his daughter had just

[1] *Essay on Satire*, dedicated to the Earl of Dorset, xiii. 16.
[2] *Ibid.*   [3] *Ibid.* 84.   [4] Dedication of the *Æneïs*, xiv. 204.

married the Duke of York in secret, begged the king to
have her instantly beheaded;[1] how the Commons, composed for the most part of Presbyterians, declared
themselves and the English people rebels, worthy of the
punishment of death; and moreover cast themselves
at the king's feet, with contrite air to beg him to pardon
the House and the nation.[2]   Dryden is no more delicate
than statesmen and legislators.   His dedications are as
a rule nauseous.   He says to the Duchess of Monmouth:
" To receive the blessings and prayers of mankind, you
need only be seen together.   We are ready to conclude,
that you are a pair of angels sent below to make virtue
amiable in your persons, or to sit to poets when they
would pleasantly instruct the age, by drawing goodness
in the most perfect and alluring shape of nature. . . .
No part of Europe can afford a parallel to your noble
Lord in masculine beauty, and in goodliness of shape." [3]
Elsewhere he says to the Duke of Monmouth : " You
have all the advantages of mind and body, and an
illustrious birth conspiring to render you an extraordinary person.   The Achilles and the Rinaldo are
present in you, even above their originals ; you only
want a Homer or a Tasso to make you equal to them.
Youth, beauty, and courage (all which you possess in
the height of their perfection) are the most desirable
gifts of Heaven." [4]   His Grace did not frown nor hold
his nose, and his Grace was right.[5]   Another author,

---

[1] See vol. ii. 332.   [2] See vol. ii. 334.

[3] Dedication of *The Indian Emperor*, ii. 261.

[4] Dedication of *Tyrannic Love*, iii. 347.

[5] He also says in the same epistle dedicatory : "All men will join
me in the adoration which I pay you." To the Earl of Rochester he
writes in a letter (xviii. 90) : "I find it is not for me to contend any
way with your Lordship, who can write better on the meanest subject

Mrs. Aphra Behn, burned a still more ill-savoured incense under the nose of Nell Gwynne : people's nerves were strong in those days, and they breathed freely where others would be suffocated. The Earl of Dorset having written some little songs and satires, Dryden swears that in his way he equalled Shakspeare, and surpassed all the ancients. And these barefaced panegyrics go on imperturbably for a score of pages; the author alternately passing in review the various virtues of his great man, always finding that the last is the finest;[1] after which he receives by way of recompense a purse of gold. Dryden in taking the money, is not more a flunkey than others. The corporation of Hull, harangued one day by the Duke of Monmouth, made him a present of six broad pieces, which were presented to Monmouth by Marvell, the member for Hull.[2] Modern scruples were not yet born. I can believe that Dryden, with all his prostrations, lacked spirit more than honour.

A second talent, perhaps the first in carnival time, is the art of saying broad things, and the Restoration was a carnival, about as delicate as a bargee's ball. There are strange songs and rather shameless prologues in Dryden's plays. His *Marriage à la Mode* opens with these verses sung by a married woman :

" Why should a foolish marriage vow,
    Which long ago was made,

than I can on the best. . . . You are above any incense I can give you." In his dedication of the *Fables* (xi. 195) he compares the Duke of Ormond to Joseph, Ulysses, Lucullus, etc. In his fourth poetical epistle (xi. 20) he compares Lady Castlemaine to Cato.

[1] Dedication of the *Essay of Dramatic Poesy*, xv. 286.
[2] See Andrew Marvell's Works, i. 210.

Oblige us to each other now,
When passion is decay'd ?
We loved, and we loved as long as we could,
' Till our love was loved out in us both.
But our marriage is dead when the pleasure is fled ;
'Twas pleasure first made it an oath." [1]

The reader may read the rest for himself in Dryden's
plays; it cannot be quoted. Besides, Dryden does not
succeed well; his mind is on too solid a basis; his
mood is too serious, even reserved, taciturn. As Sir
Walter Scott justly said, "his indelicacy was like the
forced impudence of a bashful man." [2] He wished to
wear the fine exterior of a Sedley or a Rochester, made
himself petulant of set purpose, and squatted clumsily
in the filth in which others simply sported. Nothing
is more sickening than studied lewdness, and Dryden
studies everything, even pleasantry and politeness. He
wrote to Dennis, who had praised him : "They (the
commendations) are no more mine when I receive them
than the light of the moon can be allowed to be her
own, who shines but by the reflexion of her brother.[3]
He wrote to his cousin, in a diverting narration, these
details of a fat woman, with whom he had travelled :
" Her weight made the horses travel very heavily ; but,
to give them a breathing time, she would often stop us,
. . . and tell us we were all flesh and blood." [4] It
seems that these were the sort of jokes which would
then amuse a lady. His letters are made up of
heavy official civilities, vigorously hewn compliments,
mathematical salutes; his badinage is a dissertation,

---

[1] *Marriage à la Mode*, iv. 245.   [2] Scott's *Life of Dryden*, i. 447.
[3] Letter 2, "to Mr. John Dennis," xviii. 114.
[4] Letter 29, "to Mrs. Steward," xviii. 144.

he props up his trifles with periods. I have found in his works some beautiful passages, but never agreeable ones; he cannot even argue with taste. The characters in his *Essay of Dramatic Poesy* think themselves still at college, learnedly quote Paterculus, and in Latin too, opposing the definition of the other side, and observing "that it was only *à genere et fine*, and so not altogether perfect." [1] In one of his prefaces he says in a professorial tone: "It is charged upon me that I make debauched persons my protagonists, or the chief persons of the drama; and that I make them happy in the conclusion of my play; against the law of comedy, which is to reward virtue, and punish vice." [2] Elsewhere he declares: "It is not that I would explode the use of metaphors from passion, for Longinus thinks them necessary to raise it." His great *Essay upon Satire* swarms with useless or long protracted passages, with the inquiries and comparisons of a commentator. He cannot get rid of the scholar, the logician, the rhetorician, and show the plain downright man.

But his true manliness was often apparent; in spite of several falls and many slips, he shows a mind constantly upright, bending rather from conventionality than from nature, possessing enthusiasm and afflatus, occupied with grave thoughts, and subjecting his conduct to his convictions. He was converted loyally and by conviction to the Roman Catholic creed, persevered in it after the fall of James II., lost his post of historiographer and poet-laureate, and though poor, burdened with a family, and infirm, refused to dedicate his *Virgil* to King William. He wrote to his sons:

[1] *Essay of Dramatic Poesy*, xv. 302.
[2] Preface to *An Evening's Love*, iii. 225.

"Dissembling, though lawful in some cases, is not my talent: yet, for your sake, I will struggle with the plain openness of my nature. . . . In the meantime, I flatter not myself with any manner of hopes, but do my duty, and suffer for God's sake. . . . You know the profits (of *Virgil*) might have been more; but neither my conscience nor my honour would suffer me to take them; but I can never repent of my constancy, since I am thoroughly persuaded of the justice of the cause for which I suffer."[1] One of his sons having been expelled from school, he wrote to the master, Dr. Busby, his own former teacher, with extreme gravity and nobleness, asking without humiliation, disagreeing without giving offence, in a sustained and proud style, which is calculated to please, seeking again his favour, if not as a debt to the father, at least as a gift to the son, and concluding, "I have done something, so far to conquer my own spirit as to ask it." He was a good father to his children, as well as liberal, and sometimes even generous, to the tenant of his little estate.[2] He says: "More libels have been written against me than almost any man now living. . . . I have seldom answered any scurrilous lampoon, . . . and, being naturally vindictive, have suffered in silence, and possessed my soul in quiet."[3] Insulted by Collier as a corrupter of morals, he endured this coarse reproof, and nobly confessed the faults of his youth: "I shall say the less of Mr. Collier, because in many things he has taxed me justly; and I have pleaded guilty to all thoughts and expressions of mine which can be truly argued obscenity, profaneness, or immorality, and retract them. If he be my enemy, let

---

[1] Letter 23, " to his sons at Rome," xviii. 133.
[2] Scott's *Life of Dryden*, i. 449.　　　[3] *Essay on Satire*, xiii. 80.

him triumph; if he be my friend, as I have given him
no personal occasion to be otherwise, he will be glad of
my repentance."[1]   There is some wit in what follows :
" He (Collier) is too much given to horseplay in his raillery, and comes to battle like a dictator from the plough.
I will not say ' the zeal of God's house has eaten him up,'
but I am sure it has devoured some part of his good manners and civility."[2]   Such a repentance raises a man ;
when he humbles himself thus, he must be a great man.
He was so in mind and in heart, full of solid arguments
and individual opinions, above the petty mannerism of
rhetoric and affectations of style, a master of verse, a
slave to his idea, with that abundance of thought which
is the sign of true genius : " Thoughts such as they are,
come crowding in so fast upon me, that my only difficulty is to chuse or to reject, to run them into verses,
or to give them the other harmony of prose : I have so
long studied and practised both, that they are grown
into a habit, and become familiar to me."[3]   With these
powers he entered upon his second career ; the English
constitution and genius opened it to him.

VII.

" A man," says La Bruyère, " born a Frenchman and
a Christian finds himself constrained in satire ; great
subjects are forbidden to him ; he essays them sometimes, and then turns aside to small things, which he
elevates by the beauty of his genius and his style."   It
was not so in England.   Great subjects were given up
to vehement discussion ; politics and religion, like two

---

[1] Preface to the *Fables*, xi. 238.   [2] *Ibid.*   *Ibid.* xi. 209.

arenas, invited every talent and every passion to boldness and to battle. The king, at first popular, had
roused opposition by his vices and errors, and bent before
public discontent as before the intrigue of parties. It
was known that he had sold the interests of England to
France ; it was believed that he would deliver up the
consciences of Protestants to the Papists. The lies
of Oates, the murder of the magistrate Godfrey, his
corpse solemnly paraded in the streets of London, had
inflamed the imagination and prejudices of the people ;
the judges, blind or intimidated, sent innocent Roman
Catholics to the scaffold, and the mob received with
insults and curses their protestations of innocence. The
king's brother had been dismissed from his offices, and
it was proposed to exclude him from the throne. The
pulpit, the theatre, the press, the hustings, resounded
with discussions and recriminations. The names of
Whigs and Tories arose, and the loftiest debates of
political philosophy were carried on, enlivened by the
feeling of present and practical interests, embittered
by the rancour of old and wounded passions. Dryden
plunged in ; and his poem of *Absalom and Achitophel*
was a political pamphlet. " They who can criticise
so weakly," he says in the preface, " as to imagine
that I have done my worst, may be convinced at their
own cost that I can write severely with more ease than
I can gently." A biblical allegory, suited to the taste
of the time, hardly concealed the names, and did not
hide the men. He describes the tranquil old age and
incontestable right of King David ;[1] the charm, pliant
humour, popularity of his natural son Absalom ;[2] the

---

[1] Charles II.   [2] The Duke of Monmouth.

genius and treachery of Achitophel,[1] who stirs up the son against the father, unites the clashing ambitions, and reanimates the conquered factions. There is hardly any wit here; there is no time to be witty in such contests; think of the roused people who listened, men in prison or exile who are waiting; fortune, liberty, life was at stake. The thing is to strike the nail on the head, hard, not gracefully. The public must recognise the characters, shout their names as they recognise the portraits, applaud the attacks which are made upon them, rail at them, hurl them from the high rank which they covet. Dryden passes them all in review:

[1] The Earl of Shaftesbury :

"Of these the false Achitophel was first,
A name to all succeeding ages curst :
For close designs and crooked counsels fit,
Sagacious, bold and turbulent of wit—
Restless, unfixed in principles and place,
In power unpleased, impatient of disgrace ;
A fiery soul, which working out its way,
Fretted the pigmy body to decay
And o'er-informed the tenement of clay.
A daring pilot in extremity,
Pleased with the danger, when the waves went high,
He sought the storms ; but, for a calm unfit,
Would steer too nigh the sands to boast his wit.
Great wits are sure to madness near allied
And thin partitions do their bounds divide ;.
Else, why should he, with wealth and honour blest,
Refuse his age the needful hours of rest ?
Punish a body which he could not please,
Bankrupt of life, yet prodigal of ease ?
And all to leave what with his toil he won,
To that unfeathered two-legged thing, a son,
Got, while his soul did huddled notions try,
And born a shapeless lump, like anarchy,
In friendship false, implacable in hate,
Resolved to ruin or to rule the state."

" In the first rank of these did Zimri [1] stand,
A man so various that he seemed to be
Not one, but all mankind's epitome :
Stiff in opinions, always in the wrong,
Was everything by starts and nothing long ·
But in the course of one revolving moon
Was chymist, fiddler, statesman, and buffoon ;
Then all for women, painting, rhyming, drinking,
Besides ten thousand freaks that died in thinking.
Blest madman, who could every hour employ
With something new to wish or to enjoy !
Railing and praising were his usual themes ;
And both, to show his judgment, in extremes :
So over-violent, or over-civil,
That every man with him was God or devil.
In squandering wealth was his peculiar art ;
Nothing went unrewarded but desert.
Beggared by fools whom still he found too late,
He had his jest, and they had his estate.
He laugh'd himself from Court ; then sought relief
By forming parties, but could ne'er be chief :
For spite of him, the weight of business fell
On Absalom and wise Achitophel ;
Thus wicked but in will, of means bereft,
He left not faction, but of that was left. . . .

Shimei, [2] whose youth did early promise bring
Of zeal to God and hatred to his King ;
Did wisely from expensive sins refrain
And never broke the Sabbath but for gain :
Nor ever was he known an oath to vent,
Or curse, unless against the government."

Against these attacks their chief Shaftesbury made a
stand : when accused of high treason he was declared

not guilty by the grand jury, in spite of all the efforts
of the court, amidst the applause of a great crowd;
and his partisans caused a medal to be struck, bearing
his face, and boldly showing on the reverse London
Bridge and the Tower, with the sun rising and shining
through a cloud. Dryden replied by his poem of the
Medal, and the violent diatribe overwhelmed the open
provocation :

> " Oh, could the style that copied every grace
> And plow'd such furrows for an eunuch face,
> Could it have formed his ever-changing will,
> The various piece had tired the graver's skill !
> A martial hero first, with early care,
> Blown like a pigmy by the winds, to war ;
> A beardless chief, a rebel ere a man,
> So young his hatred to his Prince began.
> Next this (how wildly will ambition steer !)
> A vermin wriggling in the usurper's ear ;
> Bartering his venal wit for sums of gold,
> He cast himself into the saint-like mould,
> Groaned, sighed, and prayed, while godliness was gain,
> The loudest bag-pipe of the squeaking train."

The same bitterness envenomed religious controversy.
Disputes on dogma, for a moment cast into the shade
by debauched and sceptical manners, had broken out
again, inflamed by the bigoted Roman Catholicism of
the prince, and by the just fears of the nation. The
poet who in *Religio Laici* was still an Anglican, though
lukewarm and hesitating, drawn on gradually by his
absolutist inclinations, had become a convert to Roman-
ism, and in his poem of *The Hind and the Panther* fought
for his new creed. " The nation," he says in the preface,
" is in too high a ferment for me to expect either fair

war or even so much as fair quarter from a reader of
the opposite party." And then, making use of medi-
æval allegories, he represents all the heretical sects as
beasts of prey, worrying a white hind of heavenly
origin; he spares neither coarse comparisons, gross
sarcasms, nor open objurgations. The argument is
close and theological throughout. His hearers were not
wits, who cared to see how a dry subject could be
adorned; they were not theologians, only by accident
and for a moment, animated by mistrustful and cautious
feelings, like Boileau in his *Amour de Dieu*. They
were oppressed men, barely recovered from a secular
persecution, attached to their faith by their sufferings,
ill at ease under the visible menaces and ominous
hatred of their restrained foes. Their poet must be a
dialectician and a schoolman; he needs all the sternness of logic; he is immeshed in it, like a recent
convert, saturated with the proofs which have separated
him from the national faith, and which support him
against public reprobation, fertile in distinctions, point-
ing with his finger at the weaknesses of an argument,
subdividing replies, bringing back his adversary to the
question, thorny and unpleasing to a modern reader,
but the more praised and loved in his own time. In
all English minds there is a basis of gravity and
vehemence; hate rises tragic, with a gloomy outbreak,
like the breakers of the North Sea. In the midst of
his public strife Dryden attacks a private enemy,
Shadwell, and overwhelms him with immortal scorn.[1]
A great epic style and solemn rhyme gave weight to
his sarcasm, and the unlucky rhymester was drawn in a
ridiculous triumph on the poetic car, whereon the muse

[1] Mac Flecknoe.

sets the heroes and the gods. Dryden represented the
Irishman Mac Flecknoe, an old king of folly, deliberating
on the choice of a worthy successor, and choosing
Shadwell as an heir to his gabble, a propagator of
nonsense, a boastful conqueror of common sense. From
all sides, through the streets littered with paper, the
nations assembled to look upon the young hero, standing
near the throne of his father, his brow surrounded with
thick fogs, the vacant smile of satisfied imbecility floating over his countenance :

> " The hoary prince in majesty appear'd,
> High on a throne of his own labours rear'd.
> At his right hand our young Ascanius sate,
> Rome's other hope, and pillar of the state ;
> His brows thick fogs instead of glories grace,
> And lambent dulness play'd around his face.
> As Hannibal did to the altars come,
> Sworn by his sire, a mortal foe to Rome ;
> So Shadwell swore, nor should his vow be vain,
> That he, till death, true dulness would maintain ;
> And, in his father's right and realm's defence,
> Ne'er to have peace with wit nor truce with sense.
> The king himself the sacred unction made,
> As king by office and as priest by trade.
> In his sinister hand, instead of ball,
> He placed a mighty mug of potent ale."

His father blesses him :

> " ' Heavens bless my son ! from Ireland let him reign
> To far Barbadoes on the western main ;
> Of his dominion may no end be known,
> And greater than his father's be his throne ;
> Beyond Love's Kingdom let him stretch his pen ! '
> He paused, and all the people cried Amen.

Then thus continued he : ' My son, advance
Still in new impudence, new ignorance.
Success let others teach, learn thou from me,
Pangs without birth and fruitless industry.
Let Virtuosos in five years be writ ;
Yet not one thought accuse thy toil of wit. . . .
Let them be all by thy own model made
Of dulness and desire no foreign aid,
That they to future ages may be known,
Not copies drawn, but issue of thy own :
Nay, let thy men of wit too be the same,
All full of thee and differing but in name. . . .
Like mine thy gentle numbers feebly creep ;
Thy tragic Muse gives smiles, thy comic sleep.
With whate'er gall thou setst thyself to write,
Thy inoffensive satires never bite ;
In thy felonious heart though venom lies,
It does but touch thy Irish pen, and dies.
Thy genius calls thee not to purchase fame
In keen Iambics, but mild Anagram.
Leave writing plays, and choose for thy command
Some peaceful province in Acrostic land.
There thou may'st wings display, and altars raise,
And torture one poor word ten thousand ways ;
Or, if thou wouldst thy different talents suit,
Set thy own songs, and sing them to thy lute.'
He said, but his last words were scarcely heard,
For Bruce and Longville had a trap prepared,
And down they set the yet declaiming bard.
Sinking he left his drugget robe behind,
Borne upwards by a subterranean wind.
The mantle fell to the young prophet's part,
With double portion of his father's art." [1]

Thus the insulting masquerade goes on, not studied

[1] Mac Flecknoe.

and polished like Boileau's *Lutrin,* but rude and pompous, inspired by a coarse poetical afflatus, as you may see a great ship enter the muddy Thames, with spread canvas, cleaving the waters.

VIII.

In these three poems, the art of writing, the mark and the source of classical literature, appeared for the first time. A new spirit was born and renewed this art, like everything else; thenceforth, and for a century to come, ideas sprang up and fell into their place after another law than that which had hitherto shaped them. Under Spenser and Shakspeare, living words, like cries or music, betrayed the internal imagination which gave them forth. A kind of vision possessed the artist; landscapes and events were unfolded in his mind as in nature; he concentrated in a glance all the details and all the forces which make up a being, and this image acted and was developed within him like the external object; he imitated his characters; he heard their words; he found it easier to represent them with every pulsation than to relate or explain their feelings; he did not judge, he saw; he was an involuntary actor and mimic; drama was his natural work, because in it the characters speak, and not the author. Then this complex and imitative conception changes colour and is decomposed: man sees things no more at a glance, but in detail; he walks leisurely round them, turning his light upon all their parts in succession. The fire which revealed them by a single illumination is extinguished; he observes qualities, marks aspects, classifies groups of actions, judges and reasons. Words, before animated, and as it were swelling with sap, are withered and dried up; they become abstractions; they cease to produce in him figures and landscapes; they only set in motion the relics of enfeebled passions; they barely shed a few flickering beams on the uniform texture of his dulled conception; they become exact, almost scientific, like numbers, and like numbers they are arranged in a series, allied by their analogies,—the first, more simple, leading up to the next, more composite,—all in the same order, so that the mind which enters upon a track, finds it level, and is never obliged to quit it. Thenceforth a new career is opened; man has the whole world resubjected to his thought; the change in his thoughts has changed all aspects, and everything assumes a new form in his metamorphosed mind. His task is to explain and to prove; this, in short, is the classical style, and this is the style of Dryden.

He develops, defines, concludes; he declares his thought, then takes it up again, that his reader may receive it prepared, and having received, may retain it. He bounds it with exact terms justified by the dictionary, with simple constructions justified by grammar, that the reader may have at every step a method of verification and a source of clearness. He contrasts ideas with ideas, phrases with phrases, so that the reader, guided by the contrast, may not deviate from the route marked out for him. You may imagine the possible beauty of such a work. This poesy is but a stronger prose. Closer ideas, more marked contrasts, bolder images, only add weight to the argument. Metre and rhyme transform the judgments into sentences. The mind, held on the stretch by the rhythm, studies itself more, and by means of reflection arrives at a noble conclusion. The judgments are enshrined in abbreviative

images, or symmetrical lines, which give them the
solidity and popular form of a dogma. General truths
acquire the definite form which transmits them to
posterity, and propagates them in the human race.
Such is the merit of these poems ; they please by their
good expressions.[1] In a full and solid web stand out
cleverly connected or sparkling threads. Here Dryden
has gathered in one line a long argument; there a
happy metaphor has opened up a new perspective under
the principal idea ;[2] further on, two similar words, united
together, have struck the mind with an unforeseen and
cogent proof ;[3] elsewhere a hidden comparison has
thrown a tinge of glory or shame on the person who
least expected it. These are all artifices or successes
of a calculated style, which chains the attention, and
leaves the mind persuaded or convinced.

[1] " Strong were our sires, and as they fought they writ,
    Conquering with force of arms and dint of wit :
    Theirs was the giant race before the flood,
    And thus, when Charles return'd, our empire stood.
    Like Janus, he the stubborn soil manured,
    With rules of husbandry the rankness cured ;
    Tamed us to manners, when the stage was rude,
    And boisterous English wit with art endured. . . .
    But what we gain'd in skill we lost in strength,
    Our builders were with want of genius curst ;
    The second temple was not like the first."
                    Epistle 12 *to Congreve*, xi. 59.

[2] " Held up the buckler of the people's cause
    Against the crown, and skulk'd against the laws. . . .
    Desire of power, on earth a vicious weed,
    Yet, sprung from high, is of celestial seed !"
                    Absalom and Achitophel, Part i.

[3] " Why then should I, encouraging the bad,
    Turn rebel, and run popularly mad ?"
                    Absalom and Achitophel, Part i.

IX.

In truth, there is scarcely any other literary merit. If Dryden is a skilled politician, a trained controversialist, well armed with arguments, knowing all the ins and outs of discussion, versed in the history of men and parties, this pamphleteering aptitude, practical and English, confines him to the low region of everyday and personal controversies, far from the lofty philosophy and speculative freedom which give endurance and greatness to the classical style of his French contemporaries. In the main, in this age, in England, all discussion was fundamentally narrow. Except the terrible Hobbes, they all lack grand originality. Dryden, like the rest, is confined to the arguments and insults of sect and fashion. Their ideas were as small as their hatred was strong; no general doctrine opened up a poetical vista beyond the tumult of the strife; texts, traditions, a sad train of rigid reasoning, such were their arms; the same prejudices and passions exist in both parties. This is why the subject-matter fell below the art of writing. Dryden had no personal philosophy to develop; he does but versify themes given to him by others. In this sterility art soon is reduced to the clothing of foreign ideas, and the writer becomes an antiquarian or a translator. In reality, the greatest part of Dryden's poems are imitations, adaptations, or copies. He translated Persius and Virgil, with parts of Horace, Theocritus, Juvenal, Lucretius, and Homer, and put into modern English several tales of Boccaccio and Chaucer. These translations then appeared to be as great works as original compositions. When he took the *Æneid* in hand, the nation, as Johnson tells us, appeared to think its honour interested in the issue. Addison furnished him with the arguments of every book, and an essay on the *Georgics;* others supplied him with editions and notes; great lords vied with one another in offering him hospitality; subscriptions flowed in. They said that the English Virgil was to give England the Virgil of Rome. This work was long considered his highest glory. Even so at Rome, under Cicero, in the early dearth of national poetry, the translators of Greek works were as highly praised as the original authors.

This sterility of invention alters or depresses the taste. For taste is an instinctive system, and leads us by internal maxims, which we ignore. The mind, guided by it, perceives connections, shuns discordances, enjoys or suffers, chooses or rejects, according to general conceptions which master it, but are not visible. These removed, we see the tact, which they engendered, disappear; the writer is clumsy, because philosophy fails him. Such is the imperfection of the stories handled by Dryden, from Boccaccio and Chaucer. Dryden does not see that fairy tales or tales of chivalry only suit a poetry in its infancy; that ingenuous subjects require an artless style; that the talk of Reynard and Chanticleer, the adventures of Palamon and Arcite, the transformations, tournaments, apparitions, need the astonished carelessness and the graceful gossip of old Chaucer. Vigorous periods, reflective antitheses, here oppress these amiable ghosts; classical phrases embarrass them in their too stringent embrace; they are lost to our sight; to find them again, we must go to their first parent, quit the too harsh light of a learned and manly age; we cannot pursue them fairly except in their first style in the dawn of credulous thought, under the mist which plays about their vague forms, with all the blushes and

smiles of morning.   Moreover, when Dryden comes on
the scene, he crushes the delicacies of his master, haul-
ing in tirades or reasonings, blotting out sincere and self-
abandoning tenderness.   What a difference between
his account of Arcite's death and Chaucer's !   How
wretched are all his fine literary words, his gallantry,
his symmetrical phrases, his cold regrets, compared to
the cries of sorrow, the true outpouring, the deep love
in Chaucer !   But the worst fault is that almost everywhere he is a copyist, and retains the faults like a literal
translator, with eyes glued on the work, powerless to
comprehend and recast it, more a rhymester than a poet.
When La Fontaine put Æsop or Boccaccio into verse,
he breathed a new spirit into them; he took their
matter only : the new soul, which constitutes the value
of his work, is his, and only his; and this soul befits
the work.   In place of the Ciceronian periods of Boccaccio, we find slim, little lines, full of delicate raillery,
dainty voluptuousness, feigned artlessness, which relish
the forbidden fruit because it is fruit, and because it is
forbidden.   The tragic departs, the relics of the middle-
ages are a thousand leagues away ; there remains nothing
but the invidious gaiety, Gallic and racy, as of a critic
and an epicurean.   In Dryden, incongruities abound;
and our author is so little shocked by them, that he
imports them elsewhere, in his theological poems,
representing the Roman Catholic Church, for instance,
as a hind, and the heresies by various animals, who
dispute at as great length and as learnedly as Oxford
graduates.[1]   I like him no better in his Epistles; as a

---

[1] " Though Huguenots contemn our ordination,
           Succession, ministerial vocation," etc.
(*The Hind and the Panther*, Part ii. x. 166), such are the harsh words
we often find in his books.

rule, they are but flatteries, almost always awkward, often mythological, interspersed with somewhat common-place sentences. "I have studied Horace," he says, "and hope the style of his Epistles is not ill imitated here."[1] But don't believe him. Horace's Epistles, though in verse, are genuine letters, brisk, unequal in move-ment, always unstudied, natural. Nothing is further from Dryden than this original and thorough man of the world, philosophical and lewd,[2] this most refined and most nervous of epicureans, this kinsman (at eighteen centuries' distance) of Alfred de Musset and Voltaire. Like Horace, an author must be a thinker and a man of the world to write agreeable morality, and Dryden was no more than his contemporaries either a man of the world or a thinker.

But other characteristics, as eminently English, sustain him. Suddenly, in the midst of the yawns which these Epistles occasioned, our eyes are arrested. A true accent, new ideas, are brought out. Dryden, writing to his cousin, a country gentleman, has lighted on an English original subject. He depicts the life of a rural squire, the referee of his neighbours, who shuns lawsuits and town doctors, who keeps himself in health by hunting and exercise. Here is his portrait:

"How bless'd is he, who leads a country life,
Unvex'd with anxious cares, and void of strife ! . . .
With crowds attended of your ancient race,
You seek the champaign sports, or sylvan chase ;
With well-breathed beagles you surround the wood,
Even then industrious of the common good ;

[1] Preface to the *Religio Laici*, x. 32.
[2] What Augustus says about Horace is charming, but cannot be quoted, even in Latin.

And often have you brought the wily fox
To suffer for the firstlings of the flocks ;
Chased even amid the folds, and made to bleed,
Like felons, where they did the murderous deed.
This fiery game your active youth maintain'd ;
Not yet by years extinguish'd though restrain'd : . . .

A patriot both the king and country serves ;
Prerogative and privilege preserves :
Of each our laws the certain limit show ;
One must not ebb, nor t'other overflow ;
Betwixt the prince and parliament we stand,
The barriers of the state on either hand ;
May neither overflow, for then they drown the land.
When both are full, they feed our bless'd abode ;
Like those that water'd once the paradise of God.
Some overpoise of sway, by turns, they share ;
In peace the people, and the prince in war :
Consuls of moderate power in calms were made ;
When the Gauls came, one sole dictator sway'd.
Patriots, in peace, assert the people's right,
With noble stubbornness resisting might ;
No lawless mandates from the court receive,
Nor lend by force, but in a body give."[1]

This serious converse shows a political mind, fed on the
spectacle of affairs, having in the matter of public and
practical debates the superiority which the French have
in speculative discussions and social conversation. So,
amidst the dryness of polemics break forth sudden
splendours, a poetic fount, a prayer from the heart's
depths ; the English well of concentrated passion is on
a sudden opened again with a flow and a spirit which
Dryden does not elsewhere exhibit :

[1] Epistle 15, xi. 75.

"Dim as the borrow'd beams of moon and stars
To lonely, weary, wand'ring travellers,
Is reason to the soul : and as on high
Those rolling fires discover but the sky,
Not light us here ; so Reason's glimm'ring ray
Was lent, not to assure our doubtful way,
But guide us upward to a better day.
And as those nightly tapers disappear
When day's bright lord ascends our hemisphere,
So pale grows Reason at Religion's sight,
So dies, and so dissolves in supernatural light." [1]

"But, gracious God ! how well dost thou provide
For erring judgments an unerring guide !
Thy throne is darkness in th' abyss of light,
A blaze of glory that forbids the sight.
O teach me to believe Thee thus conceal'd,
And search no farther than Thy self reveal'd ;
But her alone for my director take,
Whom Thou hast promised never to forsake !
My thoughtless youth was wing'd with vain desires ·
My manhood, long misled by wandering fires,
Follow'd false lights ; and when their glimpse was gone,
My pride struck out new sparkles of her own.
Such was I, such by nature still I am ;
Be Thine the glory and be mine the shame !
Good life be now my task ; my doubts are done." [2]

Such is the poetry of these serious minds. After having strayed in the debaucheries and pomps of the Restoration, Dryden found his way to the grave emotions of the inner life ; though a Romanist, he felt like a Protestant the wretchedness of man and the presence of grace : he was capable of enthusiasm. Here and there a manly and

---

[1] Beginning of *Religio Laici*, x. 37.
[2] *The Hind and the Panther*, Part. i. *l.* 64–75, x. 121.

soul-stirring verse discloses, in the midst of his reasonings, the power of conception and the inspiration of
desire.   When the tragic is met with, he takes to it as
to his own domain ; at need, he deals in the horrible.
He has described the infernal chase, and the torture of
the young girl worried by dogs, with the savage energy
of Milton." [1]   As a contrast, he loved nature : this taste
always endures in England; the sombre, reflective
passions are unstrung in the grand peace and harmony
of the fields.   Landscapes are to be met with amidst
theological disputation :

> " New blossoms flourish and new flowers arise,
>   As God had been abroad, and walking there
>   Had left his footsteps and reformed the year.
> The sunny hills from far were seen to glow
> With glittering beams, and in the meads below
> The burnished brooks appeared with liquid gold to flow.
> As last they heard the foolish Cuckoo sing,
> Whose note proclaimed the holy day of spring." [2]

Under his regular versification the artist's soul is brought
to light ; [3] though contracted by habits of classical argument, though stiffened by controversy and polemics,
though unable to create souls or to depict artless and
delicate sentiments, he is a genuine poet : he is troubled,
raised by beautiful sounds and forms ; he writes boldly
under the pressure of vehement ideas ; he surrounds

---

[1] *Theodore and Honoria,* xi. 435.
[2] *The Hind and the Panther*, Part iii. *l.* 553–560, x. 214.
[3] " For her the weeping heavens become serene,
     For her the ground is clad in cheerful green,
     For her the nightingales are taught to sing,
     And nature for her has delayed the spring."
These charming verses on the Duchess of York remind one of those of
La Fontaine in *le Songe*, addressed to the Princess of Conti.

himself willingly with splendid images; he is moved
by the buzzing of their swarms, the glitter of their
splendours; he is, when he wishes it, a musician and a
painter; he writes stirring airs, which shake all the
senses, even if they do not sink deep into the heart.
Such is his *Alexander's Feast*, an ode in honour of St.
Cecilia's day, an admirable trumpet-blast, in which
metre and sound impress upon the nerves the emotions
of the mind, a master-piece of rapture and of art, which
Victor Hugo alone has come up to.[1]   Alexander is on
his throne in the palace of Persepolis; the lovely Thais
sate by his side; before him, in a vast hall, his glorious
captains.   And Timotheus sings:

> " The praise of Bacchus, then, the sweet musician sung ;
>   Of Bacchus ever fair, and ever young.
>   The jolly God in triumph comes ;
>   Sound the trumpets, beat the drums ;
>   Flush'd with a purple grace,
>   He shews his honest face.
> Now, give the hautboys breath ; he comes, he comes.
>   Bacchus ever fair and young,
>   Drinking joys did first ordain ;
>   Bacchus' blessings are a treasure,
>   Drinking is the soldier's pleasure :
>   Rich the treasure,
>   Sweet the pleasure ;
>   Sweet is pleasure after pain."

And at the stirring sounds the king is troubled; his
cheeks are glowing; his battles return to his memory;
he defies heaven and earth.   Then a sad song depresses
him.   Timotheus mourns the death of the betrayed

---

[1] For instance, in the *Chant du Cirque.*

Darius.   Then a tender song softens him; Timotheus
lauds the dazzling beauty of Thais.   Suddenly he strikes
the lyre again :

> " A louder yet, and yet a louder strain.
>   Break his bands of sleep asunder,
>   And rouse him, like a rattling peal of thunder.
>   Hark, hark ! the horrid sound
>   Has raised up his head ;
>   As awaked from the dead,
>   And amazed, he stares around.
>   Revenge, revenge ! Timotheus cries,
>   See the furies arise ;
>   See the snakes, that they rear,
>   How they hiss in their hair !
>   And the sparkles that flash from their eyes !
>   Behold a ghastly band,
>   Each a torch in his hand !
>   Those are Grecian ghosts, that in battle were slain,
>   And unburied remain
>   Inglorious on the plain :
>   Give the vengeance due
>   To the valiant crew.
>   Behold how they toss their torches on high,
>   How they point to the Persian abodes,
>   And glittering temples of their hostile gods.—
>   The princes applaud, with a furious joy.
>   And the king seized a flambeau with zeal to destroy ;
>   Thais led the way,
>   To light him to his prey,
>   And, like another Helen, fired another Troy." [1]

Thus formerly music softened, exalted, mastered men ;
Dryden's verses acquire again its power in describing it.

---

[1] *Alexander's Feast*, xi. 183–188.

X

This was one of his last works;[1] brilliant and poetical, it was born amidst the greatest sadness. The king for whom he had written was deposed and in exile; the religion which he had embraced was despised and oppressed; a Roman Catholic and a royalist, he was bound to a conquered party, which the nation resentfully and distrustfully considered as the natural enemy of liberty and reason. He had lost the two places which were his support; he lived wretchedly, burdened with a family, obliged to support his sons abroad; treated as a hireling by a coarse publisher forced to ask him for money to pay for a watch which he could not get on credit, beseeching Lord Bolingbroke to protect him against Tonson's insults, rated by this shopkeeper when the promised page was not finished on the stated day. His enemies persecuted him with pamphlets; the severe Collier lashed his comedies unfeelingly; he was damned without pity, but conscientiously. He had long been in ill health, crippled, constrained to write much, reduced to exaggerate flattery in order to earn from the great the indispensable money which the publishers would not give him:[2] "What Virgil wrote in the vigour of his age, in plenty and at ease, I have undertaken to translate in my declining years; struggling with wants, oppressed with sickness, curbed in my genius, liable to be misconstrued in all I write; and my judges, if they are not very equitable, already prejudiced against me, by the lying

---

[1] *Alexander's Feast* was written in 1697, soon after the publication of the Virgil. In 1699 appeared Dryden's translated tales and original poems, generally known as "The Fables," in which the portrait of the English country-gentleman (see page 65) is to be found.—TR.

[2] He was paid two hundred and fifty guineas for ten thousand lines.

character which has been given them of my morals." [1]
Although he looked at his conduct from the most
favourable point of view, he knew that it had not always
been worthy, and that all his writings would not endure.
Born between two epochs, he had oscillated between
two forms of life and two forms of thought, having
reached the perfection of neither, having kept the faults
of both; having ·discovered in surrounding manners
no support worthy of his character, and in surrounding
ideas no subject worthy of his talent. If he had founded
criticism and good style, this criticism had only its
scope in pedantic treatises or unconnected prefaces;
this good style continued out of the track in inflated
tragedies, dispersed over multiplied translations, scattered in occasional pieces, in odes written to order, in
party poems, meeting only here and there an afflatus
capable of employing it, and a subject capable of sus-
taining it.   What gigantic efforts to end in such a
moderate result !   This is the natural condition of man.
The end of everything is pain and agony.   For a long
time gravel and gout left him no peace; erysipelas
seized one of his legs.   In April 1700 he tried to go
out; "a slight inflammation in one of his toes became
from neglect, a gangrene;" the doctor would have tried
amputation, but Dryden decided that what remained to
him of health and happiness was not worth the pain.
He died at the age of sixty-nine.

[1] Postscript of Virgil's Works, as translated by Dryden, xv. p. 187.

CHAPTER III.

The Revolution.

I.

WITH the constitution of 1688 a new spirit appears in England. Slowly, gradually, the moral revolution accompanies the social : man changes with the state, in the same sense and for the same causes ; character moulds itself to the situation ; and little by little, in manners and in literature, we see spring up a serious, reflective, moral spirit, capable of discipline and independence, which can alone maintain and give effect to a constitution.

II.

This was not achieved without difficulty, and at first sight it seems as though England had gained nothing by this revolution of which she is so proud. The aspect of things under William, Anne, and the first two Georges, is repulsive. We are tempted to agree with Swift in his judgment, to say that if he has depicted a Yahoo, it is because he has seen him ; naked or drawn in his carriage, the Yahoo is not beautiful. We see but corruption in high places, brutality in low, a band of intriguers leading a mob of brutes. The human beast, inflamed by political passions, gives vent to cries and violence, burns Admiral Byng in effigy, demands his death, would destroy his house and park, sways in turns from party to party, seems with its blind force ready to annihilate civil society.　When Dr. Sacheverell was tried, the butcher boys, crossing-sweepers, chimney-sweepers, costermongers, drabs, the entire scum, conceiving the Church to be in danger, follow him with yells of rage and enthusiasm, and in the evening set to work to burn and pillage the dissenter's chapels.　When Lord Bute, in defiance of public opinion, was set up in Pitt's place, he was assailed with stones, and was obliged to surround his carriage with a strong guard.　At every political crisis was heard a riotous growl, were seen disorder, blows, broken heads.　It was worse when the people's own interests were at stake.　Gin had been discovered in 1684, and about half a century later England consumed seven millions of gallons.[1]　The tavernkeepers on their signboards invited people to come and get drunk for a penny ; for twopence they might get dead drunk ; no charge for straw ; the land-lord dragged those who succumbed into a cellar, where they slept off their carouse.　A man could not walk London streets without meeting wretches, incapable of motion or thought, lying in the kennel, whom the care of the passers-by alone could prevent from being smothered in mud, or run over by carriage wheels.　A tax was imposed to stop this madness : it was in vain ; the judges dared not condemn, the informers were assassinated.　The House gave way, and Walpole, find-ing himself threatened with a riot, withdrew his law.[2]　All these bewigged and ermined lawyers, these bishops

---

[1] 1742, Report of Lord Lonsdale.

[2] In the present inflamed temper of the people, the Act could not be carried into execution without an armed force.—*Speech of Sir Robert Walpole.*

in lace, these embroidered and gold-bedizened lords, this fine government so cleverly balanced, was carried on the back of a huge and formidable brute, which as a rule would tramp peacefully though growlingly on, but which on a sudden, for a mere whim, could shake and crush it. This was clearly seen in 1780, during the riots of Lord George Gordon. Without reason or guidance at the cry of No Popery the excited mob demolished the prisons, let loose the criminals, abused the Peers, and was for three days master of London, burning, pillaging, and glutting itself. Barrels of gin were staved in and made rivers in the streets. Children and women on their knees drank themselves to death. Some became mad, others fell down besotted, and the burning and falling houses killed them, and buried them under their ruins. Eleven years later, at Birmingham, the people sacked and gutted the houses of the Liberals and Dissenters, and were found next day in heaps, dead drunk, in the roads and ditches. When instinct rebels in this over-strong and well-fed race it becomes perilous. John Bull dashed headlong at the first red rag which he thought he saw.

The higher ranks were even less estimable than the lower. If there has been no more beneficial revolution than that of 1688, there has been none that was launched or supported by dirtier means. Treachery was everywhere, not simple, but double and triple. Under William and Anne, admirals, ministers, members of the Privy Council, favourites of the antechamber, corresponded and conspired with the same Stuarts whom they had sold, only to sell them again, with a complication of bargains, each destroying the last, and a complication of perjuries, each surpassing the last, until in the end

no one knew who had bought him, or to what party
he belonged. The greatest general of the age, the Duke
of Marlborough, is one of the basest rogues in history,
supported by his mistresses, a niggard user of the pay
which he received from them, systematically plundering
his soldiers, trafficking on political secrets, a traitor to
James II., to William, to England, betraying to James
the intended plan of attacking Brest, and even, when
old and infirm, walking from the public rooms in Bath to
his lodgings, on a cold and dark night, to save sixpence
in chair-hire. Next to him we may place Bolingbroke,
a sceptic and cynic, minister in turn to Queen and
Pretender, disloyal alike to both, a trafficker in consciences, marriages, and promises, who had squandered
his talents in debauch and intrigue, to end in disgrace,
impotence, and scorn.[1] Walpole, who used to boast
that "every man had his price,"[2] was compelled to
resign, after having been prime minister for twenty
years. Montesquieu wrote in 1729:[3] "There are
Scotch members who have only two hundred pounds
for their vote, and sell it at this price. Englishmen
are no longer worthy of their liberty. They sell it to
the king; and if the king should sell it back to
them, they would sell it him again." We read in Bubb
Doddington's *Diary* the candid fashion and pretty contrivances of this great traffic. So Dr. King states:
"He (Walpole) wanted to carry a question in the House
of Commons, to which he knew there would be great
opposition. . . . As he was passing through the Court of

[1] See Walpole's terrible speech against him, 1734.
[2] See, for the truth of this statement, *Memoirs of Horace Walpole*,
2 vols., ed. E. Warburton, 1851, i. 381, note.—TR.
[3] Notes during a journey in England made in 1729 with Lord
Chesterfield.

Requests, he met a member of the contrary party, whose avarice, he imagined, would not reject a large bribe. He took him aside, and said, ' Such a question comes on this day ; give me your vote, and here is a bank-bill of two thousand pounds,' which he put into his hands. The member made him this answer : ' Sir Robert, you have lately served some of my particular friends ; and when my wife was last at court, the King was very gracious to her, which must have happened at your instance. I should therefore think myself very ungrateful (putting the bank-bill into his pocket) if I were to refuse the favour you are now pleased to ask me.' "[1] This is how a man of the world did business. Corruption was so firmly established in public manners and in politics, that after the fall of Walpole, Lord Bute, who had denounced him, was obliged to practise and increase it. His colleague Henry Fox, the first Lord Holland, changed the pay-office into a market, haggled about their price with hundreds of members, distributed in one morning twenty-five thousand pounds. Votes were only to be had for cash down, and yet at an important crisis these mercenaries threatened to go over to the enemy, struck for wages, and demanded more. Nor did the leaders miss their own share. They sold themselves for, or paid themselves with, titles, dignities, sinecures. In order to get a place vacant, they gave the holder a pension of two, three, five, and even seven thousand a year. Pitt, the most upright of politicians, the leader of those who were called patriots, gave and broke his word, attacked or defended Walpole, proposed war or peace, all to become

---

[1] Dr. W. King, *Political and Literary Anecdotes of his own Times*, 1818, 27.

or to continue a minister. Fox, his rival, was a sort of shameless sink. The Duke of Newcastle, "whose name was perfidy," "a living, moving, talking caricature," the most clumsy, ignorant, ridiculed and despised of the aristocracy, was in the Cabinet for thirty years and premier for ten years, by virtue of his connections, his wealth, of the elections which he managed, and the places in his gift. The fall of the Stuarts put the government into the hands of a few great families which, by means of rotten boroughs, bought members and high-sounding speeches, oppressed the king, moulded the passions of the mob, intrigued, lied, wrangled, and tried to swindle each other out of power.

Private manners were as lovely as public. As a rule, the reigning king detested his son; this son got into debt, asked Parliament for an increased allowance, allied himself with his father's enemies. George I. kept his wife in prison thirty-two years, and got drunk every night with his two ugly mistresses. George II., who loved his wife, took mistresses to keep up appearances, rejoiced at his son's death, upset his father's will. His eldest son cheated at cards,[1] and one day at Kensington, having borrowed five thousand pounds from Bubb Doddington, said, when he saw him from the window: "That man is reckoned one of the most sensible men in England, yet with all his parts I have just nicked him out of five thousand pounds."[2] George IV. was a sort of coachman, gamester, scandalous roysterer, unprincipled betting-man, whose proceedings all but got him excluded from the Jockey Club. The

[1] Frederick died 1751. *Memoirs of Horace Walpole*, i. 262.
[2] Walpole's *Memoirs of George II.*, ed. Lord Holland, 3 vols. 2d ed., 1847, i. 77.

only upright man was George III., a poor half-witted dullard, who went mad, and whom his mother had kept locked up in his youth as though in a cloister. She gave as her reason the universal corruption of men of quality. "The young men," she said, "were all rakes; the young women made love, instead of waiting till it was made to them." In fact, vice was in fashion, not delicate vice as in France; "Money," wrote Montesquieu, "is here esteemed above everything, honour and virtue not much. An Englishman must have a good dinner, a woman, and money. As he does not go much into society, and limits himself to this, so, as soon as his fortune is gone, and he can no longer have these things, he commits suicide or turns robber." The young men had a superabundance of coarse energy, which made them mistake brutality for pleasure. The most celebrated called themselves Mohocks, and tyrannised over London by night. They stopped people, and made them dance by pricking their legs with their swords; sometimes they would put a woman in a tub, and set her rolling down a hill; others would place her on her head, with her feet in the air; some would flatten the nose of the wretch whom they had caught, and press his eyes out of their sockets. Swift, the comic writers, the novelists, have painted the baseness of this gross debauchery, craving for riot, living in drunkenness, revelling in obscenity, issuing in cruelty, ending by irreligion and atheism.[1] This violent and excessive mood requires to occupy itself proudly and daringly in the destruction of what men respect, and what institutions protect. These men attack the clergy by the same instinct which leads them to beat the

---

[1] See the character of Birton in Voltaire's *Jenny.*

watch. Collins, Tindal, Bolingbroke, are their teachers;
the corruption of manners, the frequent practice of
treason, the warring amongst sects, the freedom of
speech, the progress of science, and the fermentation
of ideas, seemed as if they would dissolve Christianity.
"There is no religion in England," said Montesquieu.
"Four or five in the house of Commons go to prayers
or to the parliamentary sermon. . . . If any one speaks
of religion, everybody begins to laugh. A man happen-
ing to say, 'I believe this like an article of faith,'
everybody burst out laughing." In fact, the phrase
was provincial, and smacked of antiquity. The main
thing was to be fashionable, and it is amusing to see
from Lord Chesterfield in what this fashion consisted.
Of justice and honour he only speaks transiently, and
for form's sake. Before all, he says to his son, "have
manners, good breeding, and the graces." He insists
upon it in every letter, with a fulness and force of
illustration which form an odd contrast: "Mon cher
ami, comment vont les grâces, les manières, les agrémens,
et tous ces petits riens si nécessaires pour rendre un
homme aimable? Les prenez-vous? y faites-vous des
progrès? . . . A propos, on m'assure que Madame de
Blot sans avoir des traits, est jolie comme un cœur, et
que nonobstant cela, elle s'en est tenue jusqu'ici
scrupuleusement à son mari, quoi qu'il y ait déjà plus
d'un an qu'elle est mariée. Elle n'y pense pas."[1] . . .
"It seems ridiculous to tell you, but it is most certainly
true, that your dancing-master is at this time the man
in all Europe of the greatest importance to you."[2] . . .

[1] The original letter is in French. Chesterfield's *Letters to his Son*,
ed. Mahon, 4 vols. 1845; ii. April 15, 1751, p. 127.

[2] *Ibid.* ii. Jan. 3, 1751, p. 72.

"In your person you must be accurately clean; and your teeth, hands, and nails should be superlatively so. . . . Upon no account whatever put your fingers in your nose or ears.[1] What says Madame Dupin to you? For an attachment I should prefer her to la petite Blot.[2] . . . Pleasing women may in time be of service to you, They often please and govern others."[3]

And he quotes to him as examples, Bolingbroke and Marlborough, the two worst roués of the age. Thus speaks a serious man, once Lord-Lieutenant of Ireland, an ambassador and plenipotentiary, and finally a Secretary of State, an authority in matters of education and taste.[4] He wishes to polish his son, to give him a French air, to add to solid diplomatic knowledge and large views of ambition an engaging, lively, and frivolous manner. This outward polish, which at Paris is of the true colour, is here but a shocking veneer. This transplanted politeness is a lie, this vivacity is want of sense, this worldly education seems fitted only to make actors and rogues.

So thought Gay in his *Beggars' Opera*, and the

---

[1] Chesterfield's *Letters to his Son*, ed. Mahon, 4 vols., 1845; ii. Nov. 12, 1750, p. 57.　　[2] *Ibid.* ii. May 16, 1751, p. 146.

[3] *Ibid.* ii. Jan. 21, 1751, p. 81.

[4] "They (the English) are commonly twenty years old before they have spoken to anybody above their schoolmaster and the fellows of their college. If they happen to have learning, it is only Greek and Latin, but not one word of modern history or modern languages. Thus prepared, they go abroad, as they call it; but, in truth, they stay at home all that while: for, being very awkward, confoundedly ashamed, and not speaking the languages, they go into no foreign company, at least none good; but dine and sup with one another only at the tavern." *Ibid.* i., May 10, O. S., 1748, p. 136. "I could wish you would ask him (Mr. Burrish) for some letters to young fellows of pleasure or fashionable coquettes, that you may be *dans l'honnete débauche de Munich.*"—*Ibid.* ii. Oct. 3, 1753, p. 331.

polished society applauded with *furore* the portrait which he drew of it. Sixty-three consecutive nights the piece ran amidst a tempest of laughter; the ladies had the songs written on their fans, and the principal actress married a duke. What a satire! Thieves infested London, so that in 1728 the queen herself was almost robbed; they formed bands, with officers, a treasury, a commander-in-chief, and multiplied, though every six weeks they were sent by the cartload to the gallows. Such was the society which Gay put on the stage. In his opinion, it was as good as the higher society; it was hard to discriminate between them; the manners, wit, conduct, morality in both were alike. "Through the whole piece you may observe such a similitude of manners in high and low life, that it is difficult to determine whether (in the fashionable vices) the fine gentlemen imitate the gentlemen of the road, or the gentlemen of the road the fine gentlemen."[1]

Wherein, for example, is Peachum different from a great minister? Like him, he is a leader of a gang of thieves; like him, he has a register for thefts; like him, he receives money with both hands; like him, he contrives to have his friends caught and hung when they trouble him; he uses, like him, parliamentary language and classical comparisons; he has, like him, gravity, steadiness, and is eloquently indignant when his honour is suspected. It is true that Peachum quarrels with a comrade about the plunder, and takes him by the throat? But lately, Sir Robert Walpole and Lord Townsend had fought with each other on a similar question. Listen to what Mrs. Peachum says of her daughter: "Love him! (Macheath), worse and worse!

---

[1] Speech of the Beggar in the Epilogue of the *Beggars' Opera.*

I thought the girl had been better bred."[1] The daughter observes : "A woman knows how to be mercenary though she has never been in a court or at an assembly."[2] And the father remarks : "My daughter to me should be, like a court lady to a minister of state, a key to the whole gang."[3] As to Macheath, he is a fit son-in-law for such a politician. If less brilliant in council than in action, that only suits his age. Point out a young and noble officer who has a better address, or performs finer actions. He is a highwayman, that is his bravery ; he shares his booty with his friends, that is his generosity : "You see, gentlemen, I am not a mere court-friend, who professes everything and will do nothing. . . . But we, gentlemen, have still honour enough to break through the corruptions of the world."[4] For the rest he is gallant ; he has half-a-dozen wives, a dozen children ; he frequents stews, he is amiable towards the beauties whom he meets, he is easy in manners, he makes elegant bows to every one, he pays compliments to all : "Mistress Slammekin ! as careless and genteel as ever ! all you fine ladies, who know your own beauty affect undress . . . If any of the ladies chuse gin, I hope they will be so free as to call for it.— Indeed, sir, I never drink strong waters, but when I have the colic.—Just the excuse of the fine ladies ! why, a lady of quality is never without the colic."[5] Is this not the genuine tone of good society ? And does anyone doubt that Macheath is a man of quality when we learn that he has deserved to be hung, and is not ? Everything yields to such a proof. If, however, we wish for another, he would add that, "As to conscience

---

[1] Gay's *Plays*, 1772 ; *The Beggars' Opera*, i. 1.   [2] *Ibid.*
[3] *Ibid.*   [4] *Ibid.* iii. 2.   [5] *Ibid.* ii. 1.

and musty morals, I have as few drawbacks upon my pleasures as any man of quality in England; in those I am not at least vulgar."[1]   After such a speech a man must give in.   Do not bring up the foulness of these manners; we see that there is nothing repulsive in them, because fashionable society likes them.   These interiors of prisons and stews, these gambling-houses, this whiff of gin, this pander-traffic, and these pick-pockets' calculations, by no means disgust the ladies, who applaud from the boxes.   They sing the songs of Polly; their nerves shrink from no detail; they have already inhaled the filthy odours from the highly polished pastorals of the amiable poet.[2]   They laugh to see Lucy show her pregnancy to Macheath, and give Polly "rat-bane."   They are familiar with all the refinements of the gallows, and all the niceties of medicine.   Mistress Trapes expounds her trade before them, and complains of having "eleven fine customers now down under the surgeon's hands."   Mr. Filch, a prison-prop, uses words which cannot even be quoted. A cruel keenness, sharpened by a stinging irony, flows through the work, like one of those London streams whose corrosive smells Swift and Gay have described; more than a hundred years later it still proclaims the dishonour of the society which is bespattered and befouled with its mire.

---

[1] I cannot find these lines in the edition I have consulted. —Tr.

[2] In these Eclogues the ladies explain in good style that their friends have their lackeys for lovers: "Her favours Sylvia shares amongst mankind; such gen'rous Love could never be confin'd." Elsewhere the servant girl says to her mistress: "Have you not fancy'd, in his frequent kiss, th' ungrateful leavings of a filthy miss?"

III.

These were but the externals; and close observers, like Voltaire, did not misinterpret them. Betwixt the slime at the bottom and the scum on the surface rolled the great national river, which, purified by its own motion, already at intervals gave signs of its true colour, soon to display the powerful regularity of its course and the wholesome limpidity of its waters. It advanced in its native bed; every nation has one of its own, which flows down its proper slope. It is this slope which gives to each civilisation its degree and form, and it is this which we must endeavour to describe and measure.

To this end we have only to follow the travellers from the two countries who at this time crossed the Channel. Never did England regard and imitate France more, nor France England. To see the distinct current in which each nation flowed, we have but to open our eyes. Lord Chesterfield writes to his son:

" It must be owned, that the polite conversation of the men and women at Paris, though not always very deep, is much less futile and frivolous than ours here. It turns at least upon some subject, something of taste, some point of history, criticism, and even philosophy, which, though probably not quite so solid as Mr. Locke's, is however better, and more becoming rational beings, than our frivolous dissertations upon the weather or upon whist." [1]

In fact, the French became civilised by conversation; not so the English. As soon as the Frenchman quits mechanical labour and coarse material life, even before he quits it, he converses: this is his goal and his

Chesterfield's *Letters*, ii. April 22, O. S., 1751, p. 131. See, for a contrast, Swift's *Essay on Polite Conversation*.

pleasure.[1]　Barely has he escaped from religious wars
and feudal isolation, when he makes his bow and has
his say.　With the Hotel de Rambouillet we get the
fine drawing-room talk, which is to last two centuries :
Germans, English, all Europe, either novices or dullards,
listen to France open-mouthed, and from time to time
clumsily attempt an imitation.　How amiable are
French talkers !　What discrimination !　What innate
tact !　With what grace and dexterity they can persuade, interest, amuse, stroke down sickly vanity, rivet
the diverted attention, insinuate dangerous truth, ever
soaring a hundred feet above the tedium-point where
their rivals are floundering with all their native
heaviness.　But, above all, how sharp they soon have become !　Instinctively and without effort they light upon
easy gesture, fluent speech, sustained elegance, a characteristic piquancy, a perfect clearness.　Their phrases,
still formal under Guez de Balzac, are looser, lighter,
launch out, move speedily, and under Voltaire find their
wings.　Did any man ever see such a desire, such an
art of pleasing ?　Pedantic sciences, political economy,
theology, the sullen denizens of the Academy and the
Sorbonne, speak but in epigrams.　Montesquieu's *l'Esprit
des Lois* is also "*l'Esprit sur les lois.*"　Rousseau's
periods, which begat a revolution, were balanced, turned,
polished for eighteen hours in his head.　Voltaire's
philosophy breaks out into a million sparks.　Every
idea must blossom into a witticism ; people only have

---

[1] Even in 1826, Sydney Smith, arriving at Calais, writes (*Life and
Letters*, ii. 253, 254): "What pleases me is the taste and ingenuity displayed in the shops, and the good manners and politeness of the people.
Such is the state of manners, that you appear almost to have quitted a
land of barbarians.　I have not seen a cobbler who is not better bred
than an English gentleman."

flashes of thought; all truth, the most intricate and the most sacred, becomes a pleasant drawing-room conceit, thrown backward and forward, like a gilded shuttlecock, by delicate women's hands, without sullying the lace sleeves from which their slim arms emerge, or the garlands which the rosy Cupids unfold on the wainscoting. Everything must glitter, sparkle, or smile. The passions are deadened, love is rendered insipid, the proprieties are multiplied, good manners are exaggerated. The refined man becomes "sensitive." From his wadded taffeta dressing-gown he keeps plucking his worked handkerchief to whisk away the moist omen of a tear; he lays his hand on his heart, he grows tender; he has become so delicate and correct, that an Englishman knows not whether to take him for an hysterical young woman or a dancing-master.[1] Take a near view of this beribboned puppy, in his light-green dress, lisping out the songs of Florian. The genius of society which has led him to these fooleries has also led him elsewhere; for conversation, in France at least, is a chase after ideas. To this day, in spite of modern distrust and sadness, it is at table, after dinner, over the coffee especially, that deep politics and the loftiest philosophy crop up. To think, above all to think rapidly, is a recreation. The mind finds in it a sort of

---

[1] See in *Evelina*, by Miss Burney, 3 vols., 1784, the character of the poor, genteel Frenchman, M. Dubois, who is made to tremble even whilst lying in the gutter. These very correct young ladies go to see Congreve's *Love for Love;* their parents are not afraid of showing them Miss Prue. See also, in *Evelina*, by way of contrast, the boorish character of the English captain; he throws Mrs. Duval twice in the mud; he says to his daughter Molly: "I charge you, as you value my favour, that you'll never again be so impertinent as to have a taste of your own before my face" (i. 190). The change, even from sixty years ago, is surprising.

ball; think how eagerly it hastens thither. This is the source of all French culture. At the dawn of the century, the ladies, between a couple of bows, produced studied portraits and subtle dissertations; they understand Descartes, appreciate Nicole, approve Bossuet. Presently little suppers are introduced, and during the dessert they discuss the existence of God. Are not theology, morality, set forth in a noble or piquant style, pleasures for the drawing-room and adornments of luxury? Fancy finds place amongst them, floats about and sparkles like a light flame over all the subjects on which it feeds. How lofty a flight did intelligence take during this eighteenth century! Was society ever more anxious for sublime truths, more bold in their search, more quick to discover, more ardent in embracing them? These perfumed *marquises*, these laced coxcombs, all these pretty, well-dressed, gallant, frivolous people, crowd to hear philosophy discussed, as they go to hear an opera. The origin of animated beings, the eels of Needham,[1] the adventures of Jacques the Fatalist,[2] and the question of freewill, the principles of political economy, and the calculations of the Man with Forty Crowns,[3]—all is to them a matter for paradoxes and discoveries. All the heavy rocks, which the men who had made it their business, were hewing and undermining laboriously in solitude, being carried along and polished in the public torrent, roll in myriads, mingled together with a joyous clatter, hurried onwards with an ever-increasing rapidity.

[1] Needham (1713-1781), a learned English naturalist, made and published microscopical discoveries and remarks on the generation of organic bodies.—TR.

[2] The title of a philosophical novel by Diderot.—TR.

[3] The title of a philosophical tale by Voltaire.—TR.

There was no bar, no collision; they were not checked by the practicability of their plans: they thought for thinking's sake; theories could be expanded at ease. In fact, this is how in France men have always conversed. They play with general truths; they glean one nimbly from the heap of facts in which it lay concealed, and develop it; they hover above observation in reason and rhetoric; they find themselves uncomfortable and commonplace when they are not in the region of pure ideas. And in this respect the eighteenth century continues the seventeenth. The philosophers had described good breeding, flattery, misanthropy, avarice; they now instituted inquiries into liberty, tyranny, religion; they had studied man in himself; they now study him in the abstract. Religious and monarchical writers are of the same school as impious and revolutionary writers; Boileau leads up to Rousseau, Racine to Robespierre. Oratorical reasoning formed the regular theatre and classical preaching; it also produced the Declaration of Rights and the *Contrat Social*. They form for themselves a certain idea of man, of his inclinations, faculties, duties; a mutilated idea, but the more clear as it was the more reduced. From being aristocratic it becomes popular; instead of being an amusement, it is a faith; from delicate and sceptical hands it passes to coarse and enthusiastic hands. From the lustre of the drawing-room they make a brand and a torch. Such is the current on which the French mind floated for two centuries, caressed by the refinements of an exquisite politeness, amused by a swarm of brilliant ideas, charmed by the promises of golden theories, until, thinking that it touched the cloud-palace, made bright by the future, it suddenly lost its footing and fell in the storm of the Revolution.

Altogether different is the path which English civilisation has taken. It is not the spirit of society which has made it, but moral sense; and the reason is, that in England man is not as he is in France. The Frenchmen who became acquainted with England at this period were struck by it. "In France," says Montesquieu, "I become friendly with everybody; in England with nobody. You must do here as the English do, live for yourself, care for no one, love no one, rely on no one." Englishmen were of a singular genius, yet "solitary and sad. They are reserved, live much in themselves, and think alone. Most of them having wit, are tormented by their very wit. Scorning or disgusted with all things, they are unhappy amid so many reasons why they should not be so." And Voltaire, like Montesquieu, continually alludes to the sombre energy of the English character. He says that in London there are days when the wind is in the east, when it is customary for people to hang themselves; he relates shudderingly how a young girl cut her throat, and how her lover without a word redeemed the knife. He is surprised to see "so many Timons, so many splenetic misanthropes." Whither will they go? There was one path which grew daily wider. The Englishman, naturally serious, meditative, and sad, did not regard life as a game or a pleasure; his eyes were habitually turned, not outward to smiling nature, but inward to the life of the soul; he examines himself, ever descends within himself, confines himself to the moral world, and at last sees no other beauty but that which shines there; he enthrones justice as the sole and absolute queen of humanity, and

conceives the plan of disposing all his actions according
to a rigid code.   He has no lack of force in this; for
his pride comes to assist his conscience.   Having
chosen himself and by himself the route, he would blush
to quit it; he rejects temptations as his enemies; he
feels that he is fighting and conquering,[1] that he is
doing a difficult thing, that he is worthy of admiration,
that he is a man.   Moreover, he rescues himself from
his capital foe, tedium, and satisfies his craving for
action; understanding his duties, he employs his faculties and he has a purpose in life, and this gives rise to
associations, endowments, preachings; and finding more
steadfast souls, and nerves more tightly strung, it sends
them forth, without causing them too much suffering,
too long strife, through ridicule and danger.   The reflective character of the man has given a moral rule;
the militant character now gives moral force.   The
mind, thus directed, is more apt than any other to
comprehend duty; the will, thus armed, is more capable
than any other of performing its duty.   This is the
fundamental faculty which is found in all parts of
public life, concealed but present, like one of those deep
primeval rocks, which, lying far inland, give to all
undulations of the soil a basis and a support.

IV.

This faculty gives first a basis and a support to Protestantism, and it is from this structure of mind that
the Englishman is religious.   Let us find our way through

[1] " The consciousness of silent endurance, so dear to every Englishman, of standing out against something and not giving in."—*Tom
Brown's School Days.*

the knotty and uninviting bark.   Voltaire laughs at it,
and jests about the ranting of the preachers and the
austerity of the faithful.   "There is no opera, no comedy,
no concert on a Sunday in London; cards even are
expressly forbidden, so that only persons of quality,
and those who are called respectable people, play on
that day."   He amuses himself at the expense of the
Anglicans, "so scrupulous in collecting their tithes;"
the Presbyterians, "who look as if they were angry,
and preach with a strong nasal accent;" the Quakers,
"who go to church and wait for inspiration with their
hats on their heads."   But is there nothing to be
observed but these externals?   And do we suppose
that we are acquainted with a religion because we
know the details of formulary and vestment?   There
is a common faith beneath all these sectarian differences : whatever be the form of Protestantism, its object
and result are the culture of the moral sense; that is
why it is popular in England : principles and dogmas all
make it suitable to the instincts of the nation.   The
sentiment which in the Protestant is the source of everything, is qualms of conscience; he pictures perfect justice,
and feels that his uprightness, however great, cannot
stand before that.   He thinks of the Day of Judgment,
and tells himself that he will be damned.   He is
troubled, and prostrates himself; he prays God to
pardon his sins and renew his heart.   He sees that
neither by his desires, nor his deeds, nor by any ceremony
or institution, nor by himself, nor by any creature, can
he deserve the one or obtain the other.   He betakes
himself to Christ, the one Mediator; he prays to him,
he feels his presence, he finds himself justified by his
grace, elect, healed, transformed, predestinated.   Thus

understood, religion is a moral revolution; thus simpli-
fied, religion is only a moral revolution. Before this
deep emotion,. metaphysics and theology, ceremonies
and discipline, all is blotted out or subordinate, and
Christianity is simply the purification of the heart.
Look now at these men, dressed in sombre colours,
speaking through the nose on Sundays, in a box of dark
wood, whilst a man in bands, "with the air of a Cato,"
reads a psalm. Is there nothing in their heart but
theological "trash" or mechanical phrases? There
is a deep sentiment—veneration. This bare Dissenters' meeting-house, this simple service and church
of the Anglicans, leave them open to the impression of
what they read and hear. For they do hear, and they
do read; prayer in the vulgar tongue, psalms translated into the vulgar tongue, can penetrate through their
senses to their souls. They do penetrate; and this is
why they have such a collected mien. For the race is
by its very nature capable of deep emotions, disposed by
the vehemence of its imagination to comprehend the
grand and tragic; and the Bible, which is to them the
very word of eternal God, provides it. I know that to
Voltaire it is only emphatic, unconnected, ridiculous;
the sentiments with which it is filled are out of harmony
with French sentiments. In England the hearers are
on the level of its energy and harshness. The cries of
anguish or admiration of the solitary Hebrew, the
transports, the sudden outbursts of sublime passion, the
desire for justice, the growling of the thunder and the
judgments of God, shake, across thirty centuries, these
biblical souls. Their other books assist it. The Prayer
Book, which is handed down as an heirloom with the
old family Bible, speaks to all, to the dullest peasant,

or the miner, the solemn accent of true prayer. The new-born poetry, the reviving religion of the sixteenth century, have impressed their magnificent gravity upon it; and we feel in it, as in Milton himself, the pulse of the twofold inspiration which then lifted a man out of himself and raised him to heaven. Their knees bend when they listen to it. That Confession of Faith, these collects for the sick, for the dying, in case of public misfortune or private grief, these lofty sentences of impassioned and sustained eloquence, transport a man to some unknown and august world. Let the fine gentlemen yawn, mock, and succeed in not understanding: I am sure that, of the others, many are moved. The idea of dark death and of the limitless ocean, to which the poor weak soul must descend, the thought of this invisible justice, everywhere present, ever foreseeing, on which the changing show of visible things depends, enlighten them with unexpected flashes. The physical world and its laws seem to them but a phantom and a figure; they see nothing more real than justice; it is the sum of humanity, as of nature. This is the deep sentiment which on Sunday closes the theatre, discourages pleasures, fills the churches; this it is which pierces the breastplate of the positive spirit and of corporeal dulness. This shopkeeper, who all the week has been counting his bales or drawing up columns of figures; this cattle-breeding squire, who can only bawl, drink, jump a fence; these yeomen, these cottagers, who in order to amuse themselves draw blood whilst boxing, or vie with each other in grinning through a horse-collar,—all these uncultivated souls, immersed in material life, receive thus from their religion a moral life. They love it; we hear it in the yells of a mob, rising like a thunderstorm, when a rash hand touches or seems to touch the Church. We see it in the sale of Protestant devotional books; the *Pilgrim's Progress* and *The Whole Duty of Man* are alone able to force their way to the window-ledge of the yeoman and squire, where four volumes, their whole library, rest amid the fishing-tackle. We can only move the men of this race by moral reflections and religious emotions. The cooled Puritan spirit still broods underground, and is drawn in the only direction where fuel, air, fire, and action are to be found.

We obtain a glimpse of it when we look at the sects. In France, Jansenists and Jesuits seem to be puppets of another century, fighting for the amusement of this age. Here Quakers, Independents, Baptists exist, serious, honoured, recognised by the State, distinguished by their able writers, their deep scholars, their men of worth, their founders of nations.[1] Their piety causes their disputes; it is because they will believe, that they differ in belief: the only men without religion are those who do not care for religion. A motionless faith is soon a dead faith; and when a man becomes a sectarian, it is because he is fervent. This Christianity lives because it is developed; we see the sap, always flowing from the Protestant inquiry and faith, re-enter the old dogmas, dried up for fifteen hundred years. Voltaire, when he came to England, was surprised to find Arians, and amongst them the first thinkers in England— Clarke, Newton himself. Not only dogma, but feeling, is renewed; beyond the speculative Arians were the practical Methodists; behind Newton and Clarke came Whitfield and Wesley.

No history more deeply illustrates the English

[1] William Penn.

character than that of these two men. In spite of Hume and Voltaire, they founded a monastical and convulsionary sect, and triumph through austerity, and exaggeration, which would have ruined them in France. Wesley was a scholar, an Oxford student, and he believed in the devil; he attributes to him sickness, nightmare, storms, earthquakes. His family heard supernatural noises; his father had been thrice pushed by a ghost; he himself saw the hand of God in the commonest events of life. One day at Birmingham, overtaken by a hailstorm, he felt that he received this warning, because at table he had not sufficiently exhorted the people who dined with him; when he had to determine on anything, he opened the Bible at random for a text, in order to decide. At Oxford he fasted and wearied himself until he spat blood, and almost died; at sea, when he departed for America, he only ate bread, and slept on deck; he lived the life of an apostle, giving away all that he earned, travelling and preaching all the year, and every year, till the age of eighty-eight;[1] it has been reckoned that he gave away thirty thousand pounds, travelled about a hundred thousand miles, and preached forty thousand sermons. What could such a man have done in France in the eighteenth century? Here he was listened to and followed, at his death he had eighty thousand disciples; now he has a million. The qualms of conscience, which forced him in this direction, compelled others to follow in his footsteps. Nothing is more striking than the con-

---

[1] On one tour he slept three weeks on the bare boards. One day, at three in the morning, he said to Nelson, his companion: "Brother Nelson, let us be of good cheer, I have one whole side yet; for the skin is off but on one side."—Southey's *Life of Wesley*, 2 vols., 1820, ii. ch. xv. 54.

fessions of his preachers, mostly low-born and laymen. George Story had the spleen, dreamed and mused gloomily; took to slandering himself and the occupations of men. Mark Bond thought himself damned, because when a boy he had once uttered a blasphemy; he read and prayed unceasingly and in vain, and at last in despair he enlisted, with the hope of being killed. John Haime had visions, howled, and thought he saw the devil. Another, a baker, had scruples because his master continued to bake on Sunday, wasted away with anxiety, and soon was nothing but a skeleton. Such are the timorous and impassioned souls which become religious and enthusiastic. They are numerous in this land, and on them doctrine took hold. Wesley declares that "A string of opinions is no more Christian faith than a string of beads is Christian holiness. It is not an assent to any opinion, or any number of opinions." "This justifying faith implies not only the personal revelation, the inward evidence of Christianity, but likewise a sure and firm confidence in the individual believer that Christ died for *his* sin, loved *him*, and gave his life for *him*." [1] "By a Christian, I mean one who so believes in Christ, as that sin hath no more dominion over him." [2]

The faithful feels in himself the touch of a superior hand, and the birth of an unknown being. The old man has disappeared, the new man has taken his place, pardoned, purified, transfigured, steeped in joy and confidence, inclined to good as strongly as he was once drawn to evil. A miracle has been wrought, and it can be wrought at any moment, suddenly, under any circumstances, without warning. Some sinner, the oldest and

[1] Southey's *Life of Wesley*, ii. 176.   [2] *Ibid*. i. 251.

most hardened, without wishing it, without having dreamed of it, falls down weeping, his heart melted by grace.   The hidden thoughts, which fermented long in these gloomy imaginations, break out suddenly into storms, and the dull brutal mood is shaken by nervous fits which it had not known before.   Wesley, Whitefield, and their preachers went all over England preaching to the poor, the peasants, the workmen in the open air, sometimes to a congregation of twenty thousand people.   "The fire is kindled in the country."   There was sobbing and crying.   At Kingswood, Whitefield, having collected the miners, a savage race, "saw the white gutters made by the tears which plentifully fell down from their black cheeks, black as they came out from their coal-pits."[1]   Some trembled and fell; others had transports of joy, ecstasies.   Southey writes thus of Thomas Olivers: "His heart was broken, nor could he express the strong desires which he felt for righteousness. . . . He describes his feelings during a *Te Deum* at the cathedral, as if he had done with earth, and was praising God before His throne."[2]   The god and the brute, which each man carries in himself, were let loose; the physical machine was upset; emotion was turned into madness, and the madness became contagious.   An eye-witness says ·

"At Everton some were shrieking, some roaring aloud. . . . The most general was a loud breathing, like that of people half strangled and gasping for life; and, indeed, almost all the cries were like those of human creatures dying in bitter anguish. Great numbers wept without any noise; others fell down as dead. . . . I stood upon the pew-seat, as did a young man in

---

[1] Southey's *Life of Wesley*, i. ch. vi. 236.   [2] *Ibid.* ii. ch. xvii. 111.

the opposite pew, an able-bodied, fresh, healthy, countryman, but in a moment, when he seemed to think of nothing else, down he dropt, with a violence inconceivable. . . . I heard the stamping of his feet, ready to break the boards, as he lay in strong convulsions at the bottom of the pew. . . . I saw a sturdy boy, about eight years old, who roared above his fellows ; . . . his face was red as scarlet ; and almost all on whom God laid his hand, turned either very red or almost black." [1]

Elsewhere, a woman, disgusted with this madness, wished to leave, but had only gone a few steps when she fell into as violent fits as others. Conversions followed these transports ; the converted paid their debts, forswore drunkenness, read the Bible, prayed, and went about exhorting others. Wesley collected them into societies, formed " classes " for mutual examination and edification, submitted spiritual life to a methodic discipline, built chapels, chose preachers, founded schools, organised enthusiasm. To this day his disciples spend very large sums every year in missions to all parts of the world, and on the banks of the Mississippi and the Ohio their shoutings repeat the violent enthusiasm and the conversions of primitive inspiration. The same instinct is still revealed by the same signs ; the doctrine of grace survives in uninterrupted energy, and the race, as in the sixteenth century, puts its poetry into the exaltation of the moral sense.

V.

A sort of theological smoke covers and hides this glowing hearth which burns in silence. A stranger who, at this time, had visited the country, would see in this religion only a choking vapour of arguments, controversies, and sermons. All those celebrated divines and preachers, Barrow, Tillotson, South, Stillingfleet, Sher-

[1] Southey's *Life of Wesley*, ii. ch. xxiv. 320.

lock, Burnet, Baxter, Barclay, preached, says Addison,
like automatons, monotonously, without moving their
arms.   For a Frenchman, for Voltaire, who did read
them, as he read everything, what a strange reading!
Here is Tillotson first, the most authoritative of all, a
kind of father of the Church, so much admired that
Dryden tells us that he learned from him the art of
writing well, and that his sermons, the only property
which he left his widow, were bought by a publisher
for two thousand five hundred guineas.   This work has,
in fact, some weight; there are three folio volumes,
each of seven hundred pages.   To open them, a man
must be a critic by profession, or be possessed by an
absolute desire to be saved.   And now let us open
them.   "The Wisdom of being Religious,"—such is his
first sermon, much celebrated in his time, and the foundation of his success:

"These words consist of two propositions, which are not
distinct in sense; . . . So that they differ only as cause and
effect, which by a metonymy, used in all sorts of authors, are
frequently put one for another." [1]

This opening makes us uneasy.   Is this great orator a
teacher of grammar?

"Having thus explained the words, I come now to consider
the proposition contained in them, which is this:
"That religion is the best knowledge and wisdom.
"This I shall endeavour to make good these three ways:—
"1st. By a direct proof of it;
"2d. By shewing on the contrary the folly and ignorance of
irreligion and wickedness;
"3d. By vindicating religion from those common imputations
which seem to charge it with ignorance or imprudence.   I
begin with the direct proof of this." [2] . . .

[1] Tillotson's *Sermons*, 10 vols, 1760, i. 1.   [2] *Ibid.* i. 5.

Thereupon he gives his divisions. What a heavy demonstrator! We are tempted to turn over the leaves only, and not to read them. Let us examine his forty-second sermon: "Against Evil-speaking:"

"*Firstly:* I shall consider the nature of this vice, and wherein it consists.

"*Secondly:* I shall consider the due extent of this prohibition, To speak evil of no man.

"*Thirdly:* I shall show the evil of this practice, both in the causes and effects of it.

"*Fourthly:* I shall add some further considerations to dissuade men from it.

"*Fifthly:* I shall give some rules and directions for the prevention and cure of it." [1]

What a style! and it is the same throughout. There is nothing lifelike; it is a skeleton, with all its joints coarsely displayed. All the ideas are ticketed and numbered. The schoolmen were not worse. Neither rapture nor vehemence; no wit, no imagination, no original and brilliant idea, no philosophy; nothing but quotations of mere scholarship, and enumerations from a handbook. The dull argumentative reason comes with its pigeon-holed classifications upon a great truth of the heart or an impassioned word from the Bible, examines it "positively and negatively," draws thence "a lesson and an encouragement," arranges each part under its heading, patiently, indefatigably, so that sometimes three whole sermons are needed to complete the division and the proof, and each of them contains in its exordium the methodical abstract of all the points treated and the arguments supplied. Just so were the

---

[1] Tillotson's *Sermons*, iii. 2.

discussions of the Sorbonne carried on.   At the court
of Louis XIV. Tillotson would have been taken for a man
who had run away from a seminary; Voltaire would
have called him a village curé.   He has all that is
necessary to shock men of the world, nothing to attract
them.   For he does not address men of the world, but
Christians; his hearers neither need nor desire to be
goaded or amused; they do not ask for analytical
refinements, novelties in matter of feeling.   They come
to have Scripture explained to them, and morality
demonstrated.   The force of their zeal is only manifested
by the gravity of their attention.   Let others have a
text as a mere pretext; as for them, they cling to it:
it is the very word of God, they cannot dwell on it too
much.   They must have the sense of every word hunted
out, the passage interpreted phrase by phrase, in itself, by
the context, by parallel passages, by the whole doctrine.
They are willing to have the different readings, translations, interpretations expounded; they like to see the
orator become a grammarian, a Hellenist, a scholiast.
They are not repelled by all this dust of-scholarship,
which rises from the folios to settle upon their countenance.   And the precept being laid down, they
demand an enumeration of all the reasons which support
it; they wish to be convinced, carry away in their heads
a provision of good approved motives to last the week.
They came there seriously, as to their counting-house or
their field, not to amuse themselves but to do some
work, to toil and dig conscientiously in theology and
logic, to amend and better themselves.   They would
be angry at being dazzled.   Their great sense, their ordinary common sense, is much better pleased with cold
discussions; they want inquiries and methodical reports

of morality, as if it was a subject of export and import duties, and treat conscience as port wine or herrings.

In this Tillotson is admirable. Doubtless he is pedantic, as Voltaire called him; he has all " the bad manners learned at the university ;" he has not been " polished by association with women ;" he is not like the French preachers, academicians, elegant discoursers, who by a courtly air, a well-delivered Advent sermon, the refinements of a purified style, earn the first vacant bishopric and the favour of good society. But he writes like a perfectly honest man ; we can see that he is not aiming in any way at the glory of an orator ; he wishes to persuade soundly, nothing more. We enjoy this clearness, this naturalness, this preciseness, this entire loyalty. In one of his sermons he says :

" Truth and reality have all the advantages of appearance, and many more. If the show of anything be good for anything, I am sure sincerity is better ; for why. does any man dissemble, or seem to be that which he is not, but because he thinks it good to have such a quality as he pretends to ? For to counterfeit and dissemble, is to put on the appearance of some real excellency. Now, the best way in the world for a man to seem to be anything, is really to be what he would seem to be. Besides, that it is many times as troublesome to make good the pretence of a good quality, as to have it ; and if a man have it not, it is ten to one but he is discovered to want it, and then all his pains and labour to seem to have it are lost. There is something unnatural in painting, which a skilful eye will easily discern from native beauty and complexion.

" It is hard to personate and act a part long ; for where truth is not at the bottom, nature will always be endeavouring to return, and will peep out and betray herself one time or other. Therefore, if any man think it convenient to seem good, let him be so indeed. and then his goodness will appear to everybody's satisfaction ; . . . so that, upon all accounts, sincerity is true wisdom." [1]

We are led to believe a man who speaks thus ; we say to ourselves, "This is true, he is right, we must do as he says." The impression received is moral, not literary ; the sermon is efficacious, not rhetorical ; it does not please, it leads to action.

In this great manufactory of morality, where every loom goes on as regularly as its neighbour, with a monotonous noise, we distinguish two which sound louder and better than the rest—Barrow and South. Not that they were free from dulness. Barrow had all the air of a college pedant, and dressed so badly, that one day in London, before an audience who did not know him, he saw almost the whole congregation at once leave the church. He explained the word εὐχαριστεῖν in the pulpit with all the charm of a dictionary, commenting, translating, dividing, subdividing like the most formidable of scholiasts,[2] caring no more for the public than for himself ; so that once, when he had

---

[1] Tillotson's *Sermons*, iv. 15-16 ; Sermon 55, "Of Sincerity towards God and Man." John i. 47. This was the last sermon Tillotson preached ; July 29, 1694.—Tr.

[2] Barrow's *Theological Works*, 6 vols. Oxford, 1818, i. 141-142 ; Sermon viii. "The Duty of Thanksgiving," Eph. v. 20.

"These words, although (as the very syntax doth immediately discover) they bear a relation to, and have a fit coherence with, those that precede, may yet (especially considering St. Paul's style and manner of expression in the preceptive and exhortative parts of his Epistles), without any violence or prejudice on either hand, be severed from the context, and considered distinctly by themselves. . . . First, then, concerning the duty itself, *to give thanks*, or rather *to be thankful (for* εὐχαριστεῖν doth not only signify *gratias agere, reddere, dicere,* to *give, render,* or *declare thanks,* but also *gratias habere, grate affectum esse,* to be *thankfully disposed,* to entertain a grateful affection, sense, or memory. . . . I say, concerning this duty itself (abstractedly

spoken for three hours and a half before the Lord
Mayor, he replied to those who asked him if he was not
tired, " I did, in fact, begin to be weary of standing so
long." But the heart and mind were so full and so
rich, that his faults became a power. He had a geome-
trical method and clearness,[1] an inexhaustible fertility,
extraordinary impetuosity and tenacity of logic, writing
the same sermon three or four times over, insatiable
in his craving to explain and prove, obstinately
confined to his already overflowing thoughts, with a
minuteness of division, an exactness of connection, a
superfluity of explanation, so astonishing that the attention of the hearer at last gives way ; and yet the mind
turns with the vast engine, carried away and doubled
up as by the rolling weight of a flattening machine.

Let us listen to his sermon, " Of the Love of God."
Never was a more copious and forcible analysis seen in
England, so penetrating and unwearying a decomposition of an idea into all its parts, a more powerful
logic, more rigorously collecting into one network all
the threads of a subject :

"Although no such benefit or advantage can accrue to God,
which may increase his essential and indefectible happiness ;
no harm or damage can arrive that may impair it (for he can
be neither really more or less rich, or glorious, or joyful than
he is ; neither have our desire or our fear, our delight or our grief,
our designs or our endeavours any object, any ground in those
respects) ; yet hath he declared, that there be certain interests

considered), as it involves a respect to benefits or good things received ;
so in its employment about them it imports, requires, or supposes
these following particulars."

[1] He was a mathematician of the highest order, and had resigned
his chair to Newton.

and concernments, which, out of his abundant goodness and condescension, he doth tender and prosecute as his own ; as if he did really receive advantage by the good, and prejudice by the bad success, respectively belonging to them ; that he earnestly desires and is greatly delighted with some things, very much dislikes and is grievously displeased with other things : for instance, that he bears a fatherly affection towards his creatures, and earnestly desires their welfare ; and delights to see them enjoy the good he designed them ; as also dislikes the contrary events ; doth commiserate and condole their misery ; that he is consequently well pleased when piety and justice, peace and order (the chief means conducing to our welfare) do flourish ; and displeased, when impiety and iniquity, dissension and disorder (those certain sources of mischief to us) do prevail ; that he is well satisfied with our rendering to him that obedience, honour, and respect, which are due to him ; and highly offended with our injurious and disrespectful behaviour toward him, in the commission of sin and violation of his most just and holy commandments ; so that there wants not sufficient matter of our exercising good-will both in affection and action toward God ; we are capable both of wishing and (in a manner, as he will interpret and accept it) of doing good to him, by our concurrence with him in promoting those things which he approves and delights in, and in removing the contrary." [1]

This entanglement wearies us, but what a force and dash is there in this well considered and complete thought ! Truth thus supported on all its foundations can never be shaken. Rhetoric is absent. There is no art here ; the whole oratorical art consists in the desire thoroughly to explain and prove what he has to say. He is even unstudied and artless ; and it

[1] Barrow's *Theological Works*, i., Sermon xxiii. 500-501.

is just this ingenuousness which raises him to the antique level. We may meet with an image in his writings which seems to belong to the finest period of Latin simplicity and dignity :

" The middle, we may observe, and the safest, and the fairest, and the most conspicuous places in cities are usually deputed for the erections of statues and monuments dedicated to the memory of worthy men, who have nobly deserved of their countries.   In like manner should we in the heart and centre of our soul, in the best and highest apartments thereof, in the places most exposed to ordinary observation, and most secure from the invasions of worldly care, erect lively representations of, and lasting memorials unto, the divine bounty." [1]

There is here a sort of effusion of gratitude ; and at the end of the sermon, when we think him exhausted, the expansion becomes more copious by the enumeration of the unlimited blessings amidst which we move like fishes in the sea, not perceiving them, because we are surrounded and submerged by them. During ten pages the idea overflows in a continuous and similar phrase, without fear of crowding or monotony, in spite of all rules, so loaded are the heart and imagination, and so satisfied are they to bring and collect all nature as a single offering :

" To him, the excellent quality, the noble end, the most obliging manner of whose beneficence doth surpass the matter thereof, and hugely augment the benefits : who, not compelled by any necessity, not obliged by any law (or previous compact), not induced by any extrinsic arguments, not inclined by our merits, not wearied with our importunities, not instigated by troublesome passions of pity, shame, or fear (as we are wont to be), not

[1] Barrow's *Theological Works*, i. 145 ; Sermon viii., "The Duty of Thanksgiving," Eph. v. 20.

flattered with promises of recompense, nor bribed with expectation of emolument, thence to accrue unto himself; but being absolute master of his own actions, only both lawgiver and counsellor to himself, all-sufficient, and incapable of admitting any accession to his perfect blissfulness; most willingly and freely, out of pure bounty and good-will, is our Friend and Benefactor; preventing not only our desires, but our knowledge; surpassing not our deserts only, but our wishes, yea, even our conceits, in the dispensation of his inestimable and unrequitable benefits; having no other drift in the collation of them, beside our real good and welfare, our profit and advantage, our pleasure and content." [1]

Zealous energy and lack of taste; such are the features common to all this eloquence. Let us leave this mathematician, this man of the closet, this antique man, who proves too much and is too eager, and let us look out amongst the men of the world him who was called the wittiest of ecclesiastics, Robert South, as different from Barrow in his character and life as in his works and his mind; armed for war, an impassioned royalist, a partisan of divine right and passive obedience, an acrimonious controversialist, a defamer of the dissenters, a foe to the Act of Toleration, who never avoided in his enmities the license of an insult or a foul word. By his side Father Bridaine,[2] who seems so coarse to the French, was polished. His sermons are like a conversation of that time; and we know in what style they conversed then in England. South is not afraid to use any popular and impassioned image. He sets forth little vulgar facts, with their low

---

[1] Barrow's *Theological Works*, i. 159-160, Sermon viii.

[2] Jacques Bridaine ((1701–1767), a celebrated and zealous French preacher, whose sermons were always extempore, and hence not very cultivated and refined in style. —Tr.

and striking details. He never shrinks, he never minces matters; he speaks the language of the people. His style is anecdotic, striking, abrupt, with change of tone, forcible and clownish gestures, with every species of originality, vehemence, and boldness. He sneers in the pulpit, he rails, he plays the mimic and comedian. He paints his characters as if he had them before his eyes. The audience will recognise the originals again in the streets; they could put the names to his portraits. Read this bit on hypocrites:

" Suppose a man infinitely ambitious, and equally spiteful and malicious; one who poisons the ears of great men by venomous whispers, and rises by the fall of better men than himself; yet if he steps forth with a Friday look and a Lenten face, with a blessed Jesu! and a mournful ditty for the vices of the times; oh! then he is a saint upon earth: an Ambrose or an Augustine (I mean not for that earthly trash of book-learning; for, alas! such are above that, or at least that's above them), but for zeal and for fasting, for a devout elevation of the eyes, and a holy rage against other men's sins. And happy those ladies and religious dames, characterized in the 2d of Timothy, ch. iii. 6, who can have such self-denying, thriving, able men for their confessors! and thrice happy those families where they vouchsafe to take their Friday night's refreshments! and thereby demonstrate to the world what Christian abstinence, and what primitive, self-mortifying rigor there is in forbearing a dinner, that they may have the better stomach to their supper. In fine, the whole world stands in admiration of them; fools are fond of them, and wise men are afraid of them; they are talked of, they are pointed at; and, as they order the matter, they draw the eyes of all men after them, and generally something else." [1]

[1] South's *Sermons*, 1715, 11 vols., vi. 110. The fourth and last discourse from those words in Isaiah v. 20, " Woe unto them that call evil good and good evil; that put darkness for light, and light for darkness; that put bitter for sweet, and sweet for bitter!"—Tr.

A man so frank of speech was sure to commend frankness; he has done so with the bitter irony, the brutality of a Wycherley. The pulpit had the plain-dealing and coarseness of the stage; and in this picture of forcible, honest men, whom the world considers as bad characters, we find the pungent familiarity of the *Plain Dealer* :

"Again, there are some, who have a certain ill-natured stiffness (forsooth) in their tongue, so as not to be able to applaud and keep pace with this or that self-admiring, vain-glorious Thraso, while he is pluming and praising himself, and telling fulsome stories in his own commendation for three or four hours by the clock, and at the same time reviling and throwing dirt upon all mankind besides.

"There is also a sort of odd ill-natured men, whom neither hopes nor fears, frowns nor favours, can prevail upon, to have any of the cast, beggarly, forlorn nieces or kinswomen of any lord or grandee, spiritual or temporal, trumped upon them.

"To which we may add another sort of obstinate ill-natured persons, who are not to be brought by any one's guilt or greatness, to speak or write, or to swear or lie, as they are bidden, or to give up their own consciences in a compliment to those, who have none themselves.

"And lastly, there are some, so extremely ill-natured, as to think it very lawful and allowable for them to be sensible when they are injured or oppressed, when they are slandered in their good names, and wronged in their just interests ; and withal, to dare to own what they find, and feel without being such beasts of burden as to bear tamely whatsoever is cast upon them ; or such spaniels as to lick the foot which kicks them, or to thank the goodly great one for doing them all these back favours." [1]

In this eccentric style all blows tell; we might call it

---

[1] South's *Sermons*, vi. 118.

a boxing-match in which sneers inflict bruises.   But
see the effect of these churls' vulgarities.   We issue
thence with a soul full of energetic feeling; we have
seen the very objects, as they are, without disguise; we
find ourselves battered, but seized by a vigorous hand.
This pulpit is effective; and indeed, as compared with
the French pulpit, this is its characteristic.   These
sermons have not the art and artifice, the propriety and
moderation of French sermons; they are not, like the
latter, monuments of style, composition, harmony, veiled
science, tempered imagination, disguised logic, sustained
good taste, exquisite proportion, equal to the harangues
of the Roman forum and the Athenian agora.   They
are not classical.   No, they are practical.   A big work-
man-like shovel, roughly handled, and encrusted with
pedantic rust, was necessary to dig in this coarse civilisation.   The delicate French gardening would have done
nothing with it.   If Barrow is redundant, Tillotson
heavy, South vulgar, the rest unreadable, they are all
convincing; their sermons are not models of elegance, but
instruments of edification.   Their glory is not in their
books, but in their works.   They have framed morals,
not literary productions.

VI.

To form morals is not all; there are creeds to be defended.   We must combat doubt as well as vice, and
theology goes side by side with preaching.   It abounds
at this moment in England.   Anglicans, Presbyterians,
Independents, Quakers, Baptists, Antitrinitarians,
wrangle with each other, " as heartily as a Jansenist
damns a Jesuit," and are never tired of forging
weapons.   What is there to take hold of and preserve

in all this arsenal ?   In France at least theology is lofty ;
the fairest flowers of mind and genius have there grown
over the briars of scholastics ; if the subject repels, the
dress attracts.   Pascal and Bossuet, Fénelon and La
Bruyère, Voltaire, Diderot and Montesquieu, friends and
enemies, all have scattered their wealth of pearls and
gold.   Over the threadbare woof of barren doctrines the
seventeenth century has embroidered a majestic stole
of purple and silk ; and the eighteenth century, crump-
ling and tearing it, scatters it in a thousand golden
threads, which sparkle like a ball-dress.   But in England
all is dull, dry, and gloomy ; the great men themselves,
Addison and Locke, when they meddle in the defence
of Christianity, become flat and wearisome.   From
Chillingworth to Paley, apologies, refutations, exposi-
tions, discussions, multiply and make us yawn ; they
reason well, and that is all.   The theologian enters on
a campaign against the Papists of the seventeenth
century and the Deists of the eighteenth,[1] like a
tactician, by rule, taking a position on a principle,
throwing up all around a breastwork of arguments,
covering everything with texts, marching calmly underground in the long shafts which he has dug ; we
approach and see a sallow-faced pioneer creep out, with
frowning brow, stiff hands, dirty clothes ; he thinks he
is protected from all attacks ; his eyes, glued to the
ground, have not seen the broad level road beside his
bastion, by which the enemy will outflank and surprise
him.   A sort of incurable mediocrity keeps men like
him, mattock in hand, in their trenches, where no one

---

[1] I thought it necessary to look into the Socinian pamphlets,
which have swarmed so much among us within a few years.—Stillingfleet, *In Vindication of the Doctrine of the Trinity*, 1697.

is likely to pass.   They understand neither their texts
nor their formulas.   They are impotent in criticism
and philosophy.   They treat the poetic figures of
Scripture, the bold style, the approximations to impro-
visation, the mystical Hebrew emotion, the subtilties
and abstractions of Alexandrian metaphysics, with the
precision of a jurist and a psychologist.   They wish
actually to make of Scripture an exact code of prescriptions and definitions, drawn up by a convention of legislators.   Open the first that comes to hand, one of the
oldest—John Hales.   He comments on a passage of St.
Matthew, where a question arises on a matter forbidden
on the Sabbath.   What was this ?   "The disciples plucked
the ears of corn and did eat them."[1]   Then follow divisions and arguments raining down by myriads.[2]   Take
the most celebrated : Sherlock, applying the new psychology, invents an explanation of the Trinity, and imagines
three divine souls, each knowing what passes in the
others.   Stillingfleet refutes Locke, who thought that
the soul in the resurrection, though having a body,
would not perhaps have exactly the same one in which
it had lived.   Let us look at the most illustrious of all,
the learned Clarke, a mathematician, philosopher, scholar,
theologian ; he is busy patching up Arianism.   The

---

[1] John Hales of Eaton, *Works*, 3 vols, 12mo, 1765, i. 4.

[2] He examines, amongst other things, "the sin against the Holy
Ghost."   They would very much like to know in what this consists.
But nothing is more obscure.   Calvin and other theologians each gave
a different definition.   After a minute dissertation, Hales concludes
thus : "And though negative proofs from Scripture are not demonstrative, yet the general silence of the apostles may at least help
to infer a probability that the blasphemy against the Holy Ghost is
not committable by any Christian who lived not in the time of our
Saviour" (1636).   This is a training for argument.   So, in Italy, the
discussion about giving drawers to, or withholding them from the
Capuchins, developed political and diplomatic ability.—*Ibid.* i. 36.

great Newton himself comments on the Apocalypse, and proves that the Pope is Antichrist. In vain have these men genius; as soon as they touch religion, they become antiquated, narrow-minded; they make no way; they are stubborn, and obstinately knock their heads against the same obstacle. They bury themselves, generation after generation, in the hereditary hole with English patience and conscientiousness, whilst the enemy marches by, a league off. Yet in the hole they argue; they square it, round it, face it with stones, then with bricks, and wonder that, notwithstanding all these expedients, the enemy marches on. I have read a host of these treatises, and I have not gleaned a single idea. We are annoyed to see so much lost labour, and amazed that, during so many generations, people so virtuous, zealous, thoughtful, loyal, well read, well trained in discussion, have only succeeded in filling the lower shelves of libraries. We muse sadly on this second scholastic theology, and end by perceiving that if it was without effect in the kingdom of science, it was because it only strove to bear fruit in the kingdom of action.

All these speculative minds were so in appearance only. They were apologists, and not inquirers. They busy themselves with morality, not with truth.[1] They would shrink from treating God as a hypothesis, and the Bible as a document. They would see a vicious tendency in the broad impartiality of criticism and

---

[1] "The Scripture is a book of morality, and not of philosophy. Everything there relates to practice. . . . It is evident, from a cursory view of the Old and New Testament, that they are miscellaneous books, some parts of which are history, others writ in a poetical style, and others prophetical; but the design of them all, is professedly to recommend the practice of true religion and virtue."—John Clarke, Chaplain of the King, 1721. [I have not been able to find these exact words in the edition of Clarke accessible to me.—TR.]

philosophy. They would have scruples of conscience if they indulged in free inquiry without limitation. In reality there is a sort of sin in truly free inquiry, because it presupposes scepticism, abandons reverence, weighs good and evil in the same balance, and equally receives all doctrines, scandalous or edifying, as soon as they are proved. They banish these dissolving speculations; they look on them as occupations of the slothful; they seek from argument only motives and means for right conduct. They do not love it for itself; they repress it as soon as it strives to become independent; they demand that reason shall be Christian and Protestant; they would give it the lie under any other form; they reduce it to the humble position of a handmaid, and set over it their own inner biblical and utilitarian sense. In vain did free-thinkers arise in the beginning of the century; forty years later they were drowned in forgetfulness.[1] Deism and atheism were in England only a transient eruption developed on the surface of the social body, in the bad air of the great world and the plethora of native energy. Professed irreligious men, Toland, Tindal, Mandeville, Bolingbroke, met foes stronger than themselves. The leaders of experimental philosophy,[2] the most learned and accredited of the scholars of the age,[3] the most witty authors, the most beloved and able,[4] all the authority of science and genius was employed in putting them down. Refutations abound. Every year, on the foundation of Robert Boyle, men noted for their talent

---

[1] Burke, *Reflections on the Revolution in France.*
[2] Ray, Boyle, Barrow, Newton.
[3] Bentley, Clarke, Warburton, Berkeley.
[4] Locke, Addison, Swift, Johnson, Richardson.

or knowledge come to London to preach eight sermons, for proving the Christian religion against notorious infidels, viz., atheists, deists, pagans, Mohammedans, and Jews. And these apologies are solid, able to convince a liberal mind, infallible for the conviction of a moral mind. The clergymen who write them, Clarke, Bentley, Law, Watt, Warburton, Butler, are not below the lay science and intellect. Moreover, the lay element assists them. Addison writes the *Evidences of Christianity*, Locke the *Reasonableness of Christianity*, Ray the *Wisdom of God manifested in the Works of the Creation*. Over and above this concert of serious words is heard a ringing voice : Swift compliments with his terrible irony the elegant rogues who entertained the wise idea of abolishing Christianity. If they had been ten times more numerous they would not have succeeded, for they had nothing to substitute in its place. Lofty speculation, which alone could take the ground, was shown or declared to be impotent. On all sides philosophical conceptions dwindle or come to nought. If Berkeley lighted on one, the denial of matter, it stands alone, without influence on the public, as it were a theological *coup d'état*, like a pious man who wants to undermine immorality and materialism at their basis. Newton attained at most an incomplete idea of space, and was only a mathematician. Locke, almost as poor,[1] gropes about, hesitates, does little more than guess, doubt, start an opinion to advance and withdraw it by turns, not seeing its far-off consequences, nor, above all, exhausting anything. In short, he forbids himself lofty questions, and is very much inclined to forbid them to us. He has written a book to inquire

[1] "Paupertina philosophia," says Leibnitz.

what objects are within our reach, or above our comprehension.   He seeks for our limitations; he soon finds them, and troubles himself no further.   Let us shut ourselves in our own little domain, and work there diligently.   Our business in this world is not to know all things, but those which regard the conduct of our life.   If Hume, more bold, goes further, it is in the same track : he preserves nothing of lofty science; he abolishes speculation altogether.   According to him, we know neither substances, causes, nor laws.   When we affirm that an object is conjoined to another object, it is because we choose, by custom; "all events seem entirely loose and separate."   If we give them "a tie," it is our imagination which creates it;[1] there is nothing true but doubt, and even we must doubt this.   The conclusion is, that we shall do well to purge our mind of all theory, and only believe in order that we may act.   Let us examine our wings only in order to cut them off, and let us confine ourselves to walking with our legs.   So finished a pyrrhonism serves only to cast the world back upon established beliefs.   In fact, Reid, being honest, is alarmed.   He sees society broken up, God vanishing in smoke, the family evaporating in hypotheses.   He objects as a father of a family, a good citizen, a religious man, and sets up common sense as

[1] After the constant conjunction of two objects—heat and flame, for instance, weight and solidity—we are determined by custom alone to expect the one from the appearance of the other.   All inferences from experience are effects of custom, not of reasoning. . . . "Upon the whole, there appears not, throughout all nature, any one instance of connection which is conceivable by us.   All events seem entirely loose and separate ; one event follows another ; but we can never observe any tie between them.   They seem conjoined, but never connected."—Hume's *Essays*, 4 vols. 1760, iii. 117.

a sovereign judge of truth. Rarely, I think, in this world has speculation fallen lower. Reid does not even understand the systems which he discusses; he lifts his hands to heaven when he tries to expound Aristotle and Leibnitz. If some municipal body were to order a system, it would be this churchwarden-philosophy. In reality the men of this country did not care for metaphysics; to interest them it must be reduced to psychology. Then it becomes a science of observation, positive and useful, like botany; still the best fruit which they pluck from it is a theory of moral sentiments. In this domain Shaftesbury, Hutcheson, Price, Smith, Ferguson, and Hume himself prefer to labour; here they find their most original and durable ideas. On this point the public instinct is so strong, that it enrols the most independent minds in its service, and only permit them the discoveries which benefit it. Except two or three, chiefly purely literary men, and who are French or Frenchified in mind, they busy themselves only with morals. This idea rallies round Christianity all the forces which in France Voltaire ranges against it. They all defend it on the same ground—as a tie for civil society, and as a support for private virtue. Formerly instinct supported it; now opinion consecrates it; and it is the same secret force which, by a gradual labour, at present adds the weight of opinion to the pressure of instinct. Moral sense, having preserved for it the fidelity of the lower classes, conquered for it the approval of the loftier intellects. Moral sense transfers it from the public conscience to the literary world, and from being popular makes it official.

VII.

We would hardly suspect this public tendency, after taking a distant view of the English constitution; but on a closer view it is the first thing we see. It appears to be an aggregate of privileges, that is, of sanctioned injustices. The truth is, that it is a body of contracts, that is, of recognised rights. Every one, great or small, has its own, which he defends with all his might. My lands, my property, my chartered right, whatsoever it be, antiquated, indirect, superfluous, individual, public, none shall touch it, king, lords, or commons. Is it of the value of five shillings? I will defend it as if it were worth a million sterling; it is my person which they would attack. I will leave my business, lose my time, throw away my money, form associations, pay fines, go to prison, perish in the attempt; no matter; I shall show that I am no coward, that I will not bend under injustice, that I will not yield a portion of my right.

By this sentiment Englishmen have conquered and preserved public liberty. This feeling, after they had dethroned Charles I. and James II., is shaped into principles in the declaration of 1689, and is developed by Locke in demonstrations.[1] "All men," says Locke, "are naturally in a state of perfect freedom, also of

---

[1] We must read Sir Robert Filmer's *Patriarcha*, London, 1680, on the prevailing theory, in order to see from what a quagmire of follies people emerged. He said that Adam, on his creation, had received an absolute and regal power over the universe; that in every society of men there was one legitimate king, the direct heir of Adam. "Some say it was by lot, and others that Noah sailed round the Mediterranean in ten years, and divided the world into Asia, Africa, and Europe" (p. 15) —portions for his three sons. Compare Bossuet, *Politique fondée sur l'Ecriture*. At this epoch moral science was being emancipated from theology.

equality."[1]   " In the State of Nature every one has
the Executive power of the Law of Nature,"[2] *i.e.* of
judging, punishing, making war, ruling his family and
dependents.   " There only is political society where
every one of the members hath quitted this natural
Power, resign'd it up into the Hands of the Community
in all Cases that exclude him not from appealing for
Protection to the Law established by it."[3]

" Those who are united into one body and have a common
established law and judicature to appeal to, with authority . . .
to punish offenders, are in civil society one with another.[4]   As
for the ruler (they are ready to tell you), he ought to be absolute
. . . Because he has power to do more hurt and wrong, 'tis right
when he does it. . . . This is to think, that men are so foolish, that
they take care to avoid what mischiefs may be done them by pole-
cats or foxes ; but are content, nay think it safety, to be devoured
by lions.[5]   The only way whereby any one divests himself of
his natural liberty, and puts on the bonds of civil society, is by
agreeing with other men to join and unite into a community,
for their comfortable, safe, and peaceable living one amongst
another, in a secure enjoyment of their properties, and a greater
security against any, that are not of it."[6]

Umpires, rules of arbitration, this is all which their
federation can impose upon them.   They are freemen,
who, having made a mutual treaty, are still free.
Their society does not found, but guarantees their
rights.   And official acts here sustain abstract theory.
When Parliament declares the throne vacant, its first
argument is, that the king has violated the original
contract by which he was king.   When the Commons

---

[1] Locke, *Of Civil Government*, 1714, book ii. ch. ii. § 4.
[2] *Ibid.* § 13.   [3] *Ibid.* ii. ch. vii. § 87.   [4] *Ibid.*
[5] *Ibid.* ii. ch. vii. § 93.   [6] *Ibid.* ii. ch. viii. § 95.

impeach Sacheverell, it was in order publicly to maintain that the constitution of England was founded on a contract, and that the subjects of this kingdom have, in their different public and private capacities, as legal a title to the possession of the rights accorded to them by law, as the prince has to the possession of the crown. When Lord Chatham defended the election of Wilkes, it was by laying down that the rights of the greatest and of the meanest subjects now stand upon the same foundation, the security of law common to all. . . . When the people had lost their rights, those of the peerage would soon become insignificant. It was no supposition or philosophy which founded them, but an act and deed, Magna Charta, the Petition of Rights, the Habeas Corpus Act, and the whole body of the statute laws.

These rights are there, inscribed on parchments, stored up in archives, signed, sealed, authentic; those of the farmer and prince are traced on the same page, in the same ink, by the same writer; both are on an equality on this vellum; the gloved hand clasps the horny palm. What though they are unequal? It is by mutual accord; the peasant is as much a master in his cottage, with his rye-bread and his nine shillings a week,[1] as the Duke of Marlborough in Blenheim Castle, with his many thousands a year in places and pensions.

There they are, these men, standing erect and ready to defend themselves. Pursue this sentiment of right in the details of political life; the force of brutal temperament and concentrated or savage passions provides arms. If we go to an election, the first thing we see

---

[1] De Foe's estimate.

is the full tables.[1] They cram themselves at the
candidate's expense : ale, gin, brandy are set flowing
without concealment ; the victuals descend into their
electoral stomachs, and their faces grow red.   At the
same time they become furious.   " Every glass they
pour down serves to increase their animosity.   Many
an honest man, before as harmless as a tame rabbit,
when loaded with a single election dinner, has become
more dangerous than a charged culverin."[2]   The
wrangle turns into a fight, and the pugnacious instinct,
once loosed, craves for blows.   The candidates bawl
against each other till they are hoarse.   They are
chaired, to the great peril of their necks ; the mob
yells, cheers, grows warm with the motion, the defiance,
the row ; big words of patriotism peal out, anger and
drink inflame their blood, fists are clenched, cudgels are
at work, and bulldog passions regulate the greatest
interests of the country.   Let all beware how they draw
these passions down on their heads : Lords, Commons,
King, they will spare no one ; and when Government
would oppress a man in spite of them, they will compel
Government to suppress their own law.

They are not to be muzzled, they make that a
matter of pride.   With them, pride assists instinct in
defending the right.   Each feels that " his house is his

---

[1] " Their eating, indeed, amazes me ; had I five hundred heads, and
were each head furnished with brains, yet would they all be insuffi-
cient to compute the number of cows, pigs, geese, and turkies which
upon this occasion die for the good of their country ! . . . On the
contrary, they seem to lose their temper as they lose their appetites ;
every morsel they swallow serves to increase their animosity . . . The
mob meet upon the debate, fight themselves sober, and then draw
off to get drunk again, and charge for another encounter."—Goldsmith's
Citizen of the World, Letter cxii., "An Election described."   See also
Hogarth's prints.   [2] *Ibid.*

castle," and that the law keeps guard at his door. Each tells himself that he is defended against private insolence, that the public arbitrary power will never touch him, that he has "his body," and can answer blows by blows, wounds by wounds, that he will be judged by an impartial jury and a law common to all. "Even if an Englishman," says Montesquieu, "has as many enemies as hairs on his head, nothing will happen to him. The laws there were not made for one more than for another ; each looks on himself as a king, and the men of this nation are more confederates than fellow-citizens." This goes so far, "that there is hardly a day when some one does not lose respect for the king. Lately my Lady Bell Molineux, a regular virago, sent to have the trees pulled up from a small piece of land which the queen had bought for Kensington, and went to law with her, without having wished, under any pretext, to come to terms with her ; she made the queen's secretary wait three hours." [1] "When Englishmen come to France, they are deeply astonished to see the sway of ' the king's good pleasure,' the Bastille, the *lettres de cachet ;* a gentleman who dare not live on his estate in the country, for fear of the governor of the province ; a groom of the king's chamber, who, for a cut with the razor, kills a poor barber with impunity." [2] In England, "one man does not fear another." If we converse with any of them, we will find how greatly this security raises their hearts and courage. A sailor who rows Voltaire about, and may be pressed next day into the fleet, prefers his condition to that of the Frenchman, and looks on him with pity, whilst taking his five

[1] Montesquieu, *Notes sur l'Angleterre.*
[2] Smollett, *Peregrine Pickle,* ch. 40.

shillings.   The vastness of their pride breaks forth at
every step and in every page.   An Englishman, says
Chesterfield, thinks himself equal to beating three
Frenchmen.   They would willingly declare that they
are in the herd of men as bulls in a herd of cattle.
We hear them bragging of their boxing, of their meat
and ale, of all that can support the force and energy of
their virile will.   Roast-beef and beer make stronger
arms than cold water and frogs.[1]   In the eyes of the
vulgar, the French are starved wigmakers, papists, and
serfs, an inferior kind of creatures, who can neither call
their bodies nor their souls their own, puppets and
tools in the hands of a master and a priest.   As for
themselves,

> " Stern o'er each bosom reason holds her state
> With daring aims irregularly great.
> Pride in their port, defiance in their eye,
> I see the lords of human kind pass by ;
> Intent on high designs, a thoughtful band,
> By forms unfashion'd, fresh from nature's hand,
> Fierce in their native hardiness of soul,
> True to imagin'd right, above control,
> While even the peasant boasts these rights to scan,
> And learns to venerate himself as man." [2]

Men thus constituted can become impassioned in
public concerns. for they are their own concerns ; in
France, they are only the business of the king and of
Madame de Pompadour.[3]   In England, political parties
are as ardent as sects : High Church and Low Church,
capitalists and landed proprietors, court nobility and

---

[1] See Hogarth's prints.   [2] Goldsmith's *Traveller.*
[3] Chesterfield observes that a Frenchman of his time did not understand the word Country ; you must speak to him of his Prince.

county families, they have their dogmas, their theories, their manners, and their hatreds, like Presbyterians, Anglicans, and Quakers.   The country squire rails, over his wine, at the House of Hanover, drinks to the king over the water; the Whig in London, on the 30th of January, drinks to the man in the mask,[1] and then to the man who will do the same thing without a mask.   They imprisoned, exiled, beheaded each other, and Parliament resounded daily with the fury of their animadversions.   Political, like religious life, wells up and overflows, and its outbursts only mark the force of the flame which nourishes it.   The passion of parties, in state affairs as in matters of belief, is a proof of zeal; constant quiet is only general indifference; and if people fight at elections, it is because they take an interest in them.   Here "a tiler had the newspaper brought to him on the roof that he might read it."   A stranger who reads the papers "would think the country on the eve of a revolution."   When Government takes a step, the public feels itself involved in it; its honour and its property are being disposed of by the minister; let the minister beware if he disposes of them ill. With the French, M. de Conflans, who lost his fleet through cowardice, is punished by an epigram; here, Admiral Byng, who was too prudent to risk his, was shot. Every man in his due position, and according to his power, takes part in public business: the mob broke the heads of those who would not drink Dr. Sacheverell's health; gentlemen came in mounted troops to meet him.   Some public favourite or enemy is always excit-ing open demonstrations.   One day it is Pitt whom the people cheer, and on whom the municipal corpora-

[1] The executioner of Charles I.

tions bestow many gold boxes; another day it is Gren-
ville, whom people go to hiss when coming out of the
house; then again Lord Bute, whom the queen loves, who
is hissed, and who is burned under the effigy of a boot, a
pun on his name, whilst the princess of Wales was
burned under the effigy of a petticoat; or the Duke of
Bedford, whose town house is attacked by a mob, and
who is only saved by a garrison of horse and foot; Wilkes,
whose papers the Government seize, and to whom the
jury assign one thousand pounds damages. Every morning appear newspapers and pamphlets to discuss affairs,
criticise characters, denounce by name lords, orators,
ministers, the king himself. He who wants to speak
speaks. In this wrangle of writings and associations
opinion swells, mounts like a wave, and falling upon
Parliament and Court, drowns intrigue and carries away
all differences. After all, in spite of the rotten boroughs,
it is public opinion which rules. What though the
king be obstinate, the men in power band together?
Public opinion growls, and everything bends or breaks.
The Pitts rose as high as they did, only because public
opinion raised them, and the independence of the
individual ended in the sovereignty of the people.

In such a state, " all passions being free, hatred, envy,
jealousy, the fervour for wealth and distinction, would
be displayed in all their fulness." [1] We can imagine
with what force and energy eloquence must have been
implanted and flourished. For the first time since the
fall of the ancient tribune, it found a soil in which it
could take root and live, and a harvest of orators sprang
up, equal, in the diversity of their talents, the energy
of their convictions, and the magnificence of their style,

[1] Montesquieu, *De l'Esprit des lois*, book xix. ch. 27.

to that which once covered the Greek *agora* and the Roman *forum*. For a long time it seemed that liberty of speech, experience in affairs, the importance of the interests involved, and the greatness of the rewards offered, should have forced its growth; but eloquence came to nothing, encrusted in theological pedantry, or limited in local aims; and the privacy of the parliamentary sittings deprived it of half its force by removing from it the light of day. Now at last there was light; publicity, at first incomplete, then entire, gives Parliament the nation for an audience. Speech becomes elevated and enlarged at the same time that the public is polished and more numerous. Classical art, become perfect, furnishes method and development. Modern culture introduces into technical reasoning freedom of discourse and a breadth of general ideas. In place of arguing, men conversed; they were attorneys, they became orators. With Addison, Steele, and Swift, taste and genius invade politics. Voltaire cannot say whether the meditated harangues once delivered in Athens and Rome excelled the unpremeditated speeches of Windham, Carteret, and their rivals. In short, discourse succeeds in overcoming the dryness of special questions and the coldness of compassed action, which had so long restricted it; it boldly and irregularly extends its force and luxuriance; and in contrast with the fine abbés of the drawing-room, who in France compose their academical compliments, we see appear, the manly eloquence of Junius, Chatham, Fox, Pitt, Burke, and Sheridan.

I need not relate their lives nor unfold their characters; I should have to enter upon political details. Three of them, Lord Chatham, Fox, and Pitt, were ministers,[1] and their eloquence is part of their power and their acts. That eloquence is the concern of those men who may record their political history; I can simply take note of its tone and accent.

VIII.

An extraordinary afflatus, a sort of quivering of intense determination, runs through all these speeches. Men speak, and they speak as if they fought. No caution, politeness, restraint. They are unfettered, they abandon themselves, they hurl themselves onward; and if they restrain themselves, it is only that they may strike more pitilessly and more forcibly. When the elder Pitt first filled the House with his vibrating voice, he already possessed his indomitable audacity. In vain Walpole tried to "muzzle him," then to crush him; his sarcasm was sent back to him with a prodigality of outrages, and the all-powerful minister bent, smitten with the truth of the biting insult which the young man inflicted on him. A lofty haughtiness, only surpassed by that of his son, an arrogance which reduced his colleagues to the rank of subalterns, a Roman patriotism which demanded for England a universal tyranny, an ambition lavish of money and men, gave the nation its rapacity and its fire, and only saw rest in far vistas of dazzling glory and limitless power, an imagination which brought into Parliament the vehemence and declamation of the stage, the brilliancy of fitful inspiration, the bold-

---

[1] Junius wrote anonymously, and critics have not yet been able with certainty to reveal his true name. Most probably he was Sir Philip Francis

ness of poetic imagery. Such are the sources of his eloquence :

" ' *But yesterday, and* England *might have stood against the world ; now none so poor to do her reverence.*'

" My Lords, YOU CANNOT CONQUER AMERICA.

" We shall be forced ultimately to retract ; let us retract while we can, not when we must. I say we must necessarily undo these violent oppressive Acts : they must be repealed— you will repeal them ; I pledge myself for it, that you will in the end repeal them ; I stake my reputation on it. I will consent to be taken for an idiot, if they are not finally repealed.

" You may swell every expense, and every effort, still more extravagantly ; pile and accumulate every assistance you can buy or borrow ; traffic and barter with every little pitiful German prince, that sells and sends his subjects to the shambles of a foreign prince ; your efforts are for ever vain and impotent— doubly so from this mercenary aid on which you rely ; for it irritates, to an incurable resentment, the minds of your enemies. To overrun them with the mercenary sons of rapine and plunder ; devoting them and their possessions to the rapacity of hireling cruelty ! If I were an American as I am an Englishman, while a foreign troop was landed in my country, I never would lay down my arms—never—never—never !

" But, my Lords, who is the man, that in addition to these disgraces and mischiefs of our army, has dared to authorize and associate to our arms the tomahawk and scalping-knife of the savage ? To call into civilised alliance the wild and inhuman savage of the woods ; to delegate to the merciless Indian the defence of disputed rights, and to wage the horrors of barbarous war against our brethren ? My Lords, these enormities cry aloud for redress and punishment ; unless thoroughly done away, it will be a stain on the national character—it is a violation of the constitution—I believe it is against law." [1]

[1] *Anecdotes and Speeches of the Earl of Chatham,* 7th ed., 3 vols., 1810, ii. ch. 42 and 44.

There is a touch of Milton and Shakspeare in this tragic pomp, in this impassioned solemnity, in the sombre and violent brilliancy of this overstrung and overloaded style.   In such superb and blood-like purple are English passions clad, under the folds of such a banner they fall into battle array; the more powerfully that amongst them there is one altogether holy, the sentiment of right, which rallies, occupies, and ennobles them :

" I rejoice that America has resisted.   Three millions of people so dead to all the feelings of liberty, as voluntarily to submit to be slaves, would have been fit instruments to make slaves of the rest.[1]

" Let the sacredness of their property remain inviolate; let it be taxable only by their own consent given in their provincial assemblies ; else it will cease to be property.

" This glorious spirit of Whiggism animates three millions in America, who prefer poverty with liberty to gilded chains and sordid affluence, and who will die in defence of their rights as men, as freemen. . . .   The spirit which now resists your taxation in America is the same which formerly opposed loans, benevolences, and ship money in England; the same spirit which called all England on its legs, and by the Bill of Rights vindicated the English constitution ; the same spirit which established the great fundamental, essential maxim of your liberties ; that no subject of England shall be taxed but by his own consent.

" As an Englishman by birth and principle, I recognise to the Americans their supreme unalienable right in their property, a right which they are justified in the defence of to the last extremity." [2]

If Pitt sees his own right, he sees that of others

[1] *Anecdotes and Speeches of the Earl of Chatham*, ii. ch. 29.
[2] *Ibid.* ii. ch. 42.

too; it was with this idea that he moved and managed England. For it, he appealed to Englishmen against themselves; and in spite of themselves they recognised their dearest instinct in this maxim, that every human will is inviolable in its limited and legal province, and that it must put forth its whole strength against the slightest usurpation.

Unrestrained passions and the most manly sentiment of right; such is the abstract of all this eloquence. Instead of an orator, a public man, let us take a writer, a private individual; let us look at the letters of Junius, which, amidst national irritation and anxiety, fell one by one like drops of fire on the fevered limbs of the body politic. If he makes his phrases concise, and selects his epithets, it was not from a love of style, but in order the better to stamp his insult. Oratorical artifices in his hand become instruments of torture, and when he files his periods it was to drive the knife deeper and surer; with what audacity of denunciation, with what sternness of animosity, with what corrosive and burning irony, applied to the most secret corners of private life, with what inexorable persistence of . calculated and meditated persecution, the quotations alone will· show. He writes to the Duke of Bedford:

" My lord, you are so little accustomed to receive any marks of respect or esteem from the public, that if, in the following lines, a compliment or expression of applause should escape me, I fear you would consider it as a mockery of your established character, and perhaps an insult to your understanding." [1]

He writes to the Duke of Grafton:

[1] Junius' *Letters*, 2 vols., 1772, xxiii. i. 162.

"There is something in both your character and conduct which distinguishes you not only from all other ministers, but from all other men. It is not that you do wrong by design, but that you should never do right by mistake. It is not that your indolence and your activity have been equally misapplied, but that the first uniform principle, or, if I may call it, the genius of your life, should have carried you through every possible change and contradiction of conduct, without the momentary imputation or colour of a virtue ; and that the wildest spirit of inconsistency should never once have betrayed you into a wise or honourable action." [1]

Junius goes on, fiercer and fiercer; even when he sees the minister fallen and dishonoured, he is still savage.

It is vain that he confesses aloud that in the state in which he is, the Duke might "disarm a private enemy of his resentment." He grows worse :

"You have every claim to compassion that can arise from misery and distress. The condition you are reduced to would disarm a private enemy of his resentment, and leave no consolation to the most vindictive spirit, but that such an object, as you are, would disgrace the dignity of revenge. . . . For my own part, I do not pretend to understand those prudent forms of decorum, those gentle rules of discretion, which some men endeavour to unite with the conduct of the greatest and most hazardous affairs. . . . I should scorn to provide for a future retreat, or to keep terms with a man who preserves no measures with the public. Neither the abject submission of deserting his post in the hour of danger, nor even the sacred shield of cowardice, should protect him. I would pursue him through life, and try the last exertion of my abilities to preserve the perishable infamy of his name, and make it immortal." [2]

Except Swift, is there a human being who has more intentionally concentrated and intensified in his heart

---

[1] Junius' *Letters*, xii. i. 75.   [2] *Ibid*. xxxvi. ii. 56.

the venom of hatred? Yet this is not vile, for it thinks itself to be in the service of justice. Amidst these excesses, this is the persuasion which enhances them; these men tear one another; but they do not crouch; whoever their enemy be, they take their stand in front of him. Thus Junius addresses the king:

"SIR—It is the misfortune of your life, and originally the cause of every reproach and distress which has attended your government, that you should never have been acquainted with the language of truth until you heard it in the complaints of your people. It is not, however, too late to correct the error of your education. We are still inclined to make an indulgent allowance for the pernicious lessons you received in your youth, and to form the most sanguine hopes from the natural benevolence of your disposition. We are far from thinking you capable of a direct, deliberate purpose to invade those original rights of your subjects on which all their civil and political liberties depend. Had it been possible for us to entertain a suspicion so dishonourable to your character, we should long since have adopted a style of remonstrance very distant from the humility of complaint. . . . The people of England are loyal to the House of Hanover, not from a vain preference of one family to another, but from a conviction that the establishment of that family was necessary to the support of their civil and religious liberties. This, Sir, is a principle of allegiance equally solid and rational; fit for Englishmen to adopt, and well worthy of your Majesty's encouragement. We cannot long be deluded by nominal distinctions. The name of Stuart, of itself, is only contemptible :—armed with the sovereign authority, their principles are formidable. The prince who imitates their conduct, should be warned by their example; and while he plumes himself upon the security of his title to the crown, should remember that, as it was acquired by one revolution, it may be lost by another." [1]

[1] Junius' *Letters*, xxxv. ii. 29.

Let us look for less bitter souls, and try to encounter a sweeter accent. There is one man, Charles James Fox, happy from his cradle, who learned everything without study, whom his father trained in prodigality and recklessness, whom, from the age of twenty-one, the public voice proclaimed as the first in eloquence and the leader of a great party, liberal, humane, sociable, not frustrating these generous expectations, whose very enemies pardoned his faults, whom his friends adored, whom labour never wearied, whom rivals never embittered, whom power did not spoil; a lover of converse, of literature, of pleasure, who has left the impress of his rich genius in the persuasive abundance, in the fine charactei, the clearness and continuous ease of his speeches. Behold him rising to speak; think of the discretion he must use; he is a statesman, a premier, speaking in Parliament of the friends of the king, lords of the bedchamber, the noblest families of the kingdom, with their allies and connections around him; he knows that every one of his words will pierce like a fiery arrow into the heart and honour of five hundred men who sit to hear him. No matter, he has been betrayed; he will punish the traitors, and here is the pillory in which he sets " the janissaries of the bedchamber," who by the Prince's order have deserted him in the thick of the fight:

" The whole compass of language affords no terms sufficiently strong and pointed to mark the contempt which I feel for their conduct. It is an impudent avowal of political profligacy, as if that species of treachery were less infamous than any other. It is not only a degradation of a station which ought to be occupied only by the highest and most exemplary honour, but forfeits their claim to the characters of gentlemen, and reduces them to

a level with the meanest and the basest of the species; it insults
the noble, the ancient, and the characteristic independence of
the English peerage, and is calculated to traduce and vilify the
British legislature in the eyes of all Europe, and to the latest
posterity. By what magic nobility can thus charm vice into
virtue, I know not nor wish to know; but in any other thing
than politics, and among any other men than lords of the bedchamber, such an instance of the grossest perfidy would, as it
well deserves, be branded with infamy and execration." [1]

Then turning to the Commons :

"A Parliament thus fettered and controlled, without spirit
and without freedom, instead of limiting, extends, substantiates,
and establishes beyond all precedent, latitude, or condition, the
prerogatives of the crown. But though the British House of
Commons were so shamefully lost to its own weight in the constitution, were so unmindful of its former struggles and triumphs
in the great cause of liberty and mankind, were so indifferent
and treacherous to those primary objects and concerns for which
it was originally instituted, I trust the characteristic spirit of
this country is still equal to the trial; I trust Englishmen will
be as jealous of secret influence as superior to open violence; I
trust they are not more ready to defend their interests against
foreign depredation and insult, than to encounter and defeat this
midnight conspiracy against the constitution." [2]

If such are the outbursts of a nature above all
gentle and amiable, we can judge what the others must
have been. A sort of impassioned exaggeration reigns
in the debates to which the trial of Warren Hastings
and the French Revolution gave rise, in the acrimonious
rhetoric and forced declamation of Sheridan, in the
pitiless sarcasm and sententious pomp of the younger

Fox's *Speeches*, 6 vols., 1815, ii. 271 ; Dec. 17, 1783.
    [2] *Ibid.* p. 268.

Pitt.   These orators love the coarse vulgarity of gaudy colours; they hunt out accumulations of big words, contrasts symmetrically protracted, vast and resounding periods.   They do not fear to repel; they crave effect. Force is their characteristic, and the characteristic of the greatest amongst them, the first mind of the age, Edmund Burke, of whom Dr. Johnson said : " Take up whatever topic you please, he (Burke) is ready to meet you."

Burke did not enter Parliament, like Pitt and Fox, in the dawn of his youth, but at thirty-five, having had time to train himself thoroughly in all matters, learned in law, history, philosophy, literature, master of such a universal erudition, that he has been compared to Bacon.   But what distinguished him from all other men was a wide, comprehensive intellect, which, exercised by philosophical studies and writings,[1] seized the general aspects of things, and, beyond text, constitutions, and figures, perceived the invisible tendency of events and the inner spirit, covering with his contempt those pretended statesmen, a vulgar herd of common journeymen, denying the existence of everything not coarse or material, and who, far from being capable of guiding the grand movements of an empire, are not worthy to turn the wheel of a machine.

Beyond all those gifts, he possessed one of those fertile and precise imaginations which believe that finished knowledge is an inner view, which never quit a subject without having clothed it in its colours and forms, and which, passing beyond statistics and the rubbish of dry documents, recompose and reconstruct before the reader's eyes a distant country and a foreign nation, with its monuments, dresses, landscapes, and all the

[1] *An Inquiry into our Ideas of the Sublime and the Beautiful.*

shifting detail of its aspects and manners. To all these powers of mind, which constitute a man of system, he added all those energies of heart which constitute an enthusiast. Poor, unknown, having spent his youth in compiling for the publishers, he rose, by dint of work and personal merit, with a pure reputation and an unscathed conscience, ere the trials of his obscure life or the seductions of his brilliant life had fettered his independence or tarnished the flower of his loyalty. He brought to politics a horror of crime, a vivacity and sincerity of conscience, a humanity, a sensibility, which seem only suitable to a young man. He based human society on maxims of morality, insisted upon a high and pure tone of feeling in the conduct of public business, and seemed to have undertaken to raise and authorise the generosity of the human heart. He fought nobly for noble causes; against the crimes of power in England, the crimes of the people in France, the crimes of monopolists in India. He defended, with immense research and unimpeached disinterestedness, the Hindoos tyrannised over by English greed :

" Every man of rank and landed fortune being long since extinguished, the remaining miserable last cultivator who grows to the soil after having his back scored by the farmer, has it again flayed by the whip of the assignee, and is thus by a ravenous because a short-lived succession of claimants lashed from oppressor to oppressor, whilst a single drop of blood is left as the means of extorting a single grain of corn." [1]

He made himself everywhere the champion of principle and the persecutor of vice; and men saw

[1] Burke's Works, 1808, 8 vols., iv. 286, *Speech on the Nabob of Arcot's debts.*

him bring to the attack all the forces of his wonderful knowledge, his lofty reason, his splendid style, with the unwearying and untempered ardour of a moralist and a knight.

Let us read him only several pages at a time : only thus he is great ; otherwise all that is exaggerated, commonplace, and strange, will arrest and shock us ; but if we give ourselves up to him, we will be carried away and captivated. The enormous mass of his documents rolls impetuously in a current of eloquence. Sometimes a spoken or written discourse needs a whole volume to unfold the train of his multiplied proofs and courageous anger. It is either the *exposé* of an administration, or the whole history of British India, or the complete theory of revolutions, and the political conditions, which comes down like a vast, overflowing stream, to dash with its ceaseless effort and accumulated mass against some crime that men would overlook, or some injustice which they would sanction. Doubtless there is foam on its eddies, mud in its bed : thousands of strange creatures sport wildly on its surface. Burke does not select, he lavishes ; he casts forth by myriads his teeming fancies, his emphasised and harsh words, declamations and apostrophes, jests and execrations, the whole grotesque or horrible assemblage of the distant regions and populous cities which his unwearied learning or fancy has traversed. He says, speaking of the usurious loans, at forty-eight per cent, and at compound interest, by which Englishmen had devastated India, that

"That debt forms the foul putrid mucus, in which are engendered the whole brood of creeping ascarides, all the endless involutions, the eternal knot, added to a knot of those inexpugnable tape-worms which devour the nutriment, and eat up the bowels of India." [1]

Nothing strikes him as excessive in speech, neither the description of tortures, nor the atrocity of his images, nor the deafening racket of his antitheses, nor the prolonged trumpet-blast of his curses, nor the vast oddity of his jests. To the Duke of Bedford, who had reproached him with his pension, he answers :

"The grants to the house of Russell were so enormous, as not only to outrage œconomy, but even to stagger credibility. The duke of Bedford is the leviathan among all the creatures of the crown. He tumbles about his unwieldy bulk ; he plays and frolicks in the ocean of the royal bounty. Huge as he is, and whilst ' he lies floating many a rood,' he is still a creature. His ribs, his fins, his whalebone, his blubber, the very spiracles through which he spouts a torrent of brine against his origin, and covers me all over with the spray,—everything of him and about him is from the throne." [2]

Burke has no taste, nor have his compeers. The fine Greek or French deduction has never found a place among the Germanic nations ; with them all is heavy or ill-refined. It is of no use for Burke to study Cicero, and to confine his dashing force in the orderly channels of Latin rhetoric; he continues half a barbarian, battening in exaggeration and violence ; but his fire is so sustained, his conviction so strong, his emotion so warm and abundant, that we give way to him, forget our repugnance, see in his irregularities and his out-bursts only the outpourings of a great heart and a deep mind, too open and too full; and we wonder with a

---

[1] Burke's Works, iv. 282.
[2] *Ibid.* viii. 35 ; *A Letter to a Noble Lord.*

sort of strange veneration at this extraordinary overflow, impetuous as a torrent, broad as a sea, in which the inexhaustible variety of colours and forms undulates beneath the sun of a splendid imagination, which lends to this muddy surge all the brilliancy of its rays.

IX.

If you wish for a comprehensive view of all these personages, study Sir Joshua Reynolds,[1] and then look at the fine French portraits of this time, the cheerful ministers, gallant and charming archbishops, Marshal de Saxe, who in the Strasburg monument goes down to his tomb with the grace and ease of a courtier on the staircase at Versailles. In England, under skies drowned in pallid mists, amid soft, vaporous clouds, appear expressive or contemplative heads: the rude energy of the character has not awed the artist; the coarse bloated animal; the strange and ominous bird of prey; the growling jaws of the fierce bulldog—he has put them all in : levelling politeness has not in his pictures effaced individual asperities under uniform pleasantness. Beauty is there, but only in the cold decision of look, in the deep seriousness and sad nobility of the pale countenance, in the conscientious gravity and the indomitable resolution of the restrained gesture. In place of Lely's courtesans, we see by their side chaste ladies, sometimes severe and active; good mothers surrounded by their little children, who kiss them and embrace one another : morality is here, and with it the sentiment of home and family, propriety of dress, a pensive air, the correct deportment of Miss Burney's

[1] Lord Heathfield, the Earl of Mansfield, Major Stringer Lawrence, Lord Ashburton, Lord Edgecombe, and many others.

heroines. They are men who have done the work
some service: Bakewell transforms and reforms their
cattle; Arthur Young their agriculture; Howard
their prisons; Arkwright and Watt their industry;
Adam Smith their political economy; Bentham their
penal law; Locke, Hutcheson, Ferguson, Bishop Butler,
Reid, Stewart, Price, their psychology and their morality. They have purified their private manners,
they now purify their public manners. They have
settled their government, they have established themselves in their religion. Johnson is able to say with
truth, that no nation in the world better tills its soil
and its mind. There is none so rich, so free, so well
nourished, where public and private efforts are directed
with such assiduity, energy, and ability towards the
improvement of public and private affairs. One
point alone is wanting: lofty speculation. It is just
this point which, when all others are wanting, constitutes
at this moment the glory of France; and English
caricatures show, with a good appreciation of burlesque,
face to face and in strange contrast, on one side the
Frenchman in a tumbledown cottage, shivering, with
long teeth, thin, feeding on snails and a handful of
roots, but otherwise charmed with his lot, consoled by
a republican cockade and humanitarian programmes;
on the other, the Englishman, red and puffed out with
fat, seated at his table in a comfortable room, before a
dish of most juicy roast-beef, with a pot of foaming ale,
busy in grumbling against the public distress and
the treacherous ministers, who are going to ruin everything.

Thus Englishmen arrive on the threshold of the
French Revolution, Conservatives and Christians facing

the French free-thinkers and revolutionaries. Without
knowing it, the two nations have rolled onwards for two
centuries towards this terrible shock; without knowing
it, they have only been working to make it worse. All
their effort, all their ideas, all their great men have accel-
erated the motion which hurls them towards the inevi-
table conflict. A hundred and fifty years of politeness and
general ideas have persuaded the French to trust in
human goodness and pure reason. A hundred and
fifty years of moral reflection and political strife have
attached the Englishman to positive religion and an
established constitution. Each has his contrary dogma
and his contrary enthusiasm. Neither understands
and each detests the other. What one calls reform, the
other calls destruction; what one reveres as the
establishment of right, the other curses as the overthrow
of right; what seems to one the annihilation of superstition, seems to the other the abolition of morality.
Never was the contrast of two spirits and two civilisations shown in clearer characters, and it was Burke
who, with the superiority of a thinker and the hostility
of an Englishman, took it in hand to show this to the
French.

He is indignant at this "tragi-comick farce," which
at Paris is called the regeneration of humanity. He
denies that the contagion of such folly can ever poison
England. He laughs at the Cockneys, who, roused by
the pratings of democratic societies, think themselves
on the brink of a revolution :

"Because half a dozen grasshoppers under a fern make the
field ring with their importunate chink, whilst thousands of
great cattle, reposed beneath the shadow of the British oak,
chew the cud and are silent, pray do not imagine that those

who make the noise are the only inhabitants of the field ; that of course, they are many in number ; or that, after all, they are other than the little shrivelled, meagre, hopping, though loud and troublesome insects of the hour." [1]

Real England hates and detests the maxims and actions of the French Revolution : [2]

"The very idea of the fabrication of a new government is enough to fill us with disgust and horror. We wished ... to derive all we possess as an inheritance from our forefathers. ... (We claim) our franchises not as the rights of men, but as the rights of Englishmen." [3]

Our rights do not float in the air, in the imagination of philosophers ; they are put down in Magna Charta. We despise this abstract verbiage, which deprives man of all equity and respect to puff him up with presumption and theories :

"We have not been drawn and trussed, in order that we may be filled, like stuffed birds in a museum, with chaff and rags and paltry blurred shreds of paper about the rights of men." [4]

Our constitution is not a fictitious contract, like that of Rousseau, sure to be violated in three months, but a real contract, by which, king, nobles, people, church, every one holds the other, and is himself held. The crown of the prince and the privilege of the noble are as sacred as the land of the peasant and the tool of the working-man. Whatever be the acquisition or the inheritance, we respect it in every man and our law

[1] Burke's Works, v. 165 ; *Reflections on the Revolution in France.*
[2] "I almost venture to affirm, that not one in a hundred amongst us participates in the triumph of the revolution society." —Burke's *Reflections.* v. 165.   [3] *Ibid.* 75.   [4] *Ibid.* 166.

has but one object, which is, to preserve to each his property and his rights.

"We fear God; we look up with awe to kings; with affection to parliaments; with duty to magistrates; with reverence to priests; and with respect to nobility."[1]

"There is not one public man in this kingdom who does not reprobate the dishonest, perfidious, and cruel confiscation which the National Assembly has been compelled to make. . . . Church and State are ideas inseparable in our minds. . . . Our education is in a manner wholly in the hands of ecclesiasticks, and in all stages, from infancy to manhood. . . . They never will suffer the fixed estate of the church to be converted into a pension, to depend on the treasury. . . . They made their church like their nobility, independent. They can see without pain or grudging an archbishop precede a duke. They can see a Bishop of Durham or a Bishop of Winchester in possession of ten thousand a year."[2]

We will never suffer the established domain of our church to be converted into a pension, so as to place it in dependence on the treasury. We have made our church as our king and our nobility, independent. We are shocked at your robbery—first, because it is an outrage upon property; next, because it is an attack upon religion. We hold that there exists no society without belief, and we feel that, in exhausting the source, you dry up the whole stream. We have rejected as a poison the infidelity which defiled the beginning of our century and of yours, and we have purged ourselves of it, whilst you have been saturated with it.

"Who, born within the last forty years, has read one word

---

[1] Burke's *Reflections*, v. 167.   [2] *Ibid.* 188.

of Collins, and Toland, and Tindal, . . . and that whole race who called themselves Freethinkers?"[1]

"We are Protestants, not from indifference, but from zeal.

"Atheism is against not only our reason, but our instincts.

"We are resolved to keep an established church, an established monarchy, an established aristocracy, and an established democracy, each in the degree it exists, and in no greater."[2]

We base our establishment upon the sentiment of right, and the sentiment of right on reverence for God.

In place of right and of God, whom do you, Frenchmen, acknowledge as master? The sovereign people, that is, the arbitrary inconstancy of a numerical majority. We deny that the majority has a right to destroy a constitution.

"The constitution of a country being once settled upon some compact, tacit or expressed, there is no power existing of force to alter it, without the breach of the covenant, or the consent of all the parties."[3]

We deny that a majority has a right to make a constitution; unanimity must first have conferred this right on the majority. We deny that brute force is a legitimate authority, and that a populace is a nation.[4]

"A true natural aristocracy is not a separate interest in the state or separable from it. . . . When great multitudes act together under that discipline of nature, I recognise the people;

---

[1] Burke's Works, v. 172; *Reflections*.　　　　[2] *Ibid.* 175.

[3] *Ibid.* vi. 201; *Appeal from the New to the Old Whigs.*

[4] "A government of five hundred country attornies and obscure curates is not good for twenty-four millions of men, though it were chosen by eight and forty millions. . . . As to the share of power, authority, direction, which each individual ought to have in the management of the state, that I must deny to be amongst the direct original rights of man in civil society."—Burke's Works, v. 109; *Reflections.*

. . . when you separate the common sort of men from their proper chieftains so as to form them into an adverse army, I no longer know that venerable object called the people in such a disbanded race of deserters and vagabonds." [1]

We detest with all our power of hatred the right of tyranny which you give them over others, and we detest still more the right of insurrection which you give them against themselves. We believe that a constitution is a trust transmitted to this generation by the past, to be handed down to the future, and that if a generation can dispose of it as its own, it ought also to respect it as belonging to others. We hold that, "by this unprincipled facility of changing the state as often, and as much, and in as many ways as there are floating fancies and fashions, the whole chain and continuity of the commonwealth would be broken. No one generation could link with the other. Men would become little better than the flies of a summer." [2] We repudiate this meagre and coarse reason, which separates a man from his ties, and sees in him only the present, which separates a man from society, and counts him as only one head in a flock. We despise these " metaphysics of an undergraduate and the mathematics of an exciseman," by which you cut up the state and man's rights according to square miles and numerical unities. We have a horror of that cynical coarseness by which " all the decent drapery of life is to be rudely torn off," by which "now a queen is but a woman, and a woman is but an animal," [3] which cuts down chivalric and religious spirit, the two crowns of humanity, to plunge them, together with learning, into the popular

[1] Burke's Works, vi. 219 ; *Appeal from the New to the Old Whigs.*
[2] *Ibid.* v. 181 ; *Reflections*   [3] *Ibid.* 151.

mire, to be " trodden down under the hoofs of a swinish multitude." [1]   We have a horror of this systematic levelling which disorganises civil society.   Burke continues thus :

"I am satisfied beyond a doubt that the project of turning a great empire into a vestry, or into a collection of vestries, and of governing it in the spirit of a parochial administration, is senseless and absurd, in any mode, or with any qualifications. I can never be convinced that the scheme of placing the highest powers of the state in churchwardens and constables, and other such officers, guided by the prudence of litigious attornies, and Jew brokers, and set in action by shameless women of the lowest condition, by keepers of hotels, taverns, and brothels, by pert apprentices, by clerks, shop-boys, hairdressers, fiddlers, and dancers on the stage (who, in such a commonwealth as yours, will in future overbear, as already they have overborne, the sober incapacity of dull uninstructed men, of useful but laborious occupations), can never be put into any shape that must not be both disgraceful and destructive." [2]   "If monarchy should ever obtain an entire ascendency in France, it will probably be . . . the most completely arbitrary power that has ever appeared on earth.   France will be wholly governed by the agitators in corporations, by societies in the towns formed of directors in assignats, . . . attornies, agents, money-jobbers, speculators, and adventurers, composing an ignoble oligarchy founded on the destruction of the crown, the church, the nobility, and the people." [3]

This is what Burke wrote in 1790 at the dawn of the first French Revolution.[4]   Two years after the people of

[1] Burke's Works, v. 154 ; *Reflections.*

[2] *Ibid.* vi. 5 ; *Letter to a Member of the National Assembly.*

[3] *Ibid.* v. 349 ; *Reflections.*

[4] "The effect of liberty to individuals is, that they may do what they please : we ought to see what it will please them to do, before we

Birmingham destroyed the houses of some English democrats, and the miners of Wednesbury went out in a body from their pits to come to the succour of " king and church." If we compare one crusade with another, scared England was as fanatical as enthusiastic France. Pitt declared that they could not " treat with a nation of atheists." [1] Burke said that the war was not between people and people, but between property and brute force. The rage of execration, invective, and destruction mounted on both sides like a conflagration.[2] It was not the collision of the two governments, but of the two civilisations and the two doctrines. The two vast machines, driven with all their momentum and velocity, met face to face not by chance, but by fatality. A whole age of

risk congratulations which may be soon turned into complaints. . . . Strange chaos of levity and ferocity, . . . monstrous tragi-comic scene. . . . After I have read the list of the persons and descriptions elected into the Tiers-Etat, nothing which they afterwards did could appear astonishing. . . . Of any practical experience in the state, not one man was to be found. The best were only men of theory. The majority was composed of practitioners in the law, . . . active chicaners, . . . obscure provincial advocates, stewards of petty local jurisdictions, country attornies, notaries, etc."—Burke's *Reflections*, etc., v. 37 and 90. That which offends Burke, and even makes him very uneasy, was, that no representatives of the " natural landed interests " were among the representatives of the *Tiers Etat*. Let us give one quotation more, for really this political clairvoyance is akin to genius : " Men are qualified for civil liberty in exact proportion to their disposition to put moral chains upon their own appetites. . . . Society cannot exist unless a controlling power upon will and appetite be placed somewhere ; and the less of it there is within the more there must be without. It is ordained in the eternal constitution of things that men of intemperate minds cannot be free. Their passions forge their fetters."

[1] Pitt's *Speeches*, 3 vols. 1808, ii. p. 81, on negotiating for peace with France, Jan. 26, 1795. Pitt says, however, in the same speech : " God forbid that we should look on the body of the people of France as atheists."—TR.

[2] *Letters to a Noble Lord ; Letters on a Regicide Peace.*

literature and philosophy had been necessary to amass the fuel which filled their sides, and laid down the rail which guided their course.   In this thundering clash, amid these ebullitions of hissing and fiery vapour, in these red flames which licked the boilers, and whirled with a rumbling noise upwards to the heavens, an attentive spectator may still discover the nature and the accumulation of the force which caused such an outburst, dislocated such iron plates, and strewed the ground with such ruins.

CHAPTER IV.

Addison.

I.

In this vast transformation of mind which occupies
the whole eighteenth century, and gives England its
political and moral standing, two eminent men appear
in politics and morality, both accomplished writers—
the most accomplished yet seen in England ; both
accredited mouthpieces of a party, masters in the art
of persuasion and conviction ; both limited in philosophy
and art, incapable of considering sentiments in a
disinterested fashion ; always bent on seeing in things
motives for approbation or blame ; otherwise differing,
and even in contrast with one another : one happy, benevolent, beloved ; the other hated, hating, and most unfortunate : the one a partisan of liberty and the noblest
hopes of man ; the other an advocate of a retrograde
party, and an eager detractor of humanity : the one
measured, delicate, furnishing a model of the most solid
English qualities, perfected by continental culture ; the
other unbridled and formidable, showing an example of
the harshest English instincts, luxuriating without
limit or rule in every kind of devastation and amid
every degree of despair. To penetrate to the interior
of this civilisation and this people, there are no means
better than to pause and dwell upon Swift and Addison.

II.

" I have often reflected," says Steele of Addison, " after a night spent with him, apart from all the world, that I had had the pleasure of conversing with an intimate acquaintance of Terence and Catullus, who had all their wit and nature heightened with humour, more exquisite and delightful than any other man ever possessed." [1]   And Pope, a rival of Addison, and a bitter rival, adds : " His conversation had something in it more charming than I have found in any other man." [2] These sayings express the whole talent of Addison : his writings are conversations, masterpieces of English urbanity and reason ; nearly all the details of his character and life have contributed to nourish this urbanity and this reasoning.

At the age of seventeen we find him at Oxford, studious and peaceful, loving solitary walks under the elm-avenues, and amongst the beautiful meadows on the banks of the Cherwell.   From the thorny brake of school education he chose the only flower—a withered one, doubtless, Latin verse, but one which, compared to the erudition, to the theology, to the logic of the time, is still a flower.   He celebrates, in strophes or hexame-- ters, the peace of Ryswick, or the system of Dr. Burnet ; he composes little ingenious poems on a puppet-show, on the battle of the pigmies and cranes ; he learns to praise and jest—in Latin it is true—but with such suc- cess, that his verses recommend him for the rewards of the ministry, and even come to the knowledge of Boileau. At the same time he imbues himself with the Latin

---

[1] Addison's Works, ed. Hurd, 6 vols., v. 151 ; Steele's Letter to Mr. Congreve.   [2] *Ibid.* vi. 729.

poets; he knows them by heart, even the most affected,
Claudian and Prudentius; presently in Italy quotations
will rain from his pen; from top to bottom, in all its
nooks, and under all its aspects, his memory is stuffed
with Latin verses. We see that he loves them, scans
them with delight, that a fine cæsura charms him, that
every delicacy touches him, that no hue of art or emotion escapes him, that his literary tact is refined, and
prepared to relish all the beauties of thought and
expression. This inclination, too long retained, is a
sign of a little mind, I allow; a man ought not to
spend so much time in inventing centos. Addison
would have done better to enlarge his knowledge—to
study Latin prose-writers, Greek literature, Christian
antiquity, modern Italy, which he hardly knew. But
this limited culture, leaving him weaker, made him
more refined. He formed his art by studying only
the monuments of Latin urbanity; he acquired a taste
for the elegance and refinements, the triumphs and
artifices of style; he became self-contemplative, correct,
capable of knowing and perfecting his own tongue. In
the designed reminiscences, the happy allusions, the
discreet tone of his little poems, I find beforehand
many traits of the *Spectator*.

Leaving the university, he travelled for a long time
in the two most polished countries in the world, France
and Italy. He lived at Paris, in the house of the
ambassador, in the regular and brilliant society which
gave fashion to Europe; he visited Boileau, Malebranche,
saw with somewhat malicious curiosity the fine curtsies
of the painted and affected ladies of Versailles, the
grace and almost stale civilities of the fine speakers
and fine dancers of the other sex. He was amused at

the complimentary intercourse of Frenchmen, and re-
marked that when a tailor accosted a shoemaker, he con-
gratulated himself on the honour of saluting him.   In
Italy he admired the works of art, and praised them in
a letter,[1] in which the enthusiasm is rather cold, but
very well expressed.[2]   He had the fine training which
is now given to young men of the higher ranks.   And
it was not the amusements of Cockneys or the racket
of taverns which employed him.   His beloved Latin
poets followed him everywhere.   He had read them over
before setting out ; he recited their verses in the places
which they mention.   " I must confess, it was not one
of the least entertainments that I met with in travelling,
to examine these several descriptions, as it were, upon
the spot, and to compare the natural face of the country
with the landscapes that the poets have given us of
it." [3]   These were the pleasures of an epicure in literature ; there could be nothing more literary and less
pedantic than the account which he wrote on his return.[4]
Presently this refined and delicate curiosity led him to
coins.   " There is a great affinity," he says, " between
them and poetry ;" for they serve as a commentary
upon ancient authors ; an effigy of the Graces makes a
verse of Horace visible.   And on this subject he wrote
a very agreeable dialogue, choosing for personages well-
bred men : " all three very well versed in the politer

---

[1] Addison's Works, 4 vols. 4to, Tonson, 1721, vol. i. 43.   A letter
to Lord Halifax (1701).

[2] "Renowned in verse, each shady thicket grows,
    And every stream in heavenly numbers flows. . . .
    Where the smooth chisel all its force has shown,
    And softened into flesh the rugged stone. . . .
    Here pleasing airs my ravisht soul confound
    With circling notes and labyrinths of sound."—*Ibid.*

[3] Preface to *Remarks on Italy,* ii.   [4] *Remarks on Italy.*

parts of learning, and had travelled into the most
refined nations of Europe. . . . Their design was to
pass away the heat of the summer among the fresh
breezes that rise from the river (the Thames), and the
agreeable mixture of shades and fountains in which the
whole country naturally abounds." [1]   Then, with a
gentle and well-tempered gaiety, he laughs at pedants
who waste life in discussing the Latin toga or sandal,
but pointed out, like a man of taste and wit, the services
which coins might render to history and the arts.
Was there ever a better education for a literary man
of the world ?   He had already a long time ago acquired
the art of fashionable poetry, I mean the correct verses,
which are complimentary, or written to order.   In all
polite society we look for the adornment of thought;
we desire for it rare, brilliant, beautiful dress, to distinguish it from vulgar thoughts, and for this reason
we impose upon it rhyme, metre, noble expression; we
keep for it a store of select terms, verified metaphors,
suitable images, which are like an aristocratic wardrobe,
in which it is hampered but must adorn itself.   Men of
wit are bound to make verses for it, and in a certain
style just as others must display their lace, and that
after a certain pattern.   Addison put on this dress, and
wore it correctly and easily, passing without difficulty
from one habit to a similar one, from Latin to English
verse.   His principal piece, *The Campaign*,[2] is an
excellent model of the agreeable and classical style.
Each verse is full, perfect in itself, with a clever antithesis, a good epithet, or a concise picture.   Countries
have noble names; Italy is Ausonia, the Black Sea is
the Scythian Sea; there are mountains of dead, and a

[1] *First Dialogue on Medals*, i. 435.   [2] On the victory of Blenheim, i. 63.

thunder of eloquence sanctioned by Lucian; pretty
turns of oratorical address imitated from Ovid; cannons
are mentioned in poetic periphrases, as later in Delille.[1]
The poem is an official and decorative amplification,
like that which Voltaire wrote afterwards on the battle
of Fontenoy.   Addison does yet better; he wrote an
opera, a comedy, a much admired tragedy on the
death of Cato.   Such writing was always, in the
last century, a passport to a good style and to fashionable society.   A young man in Voltaire's time, on
leaving college, had to write his tragedy, as now
he must write an article on political economy; it
was then a proof that he could converse with ladies,
as now it is a proof that he can argue with men.   He
learned the art of being amusing, of touching the heart,
of talking of love; he thus escaped from dry or special
studies; he could choose among events or sentiments
those which interest or please; he was able to hold his
own in good society, to be sometimes agreeable there,
never to offend.   Such is the culture which these
works gave Addison; it is of slight importance that
they are poor.   In them he dealt with the passions,
with humour.   He produced in his opera some lively
and smiling pictures; in his tragedy some noble or

[1] " With floods of gore that from the vanquished fell
       The marshes stagnate and the rivers swell,
       Mountains of slain, etc. . . . . .

                                   Rows of hollow brass,
       Tube behind tube the dreadful entrance keep,
       Whilst in their wombs ten thousand thunders sleep. . . .

       . . . Here shattered walls, like broken rocks, from far
       Rise up in hideous views, the guilt of war;
       Whilst here the vine o'er hills of ruin climbs
       Industrious to conceal great Bourbon's crimes."—Vol. i. 63-82.

moving accents ; he emerged from reasoning and. pure dissertation ; he acquired the art of rendering morality visible and truth expressive ; he knew how to give ideas a physiognomy, and that an attractive one. Thus was the finished writer perfected by contact with ancient and modern, foreign and national urbanity, by the sight of the fine arts, by experience of the world and study of style, by continuous and delicate choice of all that is agreeable in things and men, in life and art.

His politeness received from his character a singular bent and charm. It was not external, simply voluntary and official; it came from the heart. He was gentle and kind, of refined sensibility, so shy even as to remain silent and seem dull in a large company or before strangers, only recovering his spirits before intimate friends, and confessing that only two persons can converse together. He could not endure an acrimonious discussion; when his opponent was intractable, he pretended to approve, and for punishment, plunged him discreetly into his own folly. He withdrew by preference from political arguments; being invited to deal with them in the *Spectator*, he contented himself with inoffensive and general subjects, which could interest all whilst offending none. It would have pained him to give others pain. Though a very decided and steady Whig, he continued moderate in polemics; and in an age when the winners in the political fight were ready to ruin their opponents or to bring them to the block, he confined himself to show the faults of argument made by the Tories, or to rail courteously at their prejudices. At Dublin he' went first of all to shake hands with Swift, his great and fallen adversary. Insulted bitterly by Dennis and Pope,

he refused to employ against them his influence or his
wit, and praised Pope to the end.   What can be more
touching, when we have read his life, than his essay
on kindness? we perceive that he is unconsciously
speaking of himself:

"There is no society or conversation to be kept up in the
world without good-nature, or something which must bear its
appearance, and supply its place.   For this reason mankind
have been forced to invent a kind of artificial humanity, which
is what we express by the word good-breeding. . . . The greatest
wits I have conversed with are men eminent for their humanity.
. . . Good-nature is generally born with us ; health, prosperity,
and kind treatment from the world are great cherishers of it
where they find it."[1]

It so happens that he is involuntarily describing his
own charm and his own success.   It is himself that
he is unveiling; he was very prosperous, and his good
fortune spread itself around him in affectionate
sentiments, in constant consideration for others, in
calm cheerfulness.   At College he was distinguished;
his Latin verses made him a fellow at Oxford; he
spent ten years there in grave amusements and in
studies which pleased him.   Dryden, the prince of literature, praised him in the highest terms, when Addison was
only twenty-two.   When he left Oxford, the ministry
gave him a pension of three hundred pounds to finish
his education, and prepare him for public service.   On
his return from his travels, his poem on Blenheim
placed him in the first rank of the Whigs.   He became
twice Secretary for Ireland, Under-Secretary of State, a
member of Parliament, one of the principal Secretaries
of State.   Party hatred spared him; amid the almost

[1] *Spectator*, No. 169.

universal defeat of the Whigs, he was re-elected member of Parliament; in the furious war of Whigs and Tories, both united to applaud his tragedy of *Cato;* the most cruel pamphleteers respected him; his uprightness, his talent, seemed exalted by common consent above discussion. He lived in abundance, activity, and honours, wisely and usefully, amid the assiduous admiration and constant affection of learned and distinguished friends, who could never have too much of his conversation, amid the applause of all the good men and all the cultivated minds of England. If twice the fall of his party seemed to destroy or retard his fortune, he maintained his position without much effort, by reflection and coolness, prepared for all that might happen, accepting mediocrity, confirmed in a natural and acquired calmness, accommodating himself without yielding to men, respectful to the great without degrading himself, free from secret revolt or internal suffering. These are the sources of his talent; could any be purer or finer? could anything be more engaging than worldly polish and elegance, without the factitious ardour and the complimentary falsehoods of the world? Where shall we look for more agreeable conversation than that of a good and happy man, whose knowledge, taste, and wit, are only employed to give us pleasure?

III.

This pleasure will be useful to us. Our interlocutor is as grave as he is polite; he will and can instruct as well as amuse us; his education has been as solid as it has been elegant; he even confesses in the *Spectator* that he prefers the serious to the humor-

ous style. He is naturally reflective, silent, attentive.
He has studied literature, men, and things, with the
conscientiousness of a scholar and an observer.
When he travelled in Italy, it was in the English style,
noting the difference of manners, the peculiarities of the
soil, the good and ill effects of various governments;
providing himself with precise memoirs, circumstantial statistics on taxes, buildings, minerals, climate,
harbours, administration, and on a great many other
things.[1] An English lord, who travels in Holland,
goes simply into a cheese-shop, in order to see for himself all the stages of the manufacture; he returns, like
Addison, provided with exact statistics, complete notes;
this mass of verified information is the foundation of
the common sense of Englishmen. Addison added to
it experience of business, having been successively, or
at the same time, a journalist, a member of Parliament,
a statesman, hand and heart in all the fights and
chances of party. Mere literary education only makes
good talkers, able to adorn and publish ideas which
they do not possess, and which others furnish for
them. If writers wish to invent, they must look to
events and men, not to books and drawing-rooms; the
conversation of special men is more useful to them
than the study of perfect periods; they cannot think
for themselves, but in so far as they have lived or
acted. Addison knew how to act and live. When
we read his reports, letters, and discussions, we feel
that politics and government have given him half his
mind. To exercise patronage, to handle money, to
interpret the law, to divine the motives of men, to
foresee the changes of public opinion, to be compelled

[1] See, for instance, his chapter on the Republic of San Marino.

to judge rightly, quickly, and twenty times a day, on present and great interests, looked after by the public and under the espionage of enemies; all this nourished his reason and sustained his discourses. Such a man might judge and counsel his fellows; his judgments were not amplifications arranged by a process of the brain, but observations controlled by experience: he might be listened to on moral subjects as a natural philosopher was on subjects connected with physics; we feel that he spoke with authority, and that we were instructed.

After having listened a little, people felt themselves better; for they recognised in him from the first a singularly lofty soul, very pure, so much attached to uprightness that he made it his constant care and his dearest pleasure. He naturally loved beautiful things, goodness and justice, science and liberty. From an early age he had joined the Liberal party, and he continued in it to the end, hoping the best of human virtue and reason, noting the wretchedness into which nations fell who abandoned their dignity with their independence.[1] He followed the grand discoveries of the new physical

[1] Letter from Italy to Lord Halifax;

"O Liberty, thou Goddess heavenly bright,
  Profuse of bliss, and pregnant with delight;
  Eternal pleasures in thy presence reign,
  And smiling plenty leads thy wanton train. . . .
  'Tis liberty that crowns Britannia's isle,
  And makes her barren rocks and her bleak mountains
      smile."—i. 53.

About the Republic of San Marino he writes:

"Nothing can be a greater instance of the natural love that mankind has for liberty, and of their aversion to an arbitrary government, than such a savage mountain covered with people, and the Campagna of Rome, which lies in the same country, almost destitute of inhabitants."—*Remarks on Italy*, ii. 48.

sciences, so as to give him more exalted ideas of the
works of God. He loved the deep and serious emotions
which reveal to us the nobility of our nature and the
infirmity of our condition. He employed all his talent
and all his writings in giving us the notion of what we
are worth, and of what we ought to be. Of two tragedies
which he composed or contemplated, one was on the death
of Cato, the most virtuous of the Romans; the other on
that of Socrates, the most virtuous of the Greeks. At
the end of the first he felt some scruples; and for fear of
being accused of finding an excuse for suicide, he gave
Cato some remorse. His opera of *Rosamond* ends with
the injunction to prefer pure love to forbidden joys;
the *Spectator*, the *Tatler*, the *Guardian*, are mere lay
sermons. Moreover, he put his maxims into practice.
When he was in office, his integrity was perfect; he
conferred often obligations on those whom he did not
know — always gratuitously, refusing presents, under
whatever form they were offered. When out of office,
his loyalty was perfect; he maintained his opinions
and friendships without bitterness or baseness, boldly
praising his fallen protectors,[1] fearing not thereby
to expose himself to the loss of his only remaining
resources. He possessed an innate nobility of character, and reason aided him in keeping it. He considered that there is common sense in honesty. His
first care, as he said, was to range his passions on the
side of truth. He had made for himself a portrait of
a rational creature, and he conformed his conduct to
this by reflection as much as by instinct. He rested
every virtue on an order of principles and proofs. His
logic fed his morality, and the uprightness of his mind

---

[1] Halifax, for instance.

completed the singleness of his heart. His religion, English in every sense, was after the like fashion. He based his faith on a regular succession of historical discussions :[1] he established the existence of God by a regular series of moral deductions; minute and solid demonstration was throughout the guide and foundation of his beliefs and emotions. Thus disposed, he loved to conceive God as the rational head of the world; he transformed accidents and necessities into calculations and directions; he saw order and providence in the conflict of things, and felt around him the wisdom which he attempted to establish in himself. Addison, good and just himself, trusted in God, also a being good and just. He lived willingly in His knowledge and presence, and thought of the unknown future which was to complete human nature and accomplish moral order. When the end came, he went over his life, and discovered that he had done some wrong or other to Gay : this wrong was doubtless slight, since Gay had never thought of it. Addison begged him to come to his bedside, and asked his pardon. When he was about to die, he wished still to be useful, and sent for his step-son, Lord Warwick, whose careless life had caused him some uneasiness. He was so weak that at first he could not speak. The young man, after waiting a while, said to him : "Dear sir, you sent for me, I believe; I hope that you have some commands; I shall hold them most sacred." The dying man with an effort pressed his hand, and replied gently : "See in what peace a Christian can die." [2] Shortly afterwards he expired.

[1] *Of the Christian Religion.*   [2] Addison's Works, Hurd, vi. 525.

IV.

" The great and only end of these speculations," says
Addison, in one of his *Spectators*, " is to banish vice
and ignorance out of the territories of Great Britain."
And he kept his word. His papers are wholly moral
—advices to families, reprimands to thoughtless women,
a sketch of an honest man, remedies for the passions,
reflections on God and a future life. I hardly know, or
rather I know very well, what success a newspaper full
of sermons would have in France. In England it was
extraordinary, equal to that of the most popular modern
novelists. In the general downfall of the daily and
weekly papers ruined by the Stamp Act,[1] the *Spectator*
doubled its price, and held its ground.[2] This was because it offered to Englishmen the picture of English
reason : the talent and the teaching were in harmony
with the needs of the age and of the country. Let us
endeavour to describe this reason, which became gradually eliminated from Puritanism and its rigidity, from
the Restoration and its excess. The mind attained its
balance, together with religion and the state. It conceived the rule, and disciplined its conduct ; it diverged
from a life of excess, and confirmed itself in a sensible
life ; it shunned physical and prescribed moral existence.
Addison rejects with scorn gross corporeal pleasure, the
brutal joy of noise and motion : " I would nevertheless

[1] The Stamp Act (1712 ; 10 Anne, c. 19) put a duty of a halfpenny
on every printed half-sheet or less, and a penny on a whole sheet, besides twelve pence on every advertisement. This Act was repealed in
1855. Swift writes to Stella (August 7, 1712), " Do you know that all
Grub Street is ruined by the Stamp Act."—TR.

[2] The sale of the *Spectator* was considerably diminished through its
forced increase of price, and it was discontinued in 1713, the year after
the Stamp Act was passed.—TR.

leave to the consideration of those who are the patrons of this monstrous trial of skill, whether or no they are not guilty, in some measure, of an affront to their species, in treating after this manner the human face divine."[1] "Is it possible that human nature can rejoice in its disgrace, and take pleasure in seeing its own figure turned to ridicule, and distorted into forms that raise horror and aversion? There is something disingenuous and immoral in the being able to bear such a sight."[2] Of course he sets himself against deliberate shamelessness and the systematic debauchery which were the taste and the shame of the Restoration. He wrote whole articles against young fashionable men, "a sort of vermin" who fill London with their bastards; against professional seducers, who are the "knights-errant" of vice. "When men of rank and figure pass away their lives in these criminal pursuits and practices, they ought to consider that they render themselves more vile and despicable than any innocent man can be, whatever low station his fortune or birth have placed him in."[3] He severely jeers at women who expose themselves to temptations, and whom he calls "salamanders:" "A salamander is a kind of heroine in chastity, that treads upon fire, and lives in the midst of flames without being hurt. A salamander knows no distinction of sex in those she converses with, grows familiar with a stranger at first sight, and is not so narrow-spirited as to observe whether the person she talks to be in breeches or petticoats. She admits a male visitant to her bedside, plays with him a whole afternoon at picquet, walks with him two or three hours

[1] *Spectator*, No. 173.   [2] *Tatler*, No. 108.
[3] *Guardian*, No. 123.

by moonlight." [1] He fights like a preacher against the
fashion of low dresses, and gravely demands the tucker
and modesty of olden times : "To prevent these saucy
familiar glances, I would entreat my gentle readers to
sew on their tuckers again, to retrieve the modesty of
their characters, and not to imitate the nakedness, but
the innocence, of their mother Eve. In short, modesty
gives the maid greater beauty than even the bloom of
youth; it bestows on the wife the dignity of a matron,
and reinstates the widow in her virginity." [2] We find
also lectures on masquerades which end with a rendezvous; precepts on the number of glasses people might
drink, and the dishes of which they might eat; condem-
nations of licentious professors of irreligion and immorality; all maxims now somewhat stale, but then new
and useful because Wycherley and Rochester had put
into practice and made popular the opposite maxims.
Debauchery passed for French and fashionable : this
is why Addison proscribes in addition all French fri-
volities. He laughs at women who receive visitors in
their dressing-rooms, and speak aloud at the theatre :
"There is nothing which exposes a woman to greater
dangers, than that gaiety and airiness of temper, which
are natural to most of the sex. It should be therefore
the concern of every wise and virtuous woman to keep
this sprightliness from degenerating into levity. On
the contrary, the whole discourse and behaviour of the
French is to make the sex more fantastical, or (as they
are pleased to term it) more awakened, than is consistent
either with virtue or discretion." [3] We see already in
these strictures the portrait of the sensible housewife,

[1] *Spectator*, No. 198.   [2] *Guardian*, No. 100.
[3] *Spectator*, No. 45.

the modest English woman, domestic and grave, wholly taken up with her husband and children.   Addison returns a score of times to the artifices, the pretty affected babyisms, the coquetry, the futilities of women.   He cannot suffer languishing or lazy habits.   He is full of epigrams against flirtations, extravagant toilets, useless visits.[1]   He writes a satirical journal of a man who goes to his club, learns the news, yawns, studies the barometer, and thinks his time well occupied.   He considers that time is capital, business duty, and life a task.

Is life only a task?   If Addison holds himself superior to sensual life, he falls short of philosophical life.   His morality, thoroughly English, always drags along among commonplaces, discovering no principles, making no deductions.   The fine and lofty aspects of the mind are wanting.   He gives useful advice, clear instruction, justified by what happened yesterday, useful for to-morrow.   He observes that fathers must not be inflexible, and that they often repent driving their children to despair.   He finds that bad books are pernicious, because their durability carries their poison to future ages.   He consoles a woman who has lost her sweetheart, by showing her the misfortunes of so many other people who are suffering the greatest evils at the same time.   His *Spectator* is only an honest man's manual, and is often like the *Complete Lawyer*. It is practical, its aim being not to amuse, but to correct us.   The conscientious Protestant, nourished with dissertations and morality, demands an effective monitor and guide; he would like his reading to influence his conduct, and his newspaper to suggest a

[1] *Spectator*, Nos. 317 and 323.

resolution. To this end Addison seeks motives everywhere. He thinks of the future life, but does not forget
the present; he rests virtue on interest rightly understood. He strains no principle to its limits; he accepts
them all, as they are to be met with everywhere, according to their manifest goodness, drawing from them only
the primary consequences, shunning the powerful logical
pressure which spoils all by expressing too much. Let
us observe him establishing a maxim, recommending
constancy for instance; his motives are mixed and
incongruous: first, inconstancy exposes us to scorn:
next, it puts us in continual distraction; again, it
hinders us as a rule from attaining our end; moreover,
it is the great feature of a human and mortal being;
finally, it is most opposed to the inflexible nature of
God, who ought to be our model. The whole is
illustrated at the close by a quotation from Dryden
and a verse from Horace. This medley and jumble
describe the ordinary mind which remains on the level
of its audience, and the practical mind, which knows
how to dominate over its audience. Addison persuades
the public, because he draws from the public sources of
belief. He is powerful because he is vulgar, and useful
because he is narrow.

Let us picture now this mind, so characteristically
mediocre, limited to the discovery of good motives of
action. What a reflective man, always calm and
dignified! What a store he has of resolutions and
maxims! All rapture, instinct, inspiration, and
caprice, are abolished or disciplined. No case surprises
or carries him away. He is always ready and protected; so much so, that he is like an automaton
Argument has frozen and invaded him. Consider, for

instance, how he puts us on our guard against involuntary hypocrisy, announcing, explaining, distinguishing the ordinary and extraordinary modes, dragging on with exordiums, preparations, methods, allusions to Scripture.[1] After having read six lines of this morality, a Frenchman would go out for a mouthful of fresh air. What in the name of heaven would he do, if, in order to move him to piety, he was told [2] that God's omniscience and. omnipresence furnished us with three kinds of motives, and then subdivided these motives into first, second, and third ? To put calculation at every stage ; to come with weights, scales, and figures, into the thick of human passions, to label them, classify them like bales, to tell the public that the inventory is complete ; to lead them, with the reckoning in their hand, and by the mere virtue of statistics, to honour and duty,—such is the morality of Addison and of England. It is a sort of commercial common sense applied to the interests of the soul ; a preacher here is only an economist in a white tie, who treats conscience like food, and refutes vice because its introduction is prohibited.

There is nothing sublime or chimerical in the end which he sets before us ; all is practical, that is, business-like and sensible ; the question is, how "to be easy here and happy afterwards." To be easy is a word which has no French equivalent, meaning that comfortable state of the mind, a middle state between calm satisfaction, approved action and serene conscience. Addison makes it consist in labour and manly functions, carefully and regularly discharged. We must see with what complacency he paints in the *Freeholder*

[1] *Spectator*, No. 399.   [2] *Ibid.* No. 571.

and "Sir Roger" the grave pleasures of a citizen and proprietor :

"I have rather chosen this title (the Freeholder) than any other, because it is what I most glory in, and what most effectually calls to my mind the happiness of that government under which I live. As a British freeholder, I should not scruple taking place of a French marquis ; and when I see one of my countrymen amusing himself in his little cabbage-garden, I naturally look upon him as a greater person than the owner of the richest vineyard in Champagne. . . . There is an unspeakable pleasure in calling anything one's own. A freehold, though it be but in ice and snow, will make the owner pleased in the possession, and stout in the defence of it. . . . I consider myself as one who give my consent to every law which passes. . . . A freeholder is but one remove from a legislator, and for that reason ought to stand up in the defence of those laws which are in some degree of his own making."[1]

These are all English feelings, made up of calculation and pride, energetic and austere ; and this portrait is capped by that of the married man :

"Nothing is more gratifying to the mind of man than power or dominion ; and this I think myself amply possessed of, as I am the father of a family. I am perpetually taken up in giving out orders, in prescribing duties, in hearing parties, in administering justice, and in distributing rewards and punishments. . . . I look upon my family as a patriarchal sovereignty, in which I am myself both king and priest. . . . When I see my little troop before me, I rejoice in the additions which I have made to my species, to my country, and to my religion, in having produced such a number of reasonable creatures, citizens, and Christians. I am pleased to see myself thus perpetuated ; and as there is no production comparable to that of a human

[1] *Freeholder*, No. 1.

creature, I am more proud of having been the occasion of ten such glorious productions, than if I had built a hundred pyramids at my own expense, or published as many volumes of the finest wit and learning."[1]

If now we take the man away from his estate and his household, alone with himself, in moments of idleness or reverie, we will find him just as positive. He observes, that he may cultivate his own reasoning power, and that of others; he stores himself with morality; he wishes to make the most of himself and of existence, that is the reason why he thinks of death. The northern races willingly direct their thoughts to final dissolution and the dark future. Addison often chose for his promenade gloomy Westminster Abbey, with its many tombs: "Upon my going into the church I entertained myself with the digging of a grave; and saw in every shovel-full of it that was thrown up the fragment of a bone or skull intermixt with a kind of fresh mouldering earth that some time or other had a place in the composition of a human body. . . . I consider that great day when we shall all of us be contemporaries, and make our appearance together."[2] And suddenly his emotion is transformed into profitable meditations. Underneath his morality is a pair of scales which weigh quantities of happiness. He stirs himself by mathematical comparisons to prefer the future to the present. He tries to realise, amidst an assemblage of dates, the disproportion of our short life to infinity. Thus arises this religion, a product of melancholic temperament and acquired logic, in which man, a sort of calculating Hamlet, aspires to the ideal

[1] *Spectator*, No. 500.   [2] *Ibid.* Nos. 26 and 575.

by making a good business of it, and maintains his poetical sentiments by financial calculations.

In such a subject these habits are offensive. We ought not to try and over-define or prove God; religion is rather a matter of feeling than of science; we compromise it by exacting too rigorous demonstrations, and too precise dogmas.   It is the heart which sees heaven; if a man would make me believe in it, as he makes me believe in the Antipodes, by geographical accounts and probabilities, I shall barely or not at all believe. Addison has little more than his college or edifying arguments, very like those of the abbé Pluche,[1] which let in objections at every chink, and which we can only regard as dialectical essays, or sources of emotion. When we add to these arguments, motives of interest and calculations of prudence, which can make recruits, but not converts, we possess all his proofs.   There is an element of coarseness in this fashion of treating divine things, and we like still less the exactness with which he explains God, reducing him to a mere magnified man.   This preciseness and this narrowness go so far as to describe heaven :

" Though the Deity be thus essentially present through all the immensity of space, there is one part of it in which he discovers himself in a most transcendent and visible glory. . . . It is here where the glorified body of our Saviour resides, and where all the celestial hierarchies, and the innumerable hosts of angels, are represented as perpetually surrounding the seat of God with hallelujahs and hymns of praise. . . . With how much skill must the throne of God be erected ! . . . How great must be the majesty of that place, where the whole art of

---

[1] The abbé Pluche (1688–1761) was the author of a *Système de la Nature* and several other works.—Tr.

creation has been employed, and where God has chosen to shew himself in the most magnificent manner ! What must be the architecture of infinite power under the direction of infinite wisdom ?" [1]

Moreover, the place must be very grand, and they have music there: it is a noble palace; perhaps there are antechambers. We had better not continue the quotation. The same dull and literal precision makes him inquire what sort of happiness the elect have.[2] They will be admitted into the councils of Providence, and will understand all its proceedings : "There is, doubtless, a faculty in spirits by which they apprehend one another as our senses do material objects; and there is no question but our souls, when they are disembodied, or placed in glorified bodies, will by this faculty, in whatever part of space they reside, be always sensible of the Divine Presence."[3] This grovelling philosophy repels us. One word of Addison will justify it, and make us understand it : "The business of mankind in this life is rather to act than to know." Now, such a philosophy is as useful in action as poor in science. All its faults of speculation become merits in practice. It follows in a prosy manner positive religion.[4] What support does it not attain from the authority of an ancient tradition, a national institution, an established priesthood, outward ceremonies, every-day customs ! It employs as arguments public utility, the example of great minds, heavy logic, literal interpretation, and unmistakeable texts. What better means of governing the crowd, than to degrade proofs to the vulgarity of its intelligence and needs ? It humanises the Divinity :

---

[1] *Spectator*, No. 580 ; see also No. 531.   [2] *Ibid.* Nos. 237, 571, 600.
[3] *Ibid.* No. 571; see also Nos. 237, 600.   [4] *Tatler*, No. 257.

is it not the only way to make men understand Him?
It defines almost obviously a future life : is it not the only
way to cause it to be wished for? The poetry of lofty
philosophical deductions is weak compared to the inner
persuasion, rooted by so many positive and detailed
descriptions. In this way an active piety is born; and
religion thus constructed doubles the force of the moral
spring. Addison's is admirable, because it is so strong.
Energy of feeling rescues wretchedness of dogma. Beneath his dissertations we feel that he is moved;
minutiæ, pedantry disappear. We see in him now
only a soul deeply penetrated with adoration and
respect; no more a preacher classifying God's attributes,
and pursuing his trade as a good logician; but a man
who naturally, and of his own bent, returns to a lofty
spectacle, goes with awe into all its aspects, and leaves
it only with a renewed or overwhelmed heart. The
sincerity of his emotions makes us respect even his
catechetical prescriptions. He demands fixed days of
devotion and meditation to recall us regularly to the
thought of our Creator and of our faith. He inserts
prayers in his paper. He forbids oaths, and recommends to keep always before us the idea of a sovereign
Master :

" Such an habitual homage to the Supreme Being would, in
a particular manner, banish from among us that prevailing
impiety of using his name on the most trivial occasions. . . .
What can we then think of those who make use of so tremend-
ous a name in the ordinary expressions of their anger, mirth,
and most impertinent passions? of those who admit it into the
most familiar questions, and assertions, ludicrous phrases, and
works of humour? not to mention those who violate it by
solemn perjuries! It would be an affront to reason to en-

deavour to set forth the horror and profaneness of such a practice." [1]

If a Frenchman was forbidden to swear, he would probably laugh at the first word of the admonition; in his eyes that is a matter of good taste, not of morality. But if he had heard Addison himself pronouncing what I have written, he would laugh no longer.

V.

It is no small thing to make morality fashionable. Addison did it, and it remained in fashion. Formerly honest men were not polished, and polished men were not honest; piety was fanatical, and urbanity depraved; in manners, as in literature, a man could meet only Puritans or libertines. For the first time Addison reconciled virtue with elegance, taught duty in an accomplished style, and made pleasure subservient to reason:

"It was said of Socrates that he brought Philosophy down from heaven, to inhabit among men; and I shall be ambitious to have it said of me, that I have brought Philosophy out of closets and libraries, schools and colleges, to dwell in clubs and assemblies, at tea-tables and in coffee-houses. I would therefore, in a very particular manner, recommend these my speculations to all well-regulated families, and set apart an hour in every morning for tea and bread and butter; and would earnestly advise them for their good to order this paper to be punctually served up, and to be looked upon as a part of the tea-equipage." [2]

In this passage we may detect an inclination to smile, a little irony tempers the serious idea; it is the tone of a polished man, who, at the first sign of ennui, turns

[1] *Spectator*, No. 531.   [2] *Ibid.* No. 10.

round, delicately laughs, even at himself, and tries to please.   It is Addison's general tone.

What an amount of art is necessary to please ! First, the art of making oneself understood, at once, always, completely, without difficulty to the reader, without reflection, without attention.   Let us figure to ourselves men of the world reading a page between two mouthfuls of " bohea-rolls," ladies interrupting a phrase to ask when the ball begins : three technical or learned words would make them throw the paper down.   They only desire distinct terms, in common use, into which wit enters all at once, as it enters ordinary converse ; in fact, for them reading is only a conversation, and a better one than usual.   For the select world refines language.   It does not suffer the risks and approximations of extempore and inexperienced speaking.   It requires a knowledge of style, like a knowledge of external forms.   It will have exact words to express the fine shades of thought, and measured words to preclude offensive or extreme impressions.   It wishes for developed phrases, which, presenting the same idea, under several aspects, impress it easily upon its desultory mind.   It demands harmonies of words, which, presenting a known idea in a smart form, may introduce it in a lively manner to its desultory imagination.   Addison gives it all that it desires ; his writings are the pure source of classical style ; men never spoke better in England.   Ornaments abound, and never has rhetoric a share in them. Throughout we have precise contrasts, which serve only for clearness, and are not too prolonged ; happy expressions, easily hit on, which give things a new and ingenious turn ; harmonious periods, in which the sounds flow into one another with the diversity and sweetness of a quiet stream; a fertile vein of invention and fancy, through which runs the most amiable irony. We trust one example will suffice:

"He is not obliged to attend her (Nature) in the slow advances which she makes from one season to another, or to observe her conduct in the successive production of plants and flowers. He may draw into his description all the beauties of the spring and autumn, and make the whole year contribute something to render it the more agreeable. His rose-trees, woodbines, and jessamines may flower together, and his beds be covered at the same time with lilies, violets, and amaranths. His soil is not restrained to any particular set of plants, but is proper either for oaks or myrtles, and adapts itself to the products of every climate. Oranges may grow wild in it; myrrh may be met with in every hedge; and if he thinks it proper to have a grove of spices, he can quickly command sun enough to raise it. If all this will not furnish out an agreeable scene, he can make several new species of flowers, with richer scents and higher colours, than any that grow in the gardens of nature. His concerts of birds may be as full and harmonious, and his woods as thick and gloomy as he pleases. He is at no more expense in a long vista than a short one, and can as easily throw his cascades from a precipice of half a mile high as from one of twenty yards. He has his choice of the winds, and can turn the course of his rivers in all the variety of meanders that are most delightful to the reader's imagination."[1]

I find here that Addison profits by the rights which he grants to others, and is amused in explaining to us how we may amuse ourselves. Such is the charming tone of society. Reading the *Spectator*, we fancy it still more amiable than it is: no pretension; no efforts; endless contrivances employed unconsciously, and obtained with-

[1] *Spectator*, No. 418.

out asking; the gift of being lively and agreeable; a refined banter, raillery without bitterness, a sustained gaiety; the art of finding in everything the most blooming and the freshest flower, and to smell it without bruising or sullying it; science, politics, experience, morality, bringing their finest fruits, adorning them, offering them at a chosen moment, ready to withdraw them as soon as conversation has enjoyed them, and before it is tired of them; ladies placed in the first rank,[1] arbiters of refinement, surrounded with homage, crowning the politeness of men and the brilliancy of society by the attraction of their toilettes, the delicacy of their wit, and the charm of their smiles;—such is the familiar spectacle in which the writer has formed and delighted himself.

So many advantages are not without their inconvenience. The compliments of society, which attenuate expressions, blunt the style; by regulating what is instinctive and moderating what is vehement, they make speech threadbare and uniform. We must not always seek to please, above all, to please the ear. Monsieur de Chateaubriand boasted of not admitting a single elision into the song of *Cymodocée*; so much the worse for *Cymodocée*. So the commentators who have noted in Addison the balance of his periods, do him an injustice.[2] They explain thus why he slightly wearies us. The rotundity of his phrases is a scanty merit and mars the rest. To calculate longs and shorts, to be always thinking of sounds, of final cadences,—all these classical researches

[1] *Spectator*, Nos. 423, 265.

[2] See, in the notes of No. 409 of the *Spectator*, the pretty minute analysis of Hurd, the decomposition of the period, the proportion of long and short syllables, the study of the finals. A musician could not have done better.

spoil a writer. Every idea has its accent, and all our labour ought to be to put it down free and simple on paper, as it is in our mind. We ought to copy and mark our thought with the flow of emotions and images, which raise it, caring for nothing but its exactness and clearness. One true phrase is worth a hundred periods: the first is a document which fixes for ever a movement of the heart or the senses; the other is a toy to amuse the empty heads of verse-makers. I would give twenty pages of Fléchier for three lines of Saint-Simon. Regular rhythm mutilates the impetus of natural invention; the shades of inner vision vanish; we see no more a soul which thinks or feels, but fingers which count measures whilst scanning. The continuous period is like the shears of La Quintinie,[1] which clip all the trees round under pretence of beautifying. This is why there is some coldness and monotony in Addison's style. He seems to be listening to himself. He is too measured and correct. His most touching stories, like that of *Theodosius and Constantia,* touch us only partially. Who could feel inclined to weep over such periods as these?

"Constantia, who knew that nothing but the report of her marriage could have driven him to such extremities, was not to be comforted: she now accused herself for having so tamely given an ear to the proposal of a husband, and looked upon the new lover as the murderer of Theodosius: in short, she resolved to suffer the utmost effects of her father's displeasure, rather than to comply with a marriage which appeared to her so full of guilt and horror."[2]

---

[1] La Quintinie (1626–1688) a celebrated gardener under Louis XIV., planned the gardens of Versailles. —TR.

[2] *Spectator*, No. 164.

Is this the way to paint horror and guilt ?   Where are
the passionate emotions which Addison pretends to
paint ?   The story is related, not seen.

The classical writer simply cannot see.   Always
measured and rational, his first care is to proportion and
arrange. He has his rules in his pocket, and brings them
out for everything.   He does not rise to the source of
the beautiful at once, like genuine artists, by force and
lucidity of natural inspiration ; he lingers in the middle
regions, amid precepts, subject to taste and common
sense.   This is why Addison's criticism is so solid and
so poor. They who seek ideas will do well not to read
his *Essays on Imagination*,[1] so much praised, so well
written, but so scant of philosophy, and so commonplace,
dragged down by the intervention of final causes.   His
celebrated commentary on *Paradise Lost* is little better
than the dissertations of Batteux and Bossu.   In one
place he compares, almost in a line, Homer, Virgil, and
Ovid.   The fine arrangement of a poem is with him the
highest merit.   The pure classics enjoy better arrangement and good order than artless truth and strong
originality.   They have always their poetic manual in
their hands : if we agree with the pre-arranged pattern,
we have genius; if not, we have none.   Addison, in
praise of Milton, establishes that, according to the rule
of epic poetry, the action of *Paradise Lost* is one, complete and great ; that its characters are varied and of
universal interest, and its sentiments natural, appro-
priate, and elevated ; the style clear, diversified, and
sublime.   Now we may admire Milton ; he has a testi-
monial from Aristotle.   Listen, for instance, to cold
details of classical dissertation :

[1] See *Spectator*, Nos. 411–421.

" Had I followed Monsieur Bossu's method in my first paper
on Milton, I should have dated the action of *Paradise Lost* from
the beginning of Raphael's speech in this book."[1]

" But, notwithstanding the fineness of this allegory (Sin and
Death) may atone for it (the defect in the subject of his poem)
in some measure, I cannot think that persons of such a chimerical
existence are proper actors in an epic poem." [2]

Further on Addison defines poetical machines, the
conditions of their structure, the advantage of their use.
He seems to me a carpenter inspecting a staircase.   Do
not suppose that artificiality shocks him ; on the contrary, he rather admires it.   He finds the violent
declamations of the Miltonic divinity and the royal
compliments indulged in by the persons of the Trinity,
sublime.   The camps of the angels, their bearing in
chapel and barrack, their scholastic disputes, their bitter
puritanical or pious royalistic style, do not strike him
as false or disagreeable.   Adam's pedantry and household lectures appear to him suitable to the state of
innocence.   In fact, the classics of the last two centuries
never looked upon the human mind, except in its
cultivated state.   The child, the artist, the barbarian,
the inspired man, escaped them ; so, of course, did all
who were beyond humanity : their world was limited
to the earth, and to the earth of the study and drawing-
rooms ; they rose neither to God nor nature, or if they
did, it was to transform nature into a well-regulated
garden-plot, and God into a moral scrutator.   They reduced genius to eloquence, poetry to discourse, the drama
to a dialogue.   They regarded reason as if it were beauty,
a sort of middle faculty, not apt for invention, potent
in rules, balancing imagination like conduct, and making

[1] *Spectator*, No. 327.   [2] *Ibid.* No. 273.

taste the arbiter of letters, as it made morality the arbiter
of actions.   They dispensed with the play on words, the
sensual grossness, the flights of imagination, the unlike-
lihood, the atrocities, and all the bad accompaniments
of Shakspeare ;[1] but they only half followed him in the
deep intuitions by which he pierced the human heart,
and discovered therein the god and the animal.   They
wanted to be moved, but not overwhelmed ; they allowed
themselves to be impressed, but demanded to be pleased.
To please rationally was the object of their literature.
Such is Addison's criticism, which resembles his art ;
born, like his art, of classical urbanity ; fit, like his art,
for the life of the world, having the same solidity and
the same limits, because it had the same sources, namely
order and relaxation.

VI.

But we must consider that we are in England, and that
we find there many things not agreeable to a Frenchman.   In France, the classical age attained perfection ;
so that, compared to it, other countries lack somewhat of
finish.   Addison, elegant in his own native country, is
not quite so in France.   Compared with Tillotson, he is
the most charming man possible ; compared to Montesquieu, he is only half polished.   His converse is hardly
sparkling enough ; the quick movement, the easy change
of tone, the facile smile, readily dropt and readily
resumed, are hardly visible.   He drags on in long and
too uniform phrases ; his periods are too square ; we
might cull a load of useless words.   He tells us what
he is going to say : he marks divisions and subdi-

[1] *Spectator*, Nos. 39, 40, 58.

visions; he quotes Latin, even Greek; he displays and protracts without end the serviceable and sticky plaster of his morality. He has no fear of being wearisome. That is not what Englishmen fear. Men who love demonstrative sermons three hours long are not difficult to amuse. Remember that here the women like to go to meeting, and are entertained by listening for half a day to discourses on drunkenness, or on the sliding scale for taxes : these patient creatures do not require that conversation should be always lively and piquant. Consequently they can put up with a less refined politeness and less disguised compliments. When Addison bows to them, which happens often, it is gravely, and his reverence is always accompanied by a warning. Take the following on their gaudy dresses :

" I looked with as much pleasure upon this little party-coloured assembly, as upon a bed of tulips, and did not know at first whether it might not be an embassy of Indian queens ; but upon my going about into the pit, and taking them in front, I was immediately undeceived and saw so much beauty in every face, that I found them all to be English. Such eyes and lips, cheeks and foreheads, could be the growth of no other country. The complexion of their faces hindered me from observing any further the colour of their hoods, though I could easily perceive, by that unspeakable satisfaction which appeared in their looks, that their own thoughts were wholly taken up on those pretty ornaments they wore upon their heads." [1]

In this discreet raillery, modified by an almost official admiration, we perceive the English mode of treating women : man, by her side, is always a lay-preacher :

[1] *Spectator*, No. 265.

they are for him charming children, or useful housewives, never queens of the drawing-room, or equals, as amongst the French. When Addison wishes to bring back the Jacobite ladies to the Protestant party, he treats them almost like little girls, to whom we promise, if they will be good, to restore their doll or their cake:

" They should first reflect on the great sufferings and persecutions to which they expose themselves by the obstinacy of their behaviour. They lose their elections in every club where they are set up for toasts. They are obliged by their principles to stick a patch on the most unbecoming side of their foreheads. They forego the advantage of birthday suits. . . . They receive no benefit from the army, and are never the better for all the young fellows that wear hats and feathers. They are forced to live in the country and feed their chickens; at the same time that they might show themselves at court, and appear in brocade, if they behaved themselves well. In short, what must go to the heart of every fine woman, they throw themselves quite out of the fashion. . . . A man is startled when he sees a pretty bosom heaving with such party-rage, as is disagreeable even in that sex which is of a more coarse and rugged make. And yet such is our misfortune, that we sometimes see a pair of stays ready to burst with sedition; and hear the most masculine passions expressed in the sweetest voices. . . . Where a great number of flowers grow, the ground at distance seems entirely covered with them, and we must walk into it before we can distinguish the several weeds that spring up in such a beautiful mass of colours." [1]

This gallantry is too deliberate; we are somewhat shocked to see a woman touched by such thoughtful hands. It is the urbanity of a moralist; albeit he is well-bred, he is not quite amiable; and if a Frenchman

[1] *Freeholder*, No. 26.

can receive from him lessons of pedagogy and conduct, Addison might come over to France to find models of manners and conversation.

If the first care of a Frenchman in society is to be amiable, that of an Englishman is to be dignified; their mood leads them to immobility, as ours to gestures; and their pleasantry is as grave as ours is gay. Laughter with them is inward; they shun giving themselves up to it; they are amused silently. Let us make up our mind to understand this kind of temper, it will end by pleasing us. When phlegm is united to gentleness, as in Addison, it is as agreeable as it is piquant. We are charmed to meet a lively man, who is yet master of himself. We are astonished to see these contrary qualities together. Each heightens and modifies the other. We are not repelled by venomous bitterness, as in Swift, or by continuous buffoonery, as in Voltaire. We enjoy altogether the rare union, which for the first time combines serious bearing and good humour. Read this little satire against the bad taste of the stage and the public.

"There is nothing that of late years has afforded matter of greater amusement to the town than Signor Nicolini's combat with a lion in the Haymarket, which has been very often exhibited to the general satisfaction of most of the nobility and gentry in the kingdom of Great Britain. . . . The first lion was a candle-snuffer, who being a fellow of a testy, choleric temper, overdid his part, and would not suffer himself to be killed so easily as he ought to have done. . . . The second lion was a tailor by trade, who belonged to the playhouse, and had the character of a mild and peaceable man in his profession. If the former was too furious, this was too sheepish for his part; insomuch that, after a short modest walk upon the stage, he

would fall at the first touch of Hydaspes, without grappling
with him, and giving him an opportunity of shewing his variety
of Italian trips.   It is said, indeed, that he once gave him a rip
in his flesh-coloured doublet ; but this was only to make work
for himself, in his private character of a tailor. . . . The acting
lion at present is as I am informed, a country gentleman, who
does it for his diversion, but desires his name may be concealed.
He says, very handsomely, in his own excuse, that he does not
act for gain, that he indulges an innocent pleasure in it; and
that it is better to pass away an evening in this manner than in
gaming and drinking. . . . This gentleman's temper is made
out of such a happy mixture of the mild and the choleric, that
he outdoes both his predecessors, and has drawn together greater
audiences than have been known in the memory of man. . . .
In the meantime I have related this combat of the lion, to show
what are at present the reigning entertainments of the politer
part of Great Britain.[1] "

There is much originality in this grave gaiety.   As a
rule, singularity is in accordance with the taste of the
nation ; they like to be impressed strongly by contrasts.
French literature seems to them threadbare ; and the
French find them often not very delicate.   A number of
the *Spectator* which seemed pleasant to London ladies
would have shocked people in Paris.   Thus, Addison
relates in the form of a dream the dissection of a beau's
brain :

" The pineal gland, which many of our modern philosophers
suppose to be the seat of the soul, smelt very strong of essence
and orange-flower water, and was encompassed with a kind of
horny substance, cut into a thousand little faces or mirrors,
which were imperceptible to the naked eye ; insomuch that the
soul, if there had been any here, must have been always taken
up in contemplating her own beauties.   We observed a large

[1] *Spectator*, No. 13.

antrum or cavity in the sinciput, that was filled with ribbons, lace, and embroidery. . . . We did not find anything very remarkable in the eye, saving only, that the *musculi amatorii*, or, as we may translate it into English, the ogling muscles, were very much worn, and decayed with use; whereas on the contrary, the elevator, or the muscle which turns the eye towards heaven, did not appear to have been used at all." [1]

These anatomical details, which would disgust the French, amuse a matter-of-fact mind; harshness is for him only accuracy; accustomed to precise images, he finds no objectionable odour in the medical style. Addison does not share our repugnance. To rail at a vice, he becomes a mathematician, an economist, a pedant, an apothecary. Technical terms amuse him. He sets up a court to judge crinolines, and condemns petticoats in legal formulas. He teaches how to handle a fan as if he were teaching to prime and load muskets. He draws up a list of men dead or injured by love, and the ridiculous causes which have reduced them to such a condition:

" Will Simple, smitten at the Opera by the glance of an eye that was aimed at one who stood by him.

" Sir Christopher Crazy, Bart., hurt by the brush of a whalebone petticoat.

" Ned Courtly, presenting Flavia with her glove (which she had dropped on purpose), she received it and took away his life with a curtsey.

" John Gosselin, having received a slight hurt from a pair of blue eyes, as he was making his escape, was dispatched by a smile." [2]

Other statistics, with recapitulations and tables of numbers, relate the history of the Leucadian leap:

Spectator, No. 275.   [2] *Ibid.* No. 377.

"Aridæus, a beautiful youth of Epirus, in love with Praxinoe, the wife of the Thespis, escaped without damage, saving only that two of his foreteeth were struck out, and his nose a little flatted.

"Hipparchus, being passionately fond of his own wife, who was enamoured of Bathyllus, leaped and died of his fall; upon which his wife married her gallant."[1]

We see this strange mode of painting human folly : in England it is called humour. It consists of an incisive good sense, the habit of restraint, business habits, but above all a fundamental energy of invention. The race is less refined, but stronger than the French; and the pleasures which content its mind and taste are like the liquors which suit its palate and its stomach.

This potent Germanic spirit breaks out even in Addison through his classical and Latin exterior. Albeit he relishes art, he still loves nature. His education, which loaded him with maxims, has not destroyed his virgin sentiment of truth. In his travels in France he preferred the wildness of Fontainebleau to the correctness of Versailles. He shakes off worldly refinement to praise the simplicity of the old national ballads. He explains to his public the sublime images, the vast passions, the deep religion of *Paradise Lost*. It is curious to see him, compass in hand, kept back by Bossu, fettered in endless arguments and academical phrases, attaining with one spring, through the strength of natural emotion, the lofty unexplored regions to which Milton rose by the inspiration of faith and genius. Addison does not say, as Voltaire does, that the allegory of Sin and Death is enough to make people sick. He has a foundation of grand imagination, which makes him

[1] *Spectator*, No. 233.

indifferent to the little refinements of social civilisation. He sojourns willingly amid the grandeur and marvels of the other world. He is penetrated by the presence of the Invisible, he must escape from the interests and hopes of the petty life in which we crawl.[1] This source of faith gushes from him in all directions; in vain is it enclosed in the regular channel of official dogma; the text and arguments with which it is covered do not hide its true origin. It springs from the grave and fertile imagination which can only be satisfied with a sight of what is beyond.

Such a faculty swallows a man up; and if we descend to the examination of literary qualities, we find it at the bottom as well as at the top. Nothing in Addison is more varied and rich than the changes and the scenery. The driest morality is transformed under his hand into pictures and stories. There are letters from all kinds of men, clergymen, common people, men of fashion, who keep their own style, and disguise their advice under the form of a little novel. An ambassador from Bantam jests, like Montesquieu, at the lies of European politeness. Greek or Oriental tales, imaginary travels, the vision of a Scottish seer, the memoirs of a rebel, the history of ants, the transformations of an ape, the journal of an idle man, a walk in Westminster, the genealogy of humour, the laws of ridiculous clubs; in short, an inexhaustible mass of pleasant or solid fictions. The allegories are most frequent. We feel that the author delights in this magnificent and fantastic world; he is acting for himself a sort of opera; his eyes must look on colours. Here is a paper on religions, very Protestant, but as

[1] See the last thirty numbers of the *Spectator*.

sparkling as it is ingenious : relaxation in England
does not consist, as in France, in the vivacity and
variety of tone, but in the splendour and correctness of
invention :

" The middle figure, which immediately attracted the eyes of
the whole company, and was much bigger than the rest, was
formed like a matron, dressed in the habit of an elderly woman
of quality in Queen Elizabeth's days. The most remarkable
parts of her dress were the beaver with the steeple crown, the
scarf that was darker than sable, and the lawn apron that was
whiter than ermine. Her gown was of the richest black velvet,
and just upon her heart studded with large diamonds of an
inestimable value, disposed in the form of a cross. She bore an
inexpressible cheerfulness and dignity in her aspect ; and
though she seemed in years, appeared with so much spirit and
vivacity, as gave her at the same time an air of old age and
immortality. I found my heart touched with so much love
and reverence at the sight of her, that the tears ran down my
face as I looked upon her ; and still the more I looked upon
her, the more my heart was melted with the sentiments of
filial tenderness and duty. I discovered every moment something so charming in this figure, that I could scarce take my
eyes off it. On its right hand there sat the figure of a woman
so covered with ornaments, that her face, her body, and her
hands were almost entirely hid under them. The little you
could see of her face was painted, and what I thought very odd,
had something in it like artificial wrinkles ; but I was the less
surprised at it, when I saw upon her forehead on old-fashioned
tower of grey hairs. Her head-dress rose very high by three
several stories or degrees ; her garments had a thousand colours
in them, and were embroidered with crosses in gold, silver, and
silk ; she had nothing on, so much as a glove or a slipper,
which was not marked with this figure ; nay, so superstitiously
fond did she appear of it, that she sat cross-legged. . . . The
next to her was a figure which somewhat puzzled me ; it was

that of a man looking with horror in his eyes, upon a silver bason filled with water. Observing something in his countenance that looked like lunacy, I fancied at first that he was to express that kind of distraction which the physicians call the Hydrophobia; but considering what the intention of the show was, I immediately recollected myself, and concluded it to be Anabaptism."[1]

The reader must guess what these two first figures mean. They will please a member of the Episcopal Church more than a Roman Catholic; but I think that a Roman Catholic himself cannot help recognising the fulness and freshness of the fiction.

Genuine imagination naturally ends in the invention of characters. For, if we clearly represent to ourselves a situation or an action, we will see at the same time the whole network of its connection; the passion and faculties, all the gestures and tones of voice, all details of dress, dwelling, social intercourse, which flow from it, will be connected in our mind, and bring their precedents and their consequences; and this multitude of ideas, slowly organised, will at last be concentrated in a single sentiment, from which, as from a deep spring, will break forth the portrait and the history of a complete character. There are several such in Addison; the quiet observer Will Honeycomb, the country Tory Sir Roger de Coverley, which are not satirical theses, like those of La Bruyère, but genuine individuals, like, and sometimes equal to, the characters of the great contemporary novels. In reality, he invents the novel without suspecting it, at the same time and in the same way as his most illustrious neighbours. His characters are taken from life, from the manners and

[1] *Tatler*, No. 257.

conditions of the age, described at length and minutely
in all the details of their education and surroundings,
with a precise and positive observation, marvellously
real and English. A masterpiece as well as an historical record is Sir Roger de Coverley, the country
gentleman, a loyal servant of State and Church, a
justice of the peace, with a chaplain of his own, and
whose estate shows on a small scale the structure of
the English nation. This domain is a little kingdom,
paternally governed, but still governed. Sir Roger
rates his tenants, passes them in review in church,
knows their affairs, gives them advice, assistance, commands; he is respected, obeyed, loved, because he lives
with them, because the simplicity of his tastes and
education puts him almost on a level with them;
because as a magistrate, a landed proprietor of many
years standing, a wealthy man, a benefactor and neighbour, he exercises a moral and legal, a useful and
respected authority. Addison at the same time shows
in him the solid and peculiar English character, built of
heart of oak, with all the ruggedness of the primitive
bark, which can neither be softened nor planed down,
a great fund of kindness which extends even to animals,
a love for the country and for bodily exercises, an inclination to command and discipline, a feeling of subordination and respect, much common sense and little
finesse, a habit of displaying and practising in public
his singularities and oddities, careless of ridicule, without
thought of bravado, solely because these men acknowledge no judge but themselves. A hundred traits
depict the times; a lack of love for reading, a lingering
belief in witches, rustic and sporting manners, the igno-
rances of an artless or backward mind. Sir Roger gives

the children, who answer their catechism well, a Bible for themselves, and half a flitch of bacon for their mothers. When a verse pleases him, he sings it for half a minute after the congregation has finished. He kills eight fat pigs at Christmas, and sends a pudding and a pack of cards to each poor family in the parish. When he goes to the theatre, he supplies his servants with cudgels to protect themselves from the thieves which, he says, infest London. Addison returns a score of times to the old knight, always showing some new aspect of his character, a disinterested observer of humanity, curiously assiduous and discerning, a true creator, having but one step farther to go to enter, like Richardson and Fielding, upon the great work of modern literature, the novel of manners and customs.

There is an undercurrent of poetry in all this. It has flowed through his prose a thousand times more sincere and beautiful than in his verses. Rich oriental fancies are displayed, not with a shower of sparks as in Voltaire, but in a calm and abundant light, which makes the regular folds of their purple and gold undulate.[1] The music of the vast cadenced and tranquil phrases leads the mind gently amidst romantic splendours and enchantments, and the deep sentiment of ever young nature recalls the happy quietude of Spenser. Through gentle railleries or moral essays we feel that the author's imagination is happy, delighted in the contemplation of the swaying to and fro of the forest-tops which clothe the mountains, the eternal verdure of the valleys, invigorated by fresh springs, and the wide view undulating far away on the distant horizon. Great and simple sentiments naturally join these noble images, and their measured

---

[1] See the history of *Alnaschar* in the *Spectator*, No. 535, and also that of *Hilpa* in the same paper, Nos. 584, 585.

harmony creates a unique spectacle, worthy to fascinate the heart of a good man by its gravity and sweetness. Such are the Visions of Mirza, which I will give almost entire :

" On the fifth day of the moon, which according to the custom of my forefathers I always keep holy, after having washed myself, and offered up my morning devotions, I ascended the high hills of Bagdat, in order to pass the rest of the day in meditation and prayer. As I was here airing myself on the tops of the mountains, I fell into a profound contemplation on the vanity of human life ; and passing from one thought to another : Surely, said I, man is but a shadow and life a dream. Whilst I was thus musing, I cast my eyes towards the summit of a rock that was not far from me, where I discovered one in the habit of a shepherd, with a musical instrument in his hand. As I looked upon him he applied it to his lips, and began to play upon it. The sound of it was exceeding sweet, and wrought into a variety of tunes that were inexpressibly melodious, and altogether different from anything I had ever heard. They put me in mind of those heavenly airs that are played to the departed souls of good men upon their first arrival in Paradise, to wear out the impressions of the last agonies, and qualify them for the pleasures of that happy place. My heart melted away in secret raptures. . . .

" He (the Genius) then led me to the highest pinnacle of the rock, and placing me on the top of it, Cast thy eyes eastward, said he, and tell me what thou seest. I see, said I, a huge valley, and a prodigious tide of water rolling through it. The valley that thou seest, said he, is the vale of misery, and the tide of water that thou seest is part of the great tide of Eternity. What is the reason, said I, that the tide I see rises out of a thick mist at one end, and again loses itself in a thick mist at the other ? What thou seest, said he, is that portion of Eternity which is called Time, measured out by the Sun, and reaching from the beginning of the world to its consummation. Ex-

amine now, said he, this sea that is bounded with darkness at
both ends, and tell me what thou discoverest in it. I see a
bridge, said I, standing in the midst of the tide. The bridge
thou seest, said he, is human life; consider it attentively.
Upon a more leisurely survey of it, I found that it consisted of
three score and ten entire arches, with several broken arches,
which added to those that were entire, made up the number
about an hundred. As I was counting the arches, the genius
told me that this bridge consisted at first of a thousand arches :
but that a great flood swept away the rest, and left the bridge
in the ruinous condition I now beheld it. But tell me further,
said he, what thou discoverest on it. I see multitudes of
people passing over it, said I, and a black cloud hanging on each
end of it. As I looked more attentively, I saw several of the
passengers dropping through the bridge into the great tide that
flowed underneath it ; and upon further examination, perceived
there were innumerable trap-doors that lay concealed in the
bridge, which the passengers no sooner trod upon, but they fell
through them into the tide, and immediately disappeared.
These hidden pit-falls were set very thick at the entrance of the
bridge, so that throngs of people no sooner broke through the
cloud, but many of them fell into them. They grew thinner
towards the middle, but multiplied and lay closer together
towards the end of the arches that were entire.

" There were indeed some persons, but their number was
very small, that continued a kind of hobbling march on the
broken arches, but fell through one after another, being quite
tired and spent with so long a walk.

" I passed some time in the contemplation of this wonderful
structure, and the great variety of objects which it presented.
My heart was filled with a deep melancholy to see several
dropping unexpectedly in the midst of mirth and jollity, and
catching at everything that stood by them to save themselves.
Some were looking up towards the Heavens in a thoughtful posture, and in the midst of a Speculation stumbled and fell out of

sight. Multitudes were very busy in the pursuit of bubbles that glittered in their eyes and danced before them ; but often when they thought themselves within the reach of them, their footing failed, and down they sunk. In this confusion of objects, I observed some with scimitars in their hands, and others with urinals, who ran to and fro upon the bridge, thrusting several persons on trap-doors which did not seem to lie in their way, and which they might have escaped had they not been thus forced upon them. . . .

"I here fetched a deep sigh. Alas, said I, man was made in vain ! How is he given away to misery and mortality ! tortured in life, and swallowed up in death !—The Genius, being moved with compassion towards me, bid me quit so uncomfortable a prospect. Look no more, said he, on man in the first stage of his existence, in his setting out for eternity ; but cast thine eye on that thick mist into which the tide bears the several generations of mortals that fall into it. I directed my sight as I was ordered, and (whether or no the good Genius strengthened it with any supernatural force, or dissipated part of the mist that was before too thick for the eye to penetrate) I saw the valley opening at the farther end, and spreading forth into an immense ocean, that had a huge rock of adamant running through the midst of it, and dividing it into two equal parts. The clouds still rested on one half of it, insomuch that I could discover nothing in it : but the other appeared to me a vast ocean planted with innumerable islands, that were covered with fruits and flowers, and interwoven with a thousand little shining seas that ran among them. I could see persons dressed in glorious habits, with garlands upon their heads, passing among the trees, lying down by the sides of the fountains, or resting on beds of flowers ; and could hear a confused harmony of singing birds, falling waters, human voices, and musical instruments. Gladness grew in me upon the discovery of so delightful a scene. I wished for the wings of an eagle, that I might fly away to those happy seats ; but the Genius told me there was no passage to them, except through the gates of death that I saw opening every moment upon the bridge. The islands, said he, that lie so fresh and green before thee, and with which the whole face of the ocean appears spotted as far as thou canst see, are more in number than the sands on the sea-shore ; there are myriads of islands behind those which thou here discoverest, reaching farther than thine eye, or even thine imagination, can extend itself. These are the mansions of good men after death, who according to the degree and kinds of virtue in which they excelled, are distributed among these several islands, which abound with pleasures of different kinds and degrees, suitable to the relishes and perfections of those who are settled in them : every island is a paradise accommodated to its respective inhabitants. Are not these, O Mirza, habitations, worth contending for ? Does life appear miserable, that gives thee opportunities of earning such a reward ? Is death to be feared, that will convey thee to so happy an existence ? Think not man was made in vain, who has such an eternity reserved for him.—I gazed with inexpressible pleasure on these happy islands. At length, said I, shew me now, I beseech thee, the secrets that lie hid under those dark clouds which cover the ocean on the other side of the rock of Adamant. The Genius making me no answer, I turned me about to address myself to him a second time, but I found that he had left me ; I then turned again to the vision which I had been so long contemplating : but instead of the rolling tide, the arched bridge, and the happy islands, I saw nothing but the long hollow valley of Bagdat, with oxen, sheep, and camels grazing upon the sides of it." [1]

In this ornate moral sketch, this fine reasoning, so correct and so eloquent, this ingenious and noble imagination, I find an epitome of all Addison's charac-

[1] *Spectator*, No. 159.

teristics.   These are the English tints which distinguish
this classical age from that of the French : a narrower
and more practical argument, a more poetical and less
eloquent urbanity, a structure of mind more inventive
and more rich, less sociable and less refined.

CHAPTER V.

Swift.

In 1685, in the great hall of Dublin University, the professors engaged in examining for the bachelor's degree beheld a singular spectacle : a poor scholar, odd, awkward, with hard blue eyes, an orphan, friendless, dependent on the precarious charity of an uncle, having failed once before to take his degree on account of his ignorance of logic, had come up again without having condescended to read logic. To no purpose his tutor set before him the most respectable folios—Smiglecius, Keckermannus, Burgerdiscius. He turned over a few pages, and shut them directly. When the argumentation came on, the proctor was obliged to "reduce his replies into syllogism." He was asked how he could reason well without rules ; he replied that he did reason pretty well without them. This folly shocked them ; yet he was received, though with some difficulty, *speciali gratiâ*, says the college register, and the professors went away, doubtless with pitying smiles, lamenting the feeble brain of Jonathan Swift.

I.

This was his first humiliation and his first rebellion. His whole life was like this moment, overwhelmed and made wretched by sorrow and hatred. To what excess they rose, his portrait and his history alone can show.   He fostered an exaggerated and terrible pride, and made the haughtiness of the most powerful ministers and greatest lords bend beneath his arrogance.   Though only a literary man, possessing nothing but a small Irish living, he treated them on a footing of equality. Harley, the prime minister, having sent him a bank-bill of fifty pounds for his first articles, he was offended at being taken for a hack writer, returned the money, demanded an apology, received it, and wrote in his journal: " I have taken Mr. Harley into favour again." [1]   On another occasion, having observed that the Secretary of State, St. John, looked upon him coldly, he rebuked him for it:

" One thing I warned him of, never to appear cold to me, for I would not be treated like a school-boy; that I expected every great minister who honoured me with his acquaintance, if he heard or saw anything to my disadvantage, would let me know in plain words, and not put me in pain to guess by the change or coldness of his countenance or behaviour; for it was what I would hardly bear from a crowned head; and I thought no subject's favour was worth it: and that I designed to let my Lord Keeper and Mr. Harley know the same thing, that they might use me accordingly." [2]

St. John approved of this, made excuses, said that he had passed several nights at " business, and one night at drinking," and that his fatigue might have seemed like ill-humour.   In the minister's drawing-room Swift

[1] In Swift's Works, ed. W. Scott, 19 vols. 1814; *Journal to Stella*, ii. Feb. 13 (1710–11).   He says also (Feb. 6 and 7): " I will not see him (Mr. Harley) till he makes amends. . . . I was deaf to all entreaties, and have desired Lewis to go to him, and let him know that I expect farther satisfaction.   If we let these great ministers pretend too much, there will be no governing them."

[2] *Ibid.* April 3, 1711.

went up and spoke to some obscure person, and compelled the lords to come and speak to him:

"Mr. Secretary told me the Duke of Buckingham had been talking to him much about me, and desired my acquaintance. I answered, it could not be, for he had not made sufficient advances. Then the Duke of Shrewsbury said, he thought the Duke was not used to make advances. I said, I could not help that; for I always expected advances in proportion to men's quality, and more from a duke than other men."[1]

"Saw Lord Halifax at court, and we joined and talkéd, and the Duchess of Shrewsbury came up and reproached me for not dining with her: I said that was not so soon done; for I expected more advances from ladies, especially duchesses: She promised to comply. . . . Lady Oglethorp brought me and the Duchess of Hamilton together to-day in the drawing-room, and I have given her some encouragement, but not much."[2]

He triumphed in his arrogance, and said with a restrained joy, full of vengeance: "I generally am acquainted with about thirty in the drawing-room, and am so proud that I make all the lords come up to me. One passes half an hour pleasant enough." He carried his triumph to the verge of brutality and tyranny; writing to the Duchess of Queensberry, he says: "I am glad you know your duty; for it has been a known and established rule above twenty years in England, that the first advances have been constantly made me by all ladies who aspired to my acquaintance, and the greater their quality, the greater were their advances."[3] The famous General Webb, with his crutch and cane, limped up two flights of stairs to congratulate him and invite him to dinner; Swift accepted, then an hour later withdrew his

---

[1] Swift's Works, *Journal to Stella*, ii. May 19, 1711.
[2] *Ibid.* Oct. 7, 1711.   [3] *Ibid.* xvii. p. 352.

consent, preferring to dine elsewhere. He seemed to look upon himself as a superior being, exempt from the necessity of showing his respects to any one, entitled to homage, caring neither for sex, rank, nor fame, whose business it was to protect and destroy, distributing favours, insults, and pardons. Addison, and after him Lady Gifford, a friend of twenty years' standing, having offended him, he refused to take them back into his favour until they had asked his pardon. Lord Lansdown, Secretary for War, being annoyed by an expression in the *Examiner*, Swift says: "This I resented highly that he should complain of me before he spoke to me. I sent him a peppering letter, and would not summon him by a note, as I did the rest; nor ever will have anything to say to him, till he begs my pardon." [1] He treated art like man, writing a thing ôff, scorning the wretched necessity of reading it over, putting his name to nothing, letting every piece make its way on its own merits, unassisted, without the prestige of his name, recommended by none. He had the soul of a dictator, thirsting after power, and saying openly : " All my endeavours, from a boy, to distinguish myself were only for want of a great title and fortune, that I might be treated like a lord. . . . whether right or wrong, it is no great matter ; and so the reputation of wit or great learning does the office of a blue ribbon, or of a coach and six horses." [2] But he thought this power and rank due to him; he did not ask, but expected them. " I will never beg for myself, though I often do it for others." He desired ruling power, and acted as if he had it. Hatred and misfortune find a congenial soil

[1] *Journal to Stella*, iii. March 27, 1711–12.
[2] Letter to Bolingbroke, Dublin, April 5, 1729.

in these despotic minds. They live like fallen kings, always insulting and offended, having all the miseries but none of the consolations of pride, unable to relish either society or solitude, too ambitious to be content with silence, too haughty to use the world, born for rebellion and defeat, destined by their passions and impotence to despair and to talent.

Sensitiveness in Swift's case aggravated the stings of pride. Under this outward calmness of countenance and style raged furious passions. There was within him a ceaseless tempest of wrath and desire: "A person of great honour in Ireland (who was pleased to stoop so low as to look into my mind) used to tell me that my mind was like a conjured spirit, that would do mischief, if I would not give it employment." Resentment sunk deeper in him than in other men. Listen to the profound sigh of joyful hatred with which he sees his enemies under his feet: "The whigs were ravished to see me, and would lay hold on me as a twig while they are drowning; and the great men making me their clumsy apologies." [1] "It is good to see what a lamentable confession the whigs all make of my ill-usage." [2] And soon after: "Rot them, for ungrateful dogs; I will make them repent their usage before I leave this place." [3] He is satiated and has glutted his appetite; like a wolf or a lion, he cares for nothing else.

This impetuosity led him to every sort of madness and violence. His *Drapier's Letters* had roused Ireland against the government, and the government had issued a proclamation offering a reward to any one who would denounce the Drapier. Swift came suddenly into the

---

[1] *Journal to Stella*, ii., Sept. 9, 1710.
[2] *Ibid.* Sept. 30, 1710.   [3] *Ibid.* Nov. 8, 1710.

reception-chamber, elbowed the groups, went up to the lord-lieutenant, with indignation on his countenance, and in a thundering voice, said : " So, my lord, this is a glorious exploit that you performed yesterday, in suffering a proclamation against a poor shopkeeper, whose only crime is an honest endeavour to save his country from ruin." [1] And he broke out into railing amidst general silence and amazement. The lord-lieutenant, a man of sense, answered calmly. Before such a torrent men turned aside. This chaotic and self-devouring heart could not understand the calmness of his friends ; he asked them : " Do not the corruptions and villanies of men eat your flesh, and exhaust your spirits ? " [2]

Resignation was repulsive to him. His actions, abrupt and strange, broke out amidst his silent moods like flashes of lightning. He was eccentric and violent in everything, in his pleasantry, in his private affairs, with his friends, with unknown people ; he was often taken for a madman. Addison and his friends had seen for several days at Button's coffee-house a singular parson, who laid his hat on the table, walked for half-an-hour backward and forward, paid his money, and left, having attended to nothing and said nothing. They called him the mad parson. One day this parson perceives a gentleman " just come out of the country," went straight up to him, " and in a very abrupt manner, without any previous salute, asked him, ' Pray sir, do you remember any good weather in the world ? ' The country gentleman, after staring a little at the singularity of his (Swift's) manner and the oddity of the question, answered, ' Yes, sir, I thank God, I remember a great deal of good weather in my time.' ' That is more,' said Swift,

[1] *Swift's Life*, by Roscoe, i. 56.   [2] *Swift's Life*, by W. Scott, i. 279.

'than I can say; I never remember any weather that was not too hot, or too cold, too wet or too dry; but, however God Almighty contrives it, at the end of the year 'tis all very well.'"[1]　Another day, dining with the Earl of Burlington, the Dean said to the mistress of the house, "Lady Burlington, I hear you can sing; sing me a song." The lady looked on this unceremonious manner of asking a favour with distaste, and positively refused. He said, "she should sing, or he would make her. Why, madam, I suppose you take me for one of your poor English hedge-parsons; sing when I bid you!" As the earl did nothing but laugh at this freedom, the lady was so vexed, that she burst into tears, and retired. His first compliment to her, when he saw her again, was, "Pray, madam, are you as proud and as ill-natured now as when I saw you last?"[2] People were astonished or amused at these outbursts; I see in them sobs and cries, the explosion of long, overwhelming and bitter thoughts; they are the starts of a mind unsubdued, shuddering, rebelling, breaking the barriers, wounding, crushing, or bruising every one on its road, or those who wish to stop it. Swift became mad at last; he felt this madness coming on, he has described it in a horrible manner; beforehand he has tasted all the disgust and bitterness of it; he showed it on his tragic face, in his terrible and wan eyes. This is the powerful and mournful genius which nature gave up as a prey to society and life; society and life poured all their poisons into him.

He knew what poverty and scorn were, even at that age when the mind expands, when the heart is full of

---

[1] Sheridan's *Life of Swift.*

[2] W. Scott's *Life of Swift*, i. 477.

pride,[1] when he was hardly maintained by the alms of his family, gloomy and without hope, feeling his strength and the dangers of his strength. [2] At twenty-one, as secretary to Sir William Temple, he had twenty pounds a year salary, sat at the same table with the upper servants,[3] wrote Pindaric odes in honour of his master, spent ten years amidst the humiliations of servitude and the familiarity of the servants' hall, obliged to adulate a gouty and flattered courtier, to submit to my lady his sister, acutely pained "when Sir William Temple would look cold and out of humour,"[4] lured by false hopes, forced after an attempt at independence to resume the livery which was choking him. "When you find years coming on, without hopes of a place at court, . . . I directly advise you to go upon the road which is the only post of honour left you; there you will meet many of your old comrades, and live a short life and a merry one."[5] This is followed by instructions as to the conduct servants ought to display when led

[1] At that time he had already begun the *Tale of a Tub*.

[2] He addresses his muse thus, in *Verses occasioned by Sir William Temple's late illness and recovery*, xiv. 45 :

    " Wert thou right woman, thou should'st scorn to look
       On an abandoned wretch by hopes forsook ;
       Forsook by hopes, ill fortune's last relief,
       Assign'd for life to unremitting grief ;

       To thee I owe that fatal bent of mind
       Still to unhappy restless thoughts inclined ;
       To thee, what oft I vainly strive to hide,
       That scorn of fools, by fools mistook for pride. "

[3] These assertions have been denied. See Roscoe's *Life of Swift*, i. 14.—Tr.

[4] " Don't you remember how I used to be in pain when Sir William Temple would look cold and out of humour for three or four days, and I used to suspect a hundred reasons ? I have plucked up my spirit since then, faith ; he spoiled a fine gentleman."—*Journal to Stella*, April 4, 1710–11.

[5] *Directions to Servants*, xii. ch. iii. 434.

to the gallows.   Such are his *Directions to Servants;* he was relating what he had suffered.   At the age of thirty-one, expecting a place from William III., he edited the works of his patron, dedicated them to the sovereign, sent him a memorial, got nothing, and fell back upon the post of chaplain and private secretary to the Earl of Berkeley.   He soon remained only chaplain to that nobleman, feeling all the disgust which the part of ecclesiastical valet must inspire in a man of feeling.

" You know I honour the cloth,"

Says the chambermaid in the well-known *Petition :*

> " I design to be a parson's wife. . . .
> And over and above, that I may have your excellency's letter
> With an order for the chaplain aforesaid, or instead of him a
> better." [1]

The earl, having promised him the deanery of Derry, gave it to another.   Driven to politics, he wrote a whig pamphlet, *A Discourse on the Contests and Dissensions in Athens and Rome,* received from Lord Halifax and the party leaders a score of fine promises, and was neglected.   Twenty years of insults without revenge, and humiliations without respite ; the inner tempest of fostered and crushed hopes, vivid and brilliant dreams, suddenly withered by the necessity of a mechanical duty; the habit of suffering and hatred, the necessity of concealing these, the baneful consciousness of superiority, the isolation of genius and pride, the bitterness of accumulated wrath and pent-up scorn,—these were the goads which pricked him like a bull.   More than a thousand pamphlets in four years, stung him still more, with such designations as renegade, traitor, and atheist.   He

---

[1] *Mrs. Harris' Petition,* xiv. 52.

crushed them all, set his foot on the Whig party, solaced himself with the poignant pleasure of victory. If ever a soul was satiated with the joy of tearing, outraging, and destroying, it was his. Excess of scorn, implacable irony, crushing logic, the cruel smile of the foeman, who sees beforehand the spot where he will wound his enemy mortally, advances towards him, tortures him deliberately, eagerly, with enjoyment,—such were the feelings which had leavened him, and which broke from him with such harshness that he hindered his own career;[1] and that of so many high places for which he stretched out his hands, there remained for him only a deanery in poor Ireland. The accession of George I. exiled him thither; the accession of George II., on which he had counted, confined him there. He contended there first against popular hatred, then against the victorious minister, then against entire humanity, in sanguinary pamphlets, despairing satires;[2] he tasted there once more the pleasure of fighting and wounding; he suffered there to the end, soured by the advance of years, by the spectacle of oppression and misery, by the feeling of his own impotence, enraged to have to live amongst "an enslaved people," chained and vanquished. He says: "I find myself disposed every year, or rather every month, to be more angry and revengeful; and my rage is so ignoble, that it descends even to resent the folly and baseness of the enslaved people among whom I live."[3] This cry is the epitome of his public

[1] By the *Tale of a Tub* with the clergy, and by the *Prophesy of Windsor* with the queen.

[2] *The Drapier's Letters, Gulliver's Travels, Rhapsody on Poetry, A modest Proposal for preventing the Children of poor people in Ireland from being a burden to their parents or country, and for making them beneficial to the public,* and several pamphlets on Ireland.

[3] Letter to Lord Bolingbroke, Dublin, March 21, 1728, xvii. 274.

life; these feelings are the materials which public life furnished to his talent.

He experienced these feelings also in private life, more violent and more inwardly. He had brought up and purely loved a charming, well-informed, modest young girl, Esther Johnson, who from infancy had loved and reverenced him alone. She lived with him, he had made her his confidante. From London, during his political struggles, he sent her the full journal of his slightest actions; he wrote to her twice a day, with extreme ease and familiarity, with all the playfulness, vivacity, petting and caressing names of the tenderest attachment. Yet another girl, beautiful and rich, Miss Vanhomrigh, attached herself to him, declared her passion, received from him several marks of his own, followed him to Ireland, sometimes jealous, sometimes submissive, but so impassioned, so unhappy, that her letters might have broken a harder heart: "If you continue to treat me as you do, you will not be made uneasy by me long. . . . I am sure I could have borne the rack much better, than those killing, killing words of you. . . . Oh that you may have but so much regard for me left, that this complaint may touch your soul with pity!"[1] She pined and died. Esther Johnson, who had so long possessed Swift's whole heart, suffered still more. All was changed in Swift's house. "At my first coming (at Laracor) I thought I should have died with discontent, and was horribly melancholy while they were installing me."[2] He found tears, distrust, resentment, cold silence, in place of familiarity and tenderness.

---

[1] Letter of Miss Vanhomrigh, Dublin, 1714, xix. 421.

[2] These words are taken from a letter to Miss Vanhomrigh, 8th July 1713, and cannot refer to her death, which took place in 1721.—Tr.

He married Miss Johnson from a feeling of duty, but in secret, and on condition that she should only be his wife in name. She was twelve years dying; Swift went away to England as often as he could. His house was a hell to him; it is thought that some secret physical cause had influenced his loves and his marriage. Delany, his biographer, having once found him talking with Archbishop King, saw the archbishop in tears, and Swift rushing by, with a countenance full of grief, and a distracted air. "Sir," said the prelate, "you have just met the most unhappy man upon earth; but on the subject of his wretchedness you must never ask a question." Esther Johnson died. Swift's anguish, the spectres by which he was haunted, the remembrance of the two women, slowly ruined and killed by his fault, continually encompassed him with such horrors, that only his end reveals them. "It is time for me to have done with the world ... and so I would ... and not die here in a rage, like a poisoned rat in a hole."[1] Overwork and excess of emotion had made him ill from his youth; he was subject to giddiness; he lost his hearing. He had long felt that reason was deserting him. One day he was observed "gazing intently at the top of a lofty elm, the head of which had been blasted. Upon his friend's approach, he pointed to it, significantly adding, ' I shall be like that tree, and die first at the top.'"[2] His memory left him; he received the attentions of others with disgust, sometimes with rage. He lived alone, gloomy, unable to read. It is said that he passed a whole year without uttering a word, hating the sight of a human being, walking ten hours

---

[1] Letter to Bolingbroke, Dublin, March 21, 1728, xvii. 276.
[2] Roscoe's *Life of Swift*, i. 80.

a day, a maniac, then an idiot. A tumour came on one of his eyes, so that he continued a month without sleeping, and five men were needed to prevent his tearing out the eye with his nails. One of his last words was, " I am a fool." When his will was opened, it was found that he left his whole fortune to build a madhouse.

II.

These passions and these miseries were necessary to inspire *Gulliver's Travels* and the *Tale of a Tub*.

A strange and powerful form of mind, too, was necessary, as English as his pride and his passions. Swift has the style of a surgeon and a judge, cold, grave, solid, unadorned, without vivacity or passion, manly and practical. He desired neither to please, nor to divert, nor to carry people away, nor to move the feelings; he never hesitated, nor was redundant, nor was excited, nor made an effort. He expressed his thoughts in a uniform tone, with exact, precise, often harsh terms, with familiar comparisons, levelling all within reach of his hand, even the loftiest things— especially the loftiest — with a brutal and always haughty coolness. He knows life as a banker knows accounts; and his total once made up, he scorns or knocks down the babblers who dispute it in his presence.

He knows the items as well as the sum total. He not only familiarly and vigorously seized on every object, but he also decomposed it, and kept an inventory of its details. His imagination was as minute as it was energetic. He could give you a statement of dry facts on every event and object, so connected and natural as to deceive any man. *Gulliver's Travels* read like a log-book.

Isaac Bickerstaff's predictions were taken literally by the
inquisition in Portugal. His account of M. du Baudrier
seems an authentic translation. He gives to an extravagant romance the air of a genuine history. By this
thorough knowledge of details he imports into literature
the positive spirit of men of business and experience.
Nothing could be more vigorous, narrow, unhappy, for
nothing could be more destructive. No greatness, false
or true, can stand before him; whatsoever he fathoms
and takes in hand loses at once its prestige and value.
Whilst he decomposes he displays the real ugliness,
and removes the fictitious beauty of objects. Whilst
he brings them to the level of common things, he
suppresses their real beauty, and gives them a fictitious
ugliness. He presents all their gross features, and
nothing but their gross features. Look with him into
the physical details of science, religion, state, and with
him reduce science, religion, state, to the low standing of
every-day events; with him you will see here a Bedlam
of shrivelled-up dreamers, narrow and chimerical brains,
busy in contradicting each other, picking up meaningless
phrases in mouldy books, inventing conjectures, and
crying them up for truth; there, a band of enthusiasts, mumbling phrases which they do not understand,
adoring figures of rhetoric as mysteries, attaching
ideas of holiness or impiety to lawn-sleeves or postures,
spending in persecutions or genuflexions the surplus of
sheepish or ferocious folly with which an evil fate has
crammed their brains; there, again, flocks of idiots
pouring out their blood and treasure for the whims or
plots of a carriage-drawn aristocrat, out of respect for
the carriage which they themselves have given him.
What part of human nature or existence can continue

great and beautiful, before a mind which, penetrating
all details, perceives men eating, sleeping, dressing, in
all mean and low actions, degrading everything to the
level of vulgar events, trivial circumstances of dress
and cookery? It is not enough for the positive mind
to see the springs, pulleys, lamps, and whatever there
is objectionable in the opera at which he is present; he
makes it more objectionable by calling it a show. It is
not enough not to ignore anything; we must also refuse
to admire. He treats things like domestic utensils; after
reckoning up their materials, he gives them a vile name.
Nature for him is but a caldron, and he knows the
proportion and number of the ingredients simmering in
it. In this power and this weakness we see beforehand
the misanthropy and the talent of Swift.

There are, indeed, but two modes of agreeing with
the world: mediocrity of mind and superiority of
intelligence—the one for the public and the fools, the
other for artists and philosophers: the one consists in
seeing nothing, the other in seeing all. We will
respect the respectable, if we see only the surface—if
we take them as they are, if we let ourselves be duped
by the fine show which they never fail to present.
We will revere the gold-embroidered garments with
which our masters bedizen themselves, and we will never
dream of examining the stains hidden under the
embroidery. We will be moved by the big words
which they pronounce in a sublime voice, and we will
never see in their pockets the hereditary phrase-book
from which they have taken them. We will punctili-
ously bring them our money and our services; the
custom will seem to us just, and we will accept the
goose-dogma, that a goose is bound to be roasted. But,

on the other hand, we will tolerate and even love the world, if, penetrating to its nature, we take the trouble to explain or imitate its mechanism. We will be interested in passions by an artist's sympathy or a philosopher's comprehension; we will find them natural whilst admitting their force, or we will find them necessary whilst computing their connection; we will cease to be indignant against the powers which produce fine spectacles, or will cease to be roused by the rebounds which the law of cause and effect had foretold. We will admire the world as a grand drama, or as an invincible development; and we will be preserved by imagination or by logic from slander or disgust. We will extract from religion the lofty truths which dogmas hide, and the generous instincts which superstition conceals. We will perceive in the state the infinite benefits which no tyranny abolishes, and the sociable inclinations which no wickedness uproots. We will distinguish in science the solid doctrines which discussion never shakes, the liberal notions which the shock of systems purifies and unfolds, the splendid promises which the progress of the present time opens up to the ambition of the future. We can thus escape hatred by the nullity or the greatness of the prospect, by the inability to discover contrasts, or by the power to discover the harmony of contrasts. Raised above the first, sunk beneath the last, seeing evil and disorder, ignoring goodness and harmony, excluded from love and calmness, given·up to indignation and bitterness, Swift found neither a cause to cherish, nor a doctrine to establish;[1] he employs the

[1] In his *Thoughts on Religion* (viii. 173) he says : "The want of belief is a defect that ought to be concealed, when it cannot be over-

whole force of an excellently armed mind and a thoroughly trained character in decrying and destroying : all his works are pamphlets.

III.

At this time, and in his hands, the newspaper in England attained its proper character and its greatest force. Literature entered the sphere of politics. To understand what the one became, we must understand what the other was : art depended upon political business, and the spirit of parties made the spirit of writers.

In France a theory arises—eloquent, harmonious, and generous; the young are enamoured of it, wear a cap and sing songs in its honour : at night, the citizens, while digesting their dinner, read it and delight in it ; some, hotheaded, accept it, and prove to themselves their strength of mind by ridiculing those who are behind the times. On the other hand, the established people, prudent and timid, are mistrustful : being well off, they find that everything is well, and demand that things shall continue as they are. Such are the two parties in France, very old, as we all know; not very earnest, as everybody can see. They must talk, be enthusiastic, reason on speculative opinions, glibly, about an hour a day, indulging but outwardly in this taste ; but these parties are so equally levelled, that they are at bottom all the same : when we understand them rightly, we will find in France only two parties, the men of twenty and the men of forty. English parties, on the other hand, were always compact and

come." "I look upon myself, in the capacity of a clergyman, to be one appointed by Providence for defending a post assigned me, and for gaining over as many enemies as I can."

living bodies, united by interests of money, rank, and
conscience, receiving theories only as standards or as a
balance, a sort of secondary States, which, like the two
old orders in Rome, legally endeavour to monopolise the
government. So, the English constitution was never
more than a transaction between distinct powers,
compelled to tolerate each other, disposed to encroach on
each other, occupied in treating with each other. Politics
for them are a domestic interest, for the French an
occupation of the mind; Englishmen make them a
business, the French a discussion.

Thus their pamphlets, notably Swift's, seem to us
only half literary. For an argument to be literary,
it must not address itself to an interest or a faction,
but to the pure mind: it must be based on universal
truths, rest on absolute justice, be able to touch all
human reasons; otherwise, being local, it is simply
useful: nothing is beautiful but what is general. It
must also be developed regularly by analysis, and with
exact divisions; its distribution must give a picture of
pure reason; the order of ideas must be inviolable;
every mind must be able to draw thence with ease
a complete conviction; its method, its principles, must
be sensible throughout, in all places and at all times.
The desire to prove well must be added to the art
of proving well; the writer must announce his proof,
recall it, present it under all its faces, desire to penetrate
minds, pursue them persistently in all their retreats;
but at the same time he must treat his hearers like
men worthy of comprehending and applying general
truths; his discourse must be lively, noble, polished,
and fervid, so as to suit such subjects and such minds.
It is thus that classical prose and French prose are

eloquent, and that political dissertations or religious controversies have endured as models of art.

This good taste and philosophy are wanting in the positive mind; it wishes to attain not eternal beauty, but present success. Swift does not address men in general, but certain men. He does not speak to reasoners, but to a party; he does not care to teach a truth, but to make an impression; his aim is not to enlighten that isolated part of man, called his mind, but to stir up the mass of feelings and prejudices which constitute the actual man. Whilst he writes, his public is before his eyes: fat squires, puffed out with port wine and beef, accustomed at the end of their meals to bawl loyally for church and king; gentlemen farmers, bitter against London luxury and the new importance of merchants; clergymen bred on pedantic sermons, and old-established hatred of dissenters and papists. These people have not mind enough to pursue a fine deduction or understand an abstract principle. A writer must calculate the facts they know, the ideas they have received, the interests that move them, and recall only these facts, reason only from these ideas, set in motion only these interests. It is thus Swift speaks, without development, without logical hits, without rhetorical effects, but with extraordinary force and success, in phrases whose accuracy his contemporaries inwardly felt, and which they accepted at once, because they simply told them in a clear form and openly, what they murmured obscurely and to themselves. Such was the power of the *Examiner*, which in one year transformed the opinion of three kingdoms; and particularly of the *Drapier's Letters*, which made a government withdraw one of their measures.

Small change was lacking in Ireland, and the English ministers had given a certain William Wood a patent to coin one hundred and eight thousand pounds of copper money. A commission, of which Newton was a member, verified the pieces made, found them good, and several competent judges still think that the measure was loyal and serviceable to the land. Swift roused the people against it, spoke to them in an intelligible style, and triumphed over common sense and the state.[1]

" Brethren, friends, countrymen, and fellow-subjects, what I intend now to say to you is, next to your duty to God and the care of your salvation, of the greatest concern to you and your children : your bread and clothing, and every common necessary of life depend upon it. Therefore I do most earnestly exhort you as men, as Christians, as parents, and as lovers of your country, to read this paper with the utmost attention, or get it read to you by others ; which that you may do at the less expence, I have ordered the printer to sell it at the lowest rate."[2]

We see popular distrust spring up at a glance ; this is the style which reaches workmen and peasants ; this simplicity, these details, are necessary to penetrate their belief. The author is like a draper, and they trust only men of their own condition. Swift goes on to accuse Wood, declaring that his copper pieces are not worth one-eighth their nominal value. There is no trace of proof : no proofs are required to convince the people ; it is enough to repeat the same accusation

[1] Whatever has been said, I do not think that he wrote the *Drapier's Letters*, whilst thinking the introduction of small copper coin an advantage for Ireland. It was possible, for Swift more than for another, to believe in a ministerial job. He seems to me to have been at bottom an honest man.   [2] *Drapier's Letters*, vii. ; Letter 1, 97.

again and again, to abound in intelligible examples, to strike eye and ear. The imagination once gained, they will go on shouting, convincing themselves by their own cries, and incapable of reasoning. Swift says to his adversaries :

"Your paragraph relates further that Sir Isaac Newton reported an assay taken at the Tower of Wood's metal ; by which it appears that Wood had in all respects performed his contract. His contract ! With whom ? Was it with the Parliament or people of Ireland ? Are not they to be the purchasers ? But they detest, abhor, and reject it as corrupt, fraudulent, mingled with dirt and trash." [1]

And a little further on :

" His first proposal is, that he will be content to coin no more (than forty thousand pounds), unless the *exigencies of the trade require it*, although his patent empowers him to coin a far greater quantity. . . . To which if I were to answer, it should be thus : let Mr. Wood and his crew of founders and tinkers coin on, till there is not an old kettle left in the kingdom ; let them coin old leather, tobacco-pipe clay, or the dirt in the street, and call their trumpery by what name they please from a guinea to a farthing ; we are not under any concern to know how he and his tribe of accomplices think fit to employ themselves. But I hope, and trust, that we are all, to a man, fully determined to have nothing to do with him or his ware." [2]

Swift gets angry and does not answer. In fact, this is the best way to answer ; to move such hearers we must stir up their blood and their passions ; then shop-keepers and farmers will turn up their sleeves, double their fists ; and the good arguments of their opponents will only increase their desire to knock them down.

[1] *Drapier's Letters*, vii.; Letter 2, 114.   [2] *Ibid.* vii.; Letter 2, 115.

Now see how a mass of examples makes a gratuitous assertion probable :

"Your Newsletter says that an assay was made of the coin. How impudent and insupportable is this ! Wood takes care to coin a dozen or two halfpence of good metal, sends them to the Tower, and they are approved ; and these must answer all that he has already coined, or shall coin for the future. It is true, indeed, that a gentleman often sends to my shop for a pattern of stuff; I cut it fairly off, and if he likes it, he comes or sends and compares the pattern with the whole piece, and probably we come to a bargain. But if I were to buy a hundred sheep, and the grazier should bring me one single wether, fat and well fleeced, by way of pattern, and expect the same price round for the whole hundred, without suffering me to see them before he was paid, or giving me good security to restore my money for those that were lean, or shorn, or scabby, I would be none of his customer. I have heard of a man who had a mind to sell his house, and therefore carried a piece of brick in his pocket, which he showed as a pattern to encourage purchasers ; and this is directly the case in point with Mr. Wood's assay." [1]

A burst of laughter follows; butchers and bricklayers were gained over. As a finish, Swift showed them a practical expedient, suited to their understanding and their rank in life :

"The common soldier, when he goes to the market or ale-house, will offer his money; and if it be refused, perhaps he will swagger and hector, and threaten to beat the butcher or alewife, or take the goods by force, and throw them the bad half-pence. In this and the like cases, the shopkeeper or victualler, or any other tradesman, has no more to do than to demand ten times the price of his goods, if it is to be paid in Wood's money ; for example, twenty-pence of that money for a quart of ale, and so

[1] *Drapier's Letters*, vii. ; Letter 2, 114.

in all things else, and never part with his goods till he gets the money."[1]

Public clamour overcame the English Government; they withdrew the money and paid Wood a large indemnity. Such is the merit of Swift's arguments; good tools, trenchant and handy, neither elegant nor bright, but whose value is proved by their effect.

The whole beauty of these pamphlets is in their tone. They have neither the generous fire of Pascal, nor the bewildering gaiety of Beaumarchais, nor the chiselled delicacy of Paul Louis Courier, but an overwhelming air of superiority and a bitter and terrible rancour. Vast passion and pride, like the positive " Drapier's " mind just now described, have given all the blows their force. We should read his *Public Spirit of the Whigs*, against Steele. Page by page Steele is torn to pieces with a calmness and scorn never equalled. Swift approaches regularly, leaving no part untouched, heaping wound on wound, every blow sure, knowing beforehand their reach and depth. Poor Steele, a vain, thoughtless fellow, is in his hands like Gulliver amongst the giants; it is a pity to see a contest so unequal; and this contest is pitiless. Swift crushes him carefully and easily, like an obnoxious animal. The unfortunate man, formerly an officer and a semi-literary man, had made awkward use of constitutional words :

" Upon this rock the author . . . is perpetually splitting, as often as he ventures out beyond the narrow bounds of his literature. He has a confused remembrance of words since he left the university, but has lost half their meaning, and puts them together with no regard, except to their cadence; as I re-

---

[1] *Drapier's Letters*, vii. ; Letter 1, 101.

member, a fellow nailed up maps in a gentleman's closet, some sidelong, others upside down, the better to adjust them to the pannels." [1]

When he judges he is worse than when he proves; witness his *Short Character of Thomas Earl of Wharton.* He pierces him with the formulas of official politeness; only an Englishman is capable of such phlegm and such haughtiness:

"I have had the honour of much conversation with his lordship, and am thoroughly convinced how indifferent he is to applause, and how insensible of reproach. . . . He is without the sense of shame, or glory, as some men are without the sense of smelling; and therefore, a good name to him is no more than a precious ointment would be to these. Whoever, for the sake of others, were to describe the nature of a serpent, a wolf, a crocodile or a fox, must be understood to do it without any personal love or hatred for the animals themselves. In the same manner his excellency is one whom I neither personally love nor hate. I see him at court, at his own house, and sometimes at mine, for I have the honour of his visits; and when these papers are public, it is odds but he will tell me, as he once did upon a like occasion, "that he is damnably mauled," and then, with the easiest transition in the world, ask about the weather, or time of the day; so that I enter on the work with more cheerfulness, because I am sure neither to make him angry, nor any way hurt his reputation; a pitch of happiness and security to which his excellency has arrived, and which no philosopher before him could reach. Thomas, Earl of Wharton, lord-lieutenant of Ireland, by the force of a wonderful constitution, has some years passed his grand climacteric without any visible effects of old age, either on his body or his

---

[1] *The Public Spirit of the Whigs,* iv. 405. See also in the *Examiner* the pamphlet against Marlborough under the name of Crassus, and the comparison between Roman generosity and English meanness.

mind; and in spite of a continual prostitution to those vices which usually wear out both. . . . Whether he walks or whistles, or swears, or talks bawdy, or calls names, he acquits himself in each, beyond a templar of three years' standing. With the same grace, and in the same style, he will rattle his coachman in the midst of the street, where he is governor of the kingdom; and all this is without consequence, because it is in his character, and what everybody expects. . . . The ends he has gained by lying, appear to be more owing to the frequency, than the art of them; his lies being sometimes detected in an hour, often in a day, and always in a week. . . . He swears solemnly he loves and will serve you; and your back is no sooner turned, but he tells those about him, you are a dog and a rascal. He goes constantly to prayers in the forms of his place, and will talk bawdy and blasphemy at the chapel door. He is a presbyterian in politics, and an atheist in religion; but he chooses at present to whore with a papist. In his commerce with mankind, his general rule is, to endeavour to impose on their understandings, for which he has but one receipt, a composition of lies and oaths. . . . He bears the gallantries of his lady with the indifference of a stoick; and thinks them well recompensed, by a return of children to support his family, without the fatigues of being a father. . . . He was never yet known to refuse or keep a promise, as I remember he told a lady, but with an exception to the promise he then made (which was to get her a pension), yet he broke even that, and, I confess, deceived us both. But here I desire to distinguish between a promise and a bargain; for he will be sure to keep the latter, when he has the fairest offer. . . . But here I must desire the reader's pardon, if I cannot digest the following facts in so good a manner as I intended; because it is thought expedient, for some reasons, that the world should be informed of his excellency's merits as soon as possible. . . . As they are, they may serve for hints to any person who may hereafter have a mind to write memoirs of his excellency's life." [1]

[1] Swift's Works, iv. 148.

Throughout this piece Swift's voice has remained calm; not a muscle of his face has moved; we perceive neither smile, flash of the eye, or gesture; he speaks like a statue; but his anger grows by constraint, and burns the more that it shines the less.

This is why his ordinary style is grave irony. It is the weapon of pride, meditation, and force. The man who employs it is self-contained whilst a storm is raging within him; he is too proud to make a show of his passion; he does not take the public into his confidence; he elects to be solitary in his soul; he would be ashamed to confide in any man; he means and knows how to keep absolute possession of himself. Thus collected, he understands better and suffers more; no fit of passion relieves his wrath or draws away his attention; he feels all the points and penetrates to the depths of the opinion which he detests; he multiplies his pain and his knowledge, and spares himself neither wound nor reflection. We must see Swift in this attitude, impassive in appearance, but with stiffening muscles, a heart scorched with hatred, writing with a terrible smile such pamphlets as this:

"It may perhaps be neither safe nor prudent, to argue against the abolishing of Christianity, at a juncture, when all parties appear so unanimously determined upon the point. . . . However, I know not how, whether from the affectation of singularity, or the perverseness of human nature, but so it unhappily falls out, that I cannot be entirely of this opinion. Nay, though I were sure an order were issued for my immediate prosecution by the attorney-general, I should still confess, that in the present posture of our affairs, at home or abroad, I do not yet see the absolute necessity of extirpating the Christian religion from among us. This perhaps may appear too great a paradox, even for our wise and paradoxical age to endure; therefore I shall handle it with all tenderness, and with the utmost deference to that great and profound majority, which is of another sentiment. . . . I hope no reader imagines me so weak to stand up in the defence of real Christianity, such as used, in primitive times (if we may believe the authors of those ages), to have an influence upon men's belief and actions; to offer at the restoring of that, would indeed be a wild project; it would be to dig up foundations; to destroy at one blow all the wit, and half the learning of the kingdom. . . . Every candid reader will easily understand my discourse to be intended only in defence of nominal Christianity; the other having been for some time wholly laid aside by general consent, as utterly inconsistent with our present schemes of wealth and power." [1]

Let us then examine the advantages which this abolition of the title and name of Christian might have:

" It is likewise urged, that there are, by computation, in this kingdom above ten thousand parsons, whose revenues, added to those of my lords the bishops, would suffice to maintain at least two hundred young gentlemen of wit and pleasure, and free-thinking, enemies to priestcraft, narrow principles, pedantry, and prejudices, who might be an ornament to the court and town." [2]

" It is likewise proposed as a great advantage to the public that if we once discard the system of the gospel, all religion will of course be banished for ever; and consequently along with it, those grievous prejudices of education, which under the names of virtue, conscience, honour, justice, and the like, are so apt to disturb the peace of human minds, and the notions whereof are so hard to be eradicated, by right reason, or free-thinking." [3]

---

[1] *An Argument to prove that the Abolishing of Christianity might be attended with some Inconveniences*, viii. 184. The Whigs were herein attacked as the friends of freethinkers.

[2] *Ibid.* 188.   [3] *Ibid.* 192.

Then he concludes by doubling the insult :

"I am very sensible how much the gentlemen of wit and pleasure are apt to murmur, and 'be choked at the sight of so many daggled-tail parsons, who happen to fall in their way, and offend their eyes ; but at the same time, these wise reformers do not consider what an advantage and felicity it is for great wits to be always provided with objects of scorn and contempt, in order to exercise and improve their talents, and divert their spleen from falling on each other, or on themselves ; especially when all this may be done, without the least imaginable danger to their persons. And to urge another argument of a parallel nature : if Christianity were once abolished, how could the free-thinkers, the strong reasoners, and the men of profound learning, be able to find another subject, so calculated in all points whereon to display their abilities ? what wonderful productions of wit should we be deprived of, from those, whose genius, by continual practice, has been wholly turned upon raillery and invectives, against religion, and would, therefore, never be able to shine or distinguish themselves upon any other subject ! we are daily complaining of the great decline of wit among us, and would we take away the greatest, perhaps the only topic we have left ?" [1]

"I do very much apprehend, that in six months time after the act is passed for the extirpation of the gospel, the Bank and East India stock may fall at least one per cent. And since that is fifty times more, than ever the wisdom of our age thought fit to venture, for the preservation of Christianity, there is no reason we should be at so great a loss, merely for the sake of destroying it." [2]

Swift is only a combatant, I admit ; but when we glance at this common sense and this pride, this empire over the passions of others, and this empire over

---

[1] *An Argument*, etc., viii. 196.
[2] *Ibid.* viii. 200 ; final words of the *Argument*.

himself; this force and this employment of hatred, we judge that there have rarely been such combatants. He is a pamphleteer as Hannibal was a *condottiere*.

IV.

On the night after the battle we usually unbend; we sport, we make fun, we talk in prose and verse; but with Swift this night is a continuation of the day, and the mind which leaves its trace in matters of business leaves also its trace in amusements.

What is gayer than Voltaire's *soirées*? He rails; but do we find any murderous intention in his railleries? He gets angry; but do we perceive a malignant or evil character in his passions? In him all is amiable. In an instant, through the necessity of action, he strikes, caresses, changes a hundred times his tone, his face, with abrupt movements, impetuous sallies, sometimes as a child, always as a man of the world, of taste and conversation. He wishes to entertain us; he conducts us at once through a thousand ideas, without effort, to amuse himself, to amuse us. What an agreeable host is this Voltaire, who desires to please and who knows how to please, who only dreads ennui, who does not distrust us, who is not constrained, who is always himself, who is brimful of ideas, naturalness, liveliness! If we were with him, and he rallied us, we should not be angry; we should adopt his style, we should laugh at ourselves, we should feel that he only wished to pass an agreeable hour, that he was not angry with us, that he treated us as equals and guests, that he broke out into pleasantries as a winter fire into sparks, and that he was none the less pleasant, wholesome, amusing.

Heaven grant that Swift may never jest at our

expense. The positive mind is too solid and too cold
to be gay and amiable. When such a mind takes to
ridicule, it does not sport with it superficially, but studies
it, goes into it gravely, masters it, knows all its subdivisions and its proofs. This profound knowledge can
only produce a withering pleasantry. Swift's, at bottom,
is but a *reductio ad absurdum*, altogether scientific. For
instance, *The art of Political Lying*[1] is a didactic treatise,
whose plan might serve for a model. "In the first
chapter of this excellent treatise he (the author) reasons
philosophically concerning the nature of the soul of
man, and those qualities which render it susceptible
of lies. He supposes the soul to be of the nature of
a plano-cylindrical speculum, or looking-glass. . . .
The plain side represents objects just as they are;
and the cylindrical side, by the rules of catoptrics, must
needs represent true objects false, and false objects true.
In his second chapter he treats of the nature of political
lying; in the third of the lawfulness of political lying.
The fourth chapter is wholly employed in this question,
'Whether the right of coinage of political lies be wholly
in the government.'" Again, nothing could be stranger,
more worthy of an archæological society, than the
argument in which he proves that a humorous piece of
Pope's[2] is an insidious pamphlet against the religion
of the state. His *Art of Sinking in Poetry*[3] has all
the appearance of good rhetoric; the principles are
laid down, the divisions justified; the examples chosen
with extraordinary precision and method; it is perfect
reason employed in the service of folly.

[1] vi. 415.—Arbuthnot is said to have written the whole or at least
part of it.—TR.   [2] *The Rape of the Lock.*
[3] xiii. 17.—Pope, Arbuthnot, and Swift wrote it. together.

His passions, like his mind, were too strong. If he wishes to scratch, he tears; his pleasantry is gloomy; by way of a joke, he drags his reader through all the disgusting details of sickness and death. Partridge, formerly a shoemaker, had turned astrologer; Swift, imperturbably cool, assumes an astrologer's title, writes maxims on the duties of the profession, and to inspire confidence, begins to predict:

"My first prediction is but a trifle; yet I will mention it to show how ignorant those sottish pretenders to astrology are in their own concerns: it relates to Partridge the almanack-maker; I have consulted the star of his nativity by my own rules, and find he will infallibly die upon the 29th of March next, about eleven at night, of a raging fever; therefore I advise him to consider of it, and settle his affairs in time."[1]

The 29th of March being past, he relates how the undertaker came to hang Partridge's rooms "in close mourning;" then Ned, the sexton, asking "whether the grave is to be plain or bricked;" then Mr. White, the carpenter, to screw down the coffin; then the stone-cutter with his monument. Lastly, a successor comes and sets up in the neighbourhood, saying in his printed directions, "that he lives in the house of the late ingenious Mr. John Partridge, an eminent practitioner in leather, physic, and astrology."[2] We can tell beforehand the protestations of poor Partridge. Swift in his reply proves that he is dead, and is astonished at his hard words:

[1] *Predictions for the Year* 1708 *by Isaac Bickerstaff*, ix. 156.
[2] These quotations are taken from a humorous pamphlet, *Squire Bickerstaff Detected*, written by Dr. Yalden. See Swift's Works, ix. 176.—TR.

" To call a man a fool and villain, an impudent fellow, only
for differing from him in a point merely speculative, is, in my
humble opinion, a very improper style for a person of his education. . . . I will appeal to Mr. Partridge himself, whether it
be probable I could have been so indiscreet, to begin my predictions, with the only falsehood that ever was pretended to be in
them? and this in an affair at home, where I had so many
opportunities to be exact." [1]

Mr. Partridge is mistaken, or deceives the public, or
would cheat his heirs.

This gloomy pleasantry becomes elsewhere still more
gloomy. Swift pretends that his enemy, the bookseller
Curll, has just been poisoned, and relates his agony. A
house-surgeon of a hospital would not write a more repulsive diary more coldly. The details, worked out
with the completeness of a Hogarth, are admirably
minute, but disgusting. We laugh, or rather we grin,
as before the vagaries of a madman in an asylum, but
in reality we feel sick at heart. Swift in his gaiety is
always tragical; nothing unbends him; even when he
serves, he pains you. In his *Journal to Stella* there is a
sort of imperious austerity; his condescension is that of
a master to a child. The charm and happiness of a
young girl of sixteen cannot soften him. She has just
married him, and he tells her that love is a " ridiculous
passion, which has no being but in playbooks and
romances;" then he adds, with perfect brutality:

" I never yet knew a tolerable woman to be fond of her sex;
. . . your sex employ more thought, memory, and application
to be fools than would serve to make them wise and useful. . . .
When I reflect on this, I cannot conceive you to be human
creatures, but a sort of species hardly a degree above a monkey;

[1] *A Vindication of Isaac Bickerstaff*, ix. 186.

who has more diverting tricks than any of you, is an animal less mischievous and expensive, might in time be a tolerable critic in velvet and brocade, and, for aught I know, would equally become them." [1]

Will poetry calm such a mind? Here, as elsewhere, he is most unfortunate. He is excluded from great transports of imagination, as well as from the lively digressions of conversation. He can attain neither the sublime nor the agréeable; he has neither the artist's rapture, nor the entertainment of the man of the world. Two similar sounds at the end of two equal lines have always consoled the greatest troubles: the old muse, after three thousand years, is a young and divine nurse; and her song lulls the sickly nations whom she still visits, as well as the young, flourishing races amongst whom she has appeared. The involuntary music, in which thought wraps itself, hides ugliness and unveils beauty. Feverish man, after the labours of the evening and the anguish of the night, sees at morning the beaming whiteness of the opening heaven; he gets rid of himself, and the joy of nature from all sides enters with oblivion into his heart. If misery pursues him, the poetic afflatus, unable to wipe it out, transforms it; it becomes ennobled, he loves it, and thenceforth he bears it; for the only thing to which he cannot resign himself is littleness. Neither Faust nor Manfred have exhausted human grief; they drank from the cruel cup a generous wine, they did not reach the dregs. They enjoyed themselves, and nature; they tasted the greatness which was in them, and the beauty of creation; they pressed with their bruised hands all the thorns with which

---

[1] *Letter to a very young Lady on her marriage*, ix. 420-422.

necessity has made our way thorny, but they saw them blossom with roses, fostered by the purest of their noble blood. There is nothing of the sort in Swift : what is wanting most in his verses is poetry. The positive mind can neither love nor understand it ; it sees therein only a kind of mechanism or a fashion, and employs it only for vanity and conventionality. When in his youth Swift attempted Pindaric odes, he failed lamentably. I cannot remember a line of his which indicates a genuine sentiment of nature : he saw in the forests only logs of wood, and in the fields only sacks of corn. He employed mythology, as we put on a wig, ill-timed, wearily and scornfully. His best piece, *Cadenus and Vanessa*,[1] is a poor, threadbare allegory. To praise Vanessa, he supposes that the nymphs and shepherds pleaded before Venus, the first against men, the second against women ; and that Venus, wishing to end the debates, made in Vanessa a model of perfection. What can such a conception furnish but flat apostrophes and pedantic comparisons ? Swift, who elsewhere gives a recipe for an epic poem, is here the first to make use of it. And even his rude prosaic freaks tear this Greek frippery at every turn. He puts a legal procedure into heaven ; he makes Venus use all kinds of technical terms. He introduces witnesses, " questions on the fact, bill with costs dismiss'd," etc. They talk so loud that the goddess fears to lose her influence, to be driven from Olympus, or else

> " Shut out from heaven and earth,
> Fly to the sea, my place of birth :
> There live with daggled mermaids pent,
> And keep on fish perpetual Lent."[2]

[1] *Cadenus and Vanessa*, xiv. 441.   [2] *Ibid.* 443.

When he relates the touching history of *Baucis and Philemon*,[1] he degrades it by a travesty. He does not love the ancient nobleness and beauty; the two gods become in his hands begging friars, Philemon and Baucis Kentish peasants. For a recompense, their house becomes a church, and Philemon a parson :

> " His talk was now of tithes and dues ;
> He smoked his pipe and read the news. . . .
> Against dissenters would repine,
> And stood up firm for ' right divine.' "

Wit luxuriates, incisive, in little compact verses, vigorously coined, of extreme conciseness, facility, precision ; but compared to La Fontaine, it is wine turned into vinegar. Even when he comes to the charming Vanessa, his vein is still the same : to praise her childhood, he puts her name first on the list, as a little model girl, just like a schoolmaster :

> " And all their conduct would be tried
> By her, as an unerring guide :
> Offending daughters oft would hear
> Vanessa's praise rung in their ear :
> Miss Betty, when she does a fault,
> Lets fall her knife, or spills the salt,
> Will thus be by her mother chid :
> ' 'Tis what Vanessa never did ! ' " [2]

A strange way of admiring Vanessa, and of proving his admiration for her. He calls her a nymph, and treats her like a school-girl ! Cadenus " now could praise, esteem, approve, but understood not what was love !" Nothing could be truer, and Stella felt it, like others. The verses which he writes every year on her birthday,

[1] *Baucis and Philemon*, xiv. 83.
[2] *Cadenus and Vanessa*, xiv. 448.

are a pedagogue's censures and praises; if he gives her any good marks, it is with restrictions. Once he inflicts on her a little sermon on want of patience; again, by way of compliment, he concocts this delicate warning:

> " Stella, this day is thirty-four
> (We shan't dispute a year or more).
> However, Stella, be not troubled,
> Although thy size and years are doubled
> Since first I saw thee at sixteen,
> The brightest virgin on the green;
> So little is thy form declin'd,
> Made up so largely in thy mind."

And he insists with exquisite taste:

> " O, would it please the gods to split
> Thy beauty, size, and years, and wit!
> No age could furnish out a pair
> Of nymphs so graceful, wise, and fair." [1]

Decidedly this man is an artisan, strong of arm, terrible at his work and in a fray, but narrow of soul, treating a woman as if she were a log of wood. Rhyme and rhythm are only business-like tools, which have served him to press and launch his thought; he has put nothing but prose into them: poetry was too fine to be grasped by those coarse hands.

But in prosaic subjects, what truth and force! How this masculine nakedness crushes the affected elegance and artificial poetry of Addison and Pope! There are no epithets; he leaves his thought as he conceived it, valuing it for and by itself, needing neither ornaments, nor preparation, nor extension; above the tricks of the profession, scholastic conventionalisms, the vanity of the

---

[1] *Verses on Stella's Birthday,* March 13, 1718-19, xiv. 469.

rhymester, the difficulties of the art; master of his subject and of himself. This simplicity and naturalness astonish us in verse. Here, as elsewhere, his originality is entire, and his genius creative; he surpasses his classical and timid age; he tyrannises over form, breaks it, dare utter anything, spares himself no strong word. Acknowledge the greatness of this invention and audacity; he alone is a superior being, who finds everything and copies nothing. What a biting comicality in the *Grand Question Debated !* He has to represent the entrance of a captain into a castle, his airs, his insolence, his folly, and the admiration caused by these qualities! The lady serves him first; the servants stare at him :

> " The parsons for envy are ready to burst ;
>   The servants amazed are scarce ever able
>   To keep off their eyes, as they wait at the table ;
>   And Molly and I have thrust in our nose
>   To peep at the captain in all his fine clo'es.
>   Dear madam, be sure he's a fine spoken man,
>   Do but hear on the clergy how glib his tongue ran :
> ' And madam,' says he, ' if such dinners you give,
>   You'll ne'er want for parsons as long as you live.
>   I ne'er knew a parson without a good nose ;
>   But the devil's as welcome wherever he goes ;
>   G—d—n me ! they bid us reform and repent,
>   But, z—s ! by their looks they never keep Lent :
>   Mister curate, for all your grave looks, I'm afraid
>   You cast a sheep's eye on her ladyship's maid :
>   I wish she would lend you her pretty white hand
>   In mending your cassock, and smoothing your band '
>   (For the dean was so shabby, and look'd like a ninny,
>   That the captain suppos'd he was curate to Jinny).
> ' Whenever you see a cassock and gown,
>   A hundred to one but it covers a clown.

> Observe how a parson comes into a room,
> G—d—n me, he hobbles as bad as my groom ;
> A *scholard,* when just from his college broke loose,
> Can hardly tell how to cry bo to a goose ;
> Your *Noveds* and *Bluturks* and *Omurs,*[1] and stuff,
> By G—, they don't signify this pinch of snuff :
> To give a young gentleman right education,
> The army's the only good school in the nation." [2]

This has been *seen,* and herein lies the beauty of
Swift's verses : they are personal ; they are not developed themes, but impressions felt and observations
collected. Read *The Journal of a Modern Lady, The
Furniture of a Woman's Mind,* and other pieces by the
dozen : they are dialogues transcribed or opinions put
on paper after quitting a drawing-room. *The Progress
of Marriage* represents a dean of fifty-two married
to a young worldly coquette ; do we not see in this
title alone all the fears of the bachelor of St. Patrick's ?
What diary is more familiar and more pungent than
his verses on his own death ?

> " ' He hardly breathes.' ' The Dean is dead.'
> Before the passing bell begun,
> The news through half the town has run ;
> ' O may we all for death prepare !
> What has he left ? and who's his heir ?'
> ' I know no more than what the news is ;
> 'Tis all bequeathed to public uses.'
> ' To public uses ! there's a whim !
> What had the public done for him ?
> Mere envy, avarice, and pride :
> He gave it all—but first he died.

> Ovids, Plutarchs, Homers.
> [2] *The Grand Question Debated,* xv. 153.

And had the Dean in all the nation
No worthy friend, no poor relation?
So ready to do strangers good,
Forgetting his own flesh and blood!' . . .
Poor Pope will grieve a month, and Gay
A week, and Arbuthnot a day. . . .
My female friends, whose tender hearts
Have better learn'd to act their parts,
Receive the news in doleful dumps:
The Dean is dead (pray what is trumps?)
Then, Lord, have mercy on his soul!
(Ladies, I'll venture for the vole.)
Six Deans, they say, must bear the pall.
(I wish I knew what king to call.)
Madam, your husband will attend
The funeral of so good a friend?
No, madam, 'tis a shocking sight,
And he's engaged to-morrow night:
My Lady Club will take it ill,
If he should fail her at quadrille.
He lov'd the Dean—(I lead a heart),
But dearest friends they say must part.
His time was come: he ran his race;
We hope he's in a better place." [1]

Such is the inventory of human friendships. All
poetry exalts the mind, but this depresses it; instead
of concealing reality, it unveils it; instead of creating
illusions, it removes them. When he wishes to give a
description of the morning,[2] he shows us the street-
sweepers, the "watchful bailiffs," and imitates the
different street cries. When he wishes to paint the
rain,[3] he describes "filth of all hues and odours," the

---

[1] *On the Death of Dr. Swift*, xiv. 331.   [2] Swift's Works, xiv. 93.
[3] *A Description of a City Shower*, xiv. 94.

"swelling kennels," the "dead cats," "turnip-tops," "stinking sprats," which "come tumbling down the flood." His long verses whirl all this filth in their eddies. We smile to see poetry degraded to this use; we seem to be at a masquerade; it is a queen travestied into a rough country girl. We stop, we look on, with the sort of pleasure we feel in drinking a bitter draught. Truth is always good to know, and in the splendid piece which artists show us we need a manager to tell us the number of the hired applauders and of the supernumeraries. It would be well if he only drew up such a list! Numbers look ugly, but they only affect the mind; other things, the oil of the lamps, the odours of the side scenes, all that we cannot name, remains to be told. I cannot do more than hint at the length to which Swift carries us; but this I must do, for these extremes are the supreme effort of his despair and his genius: we must touch upon them in order to measure and know him. He drags poetry not only through the mud, but into the filth; he rolls in it like a raging madman, he enthrones himself in it, and bespatters all passers-by. Compared with his, all foul words are decent and agreeable. In Aretin and Brantôme, in La Fontaine and Voltaire, there is a soupçon of pleasure. With the first, unchecked sensuality, with the others, malicious gaiety, are excuses; we are scandalised, not disgusted; we do not like to see in a man a bull's fury or an ape's buffoonery; but the bull is so eager and strong, the ape so funny and smart, that we end by looking on or being amused. Then, again, however coarse their pictures may be, they speak of the accompaniments of love: Swift touches only upon the results of digestion, and that merely with disgust and revenge; he pours them out with horror and sneering at the wretches whom he describes. He must not in this be compared to Rabelais; that good giant, that drunken doctor, rolls himself joyously about on his dung-hill, thinking no evil; the dunghill is warm, conveni-ent, a fine place to philosophise and sleep off one's wine. Raised to this enormity, and enjoyed with this heedless-ness, the bodily functions become poetical. When the casks are emptied down the giant's throat, and the viands are gorged, we sympathise with so much bodily comfort; in the heavings of this colossal belly and the laughter of this homeric mouth, we see as through a mist, the relics of bacchanal religions, the fecundity, the monstrous joy of nature; these are the splendours and disorders of its first births. The cruel positive mind, on the contrary, clings only to vileness; it will only see what is behind things; armed with sorrow and boldness, it spares no ignoble detail, no obscene word. Swift enters the dressing-room,[1] relates the disenchant-ments of love,[2] dishonours it by a medley of drugs and physic,[3] describes the cosmetics and a great many more things.[4] He takes his evening walk by solitary walls,[5] and in these pitiable pryings has his microscope ever in his hand. Judge what he sees and suffers; this is his ideal beauty and his jesting conversation, and we may fancy that he has for philosophy, as for poetry and politics, execration and disgust.

---

[1] *The Lady's Dressing-room.*   [2] *Strephon and Chloe.*
[3] *A Love Poem from a Physician.*   [4] *The Progress of Beauty.*
[5] *The Problem,* and *The Examination of Certain Abuses.*

V.

Swift wrote the *Tale of a Tub* at Sir William Temple's, amidst all kind of reading, as an abstract of truth and science. Hence this tale is the satire of all science and all truth.

Of religion first. He seems here to defend the Church of England; but what church and what creed are not involved in his attack? To enliven his subject, he profanes and reduces questions of dogma to a question of clothes. A father had three sons, Peter, Martin, and Jack; he left each of them a coat at his death,[1] warning them to wear it clean and brush it often The three brothers obeyed for some time and travelled sensibly, slaying " a reasonable quantity of giants and dragons." [2] Unfortunately, having come up to town, they adopted its manners, fell in love with several fashionable ladies, the Duchess d'Argent, Madame de Grands Titres, and the Countess d'Orgueil,[3] and to gain their favours, began to live as gallants, taking snuff, swearing, rhyming, and contracting debts, keeping horses, fighting duels, whoring, killing bailiffs. A sect was established who

"Held the universe to be a large suit of clothes, which invests everything : that the earth is invested by the air ; the air is invested by the stars, and the stars are invested by the primum mobile. . . . What is that which some call land, but a fine coat faced with green ? or the sea, but a waistcoat of water-tabby ? . . . You will find how curious journeyman Nature has been, to trim up the vegetable beaux : observe how sparkish a periwig adorns the head of a beech, and what a fine doublet of

[1] Christian truth.

[2] Persecutions and contests of the primitive church.

[3] Covetousness, ambition, and pride ; the three vices that the ancient fathers inveighed against.

white sattin is worn by the birch. . . . Is not religion a cloak ;
honesty a pair of shoes worn out in the dirt ; self-love a surtout ;
vanity a shirt ; and conscience a pair of breeches ; which,
though a cover for lewdness as well as nastiness, is easily slipt
down for the service of both ? . . . If certain ermines and furs
be placed in a certain position, we style them a judge ; and so
an apt conjunction of lawn and black sattin, we entitle a
bishop. " [1]

Others held also " that the soul was the outward, and
the body the inward clothing. . . . This last they
proved by Scripture, because in them we live, and
move, and have our being." Thus our three brothers,
having only very simple clothes, were embarrassed.
For instance, the fashion at this time was for shoulder-
knots,[2] and their father's will expressly forbade them to
" add to or diminish from their coats one thread ;

" In this unhappy case they went immediately to consult
their father's will, read it over and over, but not a word of the
shoulder-knot. . . . After much thought, one of the brothers,
who happened to be more book-learned than the other two, said,
he had found an expedient. ' It is true,' said he, ' there is
nothing in this will, *totidem verbis*, making mention of Shoulder-
Knots ; but I dare conjecture, we may find them inclusive, or
totidem syllabis.' This distinction was immediately approved
by all ; and so they fell again to examine ;[3] but their evil star
had so directed the matter, that the first syllable was not to be
found in the whole writings. Upon which disappointment, he,
who found the former evasion, took heart and said : Brothers,
there are yet hopes, for though we cannot find them *totidem
verbis*, nor *totidem syllabis*, I dare engage we shall make them
out *tertio modo* or *totidem litteris.* " This discovery was also
highly commended ; upon which they fell once more to the

[1] *A Tale of a Tub*, xi. sec. 2, 79, 81.   [2] Innovations.   [3] The Will.

scrutiny, and picked out s, h, o, u, l, d, e, r; when the same
planet, enemy to their repose, had wonderfully contrived that a
k was not to be found. Here was a weighty difficulty ; but
the distinguishing brother . . . now his hand was in, proved by
a very good argument, that k was a modern illegitimate letter,
unknown to the learned ages, nor anywhere to be found _ in
ancient manuscripts. . . . Upon this all farther difficulty
vanished ; shoulder-knots were made clearly out to be *jure
paterno*, and our three gentlemen swaggered with as large and
flaunting ones as the best. " [1]

Other interpretations admitted gold lace, and a codicil
authorised flame coloured satin linings : [2]

" Next winter a player, hired for the purpose by the corporation
of fringemakers, acted his part in a new comedy, all covered with
silver fringe, and according to the laudable custom gave rise to
that fashion. Upon which the brothers consulting their father's
will, to their great astonishment found these words : " Item, I
charge and command my said three sons to wear no sort of silver-
fringe upon or about their said coats," etc. . . . However, after
some pause, the brother so often mentioned for his erudition, who
was well skilled in criticisms, had found in a certain author,
which he said should be nameless, that the same word, which
in the will is called fringe, does also signify a broomstick : and
doubtless ought to have the same interpretation in this paragraph. This another of the brothers disliked, because of that
epithet silver, which could not, he humbly conceived, in propriety of speech, be reasonably applied to a broomstick ; but
it was replied upon him that this epithet was understood in a
mythological and allegorical sense. However, he objected again,
why their father should forbid them to wear a broomstick on
their coats, a caution that seemed unnatural and impertinent ;
upon which he was taken up short, as one who spoke irreverently
of a mystery, which doubtless was very useful and significant, but
ought not to be over-curiously pried into, or nicely reasoned upon." [3]

[1] *A Tale of a Tub*, xi. sec. 2, 83.   [2] Purgatory.
[3] *A Tale of a Tub*, 88.

In the end the scholastic brother grew weary of searching further " evasions," locked up the old will in a strong box,[1] authorised by tradition the fashions which became him, and having contrived to be left a legacy, styled himself My Lord Peter. His brothers, treated like servants, were discarded from his house ; they reopened the will of their father, and began to understand it. Martin (Luther), to reduce his clothes to the primitive simplicity, brought off a large handful of points, stripped away ten dozen yards of fringe, rid his coat of a huge quantity of gold-lace, but kept a few embroideries, which could not " be got away without damaging the cloth." Jack (Calvin) tore off all in his enthusiasm, and was found in tatters, besides being envious of Martin, and half mad.   He then joined the Æolists, or inspired admirers of the wind, who pretend that the spirit, or breath, or wind, is heavenly, and contains all knowledge :

" First, it is generally affirmed or confessed that learning puffeth men up ; and secondly they proved it by the following syllogism : words are but wind ; and learning is nothing but words ; ergo learning is nothing but wind. . . . This, when blown up to its perfection, ought not to be covetously hoarded up, stifled, or hid under a bushel, but freely communicated to mankind.   Upon these reasons, and others of equal weight, the wise Æolists affirm the gift of belching to be the noblest act of a rational creature. . . . At certain seasons of the year, you might behold the priests among them in vast number . . . linked together in a circular chain, with every man a pair of bellows applied to his neighbour's breech, by which they blew each other to the shape and size of a tun ; and for that reason with great propriety of speech, did usually call their bodies their vessels." [2]

---

[1] The prohibition of the laity's reading the Scriptures.
[2] *A Tale of a Tub*, sec. 8, 146.

After this explanation of theology, religious quarrels, and mystical inspirations, what is left, even of the Anglican Church ? She is a sensible, useful, political cloak, but what else ? Like a stiff brush used with too strong a hand, the buffoonery has carried away the cloth as well as the stain. Swift has put out a fire, I allow ; but, like Gulliver at Lilliput, the people saved by him must hold their nose, to admire the right application of the liquid, and the energy of the engine that saves them.

Religion being drowned, Swift turns against science ; for the digressions with which he interrupts his story to imitate and mock the modern sages are most closely connected with his tale. The book opens with introductions, prefaces, dedications, and other appendices generally employed to swell books—violent caricatures heaped up against the vanity and prolixity of authors. He professes himself one of them, and announces their discoveries. Admirable discoveries ! The first of their commentaries will be on

"*Tom Thumb*, whose author was a Pythagorean philosopher. This dark treatise contains the whole scheme of the Metempsychosis, deducing the progress of the soul through all her stages. *Whittington and his Cat* is the work of that mysterious rabbi Jehuda Hannasi, containing a defence of the gemara of the Jerusalem misna, and its just preference to that of Babylon, contrary to the vulgar opinion.[1] "

He himself announces that he is going to publish " A Panegyrical Essay upon the Number Three ; a General History of Ears ; a Modest Defence of the Proceedings of the Rabble in all Ages ; an Essay on the Art of Canting, philosophically, physically, and

[1] *A Tale of a Tub*, Introduction, 72.

musically considered;" and he engages his readers
to try by their entreaties to get from him these treatises,
which will change the appearance of the world.   Then,
turning against the philosophers and the critics, sifters
of texts, he proves to them, according to their own
fashion, that the ancients mentioned them.   Can we
find anywhere a more biting parody on forced interpretations :

" The types are so apposite and the applications so necessary
and natural, that it is not easy to conceive how any reader of a
modern eye or taste could overlook them. . . . `For first;
Pausanias is of opinion, that the perfection of writing correct
was entirely owing to the institution of critics ; and, that he can
possibly mean no other than the true critic, is, I think, manifest
enough from the following description. He says, they were a race of
men, who delighted to nibble at the superfluities and excrescences
of books ; which the learned at length observing, took warning,
of their own accord, to lop the luxuriant, the rotten, the dead,
the sapless, and the overgrown branches from their works.
But now, all this he cunningly shades under the following allegory ; that the Nauplians in Argos learned the art of pruning
their vines, by observing that when an ASS had browsed upon
one of them, it thrived the better and bore fairer fruits.
But Herodotus, holding the very same hieroglyph, speaks much
plainer, and almost in *terminis*.   He has been so bold as to tax
the true critics of ignorance and malice ; telling us openly, for I
think nothing can be plainer, that in the western part of Libya
there were ASSES with horns."[1]

Then follow a multitude of pitiless sarcasms.   Swift
has the genius of insult; he is an inventor of irony,
as Shakspeare of poetry ; and as beseems an extreme
force, he goes to extremes in his thought and art.

---

[1] *A Tale of a Tub,* sec. 3 ; *A Digression concerning Critics,* 97.

He lashes reason after science, and leaves nothing
of the whole human mind. With a medical seriousness he establishes that vapours are exhaled from
the whole body, which, " getting possession of the brain,"
leave it healthy if they are not abundant, but excite it
if they are; that in the first case they make peaceful
individuals, in the second great politicians, founders of
religions, and deep philosophers, that is, madmen, so that
madness is the source of all human genius and all the
institutions of the universe. This is why it is very
wrong to keep men shut up in Bedlam, and a commission appointed to examine them would find in this
academy many imprisoned geniuses "which might
produce admirable instruments for the several offices
in a state ecclesiastical, civil, and military."

"Is any student tearing his straw in piece-meal, swearing
and blaspheming, biting his grate, foaming at the mouth ? . . .
let the right worshipful commissioners of inspection give him a
regiment of dragoons, and send him into Flanders among the
rest. . . . You will find a third gravely taking the dimensions
of his kennel; a person of foresight and insight, though kept
quite in the dark. . . . He walks duly in one pace. . . . talks
much of hard times and taxes and the whore of Babylon ; bars
up the wooden window of his cell constantly at eight o'clock,
dreams of fire. . . . Now what a figure would all those acquire-
ments amount to if the owner were sent into the city among his
brethren ? . . . Now is it not amazing to think the society of
Warwick-lane should have no more concern for the recovery of so
useful a member ? . . . I shall not descend so minutely, as to
insist upon the vast number of beaux, fiddlers, poets, and politicians that the world might recover by such a reformation. . . .
Even I myself, the author of these momentous truths, am a person
whose imaginations are hard-mouthed, and exceedingly disposed
to run away with his reason, which I have observed, from long

experience, to be a very light rider, and easily shaken off; upon which account my friends will never trust me alone, without a solemn promise to vent my speculations in this, or the like manner, for the universal benefit of mankind."[1]

What a wretched man is he who knows himself and mocks himself! What madman's laughter, and what a sob in this hoarse gaiety! What remains for him but to slaughter the remainder of human invention? Who does not see here the despair from which sprang the academy of Lagado? Is there not here a foretaste of madness in this intense meditation of absurdity? His mathematician, who, to teach geometry, makes his pupils swallow wafers on which he writes his theorems; his moralist, who, to reconcile political parties, proposes to saw off the occiput and brain of each "opposite party-man," and "to let the occiputs thus cut off be interchanged;" his economist again, who tries "to reduce human excrement to its original food." Swift is akin to these, and is the most wretched of all, because he nourishes his mind, like them, on filth and folly, and because he possesses what they have not, knowledge and disgust.

It is sad to exhibit human folly, it is sadder to exhibit human perversity: the heart is more a part of ourselves than reason: we suffer less in seeing extravagance and folly than wickedness or baseness, and I find Swift more agreeable in his *Tale of a Tub* than in *Gulliver*.

All his talent and all his passions are assembled in this book; the positive mind has impressed upon it its form and force. There is nothing agreeable in the fiction or the style. It is the diary of an ordinary man, a surgeon, then a captain, who describes coolly

[1] *A Tale of a Tub; A Digression concerning Madness*, sec. 11, 167.

and sensibly the events and objects which he has just seen, but who has no feeling for the beautiful, no appearance of admiration or passion, no delivery. Sir Joseph Banks and Captain Cook relate thus. Swift only seeks the natural, and he attains it. His art consists in taking an absurd supposition, and deducing seriously the effects which it produces. It is the logical and technical mind of a mechanician, who, imagining the decrease or increase in a wheelwork, perceives the result of the changes, and writes down the record. His whole pleasure is in seeing these results clearly, and by a solid reasoning. He marks the dimensions, and so forth, like a good engineer and a statistician, omitting no trivial and positive detail, explaining cookery, stabling, politics : in this he has no equal but De Foe. The loadstone machine which sustains the flying island, the entrance of Gulliver into Lilliput, and the inventory of his property, his arrival and maintenance among the Yahoos, carry us with them ; no mind knew better the ordinary laws of nature and human life ; no mind shut itself up more strictly in this knowledge ; none was ever more exact or more limited.

But what a vehemence underneath this aridity ! How ridiculous our interests and passions seem, degraded to the littleness of Lilliput, or compared to the vastness of Brobdingnag ? What is beauty, when the handsomest body, seen with piercing eyes, seems horrible ? What is our power, when an insect, king of an ant-hill, can be called, like our princes, " sublime majesty, delight and terror of the universe ?" What is our homage worth, when a pigmy " is taller, by almost the breadth of a nail, than any of his court, which alone is enough to strike an awe into his beholders ?" Three-fourths of our sentiment are follies, and the weakness of our organs is the only cause of our veneration or love.

Society repels us still more than man. At Laputa, at Lilliput, amongst the horses and giants, Swift rages against it, and is never tired of abusing and reviling it. In his eyes, " ignorance, idleness, and vice are the proper ingredients for qualifying a legislator; laws are best explained, interpreted, and applied by those whose interest and abilities lie in perverting, confounding, and eluding them."[1] A noble is a wretch, corrupted body and 'soul, " combining in himself all the diseases and vices transmitted by ten generations of rakes and rascals. A lawyer is a hired liar, wont by twenty years of roguery to pervert the truth if he is an advocate, and to sell it if he is a judge. A minister of state is a go-between, who, having disposed of his wife," or brawled for the public good, is master of all offices ; and who, in order better to rob the money of the nation, buys members of the House of Commons with the same money. A King is a practiser of all the vices, unable to employ or love an honest man, persuaded that " the royal throne could not be supported without corruption, because that positive, confident, restive temper, which virtue infused into a man, was a perpetual clog to public business."[2] At Lilliput the king chooses as his ministers those who dance best upon the tight-rope. At Luggnagg he compels all those, who are presented to him, to crawl on their bellies and lick the dust.

" When the king has a mind to put any of his nobles to death in a gentle, indulgent manner, he commands the floor to be strewed with a certain brown powder of a deadly composition,

[1] Swift's Works, xii. *Gulliver's Travels*, Part 2, ch. 6, p. 171.
[2] *Gulliver's Travels*, Part 3, ch. 8, p. 258.

which, being licked up, infallibly kills him in twenty-four hours. But in justice to this prince's great clemency, and the care he has of his subjects' lives (wherein it were much to be wished that the monarchs of Europe would imitate him), it must be mentioned for his honour, that strict orders are given to have the infected parts of the floor well washed after every such execution. . . . I myself heard him give directions that one of his pages should be whipped, whose turn it was to give notice about washing the floor after an execution, but maliciously had omitted it; by which neglect, a young lord of great hopes coming to an audience, was unfortunately poisoned, although the King at that time had no design against his life. But this good prince was so gracious as to forgive the poor page his whipping, upon promise that he would do so no more, without special orders." [1]

All these fictions of giants, pigmies, flying islands, are means for depriving human nature of the veils with which habit and imagination cover it, to display it in its truth and its ugliness. There is still one cloak to remove, the most deceitful and familiar. Swift must take away that appearance of reason in which we deck ourselves. He must suppress the sciences, arts, combinations of societies, inventions of industries, whose brightness dazzles us. He must discover the Yahoo in man. What a spectacle!

"At last I beheld several animals in a field, and one or two of the same kind sitting in trees. Their shape was very singular and deformed. . . . Their heads and breasts were covered with a thick hair, some frizzled, and others lank; they had beards like goats, and a long ridge of hair down their backs, and the forepart of their legs and feet; but the rest of their bodies was bare, so that I might see their skins, which were of a brown

[1] *Gulliver's Travels*, Part 3, ch. 9, p. 264.

buff colour. . . . They climbed high trees as nimbly as a
squirrel, for they had strong extended claws before and behind,
terminating in sharp points and hooked. . . . The females . . .
had long lank hair on their head, but none on their faces, nor
anything more than a sort of down on the rest of their bodies.
. . . Upon the whole I never beheld in all my travels so disagreeable an animal, or one against which I naturally conceived
so great an antipathy." [1]

According to Swift, such are our brothers. He finds
in them all our instincts. They hate each other, tear
each other with their talons, with hideous contortions
and yells ! such is the source of our quarrels. If they
find a dead cow, although they are but five, and there
is enough for fifty, they strangle and wound each other :
such is a picture of our greed and our wars. They dig
up precious stones and hide them in their kennels, and
watch them " with great caution," pining and howling
when robbed : such is the origin of our love of gold.
They devour indifferently " herbs, berries, roots, the corrupted flesh of animals," preferring " what they could
get by rapine or stealth," gorging themselves till they
vomit or burst ; such is the portrait of our gluttony and
injustice. They have a kind of juicy and unwholesome
root, which they " would suck with great delight," till
they " howl, and grin, and chatter," embracing or
scratching each other, then reeling, hiccuping, wallowing
in the mud : such is a picture of our drunkenness.

" In most herds there was a sort of ruling Yahoo, who was
always more deformed in body, and mischievous in disposition,
than any of the rest : that this leader had usually a favourite
as like himself as he could get, whose employment was to lick
his master's feet, . . . and drive the female Yahoos to his

[1] *Gulliver's Travels*, Part 4, ch. 1, p. 286.

kennel; for which he was now and then rewarded with a piece of ass's flesh. . . . He usually continues in office till a worse can be found."[1]

Such is an abstract of our government. And yet he gives preference to the Yahoos over men, saying that our wretched reason has aggravated and multiplied these vices, and concluding with the king of Brobdingnag that our species is "the most pernicious race of little odious vermin that nature ever suffered to crawl upon the surface of the earth."[2]

Five years after this treatise on man, he wrote in favour of unhappy Ireland a pamphlet which is like the last effort of his despair and his genius.[3] I give it almost whole; it deserves it. I know nothing like it in any literature:

"It is a melancholy object to those who walk through this great town, or travel in the country, when they see the streets, the roads, and cabin-doors crowded with beggars of the female sex, followed by three, four, or six children, all in rags, and importuning every passenger for an alms. . . . I think it is agreed by all parties that this prodigious number of children . . . is, in the present deplorable state of the kingdom, a very great additional grievance; and therefore, whoever could find out a fair, cheap, and easy method of making these children sound, useful members of the Commonwealth, would deserve so well of the public, as to have his statue set up for a preserver of the nation. . . . I shall now, therefore, humbly propose my own thoughts, which I hope will not be liable to the least objection."[4]

[1] *Gulliver's Travels*, Part 4, ch. 7, p. 337.
[2] *Ibid.* Part 2, ch. 6, p. 172.
[3] *A Modest Proposal for preventing the children of the poor people in Ireland from being a burden to their parents or country, and for making them beneficial to the public,* 1729. [4] *Ibid.* vii. 454.

When we know Swift, such a beginning frightens us :

" I have been assured by a very knowing American of my acquaintance in London, that a young healthy child, well nursed, is, at a year old, a most delicious, nourishing, and wholesome food, whether stewed, roasted, baked, or boiled ; and I make no doubt that it will equally serve in a fricassee or a ragout.

" I do therefore humbly offer it to public consideration, that of the hundred and twenty thousand children already computed, twenty thousand may be reserved for breed, whereof only one-fourth part to be males ; . . . that the remaining hundred thousand may, at a year old, be offered in sale to the persons of quality and fortune through the kingdom ; always advising the mother to let them suck plentifully in the last month, so as to render them plump and fat for a good table. A child will make two dishes at an entertainment for friends, and when the family dines alone, the fore or hind quarter will make a reasonable dish, and seasoned with a little pepper or salt, will be very good boiled on the fourth day, especially in winter."

" I have reckoned, upon a medium, that a child just born will weigh twelve pounds, and in a solar year, if tolerably nursed, will increase to twenty-eight pounds.

" I have already computed the charge of nursing a beggar's child (in which list I reckon all cottagers, labourers, and four-fifths of the farmers), to be about two shillings per annum, rags included ; and I believe no gentleman would repine to give ten shillings for the carcass of a good fat child, which, as I have said, will make four dishes of excellent nutritive meat.

" Those who are more thrifty (as I must confess the times require), may flay the carcass ; the skin of which, artificially dressed, will make admirable gloves for ladies, and summer boots for fine gentlemen.

" As to our city of Dublin, shambles may be appointed for this purpose in the most convenient parts of it ; and butchers we may be assured will not be wanting ; although I rather recommend buying the children alive, than dressing them hot from the knife, as we do roasting pigs. . . .

"I think the advantages by the proposal which I have made, are obvious and many, as well as of the highest importance. For first, as I have already observed, it would greatly lessen the number of Papists, with whom we are yearly overrun, being the principal breeders of the nation, as well as our most dangerous enemies. . . . Thirdly, whereas the maintenance of a hundred thousand children, from two years old and upward, cannot be computed at less than ten shillings a piece per annum, the nation's stock will be thereby increased fifty thousand pounds per annum, beside the profit of a new dish introduced to the tables of all gentlemen of fortune in the kingdom, who have any refinement in taste. And the money will circulate among ourselves, the goods being entirely of our own growth and manufacture. . . . Sixthly, this would be a great inducement to marriage, which all wise nations have either encouraged by rewards, or enforced by laws and penalties. It would increase the care and tenderness of mothers toward their children, when they were sure of a settlement for life to the poor babes, provided in some sort by the public, to their annual profit or expense. . . . Many other advantages might be enumerated, for instance, the addition of some thousand carcasses in our exportation of barrelled beef; the propagation of swine's flesh, and the improvement in the art of making good bacon. . . . But this, and many others, I omit, being studious of brevity.

"Some persons of desponding spirit are in great concern about that vast number of poor people who are aged, diseased, or maimed; and I have been desired to employ my thoughts, what course may be taken to ease the nation of so grievous an encumbrance. But I am not in the least pain upon that matter; because it is very well known, that they are every day dying and rotting, by cold and famine, and filth and vermin, as fast as can be reasonably expected. And as to the young labourers, they are now in almost as hopeful a condition; they cannot get work, and consequently pine away for want of nourishment, to a degree, that, if at any time they are accidentally hired to common labour, they have not strength to perform it ; and thus the country and themselves are happily delivered from the evils to come.[1]

Swift ends with the following ironic lines, worthy of a cannibal :

"I profess, in the sincerity of my heart that I have not the least personal interest in endeavouring to promote this necessary work, having no other motive than the public good of my country, by advancing our trade, providing for infants, relieving the poor, and giving some pleasure to the rich. I have no children by which I can propose to get a single penny ; the youngest being nine years old and my wife past child-bearing."[2]

Much has been said of unhappy great men, Pascal, for instance. I think that his cries and his anguish are faint compared to this calm treatise.

Such was this great and unhappy genius, the greatest of the classical age, the most unhappy in history, English throughout, whom the excess of his English qualities inspired and consumed, having this intensity of desires, which is the main feature of the race, the enormity of pride which the habit of liberty, command, and success has impressed upon the nation, the solidity of the positive mind which habits of business have established in the country; precluded from power and action by his unchecked passions and his intractable pride ; excluded from poetry and philosophy by the clear-sightedness and narrowness of his common sense ; deprived of the consolations offered by contemplative life, and the occupation furnished by practical life ; too superior to

---

[1] *A Modest Proposal*, etc., 461.   [2] *Ibid.* 466.

embrace heartily a religious sect or a political party, too
narrow-minded to rest in the lofty doctrines which
conciliate all beliefs, or in the wide sympathies which
embrace all parties; condemned by his nature and sur-
roundings to fight without loving a cause, to write without taking a liking to literature, to think without feeling
the truth of any dogma, warring as a condottiere against
all parties, a misanthrope disliking all men, a sceptic
denying all beauty and truth. But these very surroundings, and this very nature, which expelled him from
happiness, love, power, and science, raised him, in this
age of French imitation and classical moderation, to a
wonderful height, where, by the originality and power
of his inventions, he is the equal of Byron, Milton,
and Shakspeare, and shows pre-eminently the character
and mind of his nation. Sensibility, a positive mind,
and pride, forged for him a unique style, of terrible
vehemence, withering calmness, practical effectiveness,
hardened by scorn, truth and hatred, a weapon of vengeance and war which made his enemies cry out and die
under its point and its poison. A pamphleteer against
opposition and government, he tore or crushed his
adversaries with his irony or his sentences, with the
tone of a judge, a sovereign, and a hangman. A man
of the world and a poet, he invented a cruel pleasantry,
funereal laughter, a convulsive gaiety of bitter contrasts;
and whilst dragging the mythological trappings, as if it
were rags he was obliged to wear, he created a personal poetry by painting the crude details of trivial
life, by the energy of a painful grotesqueness, by the
merciless revelation of the filth we conceal. A philosopher against all philosophy, he created a realistic
poem, a grave parody, deduced like geometry, absurd as

a dream, credible as a law report, attractive as a tale, degrading as a dishclout placed like a crown on the head of a divinity. These were his miseries and his strength : we quit such a spectacle with a sad heart, but full of admiration ; and we say that a palace is beautiful even when it is on fire. Artists will add : especially when it is on fire.

CHAPTER VI.

The Novelists.

I.

AMIDST these finished and perfect writings a new kind makes its appearance, suited to the public tendencies and circumstances of the time, the anti-romantic novel, the work and the reading of positive minds, observers and moralists, not intended to exalt and amuse the imagination, like the novels of Spain and the middle ages, not to reproduce or embellish conversation, like the novels of France and the seventeenth century, but to depict real life, to describe characters, to suggest plans of conduct, and judge motives of action. It was a strange apparition, and like the voice of a people buried underground, when, amidst the splendid corruption of high life, this severe emanation of the middle class welled up, and when the obscenities of Mrs. Aphra Behn, still the diversion of ladies of fashion, were found on the same table with De Foe's *Robinson Crusoe*.

II.

De Foe, a dissenter, a pamphleteer, a journalist, a novel-writer, successively a hosier, a tile-maker, an accountant, was one of those indefatigable labourers and obstinate combatants, who, ill-treated, calumniated, imprisoned, succeeded by their uprightness, common

sense, and energy, in gaining England over to their
side.   At twenty-three, having taken arms for Monmouth, he was fortunate in not being hung or sent out
of the country.   Seven years later he was ruined and
obliged to hide.   In 1702, for a pamphlet not rightly
understood, he was condemned to pay a fine, was set in
the pillory, imprisoned two years in Newgate, and only
the charity of Godolphin prevented his wife and six
children from dying of hunger.   Being released and
sent as a commissioner to Scotland to treat about the
union of the two countries, he narrowly escaped being
stoned.   Another pamphlet, which was again misconstrued, sent him to prison, compelled him to pay a fine
of eight hundred pounds, and only just in time he
received the Queen's pardon.   His works were copied,
he was robbed, and slandered.   He was obliged to protest
against the plagiarists, who printed and altered his works
for their benefit; against the neglect of the Whigs, who
did not find him tractable enough; against the animosity
of the Tories, who saw in him the chief champion of
the Whigs.   In the midst of his self-defence he was
struck with apoplexy, and continued to defend himself
from his bed.   Yet he lived on, but with great difficulty;
poor and burdened with a family, he turned, at fifty-five,
to fiction, and wrote successively *Moll Flanders, Captain
Singleton, Duncan Campbell, Colonel Jack,* the *History
of the Great Plague in London,* and many others.   This
vein exhausted, he diverged and tried another—the
*Complete English Tradesman, A Tour through Great
Britain.*   Death came; poverty remained.   In vain had
he written in prose, in verse, on all subjects political and
religious, accidental or moral, satires and novels,
histories and poems, travels and pamphlets, commercial

essays and statistical information, in all two hundred
and ten works, not of verbiage, but of arguments,
documents, and facts, crowded and piled one upon
another with such prodigality, that the memory, thought,
and application of one man seemed too small for such
a labour; he died penniless, in debt. However we
regard his life, we see only prolonged efforts and persecutions. Joy seems to be wanting; the idea of the
beautiful never enters. When he comes to fiction, it
is like a Presbyterian and a plebeian, with low subjects
and moral aims, to treat of the adventures, and reform
the conduct of thieves and prostitutes, workmen and
sailors. His whole delight was to think that he had a
service to perform and that he was performing it : " He
that opposes his own judgment against the current of
the times ought to be backed with unanswerable truth;
and he that has truth on his side is a fool as well as
a coward if he is afraid to own it, because of the
multitude of other men's opinions. 'Tis hard for a
man to say, all the world is mistaken but himself.
But if it be so, who can help it ? " Nobody can help
it, but then a man must walk straight ahead, and alone,
amidst blows and throwing of mud. De Foe is like
one of those brave, obscure, and useful soldiers who,
with empty belly and burdened shoulders, go through
their duties with their feet in the mud, pocket blows,
receive the whole day long the fire of the enemy, and
sometimes that of their friends into the bargain, and die
sergeants, happy if it has been their good fortune to get
hold of the legion of honour.

De Foe had the kind of mind suitable to such a hard
service, solid, exact, entirely destitute of refinement,

enthusiasm, agreeableness.[1] His imagination was that
of a man of business, not of an artist, crammed and,
as it were, jammed down with facts. He tells them
as they come to him, without arrangement or style, like
a conversation, without dreaming of producing an effect,
or composing a phrase, employing technical terms and
vulgar forms, repeating himself at need, using the
same thing two or three times, not seeming to imagine
that there are methods of amusing, touching, engrossing,
or pleasing, with no desire but to pour out on paper
the fulness of the information with which he is charged.
Even in fiction his information is as precise as in
history. He gives dates, year, month, and day; notes
the wind, north-east, south-west, north-west; he writes
a log-book, an invoice, attorneys' and shopkeepers' bills,
the number of moidores, interest, specie payments,
payments in kind, cost and sale prices, the share of the
king, of religious houses, partners, brokers, net totals,
statistics, the geography and hydrography of the island,
so that the reader is tempted to take an atlas and draw
for himself a little map of the place, to enter into all
the details of the history, and to see the objects as clearly
and fully as the author. It seems as though our author
had performed all Crusoe's labours, so. exactly does he
describe them, with numbers, quantities, dimensions, like
a carpenter, potter, or an old tar. Never was such a sense
of the real before or since. Our realists of to-day, painters,
anatomists, who enter deliberately on their business,
are very far from this naturalness; art and calculation
crop out amidst their too minute descriptions. De Foe
creates illusion; for it is not the eye which deceives us,

---

[1] See his dull poems, amongst others *Jure divino*, a poem in twelve
books, in defence of every man's birthright by nature.

but the mind, and that literally : his account of the great plague has more than once passed for true; and Lord Chatham mistook his *Memoirs of a Cavalier* for an authentic narrative. This was his aim. In the preface to the old edition of *Robinson Crusoe* it is said : " The story is told . . . to the instruction of others by this example, and to justify and honour the wisdom of Providence. The editor believes the thing to be a just history of facts ; neither is there any appearance of fiction in it." All his talents lie in this, and thus even his imperfections aid him; his lack of art becomes a profound art ; his negligence, repetitions, prolixity, contribute to the illusion : we cannot imagine that such and such a detail, so minute, so dull, is invented ; an inventor would have suppressed it ; it is too tedious to have been put in on purpose : art chooses, embellishes, interests ; art, therefore, cannot have piled up this heap of dull and vulgar accidents ; it is the truth.

Read, for instance, *A True Relation of the Apparition of one Mrs. Veal, the next Day after her Death, to one Mrs. Bargrave, at Canterbury, the 8th of September* 1705 ; *which Apparition recommends the perusal of Drelincourt's Book of Consolation against the Fear of Death.*[1] The old little chap books, read by aged needlewomen, are not more monotonous. There is such an array of circumstantial and guaranteed details, such a file of witnesses quoted, referred to, registered, compared, such a perfect appearance of tradesman-like honesty, plain, vulgar common sense, that a man would take the author for an honest retired hosier, with too little brains to invent a story; no writer careful of his

---

[1] Compare another story of an apparition, Edgar Poe's *Case of M. Waldemar.* The American is a suffering artist ; De Foe a citizen, who has common sense.

reputation would have printed such nonsense. In fact, it was not his reputation that De Foe cared for; he had other motives in his head; we literary men of the present time cannot guess them, being literary men only. But he wanted to sell a pious book of Drelincourt, which would not sell of itself, and in addition, to confirm people in their religious belief by advocating the appearance of ghosts. It was the grand proof then brought to bear on sceptics. Grave Dr. Johnson himself tried to see a ghost, and no event of that time was more suited to the belief of the middle class. Here, as elsewhere, De Foe, like Swift, is a man of action; effect, not noise touches him; he composed *Robinson Crusoe* to warn the impious, as Swift wrote the life of the last man hung to inspire thieves with terror! In that positive and religious age, amidst these political and puritanic citizens, practice was of such importance as to reduce art to the condition of its tool.

Never was art the tool of a more moral or more thoroughly English work. Robinson Crusoe is quite a man of his race, and might instruct it even in the present day. He has that force of will, inner enthusiasm, hidden ferment of a violent imagination which formerly produced the sea-kings, and now produces emigrants and squatters. The misfortunes of his two brothers, the tears of his relatives, the advice of his friends, the remonstrances of his reason, the remorse of his conscience, are all unable to restrain him: there was "a something fatal in his nature;" he had conceived the idea, he must go to sea. To no purpose is he seized with repentance during the first storm; he drowns in punch these "fits" of conscience. To no purpose is he warned by shipwreck and a narrow escape from death; he is hardened, and grows obstinate. To no purpose captivity among the Moors and the possession of a fruitful plantation invite repose; the indomitable instinct returns; he was born to be his own destroyer, and embarks again. The ship goes down; he is cast alone on a desert island; then his native energy found its vent and its employment; like his descendants, the pioneers of Australia and America, he must recreate and re-master one by one the inventions and acquisitions of human industry; one by one he does so. Nothing represses his effort; neither possession nor weariness:

"I had the biggest magazine of all kinds now that ever was laid up, I believe, for one man; but I was not satisfied still; for, while the ship sat upright in that posture, I thought I ought to get everything out of her that I could. . . . I got most of the pieces of cable ashore, and some of the iron, though with infinite labour; for I was fain to dip for it into the water; a work which fatigued me very much. . . . I believe, verily, had the calm weather held, I should have brought away the whole ship, piece by piece." [1]

In his eyes, work is natural. When, in order "to barricade himself, he goes to cut the piles in the woods, and drives them into the earth, which cost a great deal of time and labour," he says: "A very laborious and tedious work. But what need I have been concerned at the tediousness of anything I had to do, seeing I had time enough to do it in? . . . My time or labour was little worth, and so it was as well employed one way as another." [2] Application and fatigue of head and arms give occupation to his superfluous activity and force; the mill-stone must find grist to grind, without

---

[1] De Foe's Works, 20 vols., 1819 21. *The Life and Adventures of Robinson Crusoe,* i. ch. iv. 65.   [2] *Ibid.* 76.

which, turning round empty, it would wear itself away. He works, therefore, all day and night, at once carpenter, oarsman, porter, hunter, tiller of the ground, potter, tailor, milkman, basketmaker, grinder, baker, invincible in difficulties, disappointments, expenditure of time and toil. Having but a hatchet and an adze, it took him forty-two days to make a board. He occupied two months in making his first two jars; five months in making his first boat; then, " by dint of hard labour," he levelled the ground from his timber-yard to the sea, then, not being able to bring his boat to the sea, he tried to bring the sea up to his boat, and began to dig a canal; then, reckoning that he would require ten or twelve years to finish the task, he builds another boat at another place, with another canal half-a-mile long, four feet deep, six wide. He spends two years over it : " I bore with this. . . . I went through that by dint of hard labour. . . . Many a weary stroke it had cost. . . . This will testify that I was not idle. . . . As I had learned not to despair of anything. I never grudged my labour." These strong expressions of indomitable patience are ever recurring. These stout-hearted men are framed for labour, as their sheep are for slaughter and their horses for racing. Even now we may hear their mighty hatchet and pickaxe sounding in the claims of Melbourne and in the log-houses of the Salt Lake. The reason of their success is the same there as here ; they do everything with calculation and method ; they rationalise their energy, which is like a torrent they make a canal for. Crusoe sets to work only after deliberate calculation and reflection. When he seeks a spot for his tent, he enumerates the four conditions of the place he requires. When he wishes to escape despair, he draws

up impartially, "like debtor and creditor," the list
of his advantages and disadvantages, putting them in
two columns, active and passive, item for item, so that
the balance is in his favour. His courage is only the
servant of his common sense : " By stating and squaring
everything by reason, and by making the most rational
judgment of things, every man may be in time master
of every mechanic art. I had never handled a tool in
my life, and yet in time, by labour, application, and
contrivance, I found at last that I wanted nothing but
I could have made it, especially if I had had tools."[1]
There is a grave and deep pleasure in this painful
success, and in this personal acquisition. The squatter,
like Crusoe, takes pleasure in things, not only because
they are useful, but because they are his work. He
feels himself a man, whilst finding everywhere about him
the sign of his labour and thought ; he is pleased : " I
had everything so ready at my hand, that it was a great
pleasure to me to see all my goods in such order; and
especially to find my stock of all necessaries so great."[2]
He returns to his home willingly, because he is there a
master and creator of all the comforts he has around him ;
he takes his meals there gravely and " like a king."

Such are the pleasures of home. A guest enters
there to fortify these natural inclinations by the ascendency of duty. Religion appears, as it must, in emotions
and visions : for this is not a calm soul ; imagination
breaks out into it at the least shock, and carries it to
the threshold of madness. On the day when Robinson
Crusoe saw the " print of a naked man's foot on the
shore," he stood " like one thunderstruck," and fled
" like a hare to cover ;" his ideas are in a whirl, he is

<hr>

[1] *Robinson Crusoe*, ch. iv. 79.   [2] *Ibid.* 80.

no longer master of them; though he is hidden and barricaded, he thinks himself discovered; he intends " to throw down the enclosures, turn all the tame cattle wild into the woods, dig up the corn-fields." He has all kind of fancies; he asks himself if it is not the devil who has left this footmark; and reasons upon it :

> "I considered that the devil might have found out abundance of other ways to have terrified me; . . . that, as I lived quite on the other side of the island, he would never have been so simple to leave a mark in a place, where it was ten thousand to one whether I should ever see it or not, and in the sand too, which the first surge of the sea upon a high wind would have defaced entirely. All this seemed inconsistent with the thing itself, and with all notions we usually entertain of the subtlety of the devil."[1]

In this impassioned and uncultivated mind, which for eight years had continued without a thought, and as it were stupid, engrossed in manual labour and bodily wants, belief took root, fostered by anxiety and solitude. Amidst the risks of all-powerful nature, in this great uncertain upheaving, a Frenchman, a man bred as we are, would cross his arms gloomily like a Stoic, or would wait like an Epicurean for the return of physical cheerfulness. As for Crusoe, at the sight of the ears of barley which have suddenly made their appearance, he weeps, and thinks at first " that God had miraculously caused this grain to grow." Another day he has a terrible vision : in a fever of excitement he repents of his sins ; he opens the Bible, and finds these words, which " were very apt to his case :" " Call upon me in the day of trouble ; I will deliver thee, and thou shalt glorify me."[2] Prayer then rises to his

---

[1] *Robinson Crusoe,* ch. xi. 184.   [2] *Ibid.* 187. Ps. l. 15.

lips, true prayer, the converse of the heart with a God who answers, and to whom we listen. He also read the words: "I will never leave thee nor forsake thee."[1] "Immediately it occurred that these words were to me. Why else should they be directed in such a manner, just at the moment when I was mourning over my condition, as one forsaken of God and man?"[2] Thenceforth spiritual life begins for him. To reach its very foundation, the squatter needs only his Bible; with it he carries about his faith, his theology, his worship; every evening he finds in it some application to his present condition: he is no longer alone: God speaks to him, and provides for his energy matter for a second labour to sustain and complete the first. For he now undertakes against his heart the combat which he has maintained against nature; he wants to conquer, transform, ameliorate, pacify the one as he has done with the other. Robinson Crusoe fasts, observes the Sabbath, three times a day he reads the Scripture, and says: ".I gave humble and hearty thanks . . . that he (God) could fully make up to me the deficiencies of my solitary state, and the want of human society by his presence, and the communication of his grace to my soul, supporting, comforting, and encouraging me to depend upon his providence, and hope for his eternal presence hereafter."[3] In this disposition of mind there is nothing a man cannot endure or do; heart and hand come to the assistance of the arms; religion consecrates labour, piety feeds patience; and man, supported on one side by his instincts, on the other by his belief, finds himself able to clear the land, to people, to organise and civilise continents.

[1] Heb. xiii. 5.   [2] *Robinson Crusoe*, ch. viii. 134.   [3] *Ibid*. ch. viii. 133.

III.

It was by chance that De Foe, like Cervantes, lighted on a novel of character: as a rule, like Cervantes, he only wrote novels of adventure; he knew life better than the soul, and the general course of the world better than the idiosyncrasies of an individual. But the impulse was given, nevertheless, and now the rest followed. Chivalrous manners had been blotted out, carrying with them the poetical and picturesque drama. Monarchical manners had been blotted out, carrying with them the witty and licentious drama. Citizen manners had been established, bringing with them domestic and practical reading. Like society, literature changed its course. Books were needed to read by the fireside, in the country, amongst the family: invention and genius turn to this kind of writing. The sap of human thought, abandoning the old dried-up branches, flowed into the unseen boughs, which it suddenly made to grow and turn green, and the fruits which it produced bear witness at the same time to the surrounding temperature and the native stock. Two features are common and proper to them. All these novels are character novels. Englishmen, more reflective than others, more inclined to the melancholy pleasure of concentrated attention and inner examination, find around them human medals more vigorously struck, less worn by friction with the world, whose uninjured face is more visible than that of others. All these novels are works of observation, and spring from a moral design. The men of this time, having fallen away from lofty imagination, and being immersed in active life, desire to cull from books solid instruction, just examples, powerful emotions, feelings of practical admiration, and motives of action.

We have but to look around; the same inclination begins on all sides the same task. The novel springs up everywhere, and shows the same spirit under all forms. At this time [1] appear the *Tatler*, *Spectator*, *Guardian*, and all those agreeable and serious essays which, like the novel, look for readers at home, to supply them with examples and provide them with counsels; which, like the novel, describe manners, paint characters, and try to correct the public; which, finally, like the novel, turn spontaneously to fiction and portraiture. Addison, like a delicate amateur of moral curiosities, complacently follows the amiable oddities of his darling Sir Roger de Coverley, smiles, and with discreet hand guides the excellent knight through all the awkward predicaments which may bring out his rural prejudices and his innate generosity; whilst by his side the unhappy Swift, degrading man to the instincts of the beast of prey and beast of burden, tortures humanity by forcing it to recognise itself in the execrable portrait of the Yahoo. Although they differ, both authors are working at the same task. They only employ imagination in order to study characters, and to suggest plans of conduct. They bring down philosophy to observation and application. They only dream of reforming or chastising vice. They are only moralists and psychologists. They both confine themselves to the consideration of vice and virtue; the one with calm benevolence, the other with savage indignation. The same point of view produces the graceful portraits of Addison and the slanderous pictures

[1] 1709, 1711, 1713.

of Swift. Their successors do the like, and all diversities of mood and talent do not hinder their works from acknowledging a similar source, and concurring in the same effect.

Two principal ideas can rule, and have ruled, morality in England. Now it is conscience which is accepted as a sovereign; now it is instinct which is taken for guide. Now they have recourse to grace; now they rely on nature. Now they wholly enslave everything to rule; now they give everything up to liberty. The two opinions have successively reigned in England; and the human frame, at once too vigorous and too unyielding, successively justifies their ruin and their success. Some, alarmed by the fire of an over-fed temperament, and by the energy of unsocial passions, have regarded nature as a dangerous beast, and placed conscience with all its auxiliaries, religion, law, education, proprieties, as so many armed sentinels to repress its least outbreaks. Others, repelled by the harshness of an incessant constraint, and by the minuteness of a morose discipline, have overturned guards and barriers, and let loose captive nature to enjoy the free air and sun, deprived of which it was being choked. Both by their excesses have deserved their defeats and raised up their adversaries. From Shakspeare to the Puritans, from Milton to Wycherley, from Congreve to De Foe, from Sheridan to Burke, from Wilberforce to Lord Byron, irregularity has provoked constraint and tyranny revolt. This great contest of rule and nature is developed again in the writings of Fielding and Richardson.

IV.

"*Pamela, or Virtue rewarded,* in a series of familiar letters from a beautiful young damsel to her parents, published in order to cultivate the principles of virtue and religion in the minds of the youth of both sexes; a narrative which has its foundation in truth and at the same time that it agreeably entertains by a variety of curious and affecting incidents, is entirely divested of all those images which, in too many pieces calculated for amusement only, tend to inflame the minds they should instruct."[1] We can make no mistake, the title is clear. The preachers rejoiced to see assistance coming to them from the very spot where there was danger; and Dr. Sherlock, from his pulpit, recommended the book. Men inquired about the author. He was a printer and bookseller, a joiner's son, who, at the age of fifty, and in his leisure moments, wrote in his shop parlour: a laborious man, who, by work and good conduct, had raised himself to a competency and had educated himself; delicate moreover, gentle, nervous, often ill, with a taste for the society of women, accustomed to correspond for and with them, of reserved and retired habits, whose only fault was a timid vanity. He was severe in principles, and had acquired perspicacity by his rigour. In reality, conscience is a lamp; a moralist is a psychologist; Christian casuistry is a sort of natural history of the soul. He who through anxiety of conscience busies himself in drawing out the good or evil motives of his manifest actions, who sees vices and virtues at their birth, who follows the gradual

---

[1] 1741. The translator has consulted the tenth edition, 1775, 4 vols.

progress of culpable thoughts, and the secret con-
firmation of good resolves, who can mark the force,
nature, and moment of temptation and resistance,
holds in his hand almost all the moving strings of
humanity, and has only to make them vibrate regularly
to draw from them the most powerful harmonies.   In
this consists the art of Richardson; he combines whilst
he observes; his meditation develops the ideas of the
moralist.   No one in this age has equalled him in
these detailed and comprehensive conceptions, which,
grouping to a single end the passions of thirty characters, twine and colour the innumerable threads of the
whole canvas, to bring out a figure, an action, or a
lesson.

This first novel is a flower—one of those flowers
which only bloom in a virgin imagination, at the dawn
of original invention, whose charm and freshness surpass
all that the maturity of art and genius can afterwards
cultivate or arrange.   Pamela is a child of fifteen,
brought up by an old lady, half servant and half
favourite, who, after the death of her mistress, finds
herself exposed to the growing seductions and persecutions of the young master of the house.   She is a
genuine child, frank and artless as Goethe's Margaret,
and of the same family.   After twenty pages, we
involuntarily see this fresh rosy face, always blushing,
and her laughing eyes, so ready with tears.   At the
smallest kindness she is confused; she knows not
what to say; she changes colour, casts down her eyes,
as she makes a curtsey; the poor innocent heart
is troubled or melts.[1]   No trace of the bold vivacity,

---

[1] "To be sure I did think nothing but curt'sy and cry, and was all
in confusion at his goodness."

the nervous coolness, which are the elements of a French girl. She is "a lambkin," loved, loving, without pride, vanity, bitterness; timid, always humble. When her master tries forcibly to kiss her, she is astonished; she will not believe that the world is so wicked. "This gentleman has degraded himself to offer freedoms to his poor servant." [1] She is afraid of being too free with him; reproaches herself, when she writes to her relatives, with saying too often *he* and *him* instead of his honour; "but it is his fault if I do, for why did he lose all his dignity with me?" [2] No outrage exhausts her submissiveness: he has kissed her, and took hold of her arm so rudely that it was "black and blue;" he has tried worse, he has behaved like a ruffian and a knave. To cap all, he slanders her circumstantially before the servants; he insults her repeatedly, and provokes her to speak; she does not speak, will not fail in her duty to her master. "It is for you, sir, to say what you please, and for me only to say, God bless your honour!" [3] She falls on her knees, and thanks him for sending her away. But in so much submission what resistance! Everything is against her; he is her master; he is a justice of the peace, secure against all intervention—a sort of divinity to her, with all the superiority and authority of a feudal prince. Moreover, he has the brutality of the times; he rates her, speaks to her like a slave, and yet thinks himself very kind. He shuts her up alone for several months, with "a wicked creature," his housekeeper, who beats

---

"I was so confounded at these words, you might have beat me down with a feather. . . . So, like a fool, I was ready to cry, and went away curt'sying, and blushing, I am sure, up to the ears."

[1] *Pamela*, vol. i. Letter x.   [2] *Ibid.*   [3] *Ibid.* Letter xxvii.

and threatens her.   He tries on her the influence of fear, loneliness, surprise, money, gentleness. And what is more terrible, her own heart is against her: she loves him secretly; her virtues injure her; she dare not lie, when she most needs it;[1] and piety keeps her from suicide, when that seems her only resource. One by one the issues close around her, so that she loses hope, and the readers of her adventures think her lost and ruined. But this native innocence has been strengthened by Puritanic faith. She sees temptations in her weaknesses; she knows that "Lucifer always is ready to promote his own work and workmen;"[2] she is penetrated by the great Christian idea, which makes all souls equal before the common salvation and the final judgment. She says: "My soul is of equal importance to the soul of a princess, though my quality is inferior to that of the meanest slave."[3] Wounded, stricken, abandoned, betrayed, still the knowledge and thought of a happy or an unhappy eternity are two defences which no assault can carry. She knows it well; she has no other means of explaining vice than to suppose them absent. She considers that wicked Mrs. Jewkes is an atheist. Belief in God, the heart's belief—not the wording of the catechism, but the inner feeling, the habit of picturing justice as ever living and ever present—this is the fresh blood which the Reformation caused to flow into the veins of the old world, and which alone could give it a new life and a new youth.

She is, as it were, animated by this feeling; in the most perilous as in the sweetest moments, this grand sentiment returns to her, so much is it entwined with

---

[1] "I dare not tell a wilful lie."
[2] *Pamela*, i. Letter xxv.   [3] *Ibid.* Letter to Mr. Williams, i. 208.

all the rest, so much has it multiplied its tendrils and
buried its roots in the innermost folds of her heart.
Her young master thinks of marrying her now, and
wishes to be sure that she loves him. She dares not
say so, being afraid to give him a hold upon her. She
is greatly troubled by his kindness, and yet she must
answer. Religion comes to veil love in a sublime
half-confession : " I fear not, sir, the grace of God
supporting me, that any acts of kindness would make
me forget what I owe to my virtue; but . . . my
nature is too frank and open to make me wish to be
ungrateful ; and if I should be taught a lesson I never
yet learnt, with what regret should I descend to the
grave, to think that I could not hate my undoer ; and
that, at the last great day, I must stand up as an
accuser of the poor unhappy soul, that I could wish it
in my power to save !" [1] He is softened and vanquished,
descends from that vast height where aristocratic
customs placed him, and thenceforth, day by day, the
letters of the happy child record the preparations for
their marriage. Amidst this triumph and happiness
she continues humble, devoted, and tender ; her heart
is full, and gratitude fills it from every source : " This
foolish girl must be, after twelve o'clock this day, as
much his wife as if he were to marry a duchess." [2]
She " had the boldness to kiss his hand." [3] " My heart
is so wholly yours, that I am afraid of nothing but
that I may be forwarder than you wish." [4] Shall the
marriage take place Monday, or Tuesday, or Wednesday ?
She dare not say Yes ; she blushes and trembles : there
is a delightful charm in this timid modesty, these
restrained effusions. For a wedding present she obtains

[1] *Pamela*, i. 290. [2] *Ibid.* ii. 167. [3] *Ibid.* ii. 78. [4] *Ibid.* ii. 148.

the pardon of the wicked creatures who have ill-treated her : " I clasped my arms about his neck, and was not ashamed to kiss him once, and twice, and three times, once for each forgiven person." [1]   Then they talk over their plans : she shall remain at home ; she will not frequent grand parties ; she is not fond of cards ; she will keep the " family accounts," and distribute her husband's charities ; she will help the housekeeper in " the making jellies, comfits, sweetmeats, marmalades, cordials, and to pot, and candy, and preserve," [2] to get up the linen ; she will look after the breakfast and dinner, especially when there are guests ; she knows how to carve ; she will wait for her husband, who perhaps will be so good as now and then to give her an hour or two of his " agreeable conversation," " and will be indulgent to the impertinent overflowings of my grateful heart." [3]   In his absence she will read—" that will help to polish my mind, and make me worthier of your company and conversation ; " [4] and she will pray to God, she says, in order " that I may be enabled to discharge my duty to my husband." [5]   Richardson has sketched here the portrait of the English wife—a good house-keeper and sedentary, studious and obedient, loving and pious—and Fielding will finish it in his *Amelia*.

Pamela's adventures describe a contest : the novel of Clarissa Harlowe represents one still greater. Virtue, like force of every kind, is proportioned according to its power of resistance ; and we have only to subject it to more violent tests, to give it its greatest prominence.   Let us look in passions of the English for foes capable of assailing virtue, calling it forth,

[1] *Pamela*, ii. 194.   [2] *Ibid*. ii. 62.   [3] *Ibid*.
[4] *Ibid*. ii. 63.   [5] *Ibid*.

and strengthening it. The evil and the good of the English character is a too strong will.[1] When tenderness and lofty reason fail, the native energy becomes sternness, obstinacy, inflexible tyranny, and the heart a den of malevolent passions, eager to rave and tear each other. Against a family, having such passions, Clarissa Harlowe has to struggle. Her father never would be "controuled, nor yet persuaded." [2] He never "did give up one point he thought he had a right to carry." [3] He has broken down the will of his wife, and degraded her to the part of a dumb servant : he wishes to break down the will of his daughter, and to give her for a husband a coarse and heartless fool. He is the head of the family, master of all his people, despotic and ambitious as a Roman patrician, and he wishes to found a house. He is stern in these two harsh resolves, and inveighs against the rebellious daughter. Above the outbursts of his voice we hear the loud wrath of his son, a sort of plethoric, over-fed bull-dog, excited by his greed, his youth, his fiery temper, and his premature authority ; the shrill outcry of the eldest daughter, a coarse, plain-looking girl, with "a plump, high-fed face," exactingly jealous, prone to hate, who, being neglected by Lovelace, revenges herself on her beautiful sister ; the churlish growling of the two uncles, narrow-minded old bachelors, vulgar, pig-headed, through their notions of male authority ; the grievous importunities of the mother, the aunt, the old nurse, poor timid slaves, reduced one by one to become instruments of persecution. The whole family have bound themselves to favour Mr. Solmes'

---

[1] See in *Pamela* the characters of Squire B. and Lady Davers.
[2] *Clarissa Harlowe*, 4th ed. 1751, 7 vols. i. 92.   [3] *Ibid.* i. 105.

proposal to marry Clarissa. They do not reason, they simply express their will. By dint of repetition, only one idea has fixed itself in their brain, and they become furious when any one endeavours to oppose it. " Who at the long run must submit ? " asks her mother ; " all of us to you, or you to all of us ? " [1] Clarissa offers to remain single, never to marry at all ; she consents to give up her property. But her family answered : " They had a right to her obedience upon their own terms ; her proposal was an artifice, only to gain time ; nothing but marrying Mr. Solmes should do ; . . . they should not be at rest till it was done." [2] It must be done, they have promised it ; it is a point of honour with them. A girl, a young, inexperienced, insignificant girl, to resist men, old men, people of position and consideration, nay, her whole family— monstrous ! So they persist, like brutes as they are, blindly, putting on the screw with all their stupid hands together, not seeing that at every turn they bring the child nearer to madness, dishonour, or death. She begs them, implores them, one · by one, with every argument and prayer ; racks herself to discover concessions, goes on her knees, faints, makes them weep. It is all useless. The indomitable, crushing will oppresses her with its daily increasing mass. There is no example of such a varied moral torture, so incessant, so obstinate. They persist in it, as if it were a task, and are vexed to find that she makes their task so long. They refuse to see her, forbid her to write, are afraid of her tears. Her sister Arabella, with the venomous bitterness of an offended, ugly woman, tries to make her insults more stinging :

[1] *Clarissa Harlowe*, i. Letter xx. 125.   [2] *Ibid.* i. Letter xxxix. 253.

" ' The *witty*, the *prudent*, nay the *dutiful* and pi-ous (so she sneeringly pronounced the word) Clarissa Harlowe, should be so strangely fond of a profligate man, that her parents were forced to lock her up, in order to hinder her from running into his arms.' ' Let me ask you, my dear,' said she, ' how you now keep your account of the disposition of your time ? How many hours in the twenty-four do you devote to your needle ? How many to your prayers ? How many to letter-writing ? And how many to love ? - I doubt, I doubt, my little dear, the latter article is like Aaron's rod, and swallows up all the rest. . . . You must therefore bend or break, that is all, child.'[1] . . .

" ' What, not speak yet ? Come, my sullen, silent dear, speak one word to me. You must say *two* very soon to Mr. Solmes, I can tell you that. . . . Well, well (insultingly wiping my averted face with her handkerchief) . . . Then you think you may be brought to speak the two words.' "[2]

She continues thus :

" ' *This*, Clary, is a pretty pattern enough. But *this* is quite charming ?—And *this*, were I you, should be my wedding night-gown.—But, Clary, won't you have a velvet suit ? It would cut a great figure in a country church, you know. Crimson velvet, suppose ! Such a fine complexion as yours, how it would be set off by it !—And do you sigh, love ? Black velvet, so fair as you are, with those charming eyes, gleaming through a wintry cloud, like an April sun. Does not Lovelace tell you they are charming eyes ? ' "[3]

Then, when Arabella is reminded that, three months ago, she did not find Lovelace so worthy of scorn, she nearly chokes with passion ; she wants to beat her sister, cannot speak, and says to her aunt, " with great violence :" " Let us go, madam ; let us leave the crea-

---

[1] *Clarissa Harlowe*, i. Letter xlii. 278.   [2] *Ibid.* i. Letter xliii. 295.
[3] *Ibid.* i. Letter xlv. 308.

ture to swell till she bursts with her own poison."[1]   It
reminds us of a pack of hounds in full cry after a deer,
which is caught, and wounded; whilst the pack grow
more eager and more ferocious, because they have tasted
blood.

At the last moment, when she thinks to escape them,
a new chase begins, more dangerous than the other.
Lovelace has all the evil passions of Harlowe, and in
addition a genius which sharpens and aggravates them.
What a character!   How English! how different from
the Don Juan of Mozart or of Molière!   Before everything he wishes to have the cruel fair one in his power:
then come the desire to bend others, a combative spirit,
a craving for triumph; only after all these come the
senses.   He spares an innocent, young girl, because he
knows she is easy to conquer, and the grandmother
" has besought him to be merciful to her."   " The
Del ellare superbos should be my motto,"[2] he writes to
his friend Belford; and in another letter he says, " I
always considered opposition and resistance as a chal-
lenge to do my worst."[3]   At bottom, pride, infinite, insatiable, senseless, is the mainspring, the only motive
of all his actions.   He acknowledges " that he only
wanted Cæsar's outsetting to make a figure among his
contemporaries,"[4] and that he only stoops to private
conquests out of mere whim.   He declares that he
would not marry the first princess on earth, if he but
thought she balanced a minute in her choice of him or
of an emperor.   He is held to be gay, brilliant, con-
versational; but this petulance of animal vigour is only
external; he is cruel, jests savagely, in cool blood, like

---

[1] *Clarissa Harlowe*, i. Letter xlv. 309.   [2] *Ibid.* Letter xxxiv. 223.
[3] *Ibid.* ii. Letter xliii. 315.   [4] *Ibid.* i. Letter xii. 65.

a hangman, about the harm which he has done or
means to do. He reassures a poor servant who is
troubled at having given up Clarissa to him in the following words: " The affair of Miss Betterton was a
youthful frolick. . . . I went into mourning for her,
though abroad at the time,—a distinction I have
ever paid to those worthy creatures who died in child-
bed by me. . . . Why this squeamishness, then, honest
Joseph?"[1] The English roysterers of those days threw
the human body in the sewers. One gentleman, a friend
of Lovelace, " tricked a farmer's daughter, a pretty girl,
up to town, . . . drank her light-hearted, . . . then
to the play, . . . then to the bagnio, ruined her; kept
her on a fortnight or three weeks; then left her to the
mercy of the people of the bagnio (never paying for
anything), who stript her of all her cloaths, and because
she would not take on, threw her into prison, where
she died in want and in despair."[2] The rakes in
France were only rascals,[3] here they were villains;
wickedness with them poisoned love. Lovelace hates
Clarissa even more than he loves her. He has a book
in which he sets down, he says, " all the family faults
and the infinite trouble she herself has given me.
When my heart is soft, and all her own, I can but turn
to my memoranda, and harden myself at once."[4] He
is angry because she dares to defend herself, says that
he'll teach her to vie with him in inventions, to make
plots against and for her conqueror. It is a struggle
between them without truce or halting. Lovelace says

---

[1] *Clarissa Harlowe*, iii. Letter xviii. 89.
[2] *Ibid.* vii. Letter xxxviii. 122.
[3] See the *Mémoires* of the Marshal de Richelieu.
[4] *Clarissa Harlowe*, ii. Letter xxxix. 294.

of himself : " What an industrious spirit have I ! Nobody can say that I eat the bread of idleness ; . . .
certainly, with this active soul, I should have made a
very great figure in whatever station I had filled." [1]
He assaults and besieges her, spends whole nights
outside her house, gives the Harlowes servants of his
own, invents stories, introduces personages under a false
name, forges letters.   There is no expense, fatigue, plot,
treachery which he will not undertake.   All weapons
are the same to him.   He digs and plans even when
away, ten, twenty, fifty saps, which all meet in the
same mine.   He provides against everything; he is
ready for everything ; divines, dares everything, against
all duty, humanity, common sense, in spite of the
prayers of his friends, the entreaties of Clarissa, his
own remorse.   Excessive will, here as with the Harlowes, becomes an iron wheel, which twists out of shape
and breaks to pieces what it ought to bend, so that at
last, by blind impetuosity, it is broken by its own
impetus, over the ruins it has made.

Against such assaults what resources has Clarissa ?
A will as determined as Lovelace's.   She also is armed
for war, and admits that she has as much of her father's
spirit as of her mother's gentleness.   Though gentle,
though readily driven into Christian humility, she has
pride ; she " had hoped to be an example to young persons " of her sex ; she possesses the firmness of a man,
and above all a masculine reflection. [2]   What self-scru-
tiny ! what vigilance ! what minute and indefatigable
observation of her conduct, and of that of others ! [3]

[1] *Clarissa Harlowe*, iv. xxxiii. 232.
[2] See (vol vii. Letter xlix.) among other other things her last Will.
[3] She makes out statistics and a classification of Lovelace's merits

No action, or word, involuntary or other gesture of Lovelace is unobserved by her, uninterpreted, unjudged, with the perspicacity and clearness of mind of a diplomatist and a moralist ! We must read these long conversations, in which no word is used without calculation, genuine duels daily renewed, with death, nay, with dishonour before her.   She knows it, is not disturbed, remains ever mistress of herself, never exposes herself, is not dazed, defends every inch of ground, feeling that all the world is on his side, no one for her, that she loses ground, and will lose more, that she will fall, that she is falling.   And yet she bends not.   What a change since Shakspeare ! Whence comes this new and original idea of woman ? Who has encased these yielding and tender innocents with such heroism and calculation ?   Puritanism transferred to the laity.   Clarissa " never looked upon any duty, much less a voluntary vowed one, with indifference." She has passed her whole life in looking at these duties.   She has placed certain principles before her, has reasoned upon them, applied them to the various circumstances of life, has fortified herself on every point with maxims, distinctions, and arguments.   She has set round her, like bristling and multiplied ramparts, a numberless army of inflexible precepts.   We can only reach her by turning over her whole mind and her whole past.   This is her force, and also her weakness ; for she is so carefully defended by her fortifications,

and faults, with subdivisions and numbers.   Take an example of this positive and practical English logic : "That such a husband might unsettle me in all my own principles, and hazard my future hopes. That he has a very immoral character to women.   That knowing this, it is a high degree of impurity to think of joining in wedlock with such a man."   She keeps all her writings, her memorandums, summaries or analyses of her own letters.

that she is a prisoner; her principles are a snare to her, and her virtue destroys her. She wishes to preserve too much decorum. She refuses to apply to a magistrate, for it would make public the family quarrels. She does not resist her father openly; that would be against filial humility. She does not repel Solmes violently, like a hound, as he is; it would be contrary to feminine delicacy. She will not leave home with Miss Howe; that might injure the character of her friend. She reproves Lovelace when he swears,[1] a good Christian ought to protest against scandal. She is argumentative and pedantic, a politician and a preacher; she wearies us, she does not act like a woman. When a room is on fire, a young girl flies barefooted, and does not do what Miss Clarissa does—ask for her slippers. I am very sorry for it, but I say it with bated breath, the sublime Clarissa had a little mind; her virtue is like the piety of devotees, literal and over-nice. She does not carry us away, she has always her guide of deportment in her hand; she does not discover her duties, but follows instructions; she has not the audacity of great resolutions, she possesses more conscience and firmness than enthusiasm and genius.[2] This is the disadvantage of morality pushed to an extreme, no matter what the school or the aim is. By dint of regulating man, we narrow him.

Poor Richardson, unsuspiciously, has been at pains to set the thing forth in broad light, and has created Sir Charles Grandison "a man of true honour." I

---

[1] "Swearing is a most unmanly vice, and cursing as poor and low a one, since it proclaims the profligate's want of power and his wickedness at the same time; for could such a one punish as he speaks, he would be a fiend."—Vol. ii. Letter xxxviii. 282.

[2] The contrary is the case with the heroines of George Sand's novels.

cannot say whether this model has converted many.
There is nothing so insipid as an edifying hero. This
Sir Charles is as correct as an automaton; he passes
his life in weighing his duties, and "with an air of
gallantry."[1] When he goes to visit a sick person, he
has scruples about going on a Sunday, but reassures his
conscience by saying, "I am afraid I must borrow of
the Sunday some hours on my journey; but visiting
the sick is an act of mercy."[2] Would any one believe
that such a man could fall in love? Such is the case,
however, but in a manner of his own. Thus he writes to
his betrothed: "And now, loveliest and dearest of women,
allow me to expect the honour of a line, to let me know
how much of the tedious month from last Thursday you
will be so good to abate. . . . My utmost gratitude
will ever be engaged by the condescension, whenever
you shall distinguish the day of the year, distinguished
as it will be to the end of my life that shall give me
the greatest blessing of it and confirm me—for ever
yours, Charles Grandison."[3] A wax figure could not
be more proper. All is in the same taste. There are
eight wedding-coaches, each with four horses; Sir
Charles is attentive to old people; at table, the gentlemen, each with a napkin under his arm, wait upon the
ladies; the bride is ever on the point of fainting; he
throws himself at her feet with the utmost politeness:
"What, my love! In compliment to the best of parents
resume your usual presence of mind. I, else, who shall
glory before a thousand witnesses in receiving the

---

[1] See *Sir Charles Grandison*, 7 vols. 1811, iii. Letter xvi. 142:
"He received the letters, standing up, bowing; and kissed the papers
with an air of gallantry, that I thought greatly became him."

[2] *Ibid.* vi. Letter xxxi. 236. [3] *Ibid.* vi. Letter xxxiii. 252.

honour of your hand, shall be ready to regret that I
acquiesced so cheerfully with the wishes of those
parental friends for a public celebration." [1] Courtesies
begin, compliments fly about; a swarm of proprieties
flutters around, like a troop of little love-cherubs, and
their devout wings serve to sanctify the blessed tender-
nesses of the happy couple. Tears abound; Harriet
bemoans the fate of Sir Hargrave Pollexfen, whilst Sir
Charles, "in a soothing, tender, and respectful manner,
put his arm round me, and taking my own handkerchief,
unresisted, wiped away the tears as they fell on my cheek.
Sweet humanity! Charming sensibility! Check not
the kindly gush. Dewdrops of heaven! (wiping away
my tears, and kissing the handkerchief), dew-drops of
heaven, from a mind like that heaven mild and gracious!" [2] It is too much; we are surfeited, we say to
ourselves that these phrases should be accompanied by
a mandoline. The most patient of mortals feels himself
sick at heart when he has swallowed a thousand pages
of this sentimental twaddle, and all the milk and water
of love. To crown all, Sir Charles, seeing Harriet
embrace her rival, sketches the plan of a little temple,
dedicated to Friendship, to be built on the very spot;
it is the triumph of mythological bad taste. At the end,
bouquets shower down as at the opera; all the characters sing in unison a chorus in praise of Sir Charles, and
his wife says : "But could he be otherwise than the best
of husbands, who was the most dutiful of sons, who is
the most affectionate of brothers; the most faithful of
friends : who is good upon principle in every relation
of life!" [3] He is great, he is generous, delicate, pious,

. [1] *Sir Charles Grandison*, vi. Letter lii. 358.
[2] *Ibid.* vi. Letter xxxi. 233.   [3] *Ibid.* vii. Letter lxi. 336.

irreproachable; he has never done a mean action, nor made a wrong gesture. His conscience and his wig are unsullied. Amen! Let us canonise him, and stuff him with straw.

Nor, my dear Richardson, have you, great as you are, exactly all the wit which is necessary in order to have enough. By seeking to serve morality, you prejudice it. Do you know the effect of these edifying advertisements which you stick on at the beginning or end of your books? We are repelled, feel our emotion diminish, see the black-gowned preacher come snuffling out of the worldly dress which he had assumed for an hour; we are annoyed by the deceit. Insinuate morality, but do not inflict it. Remember there is a substratum of rebellion in the human heart, and that if we too openly set ourselves to wall it up with discipline, it escapes and looks for free air outside. You print at the end of *Pamela* the catalogue of the virtues of which she is an example; the reader yawns, forgets his pleasure, ceases to believe, and asks himself if the heavenly heroine was not an ecclesiastical puppet, trotted out to give him a lesson. You relate at the end of *Clarissa Harlowe* the punishment of all the wicked, great and small, sparing none; the reader laughs, says that things happen otherwise in this world, and bids you put in here like Arnolphe,[1] a description " of the cauldrons in which the souls of those who have led evil lives are to boil in the infernal regions." We are not such fools as you take us for. There is no need that you should shout to make us afraid; that you should write out the lesson by itself, and in capitals, in order to distinguish it. We

A selfish and misanthropical cynic in Moliére's *École des Femmes.*
—Tr.

love art, and you have a scant amount of it; we want
to be pleased, and you don't care to please us. You
copy all the letters, detail the conversations, tell everything, prune nothing; your novels fill many volumes;
spare us, use the scissors; be a skilled literary workman,
not a registrar of the Rolls office. Do not pour out your
library of documents on the high-road. Art is different
from nature; the latter draws out, the first condenses.
Twenty letters of twenty pages do not display a character; but one brilliant saying does. You are weighed
down by your conscience, which compels you to move
step by step and slow; you are afraid of your genius;
you rein it in; you dare not use loud cries and
free speech at the very moment when passion is most
virulent. You flounder into emphatic and well-written
phrases;[1] you will not show nature as it is, as Shakspeare shows it, when, stung by passion as by a hot
iron, it cries out, rears, and bounds over your barriers.
You cannot love it, and your punishment is that you
cannot see it.[2]

[1] Clarissa and Pamela employ too many.

[2] In *Novels and Novelists*, by W. Forsyth, 1871, it is said, ch. vii.:
"To me, I confess, *Clarissa Harlowe* is an unpleasant, not to say odious
book. . . . If any book deserved the charge of sickly sentimentality, it
is this ; and that it should have once been so widely popular, and
thought admirably adapted to instruct young women in lessons of virtue
and religion, shows a strange and perverted state of the public taste,
not to say public morals." Mrs. Oliphant, in her *Historical Sketches
of the Reign of George Second*, 1869, says of the same novel (ii. x. 264) :
"Richardson was a respectable tradesman, . . . a good printer, . . . a
comfortable soul, . . . never owing a guinea nor transgressing a rule of
morality ; and yet so much a poet, that he has added at least one
character (Clarissa Harlowe) to the inheritance of the world, of which
Shakspeare need not have been ashamed—the most celestial thing, the
highest effort of his generation."—Tr.

V.

Fielding protests on behalf of nature; and certainly, to see his actions and his persons, we might think him made expressly for that purpose: a robust, strongly built man, above six feet high, sanguine, with an excess of good humour and animal spirits, loyal, generous, affectionate, and brave, but imprudent, extravagant, a drinker, a roysterer, ruined as his father was before him, having seen the ups and downs of life, not always clean but always jolly. ·Lady Wortley Montague says of him: "His happy constitution made him forget everything when he was before a venison pasty, or over a flask of champagne."[1] Natural impulse, somewhat coarse but generous, sways him. It does not restrain itself, it flows freely, it follows its own bent, not too choice in its course, not confining itself to banks, miry but copious, and in a broad channel. From the outset an abundance of health and physical impetuosity plunges Fielding into gross jovial excess, and the immoderate sap of youth bubbles up in him until he marries and becomes ripe in years. He is gay, and seeks gaiety; he is careless, and has not even literary vanity. One day Garrick begged him to cut down an awkward scene, and told him "that a repulse would flurry him so much, he should not be able to do justice to the part." "If the scene is not a good one, let them find that out," said Fielding; just as was foreseen, the house made a violent uproar, and the performer tried to quell it by retiring to the green-room, where the author was supporting his spirits with a bottle of champagne. "What is the matter, Garrick? are they hissing me

[1] *Lady Montague's Letters*, ed. Lord Wharncliffe, 2d ed. 3 vols. 1837 ; Letter to the Countess of Bute, iii. 120.

now ?" " Yes, just the same passage that I wanted you
to retrench." " Oh," replied the author, " I did not give
them credit for it : they have found it out, have they ?"[1]
In this easy manner he took all mischances. He went
ahead without feeling the bruises much, like a confident
man, whose heart expands and whose skin is thick.
When he inherited some money he feasted, gave dinners
to his neighbours, kept a pack of hounds and a lot of
magnificent lackeys in yellow livery. In three years
he had spent it all ; but courage remained, he finished
his law studies, prepared a voluminous Digest of the
Statutes at Large, in two folio volumes, which remained
unpublished, became a magistrate, destroyed bands of
robbers, and earned in the most insipid of labours " the
dirtiest money upon earth." Disgust, weariness did
not affect him ; he was too solidly made to have the
nerves of a woman. Force, activity, invention, tenderness, all overflowed in him. He had a mother's fond-
ness for his children, adored his wife, became almost
mad when he lost her, found no other consolation than
to weep with his maid-servant, and ended by marrying
that good and honest girl, that he might give a mother
to his children ; the last trait in the portrait of this
valiant plebeian heart, quick in telling all, having no
dislikes, but all the best parts of man, except delicacy.
We read his books as we drink a pure, wholesome, and
rough wine, which cheers and fortifies us, and which
wants nothing but bouquet.

Such a man was sure to dislike Richardson. He who
loves expansive and liberal nature, drives from him like
foes the solemnity, sadness, and pruderies of the Puritans. His first literary work was to caricature Richardson.

[1] Roscoe's *Life of Fielding*, p. xxv.

His first hero, Joseph, is the brother of Pamela, and resists the proposals of his mistress, as Pamela does those of her master. The temptation, touching in the case of a girl, becomes comical in that of a young man, and the tragic turns into the grotesque. Fielding laughs heartily, like Rabelais, or Scarron. He imitates the emphatic style; ruffles the petticoats and bobs the wigs; upsets with his rude jests all the seriousness of conventionality. If we are refined, or simply well dressed, don't let us go along with him. He will take us to prisons, inns, dunghills, the mud of the roadside; he will make us flounder among rollicking, scandalous, vulgar adventures, and crude pictures. He has plenty of words at command, and his sense of smell is not delicate. Mr. Joseph Andrews, after leaving Lady Booby, is felled to the ground, left naked in a ditch, for dead; a stage-coach came by; a lady objects to receive a naked man inside; and the gentlemen, " though there were several greatcoats about the coach," could not spare them; the coachman, who had two greatcoats spread under him, refused to lend either, lest they should be made bloody.[1] This is but the out-set, judge of the rest. Joseph and his friend, the good Parson Adams, give and receive a vast number of cuffs; blows resound; cans of pig's blood are thrown at their heads; dogs tear their clothes to pieces; they lose their horse. Joseph is so good-looking, that he is assailed by the maid-servant, " obliged to take her in his arms and to shut her out of the room;"[2] they have never any money; they are threatened with being sent to prison. Yet they go on in a merry fashion, like their

---

[1] *The Adventures of Joseph Andrews*, bk. i. ch. xii.
[2] *Ibid.* i. ch. xviii.

brothers in Fielding's other novels, Captain Booth and
Tom·Jones. These hailstorms of blows, these tavern
brawls, this noise of broken warming-pans and basins
flung at heads, this medley of incidents and down-
pouring of mishaps, combine to make the most joyous
music. All these honest folk fight well, walk well, eat
well, drink still better. It is a pleasure to observe these
potent stomachs; roast-beef goes down into them as to
its natural place. Let us not say that these good arms
practise too much on their neighbours' skins: the
neighbours' hides are tough, and always heal quickly.
Decidedly life is a good thing, and we will go along with
Fielding, smiling by the way, with a broken head and
a bellyful.

Shall we merely laugh? There are many things to
be seen on our journey: the sentiment of nature is a
talent, like the understanding of certain rules; and
Fielding, turning his back on Richardson, opens up a
domain as wide as that of his rival. What we call
nature is this brood of secret passions, often malicious,
generally vulgar, always blind, which tremble and fret
within us, ill-covered by the cloak of decency and reason
under which we try to disguise them; we think we
lead them, and they lead us; we think our actions our
own, they are theirs. They are so many, so strong, so
interwoven, so ready to rise, break forth, be carried
away, that their movements elude all our reasoning and
our grasp. This is Fielding's domain; his art and
pleasure, like Molière's are in lifting a corner of the
cloak; his characters parade with a rational air, and
suddenly, through a vista, the reader perceives the inner
turmoil of vanities, follies, lusts, and secret rancours
which make them move. Thus, when Tom Jones' arm

is broken, philosopher Square comes to console him by an application of stoical maxims ; but in proving to him that " pain was the most contemptible thing in the world," he bites his tongue, and lets slip an oath or two ; whereupon Parson Thwackum, his opponent and rival, assures him that his mishap, is a warning of Providence, and both in consequence are nearly coming to blows.[1] In *the Life of Mr. Jonathan Wild*, the prison chaplain having aired his eloquence, and entreated the condemned man to repent, accepts from him a bowl of punch, because " it is nowhere spoken against in Scripture ;" and after drinking, repeats his last sermon against the pagan philosophers. Thus unveiled, natural impulse has a grotesque appearance ; the people advance gravely, cane in hand, but in our eyes they are all naked. Understand, they are every whit naked ; and some of their attitudes are very lively. Ladies will do well not to enter here. This powerful genius, frank and joyous, loves boorish feasts like Rubens ; the red faces, beaming with good humour, sensuality, and energy, move about his pages, flutter hither and thither, and jostle each other, and their overflowing instincts break forth in violent actions. Out of such he creates his chief characters. He has none more lifelike than these, more broadly sketched in bold and dashing outline, with a more wholesome colour. If sober people like Allworthy remain in a corner of his vast canvas, characters full of natural impulse, like Western, stand out with a relief and brightness, never seen since Falstaff. Western is a country squire, a good fellow in the main, but a drunkard, always in the saddle, full of oaths, ready with coarse language, blows, a sort of dull carter, hardened

---

[1] *History of a Foundling*, bk. v. ch. ii.

and excited by the brutality of the race, the wildness
of a country life, by violent exercise, by abuse of coarse
food and strong drink, full of English and rustic pride
and prejudice, having never been disciplined by the
constraint of the world, because he lives in the country;
nor by that of education, since he can hardly read;
nor of reflection, since he cannot put two ideas together;
nor of authority, because he is rich and a justice of the
peace, and given up, like a noisy and creaking weather-
cock, to every gust of passion. When contradicted, he
grows red, foams at the mouth, wishes to thrash some
one. "Doff thy clothes." They are even obliged to
stop him by main force. He hastens to go to Allworthy to complain of Tom Jones, who has dared to
fall in love with his daughter: "It's well for un I
could not get at un: I'd a licked un; I'd a spoiled his
caterwauling; I'd a taught the son of a whore to meddle
with meat for his master. He shan't ever have a morsel of meat of mine, or a varden to buy it. If she will
ha un, one smock shall be her portion. I'd sooner give
my estate to the sinking fund, that it may be sent to
Hanover, to corrupt our nation with."[1] Allworthy says
he is very sorry for it: "Pox o' your sorrow. It will
do me abundance of good, when I have lost my only
child, my poor Sophy that was the joy of my heart, and
all the hope and comfort of my age. But I am resolved
I will turn her out o' doors; she shall beg, and starve,
and rot in the streets. Not one hapenny, not a hapenny
shall she ever hae o' mine. The son of a bitch was
always good at finding a hare sitting and be rotted to'n;
I little thought what puss he was looking after. But
it shall be the worst he ever vound in his life. She

[1] *History of a Foundling*, bk. vi. ch. x.

shall be no better than carrion; the skin o'er it is all
he shall ha, and zu you may tell un."[1]   His daughter
tries to reason with him; he storms.   Then she speaks
of tenderness and obedience; he leaps about the room
for joy, and tears come to his eyes.   Then she recom-
mences her prayers; he grinds his teeth, clenches his
fists, stamps his feet; "I am determined upon this
match, and ha him[2] you shall, damn me, if shat unt.
Damn me, if shat unt, though dost hang thyself the
next morning."[3]   He can find no reason; he can only
tell her to be a good girl.   He contradicts himself,
defeats his own plans; is like a blind bull, which butts
to right and left, doubles on his path, touches no one,
and paws the ground.   At the least sound he rushes
head foremost, offensively, not knowing why.   His
ideas are only starts or transports of flesh and blood.
Never has the animal so completely covered and
absorbed the man.   It makes him grotesque; he is so
natural and so brute-like: he allows himself to be led,
and speaks like a child.   He says: "I don't know how
'tis, but, Allworthy, you make me do always just as you
please; and yet I have as good an estate as you, and
am in the commission of the peace just as yourself."[4]
Nothing holds or lasts with him; he is impulsive in
everything; he lives but for the moment.   Rancour,
interest, no passions of long continuance affect him.
He embraces people whom he just before wanted to
knock down.   Everything with him disappears in the
fire of the momentary passion, which floods his brain,
as it were, in sudden waves, and drowns the rest.
Now that he is reconciled to Tom Jones, he cannot rest

[1] *History of a Foundling*, bk. vi. ch. x.   [2] Blifil.
[3] *History of a Foundling*, xvi. ch. ii.   [4] *Ibid.* xviii. ch. ix.

until Tom marries his daughter : "To her, boy, to her,
go to her. That's it, little honeys, O that's it. Well,
what, is it all over? Hath she appointed the day,
boy? What, shall it be to-morrow or next day? I
shan't be put off a minute longer than next day; I am
resolved. . . . I tell thee it is all flimflam. Zoodikers!
she'd have the wedding to-night with all her heart.
Would'st not, Sophy? . . . Where the devil is Allworthy;
. . . Harkee, Allworthy, I'll bet thee five pounds to a
crown, we have a boy to-morrow nine months. But
prithee, tell me what wut ha? Burgundy, champagne,
or what? For please Jupiter, we'll make a night on't."[1]
And when he becomes a grandfather, he spends his time
in the nursery, "where he declares the tattling of his
little granddaughter, who is above a year and a half old, is
sweeter music than the finest cry of dogs in England."[2]
This is pure nature, and no one has displayed it more
free, more impetuous, ignoring all rule, more abandoned
to physical passions than Fielding.

It is not because he loves it like the great impartial
artists, Shakspeare and Goethe; on the contrary, he is
eminently a moralist; and it is one of the great marks
of the age, that reformatory designs are as decided with
him as with others. He gives his fictions a practical
aim, and commends them by saying that the serious
and tragic tone sours, whilst the comic style disposes
men to be "more full of good humour and benevolence."[3]
Moreover, he satirises vice; he looks upon the passions
not as simple forces, but as objects of approbation or
blame. At every step he suggests moral conclusions;

[1] *History of a Foundling*, xviii. ch. xii.
[2] Last chapter of the *History of a Foundling*.
[3] Preface to *Joseph Andrews*

he wants us to take sides; he discusses, excuses, or condemns. He writes an entire novel in an ironical style,[1] to attack and destroy rascality and treason. He is more than a painter, he is a judge, and the two parts agree in him. For a psychology produces a morality: where there is an idea of man, there is an ideal of man; and Fielding, who has seen in man nature as opposed to rule, praises in man nature as opposed to rule; so that, according to him, virtue is but an instinct. Generosity in his eyes is, like all sources of action, a primitive inclination; like all sources of action, it flows on receiving no good from catechisms and phrases; like all sources of action, it flows at times too copious and quick. Take it as it is, and do not try to oppress it under a discipline, or to replace it by an argument. Mr. Richardson, your heroes, so correct, constrained, so carefully made up with their impedimenta of maxims, are cathedral vergers, of use but to drone in a procession. Square or Thwackum, your tirades on philosophical or Christian virtue are mere words, only fit to be heard after dinner. Virtue is in the mood and the blood; a gossipy education and cloistral severity do not assist it. Give me a man, not a show-mannikin or a mere machine, to spout phrases. My hero is the man who is born generous, as a dog is born affectionate, and a horse brave. I want a living heart, full of warmth and force, not a dry pedant, bent on squaring all his actions. This ardent and impulsive character will perhaps carry the hero too far; I pardon his escapades. He will get drunk unawares; he will pick up a girl on his way; he will hit out with a zest; he will not refuse a duel; he will suffer a fine lady to appreciate him, and will accept

[1] *Jonathan Wild.*

her purse; he will be imprudent, will injure his reputation, like Tom Jones; he will be a bad manager, and will get into debt, like Captain Booth.   Pardon him for having muscles, nerves, senses, and that overflow of anger or ardour which urges forward animals of a noble breed. But he will let himself be beaten till the blood flows, before he betrays a poor gamekeeper.   He will pardon his mortal enemy readily, from sheer kindness, and will send him money secretly.   He will be loyal to his mistress, and will be faithful to her, spite of all offers, in the worst destitution, and without the least hope of winning her.   He will be liberal with his purse, his trouble, his sufferings, his blood; he will not boast of it; he will have neither pride, vanity, affectation, nor dissimulation; bravery and kindness will abound in his heart, as good water in a good spring.   He may be stupid like Captain Booth, a gambler even, extravagant, unable to manage his affairs, liable one day through temptation to be unfaithful to his wife; but he will be so sincere in his repentance, his error will be so involuntary, he will be so carefully, genuinely tender, that she will love him exceedingly,[1] and in good truth he will deserve it.   He will be a nurse to her when she is ill, behave as a mother to her; he will himself see to her lying-in; he will feel towards her the adoration of a lover, always, before all the world, even

---

[1] Amelia is the perfect English wife, an excellent cook, so devoted as to pardon her husband his accidental infidelities, always looking forward to the accoucheur. She says even (bk. iv. ch. vi.), "Dear Billy, though my understanding be much inferior to yours." She is excessively modest, always blushing and tender. Bagillard having written her some love-letters, she throws them away, and says (bk. iii. ch. ix.): "I would not have such a letter in my possession for the universe; I thought my eyes contaminated with reading it."

before Miss Matthews, who seduced him.   He says " If
I had the world, I was ready to lay it at my Amelia's
feet; and so, heaven knows, I would ten thousand
worlds."[1]   He weeps like a child on thinking of her;
he listens to her like a little child.   " I believe I am
able to recollect much the greatest part (of what she
uttered); for the impression is never to be effaced from
my memory."[2]   He dressed himself " with all the
expedition imaginable, singing, whistling, hurrying,
attempting by every method to banish thought,"[3] and
galloped away, whilst his wife was asleep, because he
cannot endure her tears.   In this soldier's body,
under this brawler's thick breastplate, there is a true
woman's heart, which melts, which a trifle disturbs,
when she whom he loves is in question; timid in its
tenderness, inexhaustible in devotion, in trust, in self-
denial, in the communication of its feelings.   When a
man possesses this, overlook the rest; with all his
excesses and his follies, he is better than your well-
dressed devotees.

To this we reply; You do well to defend nature, but
let it be on condition that you suppress nothing.   One
thing is wanting in your strongly-built folks—refinement; delicate dreams, enthusiastic elevation, and
trembling delicacy exist in nature equally with coarse
vigour, noisy hilarity, and frank kindness.   Poetry is
true, like prose; and if there are eaters and boxers,
there are also knights and artists.   Cervantes, whom
you imitate, and Shakspeare, whom you recall, had this
refinement, and they have painted it; in this abundant
harvest, which you have gathered so plentifully, you

Amelia, bk. ii. ch. viii.   [2] *Ibid*. bk. iii. ch. i.

[3] *Ibid*. bk. iii. ch. ii.

have. forgotten the flowers. We tire at last of your fisticuffs and tavern bills. You flounder too readily in cowhouses, among the ecclesiastical pigs of Parson Trulliber. We would fain see you have more regard for the modesty of your heroines; wayside accidents raise their tuckers too often; and Fanny, Sophia, Mrs. Heartfree, may continue pure, yet we cannot help remembering the assaults which have lifted their petticoats. You are so coarse yourself, that you are insensible to what is atrocious. You persuade Tom Jones falsely, yet for an instant, that Mrs. Waters, whom he has made his mistress, is his own mother, and you leave the reader during a long time buried in the shame of this supposition. And then you are obliged to become unnatural in order to depict love; you can give but constrained letters; the transports of your Tom Jones are only the author's phrases. For want of ideas he declaims odes. You are only aware of the impetuosity of the senses, the upwelling of the blood, the effusion of tenderness,.but you are unacquainted with nervous exaltation and poetic rapture. Man, such as you conceive him, is a good buffalo; and perhaps he is the hero required by a people which gives itself the nickname "John Bull."

VI.

At all events this hero is powerful and formidable; and if at this period we collect in our mind the scattered features of the faces which the novel-writers have made pass before us, we will feel ourselves transported into a half-barbarous world, and to a race whose energy must terrify or revolt all our gentleness. Now let us open a more literal copyist of life: they are doubtless all such,

and declare—Fielding amongst them—that if they imagine a feature, it is because they have seen it; but Smollett has this advantage, that, being mediocre, he chalks
out the figures tamely, prosaically, without transforming
them by the illumination of genius : the joviality of
Fielding and the rigour of Richardson are not there to
light up or ennoble the pictures.   Let us observe carefully Smollett's manners; let us listen to the confessions
of this imitator of Le Sage, who reproaches that author
with being gay, and jesting with the mishaps of his
hero.   He says: " The disgraces of Gil Blas are, for
the most part, such as rather excite mirth than compassion : he himself laughs at them, and his transitions
from distress to happiness, or at least ease, are so sudden
that neither the reader has time to pity him, nor himself to be acquainted with affliction.   This conduct . . .
prevents that generous indignation which ought to
animate the reader against the sordid and vicious
disposition of the world.   I have attempted to represent modest merit struggling with every difficulty to
which a friendless orphan is exposed from his own
want of experience as well as from the selfishness,
envy, malice, and base indifference of mankind." [1]   We
hear no longer merely showers of blows, but also
knife and sword thrusts, as well as pistol shots.   In
such a world, when a girl goes out she runs the risk of
coming back a woman; and when a man goes out, he
runs the risk of not coming back at all.   The women
bury their nails in the faces of the men; the well-bred
gentlemen, like Peregrine Pickle, whip other gentlemen
soundly.   Having deceived a husband, who refuses to
demand satisfaction, Peregrine calls his two servants,

[1] Preface to *Roderick Random.*

" and ordered them to duck him in the canal." [1]
Misrepresented by a curate, whom he has horsewhipped,
he gets an innkeeper " to rain a shower of blows upon
his (the parson's) carcase," who also " laid hold of one
of his ears with his teeth, and bit it unmercifully." [2]
I could quote from memory a score more of outrages
begun or completed. Savage insults, broken jaws,
men on the ground beaten with sticks, the churlish
sourness of conversations, the coarse brutality of jests
give an idea of a pack of bull-dogs eager to fight each
other, who, when they begin to get lively, still amuse
themselves by tearing away pieces of flesh. A Frenchman can hardly endure the story of *Roderick Random*,
or rather that of Smollett, when he is on board a man-
of-war. He is pressed, that is to say, carried off by
force, knocked down, attacked with "cudgels and drawn
cutlasses," " pinioned like a malefactor," and rolled on
board, covered with blood, before the sailors, who laugh
at his wounds; and one of them, " seeing my hair
clotted together with blood, as it were, into distinct
cords, took notice that my bows were manned with the
red ropes, instead of my side." [3] Roderick " desired
one of his fellow-captives, who was unfettered, to take
a handkerchief out of his pocket, and tie it round his
head to stop the bleeding; he (the fellow) pulled out
my handkerchief, 'tis true, but sold it before my face
to a bum-boat woman for a quart of gin." Captain
Oakum declares he will have no more sick in his ship,
ordered them to be brought on the quarter-deck,
commanded that some should receive a round dozen;
some spitting blood, others fainting from weakness,
whilst not a few became delirious; many died, and of

[1] *Peregrine Pickle*, ch. lx.   [2] *Ibid.* ch. xxix.   [3] *Ibid.* ch. xxiv.

the sixty-one sick, only a dozen remained alive.[1] To
get into this dark, suffocating hospital, swarming with
vermin, it is necessary to creep under the close ham-
mocks, and forcibly separate them with the shoulders,
before the doctor can reach his patients. Read the
story of Miss Williams, a wealthy young girl, of good
family, reduced to become a prostitute, robbed, hungry,
sick, shivering, strolling about the streets in the
long winter nights, amongst " a number of naked
wretches reduced to rags and filth, huddled together
like swine, in the corner of a dark alley," who depend
" upon the addresses of the lowest class, and are fain
to allay the rage of hunger and cold with gin ; degene-
rate into a brutal insensibility, rot and die upon a
dunghill.".[2]   She was thrown into Bridewell, where,
she says, " in the midst of a hellish crew I was subjected
to the tyranny of a barbarian, who imposed upon me
tasks that I could not possibly perform, and then
punished my incapacity with the utmost rigour and
inhumanity. I was often whipped into a swoon, and
lashed out of it, during which miserable intervals I was
robbed by my fellow-prisoners of everything about me,
even to my cap, shoes, and stockings : I was not only
destitute of necessaries, but even of food, so that my
wretchedness was extreme." One night she tried to
hang herself. Two of her fellow-prisoners, who watched
her, prevented her.   " In the morning my attempt was
published among the prisoners, and punished with
thirty stripes, the pain of which co-operating with my
disappointment and disgrace, bereft me of my senses,
and threw me into an ecstasy of madness, during which
I tore the flesh from my bones with my teeth, and

---

[1] *Peregrine Pickle*, ch. xxvii.   [2] *Ibid.* ch. xxiii.

dashed my head against the pavement." [1]   In vain we
turn our eyes on the hero of the novel, Roderick Random,
to repose a little after such a spectacle.   He is sensual
and coarse, like Fielding's heroes, but not good and
jovial as these.   Pride and resentment are the two
principal points in his character.   The generous wine
of Fielding, in Smollett's hands becomes common
brandy.   His heroes are selfish ; they revenge themselves
barbarously.   Roderick oppresses the faithful Strap,
and ends by marrying him to a prostitute.   Peregrine
Pickle attacks by a most brutal and cowardly plot the
honour of a young girl, whom he wants to marry, and
who is the sister of his best friend.   We get to hate
his rancorous, concentrated, obstinate character, which
is at once that of an absolute king accustomed to please
himself at the expense of others' happiness, and that
of a boor with only the varnish of education.   We
should be uneasy at living near him ; he is good for
nothing but to. shock or tyrannise over others.   We
avoid him as we would a dangerous beast ; the sudden
rush of animal passion and the force of his firm will
are so overpowering in him, that when he fails he
becomes outrageous.   He draws his sword against an
innkeeper ; he must bleed him, grows mad.   Everything,
even to his generosities, is spoilt by pride ; all, even to
his gaieties, is clouded by harshness.   Peregrine's
amusements are barbarous, and those of Smollett are
after the same style.   He exaggerates caricature ; he
thinks to amuse us by showing us mouths gaping to
the ears, and noses half-a-foot long ; he magnifies a
national prejudice or a professional trick until it absorbs
the whole character; he jumbles together the most

[1] *Peregrine Pickle*, ch. xxiii.

repulsive oddities, — a Lieutenant Lismahago half roasted by Red Indians; old jack-tars who pass their life in shouting and travestying all sorts of ideas into their nautical jargon; old maids as ugly as monkeys, as fleshless as skeletons, and as sour as vinegar; eccentric people steeped in pedantry, hypochondria, misanthropy, and silence. Far from sketching them slightly, as Le Sage does in *Gil Blas*, he brings into prominent relief each disagreeable feature, overloads it with details, without considering whether they are too numerous, without recognising that they are excessive, without feeling that they are odious, without perceiving that they are disgusting. The public whom he addresses is on a level with his energy and his coarseness; and in order to move such nerves, a writer cannot strike too hard.[1]

But, at the same time, to civilise this barbarity and to control this violence, a faculty appears, common to all, authors and public: serious reflection intent to observe character. Their eyes are turned toward the inner man. They note exactly the individual pecu-

In *Novels and Novelists*, by W. Forsyth, the author says, ch. v. 159 : "What is the character of most of these books (novels) which were to correct follies and regulate morality? Of a great many of them, and especially those of Fielding and Smollett, the prevailing features are grossness and licentiousness. Love degenerates into a mere animal passion. . . . The language of the characters abounds in oaths and gross expressions. . . . The heroines allow themselves to take part in conversations which no modest woman would have heard without a blush. And yet these novels were the delight of a bygone generation, and were greedily devoured by women as well as men. Are we therefore to conclude that our great-great-grandmothers . . . were less chaste and moral than their female posterity? I answer, certainly not; but we must infer that they were inferior to them in delicacy and refinement. They were accustomed to hear a spade called a spade, and words which would shock the more fastidious ear in the reign of Queen Victoria were then in common and daily use."—TR.

liarities, and stamp them with such a precise mark that
their personage becomes a type, which cannot be
forgotten. They are psychologists. The title of a
comedy, of old Ben Jonson's *Every Man in his
Humour*, indicates how old and national this taste
is amongst them. Smollett writes a whole novel,
Humphrey Clinker, on this idea. There is no action in
it; the book is a collection of letters written during a
tour in Scotland and England. Each of the travellers,
after his bent of mind, judges variously of the same
objects. A generous, grumbling old gentleman, who
employs his spare time by thinking himself ill, a crabbed
old maid in search of a husband; a lady's maid, simple
and vain, who bravely bungles her spelling; a series of
eccentric people, who one after another bring their
oddities on the scene,—such are the characters: the
pleasure of the reader consists in recognising their
humour in their style, in foreseeing their follies, in perceiving the thread which pulls each of their motions, in
verifying the connection between their ideas and their
actions. When we push this study of human peculiarities
to excess we will come upon the origin of Sterne's talent.

VII.

Let us figure to ourselves a man who goes on a
journey, with a pair of marvellously magnifying spectacles on his eyes. A hair on his hand, a speck on a
tablecloth, a fold of a moving garment, will interest
him: at this rate he will not go very far; he will go
six steps in a day, and will not quit his room. So
Sterne writes four volumes to record the birth of his
hero. He perceives the infinitely little, and describes
the imperceptible. A man parts his hair on one side;

this, according to Sterne, depends on his whole character, which is 'of a piece with that of his father, his
mother, his uncle, and his whole ancestry; it depends
on the structure of his brain, which depends on the
circumstances of his conception and his birth, and these
on the hobbies of his parents, the humour of the moment,
the talk of the preceding hour, the difficulties of the
parson, a cut thumb, twenty knots made on a bag; I
know not how many things besides.   The six or eight
volumes of *Tristram Shandy* are employed in summing
them up; for the smallest and dullest incident, a sneeze,
a badly-shaven beard, drags after it an inextricable
network of inter-involved causes, which from above,
below, right and left, by invisible prolongations and
ramifications, sink into the depths of a character and in
the remote vistas of events.   Instead of extracting, like
the novel-writers, the principal root, Sterne, with
marvellous devices and success, devotes himself to
drawing out the tangled skein of numberless threads,
which are sinuously immersed and dispersed, so as to
suck in from all sides the sap and the life.   Slender,
intertwined, buried as they are, he finds them; he ex-
tricates them without breaking, brings them to the
light; and there, where we fancied but a stalk, we see
with wonder the underground mass and vegetation of
the multiplied fibres and fibrils, by which the visible
plant grows and is supported.

This is truly a strange talent, made up of blindness
and insight, which resembles those diseases of the retina
in which the over-excited nerve becomes at once dull
and penetrating, incapable of seeing what the most
ordinary eyes perceive, capable of observing what the
most piercing sight misses.   In fact, Sterne is a sickly

and eccentric humorist, a clergyman and a libertine, a
fiddler and a philosopher, who preferred " whining over
a dead ass to relieving a living mother,"[1] selfish in act,
selfish in word, who in everything takes a contrary view
of himself and of others.   His book is like a great store-
house of articles of *virtu*, where curiosities of all ages,
kinds, and countries lie jumbled in a heap; forms of
excommunication, medical consultations, passages of unknown or imaginary authors, scraps of scholastic erudition, strings of absurd histories, dissertations, addresses to
the reader.   His pen leads him; he has neither sequence
nor plan; nay, when he lights upon anything orderly, he
purposely contorts it; with a kick he sends the pile of
folios next to him over the history he has commenced, and
dances on the top of them.   He delights in disappoint-
ing us, in sending us astray by interruptions and delays.[2]
Gravity displeases him, he treats it as a hypocrite : to
his liking folly is better, and he paints himself in Yorick.
In a well-constituted mind ideas march one after
another, with uniform motion or acceleration; in this
odd brain they jump about like a rout of masks at a
carnival, in troops, each dragging his neighbour by the
feet, head, coat, amidst the most general and unforeseen
hubbub.   All his little lopped phrases are somersaults;
we pant as we read.   The tone is never for two minutes
the same; laughter comes, then the beginning of emotion,
then scandal, then wonder, then sensibility, then laughter
again.   The mischievous joker pulls and entangles the
threads of all our feelings, and makes us go hither,

[1] Byron's Works, ed. Moore, 17 vols. 1832 ; *Life*, iii. 127, note.

[2] There is a distinct trace of a spirit similar to that which is here
sketched, in a select few of the English writers.   Pultock's *Peter
Wilkins the Flying Man*, Amory's *Life of John Buncle*, and Southey's
Doctor, are instances of this.   Rabelais is probably their prototype.—TR.

thither, in a whimsical manner, like puppets. Amongst
these various threads there are two which he pulls more
willingly than the rest. Like all men who have nerves,
he is subject to sensibility; not that he is really
kindly and tender-hearted; on the contrary, his life is
that of an egotist; but on certain days he must needs
weep, and he makes us weep with him. He is moved
on behalf of a captive bird, of a poor ass, which, accustomed to blows, "looked up pensive," and seemed to say,
" Don't thrash me with it (the halter); but if you will,
you may." [1] He will write a couple of pages on the
attitude of this donkey, and Priam at the feet of
Achilles was not more touching. Thus in a silence, in
an oath, in the most trifling domestic action, he hits
upon exquisite refinements and little heroisms, a variety
of charming flowers, invisible to everybody else, which
grow in the dust of the driest road. One day Uncle
Toby, the invalided captain, catches, after "infinite
attempts," a big buzzing fly, who has cruelly tormented
him all dinner-time; he gets up, crosses the room on
his suffering leg, and opening the window, cries: "Go,
poor devil, get thee gone; why should I hurt thee?
This world surely is wide enough to hold both thee and
me." [2] This womanish sensibility is too fine to be described; we should have to give a whole story—that
of Lefevre, for instance—that the perfume might be
inhaled; this perfume evaporates as soon as we touch
it, and is like the weak fleeting odour of flowers,
brought for one moment into a sick-chamber. What
still more increases this sad sweetness is the contrast
of the free and easy waggeries which, like a hedge of

[1] Sterne's Works, 7 vols., 1783, 3; *The Life and Opinions of Tristram Shandy*, vii. ch. xxxii.   [2] *Ibid.* 1, ii. ch. xii.

nettles, encircles them on all sides. Sterne, like all
men whose mechanism is over-excited, has odd desires.
He loves the nude, not from a feeling of the beautiful,
and in the manner of painters, not from sensuality
and frankness like Fielding, not from a search after
pleasure like Dorat, Boufflers, and all those refined
epicures, who at that time were rhyming and enjoying themselves in France. If he goes into dirty
places, it is because they are forbidden and not frequented. What he seeks there is singularity and
scandal. The allurement of this forbidden fruit is not
the fruit, but the prohibition; for he bites by preference
where the fruit is half rotten or worm-eaten. That an
epicurean delights in detailing the pretty sins of a
pretty woman is nothing wonderful; but that a novelist
takes pleasure in watching the bedroom of a musty,
fusty old couple, in observing the consequences of the
fall of a burning chestnut in a pair of breeches,[1] in
detailing the questions of Mrs. Wadman on the consequences of wounds in the groin,[2] can only be explained
by the aberration of a perverted fancy, which finds its
amusement in repugnant ideas, as spoiled palates are
pleased by the pungent flavour of decayed cheese.[3] Thus,
to read Sterne we should wait for days when we are in
a peculiar kind of humour, days of spleen, rain, or when

---

[1] *Tristram Shandy*, 2, iv. ch. xxvii.   [2] *Ibid.* 3, ix. ch. xx.

[3] Sterne, Goldsmith, Burke, Sheridan, Moore, have a tone of their
own, which comes from their blood, or from their proximate or distant
parentage—the Irish tone. So Hume, Robertson, Smollett, Scott,
Burns, Beattie, Reid, D. Stewart, and others, have the Scottish tone.
In the Irish or Celtic tone we find an excess of chivalry, sensuality,
expansion; in short, a mind less equally balanced, more sympathetic
and less practical. The Scotsman, on the other hand, is an Englishman, either slightly refined or narrowed, because he has suffered more
and fasted more.

through nervous irritation we are disgusted with ration-
ality. In fact his characters are as unreasonable as
himself. He sees in man nothing but fancy, and what
he calls the hobby-horse—Uncle Toby's taste for
fortifications, Mr. Shandy's fancy for oratorical tirades
and philosophical systems. This hobby-horse, according
to him, is like a wart, so small at first that we hardly
perceive it, and only when it is in a strong light; but
it gradually increases, becomes covered with hairs, grows
red, and buds out all around: its possessor, who is
pleased with and admires it, nourishes it, until at last
it is changed into a vast wen, and the whole face
disappears under the invasion of the parasite excre-
scence. No one has equalled Sterne in the history of
these human hypertrophies; he puts down the seed, feeds
it gradually, makes the propagating threads creep round
about, shows the little veins and microscopic arteries
which inosculate within, counts the palpitations of the
blood which passes through them, explains their changes
of colour and increase of bulk. Psychological observation attains here one of its extreme developments.
A far advanced art is necessary to describe, beyond the
confines of regularity and health, the exception or the
degeneration; and the English novel is completed here
by adding to the representation of form the picture of
malformations.

VIII.

The moment approaches when purified manners will,
by purifying the novel, give it its final impress and
character. Of the two great tendencies manifested by
it, native brutality and intense reflection, one at last
conquers the other; when literature became severe it
expelled from fiction the coarseness of Smollett and the

indecencies of Sterne; and the novel, in every respect
moral, before falling into the almost prudish hands of
Miss Burney, passes into the noble hands of Goldsmith.
His *Vicar of Wakefield* is "a prose idyl," somewhat
spoilt by phrases too rhetorical, but at bottom as
homely as a Flemish picture. Observe in Terburg's
or Mieris' paintings a woman at market or a burgo-
master emptying his long glass of beer: the faces are
vulgar, the ingenuousness is comical, the cookery occupies
the place of honour; yet these good folk are so peaceful,
so contented with their small ordinary happiness, that
we envy them. The impression left by Goldsmith's
book is pretty much the same. The excellent Dr.
Primrose is a country clergyman, the whole of whose
adventures have for a long time consisted in "migrations
from the blue bed to the brown." He has cousins,
"even to the fortieth remove," who come to eat his
dinner and sometimes to borrow a pair of boots. His
wife, who has all the education of the time, is a perfect
cook, can almost read, excels in pickling and preserving,
and at dinner gives the history of every dish. His
daughters aspire to elegance, and even "make a wash
for the face over the fire." His son Moses gets cheated
at the fair, and sells a colt for a gross of green spectacles.
Dr. Primrose himself writes pamphlets, which no one
buys, against second marriages of the clergy; writes
beforehand in his wife's epitaph, though she was still
living, that she was "the only wife of Dr. Primrose," and
by way of encouragement, places this piece of eloquence
in an elegant frame over the chimney-piece. But the
household continues the even tenor of its way; the
daughters and the mother slightly domineer over the
father of the family; he lets them do so, because he is

an easy-going man; now and again fires off an innocent
jest, and busies himself in his new farm, with his two
horses, wall-eyed Blackberry and the other without a
tail: "Nothing could exceed the neatness of my
enclosures, the elms and hedge-rows appearing with
inexpressible beauty. . . . Our little habitation was
situated at the foot of a sloping hill, sheltered with a
beautiful underwood behind, and a prattling river
before; on one side a meadow, on the other a green.
. . . (It) consisted but of one storey, and was covered
with thatch, which gave it an air of great snugness;
the walls on the inside were nicely whitewashed. . . .
Though the same room served us for parlour and
kitchen, that only made it the warmer. Besides, as it
was kept with the utmost neatness, the dishes, plates,
and coppers, being well scoured, and all disposed in
bright rows on the shelves, the eye was agreeably
relieved, and did not want richer furniture."[1] They
make hay all together, sit under the honeysuckle to
drink a bottle of gooseberry wine; the girls sing, the
two little ones read; and the parents "would stroll
down the sloping field, that was embellished with blue
bells and centaury:" "But let us have one bottle more,
Deborah, my life, and 'Moses, give us a good song.
What thanks do we not owe to heaven for thus
bestowing tranquillity, health, and competence! I
think myself happier now than the greatest monarch
upon earth. He has no such fireside, nor such pleasant
faces about it."[2]

Such is moral happiness. Their misfortune is no
less moral. The poor vicar has lost his fortune, and,
removing to a small living, turns farmer. The squire

---

[1] *The Vicar of Wakefield*, ch. iv.   [2] *Ibid.* ch. xvii.

of the neighbourhood seduces and carries off his, eldest daughter; his house takes fire; his arm was burnt in a terrible manner in saving his two little children. He is put in prison for debt, amongst wretches and rogues, who swear and blaspheme, in a vile atmosphere, sleeping on straw, feeling that his illness increases, foreseeing that his family will soon be without bread, learning that his daughter is dying. Yet he does not give way: he remains a priest and the head of a family, prescribes to each of them his duty; encourages, consoles, provides for, orders, preaches to the prisoners, endures their coarse jests, reforms them; establishes in the prison useful work, and "institutes fines for punishment and rewards for industry." It is not hardness of heart nor a morose temperament which gives him strength; he has the most paternal soul, the most sociable, humane, open to gentle emotions and familiar tenderness. He says: "I have no resentment now; and though he (the squire) has taken from me what I held dearer than all his treasures, though he has wrung my heart (for I am sick almost to fainting, very sick, my fellow-prisoner), yet that shall never inspire mé with vengeance. . . . If this (my) submission can do him any pleasure, let him know, that if I have done him any injury, I am sorry for it. . . . I should detest my own heart, if I saw either pride or resentment lurking there. On the contrary, as my oppressor has been once my parishioner, I hope one day to present him up an unpolluted soul at the eternal tribunal."[1] But the hard-hearted squire haughtily repulses the noble application of the vicar, and in addition causes his second daughter to be carried off, and the eldest son to be thrown into prison under a false

[1] *The Vicar of Wakefield*, ch. xxviii.

accusation of murder. At this moment all the affections
of the father are wounded, all his consolations lost, all
his hopes ruined. " His heart weeps to behold" all
this misery, he was going to curse the cause of it all;
but soon, returning to his profession and his duty, he
thinks how he will prepare to fit his son and himself
for eternity, and by way of being useful to as many
people as he can, he wishes at the same time to exhort
his fellow-prisoners. He " made an effort to rise on
the straw, but wanted strength, and was able only to
recline against the wall; my son and his mother
supported me on either side." [1] In this condition he
speaks, and his sermon, contrasting with his condition,
is the more moving. It is a dissertation in the English
style, made up of close reasoning, seeking only to
establish that " Providence has given to the wretched
two advantages over the happy in this life," greater
felicity in dying; and in heaven all that superiority of
pleasure which arises from contrasted enjoyments.[2]
We see the sources of this virtue, born of Christianity
and natural kindness, but long nourished by inner
reflection. Meditation, which usually produces only
phrases, results with Dr. Primrose in actions. Verily
reason has here taken the helm, and it has taken it
without oppressing other feelings; a rare and eloquent
spectacle, which, uniting and harmonising in one character the best features of the manners and morals of that
time and country, creates an admiration and love for
pious and orderly, domestic and disciplined, laborious
and rural life. Protestant and English virtue has not
a more approved and amiable exemplar. Religious,
affectionate, rational, the Vicar unites predilections

---

[1] *The Vicar of Wakefield,* ch. xxviii.   [2] *Ibid.* ch. xxix.

which seemed irreconcilable; a clergyman, a farmer, a head of a family, he enhances those characters which appeared fit only for comic or homely parts.

IX.

We now come upon a strange character, the most esteemed of his time, a sort of literary dictator. Richardson was his friend, and gave him essays for his paper; Goldsmith, with an artless vanity, admires him, whilst suffering to be continually outshone by him; Miss Burney imitates his style, and reveres him as a father. Gibbon the historian, Reynolds the painter, Garrick the actor, Burke the orator, Sir William Jones the Orientalist, come to his club to converse with him. Lord Chesterfield, who had lost his favour, vainly tried to regain it, by proposing to assign to him, on every word in the language, the authority of a dictator.[1] Boswell dogs his steps, sets down his opinions, and at night fills quartos with them. His criticism becomes law; men crowd to hear him talk; he is the arbiter of style. Let us transport in imagination this ruler of mind, Dr. Samuel Johnson, into France, among the pretty drawing-rooms, full of elegant philosophers and epicurean manners; the violence of the contrast will mark better than all argument the bent and predilections of the English mind.

There appears then before us a man whose "person was large, robust, approaching to the gigantic, and grown unwieldy from corpulency,"[2] with a gloomy and

---

[1] See, in Boswell's *Life of Johnson*, ed. Croker, 1853, ch. xi. p. 85, Chesterfield's complimentary paper on Johnson's *Dictionary*, printed in the *World*.   [2] *Ibid.* ch. xxx. 269.

unpolished air, "his countenance disfigured by the king's evil," and blinking with one of his eyes, "in a full suit of plain brown clothes," and with not overclean linen, suffering from morbid melancholy since his birth, and moreover a hypochondriac.[1] In company he would sometimes retire to a window or corner of a room, and mutter a Latin verse or a prayer.[2] At other times, in a recess, he would roll his head, sway his body backward and forward, stretch out and then convulsively draw back his leg. His biographer relates that it "was his constant anxious care to go out or in at a door or passage, . . . so as that either his right or his left foot should constantly make the first actual movement; . . . when he had neglected or gone wrong in this sort of magical movement, I have seen him go back again, put himself in the proper posture to begin the ceremony, and having gone through it, walk briskly on and join his companion."[3] People are sitting at table, when suddenly, in a moment of abstraction, he stoops, and clenching hold of the foot of a lady, draws off her shoe.[4] Hardly is the dinner served when he darts on the food; "his looks seemed rivetted to his plate; nor would he, unless when in very high company, say one word, or even pay the least attention to what was said by others; (he) indulged with such intenseness, that, while in the act of eating, the veins of his forehead swelled, and generally a strong perspiration was visible."[5] If by chance the hare was high, or the pie had been made with rancid butter, he no longer ate, but devoured. When at last his appetite was satisfied, and he con-

---

[1] *Life of Johnson*, ch. iii. 14 and 15.   [2] *Ibid.* ch. xviii. 165, n. 4.
[3] *Ibid.* ch. xviii. 166.   [4] *Ibid.* ch. xlviii. 439, n. 3.
[5] *Ibid.* ch. xvii. 159.

sented to speak, he disputed, shouted, made a sparring-match of his conversation, triumphed no matter how, laid down his opinion dogmatically, and ill-treated those whom he was refuting. " Sir, I perceive you are a vile Whig." [1] " My dear lady (to Mrs. Thrale), talk no more of this; nonsense can be defended but by nonsense." [2] " One thing I know, which you don't seem to know, that you are very uncivil." [3] " In the intervals of articulating he made various sounds with his mouth, sometimes as if ruminating, . . . sometimes giving a half whistle, sometimes making his tongue play backwards from the roof of his mouth, as if clucking like a hen. . . . Generally, when he had concluded a period, in the course of a dispute, . . . he used to blow out his breath like a whale," [4] and swallow several cups of tea.

Then in a low voice, cautiously, men would ask Garrick or Boswell the history and habits of this strange being. He had lived like a cynic and an eccentric, having passed his youth reading miscellaneously, especially Latin folios, even those least known, such as Macrobius; he had found on a shelf in his father's shop the Latin works of Petrarch, whilst he was looking for apples, and had read them; [5] " he published proposals for printing by subscription the Latin poems of Politian." [6] At twenty-five he had married for love a woman of about fifty, " very fat, with swelled cheeks, of a florid red, produced by thick painting, flaring and fantastic in her dress," [7] and who had children as old as

[1] *Life of Johnson*, ch. xxvi. 236.   [2] *Ibid.* ch. xxii. 201.
[3] *Ibid.* ch. lxviii. 628.   [4] *Ibid.* ch. xviii. 166.
[5] *Ibid.* ch. ii. 12.   [6] *Ibid.* ch. iv. 22.
[7] *Ibid.* ch. iv. 26.

himself. Having come to London to earn his bread, some people, seeing his convulsive grimaces, took him for an idiot; others, seeing his robust frame, advised him to buy a porter's knot.[1] For thirty years he worked like a hack for the publishers, whom he used to thrash when they became impertinent;[2] always shabby, having once fasted two days;[3] content when he could dine on "a cut of meat for sixpence, and bread for a penny;"[4] having written *Rasselas* in eight nights, to pay for his mother's funeral. Now pensioned [5] by the king, freed from his daily labours, he gave way to his natural indolence, lying in bed often till mid-day and after. He is visited at that hour. We mount the stairs of a gloomy house on the north side of Fleet Street, the busy quarter of London, in a narrow and obscure court; and as we enter, we hear the scoldings of four old women and an old quack doctor, poor penniless creatures, bad in health and in disposition, whom he has rescued, whom he supports, who vex or insult him. We ask for the doctor, a negro opens the door; we gather round the master's bed; there are always many distinguished people at his levee, including even ladies. Thus surrounded, " he declaims, then went to dinner at a tavern, where he commonly stays late," [6] talks all the evening, goes out to enjoy in the streets the London mud and fog, picks up a friend to talk again, and is

---

[1] *Life of Johnson*, ch. v. 28, note 2. [2] *Ibid.* ch. vii. 46.
[3] *Ibid.* ch. xvii. 159. [4] *Ibid.* ch. v. 28.
[5] He had formerly put in his *Dictionary* the following definition of the word pension : " *Pension*—an allowance made to any one without an equivalent. In England it is generally understood to mean pay given to a state-hireling for treason to his country." This drew of course afterwards all the sarcasms of his adversaries upon himself.
[6] Boswell's *Life*, ch. xxiv. 216.

busy pronouncing oracles and maintaining his opinion till four in the morning.

Whereupon we ask if it is the freedom of his opinions which is fascinating. His friends answer, that there is no more indomitable partisan of order. He is called the Hercules of Toryism. From infancy he detested the Whigs, and he never spoke of them but as public male-factors. He insults them even in his *Dictionary*. He exalts Charles the Second and James the Second as two of the best kings who have ever reigned.[1] He justifies the arbitrary taxes which Government presumes to levy on the Americans.[2] He declares that "Whiggism is a negation of all principle;"[3] that "the first Whig was the devil;"[4] that "the Crown has not power enough;"[5] that "mankind are happier in a state of inequality and subordination."[6] Frenchmen of the present time, admirers of the *Contrat Social*, soon feel, on reading or hearing all this, that they are no longer in France. And what must they feel when, a few moments later, the Doctor says: "I think him (Rousseau) one of the worst of men; a rascal who ought to be hunted out of society, as he has been. . . . I would sooner sign a sentence for his transportation, than that of any felon who has gone from the Old Bailey these many years. Yes, I should like to have him work in the plantations."[7] . . . .

It seems that in England people do not like philoso-phical innovators. Let us see if Voltaire will be treated better: "It is difficult to settle the proportion of

---

[1] Boswell's *Life*, ch. xlix. 444.   [2] *Ibid*. ch. xlviii. 435.
[3] *Ibid*. ch. xvi. 148.   [4] *Ibid*. ch. lxvi. 606.
[5] *Ibid*. ch. xxvi. 236.   [6] *Ibid*. ch. xxviii. 252.
[7] *Ibid*. ch. xix. 175.

iniquity between them (Rousseau and Voltaire)."[1] In good sooth, this is clear. But can we not look for truth outside an Established Church? No; "no honest man could be a Deist; for no man could be so after a fair examination of the proofs of Christianity."[2] Here is a peremptory Christian; there are scarcely any in France so decisive. Moreover, he is an Anglican, with a passion for the hierarchy, an admirer of established order, an enemy of Dissenters. We see him bow to an archbishop with peculiar veneration.[3] We hear him reprove one of his friends "for saying grace without mention of the name of our Lord Jesus Christ."[4] If we speak to him of a Quaker's meeting, and of a woman preaching, he will tell us that "a woman preaching is like a dog's walking on his hind legs; it is not done well, but you are surprised to find it done at all."[5] He is a Conservative, and does not fear being considered antiquated. He went at one o'clock in the morning into St. John's Church, Clerkenwell, to interrogate a tormented spirit, which had promised to "give a token of her presence there by a knock upon her coffin."[6] If we look at Boswell's life of him, we will find there fervent prayers, examinations of conscience, and rules of conduct. Amidst prejudices and ridicule he has a deep conviction, an active faith, a severe moral piety. He is a Christian from his heart and conscience, reason and practice. The thought of God, the fear of the last judgment, engross and reform him. He said one day to Garrick: "I'll come no more behind your scenes, David, for the silk stockings and white bosoms of your actresses

---

[1] Boswell's *Life*, ch. xix. 176.
[3] *Ibid.* ch. lxxv. 723.
[5] *Ibid.* ch. xvii. 157.

[2] *Ibid.* ch. xix. 174.
[4] *Ibid.* ch. xxiv. 218.
[6] *Ibid.* ch. xv. 138, note 3.

excite my amorous propensities." He reproaches himself
with his indolence, implores God's pardon, is humble,
has scruples. All this is very strange. We ask men
what can please them in this grumbling bear, with the
manners of a beadle and the inclinations of a constable?
They answer, that in London people are less exacting
than in Paris, as to manners and politeness; that in
England they allow energy to be rude and virtue odd;
that they put up with a combative conversation; that
public opinion is all on the side of the constitution and
Christianity; and that society was right to take for its
master a man who, by his style and precepts, best suited
its bent.

We now send for his books, and after an hour we
observe, that whatever the work be, tragedy or dictionary, biography or essay, he always writes in the same
style. "Dr. Johnson," Goldsmith said one day to him,
"if you were to make little fishes talk, they would talk
like whales."[1] In fact, his phraseology rolls ever in
solemn and majestic periods, in which every substantive
marches ceremoniously, accompanied by its epithet;
grand, pompous words peal like an organ; every proposition is set forth balanced by a proposition of
equal length; thought is developed with the compassed regularity and official splendour of a procession. Classical prose attains its perfection in him, as
classical poetry in Pope. Art cannot be more finished, or nature more forced. No one has confined
ideas in more strait compartments; none has given
stronger relief to dissertation and proof; none has imposed more despotically on story and dialogue the forms
of argumentation and violent declamation; none has

[1] Boswell's *Life*, ch. xxviii. 256.

more generally mutilated the flowing liberty of conversation and life by antitheses and technical words. It is the completion and the excess, the triumph and the tyranny of oratorical style.[1] We understand now that an oratorical age would recognise him as a master, and attribute to him in eloquence the mastery which it attributed to Pope in verse.

We wish to know what ideas have made him popular. Here the astonishment of a Frenchman redoubles. We vainly turn over the pages of his *Dictionary*, his eight volumes of essays, his many volumes of biographies, his numberless articles, his conversation so carefully collected; we yawn. His truths are too true; we already know his precepts by heart. We learn from him that life is short, and we ought to improve the few moments granted to us;[2] that a mother ought not to bring up her son as a fop; that a man ought to repent of his faults, and yet avoid superstition; that in everything we ought to be active, and not hurried. We thank him for these sage counsels, but we mutter to ourselves that we could have done very well without them. We should like to know who could have been the lovers of *ennui* who have bought up thirteen thousand copies of his works.

---

[1] Here is a celebrated phrase, which will give some idea of his style (Boswell's *Journal*, ch. xliii. 381): "We were now treading that illustrious island, which was once the luminary of the Caledonian regions, whence savage clans and roving barbarians derived the benefits of knowledge and the blessings of religion. To abstract the mind from all local emotion would be impossible if it were endeavoured, and would be foolish if it were possible. . . . Far from me and from my friends be such frigid philosophy as may conduct us indifferent and unmoved over any ground which has been dignified by wisdom, bravery, or virtue. That man is little to be envied, whose patriotism would not gain force upon the plain of Marathon, or whose piety would not grow warmer among the ruins of Iona." [2] *Rambler*, 108, 109, 110, 111.

We then remember that sermons are liked in England, and that these *Essays* are sermons. We discover that men of reflection do not need bold or striking ideas, but palpable and profitable truths. They desire to be furnished with a useful provision of authentic examples on man and his existence, and demand nothing more. No matter if the idea is vulgar; meat and bread are vulgar too, and are no less good. They wish to be taught the kinds and degrees of happiness and unhappiness, the varieties and results of character and condition, the advantages and inconveniences of town and country, knowledge and ignorance, wealth and moderate circumstances, because they are moralists and utilitarians.; because they look in a book for the knowledge to turn them from folly, and motives to confirm them in uprightness; because they cultivate in themselves sense, that is common, practical reason. A little fiction, a few portraits, the least amount of amusement, will suffice to adorn it. This substantial food only needs a very simple seasoning. It is not the novelty of the dishes, nor dainty cookery, but solidity and wholesomeness, which they seek. For this reason *Essays* are Johnson's national food. It is because they are insipid and dull for Frenchmen that they suit the taste of an Englishman. We understand now why they take for a favourite the respectable, the tiresome Dr. Samuel Johnson.

X.

I would fain bring together all these features, see these figures; only colours and forms complete an idea; in order to know, we must see. Let us go to the picture-gallery. Hogarth, the national painter, the friend of

Fielding, the contemporary of Johnson, the exact imitator of manners, will show us the outward, as these
authors have shown us the inward.

We enter these great galleries of art. Painting is a
noble thing! It embellishes all, even vice. On the
four walls, under transparent and brilliant glass, the
torsos rise, flesh palpitates, the blood's warm current
circulates under the veined skin, speaking likenesses
stand out in the light; it seems that the ugly, the
vulgar, the odious, have disappeared from the world.
I no more criticise characters; I have done with moral
rules. I am no longer tempted to approve or to hate.
A man here is but a smudge of colour, at most a handful
of muscles; I know no longer if he be a murderer.

Life, the happy, complete, overflowing display, the
expansion of natural and corporal powers; this from all
sides floods and rejoices our eyes. Our limbs instinctively move by contagious imitation of movements and
forms. Before these lions of Rubens, whose deep growls
rise like thunder to the mouth of the cave, before these
colossal writhing torsos, these snouts which grope about
skulls, the animal within us quivers through sympathy,
and it seems as if we were about to emit from our
chests a roar to equal their own.

What though art has degenerated even amongst
Frenchmen, epigrammatists, the bepowdered abbés of
the eighteenth century, it is art still. Beauty is
gone, elegance remains. These pretty arch faces, these
slender waspish waists, these delicate arms buried in a
nest of lace, these careless wanderings amongst thickets
and warbling fountains, these gallant dreams in a lofty
chamber festooned with garlands, all this refined and
coquettish society is still charming. The artist, then

as always, gathers the flower of things, and cares not for the rest.

But what was Hogarth's aim? who ever saw such a painter? Is he a painter? Others make us wish to see what they represent; he makes us wish not to see it.

Is there anything more agreeable to paint than a drunken debauch by night? the jolly, careless faces; the rich light, drowned in shadows which flicker over rumpled garments and weighed-down bodies. With Hogarth, on the other hand, what figures! Wickedness, stupidity, all the vile poison of the vilest human passions, drops and distils from them. One is shaking on his legs as he stands, sick, whilst a hiccup half opens his belching lips; another howls hoarsely, like a wretched cur; another, with bald and broken head, patched up in places, falls forward on his chest, with the smile of a sick idiot. We turn over the leaves of Hogarth's works, and the train of odious or bestial faces appears to be inexhaustible; features distorted or deformed, foreheads lumpy or puffed out with perspiring flesh, hideous grins distended by ferocious laughter: one has had his nose bitten off; the next, one-eyed, square-headed, spotted over with bleeding warts, whose red face looks redder under the dazzling white wig, smokes silently, full of rancour and spleen; another, an old man with a crutch, scarlet and bloated, his chin falling on his breast, gazes with the fixed and starting eyes of a crab. Hogarth shows the beast in man, and worse, a mad and murderous, a feeble or enraged beast. Look at this murderer standing over the body of his butchered mistress, with squinting eyes, distorted mouth, grinding his teeth at the thought of the blood which stains and denounces him; or this ruined gambler, who has torn off his wig and kerchief, and is crying on his knees, with closed teeth, and fist raised against heaven. Look again at this madhouse: the dirty idiot, with muddy face, filthy hair, stained claws, who thinks he is playing on the violin, and has a sheet of music for a cap; the religious madman, who writhes convulsively on his straw, with clasped hands, feeling the claws of the devil in his bowels; the naked and haggard raving lunatic whom they are chaining up, and who is tearing out his flesh with his nails. Detestable Yahoos who presume to usurp the blessed light of heaven, in what brain can you have arisen, and why did a painter sully our eyes with your picture?

It is because his eyes were English, and because the senses in England are barbarous. Let us leave our repugnance behind us, and look at things as Englishmen do, not from without, but from within. The whole current of public thought tends here towards observation of the soul, and painting is dragged along with literature in the same course. Forget then the forms, they are but lines; the body is here only to translate the mind.[1] This twisted nose, these pimples on a vinous cheek, these stupefied gestures of a drowsy brute, these wrinkled features, these degraded forms, only make the character, the trade, the whim, the habit stand out more clearly. The artist shows us no longer limbs and heads, but debauchery, drunkenness, brutality, hatred, despair, all the diseases and deformities of these too harsh and

---

[1] When a cnaracter is strongly marked in the living face, it may be considered as an index to the mind, to express which with any degree of justness in painting, requires the utmost efforts of a great master. —*Analysis of Beauty.*

unbending wills, the mad menagerie of all the passions.
Not that he lets them loose; this rude, dogmatic, and
Christian citizen handles more vigorously than any of
his brethren the heavy club of morality. He is a beef-
eating policeman charged with instructing and correcting
drunken pugilists. From such a man to such men
ceremony would be superfluous. At the bottom of
every cage where he imprisons a vice, he writes its name
and adds the condemnation pronounced by Scripture; he
displays that vice in its ugliness, buries it in its filth,
drags it to its punishment, so that there is no conscience
so perverted as not to recognise it, none so hardened as
not to be horrified at it.

Let us look well, these are lessons which bear fruit.
This one is against gin: on a step, in the open street,
lies a drunken woman, half naked, with hanging breasts,
scrofulous legs; she smiles idiotically, and her child,
which she lets fall on the pavement, breaks its skull.
Underneath, a pale skeleton, with closed eyes, sinks
down with a glass in his hand. Round about, dissipa-
tion and frenzy drive the tattered spectres one against
another. A wretch who has hung himself sways to
and fro in a garret. Gravediggers are putting a naked
woman into a coffin. A starveling is gnawing a bare
bone side by side with a dog. By his side little girls
are drinking with one another, and a young woman is
making her suckling swallow gin. A madman pitchforks
his child, and raises it aloft; he dances and laughs, and
the mother sees it.

Another picture and lesson, this time against cruelty.
A young murderer has been hung, and is being dissected.
He is there, on a table, and the lecturer calmly points
out with his wand the places where the students are to

work. At this sign the dissectors cut the flesh and pull. One is at the feet; the second man of science, a sardonic old butcher, seizes a knife with a hand that looks as if it would do its duty, and thrusts the other hand into the entrails, which, lower down, are being taken out to be put into a bucket. The last medical student takes out the eye, and the distorted mouth seems to howl under his hand. Meanwhile a dog seizes the heart, which is trailing on the ground; thighbones and skull boil, by way of concert, in a copper; and the doctors around coolly exchange surgical jokes on the subject which, piecemeal, is passing away under their scalpels.

Frenchmen will say that such lessons are good for barbarians, and that they only half-like these official or lay preachers, De Foe, Hogarth, Smollett, Richardson, Johnson, and the rest. I reply that moralists are useful, and that these have changed a state of barbarism into one of civilisation.

CHAPTER VII.

The Poets.

I.

WHEN we take in at one view the vast literary region in England, extending from the restoration of the Stuarts to the French Revolution, we perceive that all the productions, independently of the English character, bear a classical impress, and that this impress, special to this region, is met with neither in the preceding nor in the succeeding time. This dominant form of thought is imposed on all writers from Waller to Johnson, from Hobbes and Temple to Robertson and Hume: there is an art to which they all aspire; the work of a hundred and fifty years, practice and theory, inventions and imitations, examples and criticism, are employed in attaining it. They comprehend only one kind of beauty; they establish only the precepts which may produce it; they re-write, translate, and disfigure on its pattern the great works of other ages; they carry it into all the different kinds of literature, and succeed or fail in them according as it is adapted to them or not. The sway of this style is so absolute, that it is imposed on the greatest, and condemns them to impotence when they would apply it beyond its domain. The possession of this style is so universal, that it is met with in the weakest authors, and raises them to the height of talent, when they apply it in its domain.[1] This it is which brings to perfection prose, discourse, essay, dissertation, narration, and all the productions which form part of conversation and eloquence. This it is which destroyed the old drama, debased the new, impoverished and diverted poetry, produced a correct, agreeable, sensible, colourless, and narrow-minded history. This spirit, common to England and France, impressed its form on an infinite diversity of literary works, so that in its universal manifest ascendency we cannot but recognise the presence of one of those internal forces which bend and govern the course of human genius.

In no branch was it displayed more manifestly than in poetry, and at no time did it appear more clearly than in the reign of Queen Anne. The poets have just attained to the art which they had before dimly discerned. For sixty years they were approaching it; now they possess it, handle it; they use and exaggerate it. The style is at the same time finished and artificial. Let us open the first that comes to hand, Parnell or Philips, Addison or Prior, Gay or Tickell, we find a certain turn of mind, versification, language. Let us pass to a second, the same form reappears; we might say that they were imitations of one another. Let us go on to a third; the same diction, the same apostrophes, the same fashion of arranging an epithet and rounding a period. Let us turn over the whole lot; with little individual differences, they seem to be all cast in the same mould; one is more epicurean, another more moral, another more biting; but a noble language, an oratorical pomp, a classical correctness, reign through-

[1] Paul Louis Courier (1772-1825) says, "a lady's maid, in Louis XIV's. time, wrote better than the greatest of modern writers."

out; the substantive is accompanied by its adjective, its knight of honour; antithesis balances its symmetrical architecture; the verb, as in Lucan or Statius, is displayed, flanked on each side by a noun decorated by an epithet; we would say that it is of a uniform make, as if fabricated by a machine; we forget what it wishes to make known; we are tempted to count the measure on our fingers; we know beforehand what poetical ornaments are to embellish it. There is a theatrical dressing, contrasts, allusions, mythological elegance, Greek or Latin quotations. There is a scholastic solidity, sententious maxims, philosophic commonplaces, moral developments, oratorical exactness. We might imagine ourselves to be before a family of plants; if the size, colour, accessories, names differ, the fundamental type does not vary; the stamens are of the same number, similarly inserted around similar pistils, above leaves arranged on the same plan; a man who knows one knows all; there is a common organism and structure which involves the uniformity of the rest. If we review the whole family, we will doubtless find there some characteristic plant which displays the type in a clear light, whilst all around it and by degrees it alters, degenerates, and at last loses itself in the surrounding families. So here we see classical art find its centre in the neighbours of Pope, and above all in Pope himself; then, after being half effaced, mingle with foreign elements until it disappears in the poetry which succeeded it.[1]

---

[1] The Rev. Whitwell Elwin, in his second volume of the *Works of Alexander Pope*, at the end of his introduction to *An Essay on Man*, p. 338, says : "'M. Taine asserts that from the Restoration to the French Revolution, from Waller to Johnson, from Hobbes and Temple

II.

In 1688, at a linen draper's in Lombard Street, London, was born a little, delicate, and sickly creature, by nature artificial, constituted beforehand for a studious existence, having no taste but for books, who from his early youth derived his whole pleasure from the contemplation of printed books. He copied the letters, and thus learned to write. He passed his infancy with them, and was a verse-maker as soon as he knew how to speak. At the age of twelve he had written a little tragedy out of the *Iliad,* and an *Ode on Solitude.* From thirteen to fifteen he composed a long epic of four thousand verses, called *Alcander.* For eight years shut up in a little house in Windsor Forest, he read all the best critics, almost all the English, Latin, and French poets who had a reputation, Homer, the Greek poets, and a few of the great ones in the original, Tasso and Ariosto in translations, with such assiduity, that he nearly died from it. He did not search in them for passions, but style : there was never a more devoted adorer, never a more precocious master of form. Already his taste showed itself : amongst all

to Robertson and Hume, all our literature, both prose and verse, bears the impress of classic art. The mode, he says, culminated in the reign of Queen Anne, and Pope, he considers, was the extreme example of it. . . . Many of the most eminent authors who flourished between the English Restoration wrote in a style far removed from that which M. Taine calls classical. . . . The verse differs like the prose, though in a less degree, and is not "of a uniform make, as if fabricated by a machine." . . . Neither is the substance of the prose and verse, from the Restoration to the French Revolution, an invariable common-sense mediocrity. . . . There is much truth in his (M. Taine's) view, that there was a growing tendency to cultivate style, and in some writers the art degenerated into the artificial."—Tr.

the English poets his favourite was Dryden, the least
inspired and the most classical. He perceived his
career. He states that Mr. Walsh told him there was
one way left of excelling. "We had several great
poets," he said, "but we never had one great poet that
was correct; and he advised me to make that my study
and aim."[1] He followed this advice, tried his hand in
translations of Ovid and Statius, and in recasting parts
of old Chaucer. He appropriated all the poetic elegancies
and excellences, stored them up in his memory; he
arranged in his head a complete dictionary of all
happy epithéts, all ingenious turns of expression, all
sonorous rhythms by which a poet may exalt, render
precise, illuminate an idea. He was like those little
musicians, infant prodigies, who, brought up at the
piano, suddenly acquire a marvellous touch, roll out
scales, brilliant shakes, make the octaves vault with an
agility and accuracy which drive off the stage the most
famous performers. At seventeen, becoming acquainted
with old Wycherley, who was sixty-nine, he undertook,
at his request, to correct his poems, and corrected them
so well, that the other was at once charmed and morti-
fied. Pope blotted out, added, recast, spoke frankly,
and eliminated firmly. The author, in spite of himself,
admired the corrections secretly, and tried openly to
make light of them, until at last his vanity, wounded
at owing so much to so young a man, and at finding a
master in a scholar, ended by breaking off an intercourse
by which he profited and suffered too much. For the
scholar had at the outset carried the art beyond any of
the masters. At sixteen[2] his Pastorals bore witness to

[1] R. Carruthers, *Life of Alexander Pope*, 2d ed. 1857, ch. i. 33.
[2] It is very doubtful whether Pope was not older than sixteen when

a correctness which no one had possessed, not even
Dryden. When people observed these choice words,
these exquisite arrangements of melodious syllables, this
science of division and rejection, this style so fluent and
pure, these graceful images rendered still more graceful
by the diction, and all this artificial and many-tinted
garland of flowers which Pope called pastoral, they
thought of the first eclogues of Virgil. Mr. Walsh
declared " that it is not flattery at all to say that Virgil
had written nothing so good at his age." [1] When later
they appeared in a volume, the public was dazzled.
" You have only displeased the critics," wrote Wycherley, " by pleasing them too well." [2] The same year the
poet of twenty-one finished his *Essay on Criticism*, a
sort of *Ars Poetica* : it is the kind of poem a man
might write at the end of his career, when he has
handled all modes of writing, and has grown grey in
criticism ; and in this subject, of which the treatment
demands the experience of a whole literary life, he was
at the first onset as ripe as Boileau.

What will this consummate musician, who begins
by a treatise on harmony, make of his incomparable
mechanism and his science as a teacher ? It is well
to feel and think before writing ; a full source of living
ideas and real passions is necessary to make a genuine
poet, and in him, seen closely, we find that everything,
to his very person, is scanty and artificial ; he was a
dwarf, four feet high, contorted, hunchbaeked, thin,
valetudinarian, appearing, when he arrived at maturity,
no longer capable of existing. He could not get up

he wrote the Pastorals. See, on this subject, Pope's Works, ed. Elwin,
London 1871, i. 239 *et passim.*—TR.

[1] Pope's Works. ed. Elwin, i. 233.   [2] *Ibid.* i. 242.

himself, a woman dressed him; he wore three pairs of stockings, drawn on one over the other, so slender were his legs; "when he rose, he was invested in bodice made of stiff canvas, being scarce able to hold himself erect till they were laced, and he then put on a flannel waistcoat;"[1] next came a sort of fur doublet, for the least thing made him shiver; and lastly, a thick linen shirt, very warm, with fine sleeves. Over all this he wore a black garment, a tye-wig, a little sword; thus equipped, he went and took his place at the table of his great friend, the Earl of Oxford. He was so small, that he had to be raised on a chair of his own; so bald, that when he had no company he covered his head with a velvet cap; so punctilious and exacting, that the footmen evaded going his errands, and the Earl had to discharge several "for their resolute refusal of his messages." At dinner he ate too much; like a spoiled child, he would have highly seasoned dishes, and thus "would oppress his stomach with repletion." When cordials were offered him, he got angry, but did not refuse them. He had all the appetite and whims of an old child, an old invalid, an old author, an old bachelor. We are prepared to find him whimsical and susceptible. He often, without saying a word, and without any known cause, quitted the house of Lord Oxford, and the footmen had to go repeatedly with messages to bring him back. If Lady Mary Wortley, his former poetical divinity, were unfortunately at table, there was no dining in peace; they would not fail to contradict, peck at each other, quarrel; and one or other would leave the room. He would be sent for

---

[1] Johnson, *Lives of the most eminent English Poets*, 3 vols., ed. Cunningham, 1854 A. Pope, iii. 96.

and would return, but he brought his hobbies back with him. He was as crafty and malignant as a nervous abortion, which he was; when he wanted anything, he dared not ask for it plainly; with hints and contrivances of speech he induced people to mention it, to bring it forward, after which he would make use of it. "Thus he teased Lord Orrery till he obtained a screen. He hardly drank tea without a stratagem. Lady Bolingbroke used to say that ' he played the politician about cabbages and turnips.'"[1]

The rest of his life is not much more noble. He wrote libels on the Duke of Chandos, Aaron Hill, Lady Mary Wortley, and then lied or equivocated to disavow them. He had an ugly liking for artifice, and played a disloyal trick on Lord Bolingbroke, his greatest friend. He was never frank, always acting a part; he aped the *blasé* man, the impartial great artist, a contemner of the great, of kings, of poetry itself. The truth is, that he thought of nothing but his phrases, his author's reputation, and "a little regard shown him by the Prince of Wales melted his obduracy."[2] When we read his correspondence, we find that there are not more than about ten genuine letters; he is a literary man even in the moments when he opened his heart; his confidences are formal rhetoric; and when he conversed with a friend he was always thinking of the printer, who would give his effusions to the public. Through this very pretentiousness he grew awkward, and unmasked himself. One day Richardson and his father, the painter, found him reading a pamphlet that Cibber had written against him. "These things," said

---

[1] Johnson, *Lives of the most eminent English Poets;* A. Pope, iii. 99.
[2] Boswell's *Life of Johnson,* ch. lxxi. 670.

Pope, " are my diversion." " They sat by him while
he perused it, and saw his features writhing with
anguish ; and young Richardson said to his father,
when they returned, that he hoped to be preserved
from such diversion."[1] After all, his great cause for
writing was literary vanity : he wished to be admired,
and nothing more ; his life was that of a coquette
studying herself in a glass, painting her face, smirking,
receiving compliments from any one, yet declaring that
compliments weary her, that paint makes her dirty, and
that she has a horror of affectation.   Pope has no dash,
no naturalness or manliness ; he has no more ideas than
passions ; at least such ideas as a man feels it necessary
to write, and in connection with which we lose thought
of words.   Religious controversy and party quarrels
resound about him ; he studiously avoids them ; amidst
all these shocks his chief care is to preserve his writing-
desk ; he is a very lukewarm Catholic, all but a deist,
not well aware what deism means ; and on this point
he borrows from Bolingbroke ideas whose scope he
cannot see, but which he thinks suitable to be put into
verse.   In a letter to Atterbury (1717) he says : " In
my politics, I think no further than how to prefer the
peace of my life, in any government under which I
live ; nor in my religion, than to preserve the peace of
my conscience in any church with which I com-
municate.   I hope all churches and governments are
so far of God, as they are rightly understood and
rightly administered ; and where they err, or may be
wrong, I leave it to God alone to mend or reform
them."[2] Such convictions do not torment a man.   In
reality, he did not write because he thought, but

---

[1] Carruthers' *Life of Pope*, ch. x. 377.   [2] *Ibid.* ch. iv. 164.

thought in order to write; manuscript and the noise
it makes in the world, when printed, was his idol; if
he wrote verses, it was merely for the sake of doing so.

This is the best training for versification. Pope
gave himself up to it; he was a man of leisure, his
father had left him a very fair fortune; he earned a
large sum by translating the *Iliad* and *Odyssey;* he had
an income of eight hundred pounds. He was never in
the pay of a publisher; he looked from an eminence
upon the beggarly authors grovelling in their free and
easy life, and, calmly seated in his pretty house at
Twickenham, in his grotto, or in the fine garden which
he had himself planned, he could polish and file his
writings as long as he chose. He did not fail to do so.
When he had written a work, he kept it at least two
years in his desk. From time to time he re-read and
corrected it; took counsel of his friends, then of his
enemies; no new edition was unamended; he altered
without wearying. His first outburst became so recast and transformed, that it could not be recognised
in the final copy. The pieces which seem least
retouched are two satires, and Dodsley says that in the
manuscript " almost every line was written twice over;
I gave him a clean transcript, which he sent some time
afterwards to me for the press, with almost every line
written twice over a second time."[1] Dr. Johnson says:
" From his attention to poetry he was never diverted.
If conversation offered anything that could be improved,
he committed it to paper; if a thought, or perhaps an
expression, more happy than was common, rose to his
mind, he was careful to write it; an independent
distich was preserved for an opportunity of insertion;

[1] Johnson, *The Lives of the English Poets;* Alexander Pope, iii. 114.

and some little fragments have been found containing lines, or parts of lines, to be wrought upon at some other time."[1] His writing-desk had to be placed upon his bed before he rose. "Lord Oxford's domestic related that, in the dreadful winter of 1740, she was called from her bed by him four times in one night to supply him with paper, lest he should lose a thought."[2] Swift complains that he was never at leisure for conversation, because he "had always some poetical scheme in his head." Thus nothing was lacking for the attainment of perfect expression; the practice of a lifetime, the study of every model, an independent fortune, the company of men of the world, an immunity from turbulent passions, the absence of dominant ideas, the facility of an infant prodigy, the assiduity of an old man of letters. It seems as though he were expressly endowed with faults and good qualities, here enriched, there impoverished, at once narrowed and developed, to set in relief the classical form by the diminution of the classical depth, to present the public with a model of a worn-out and accomplished art, to reduce to a brilliant and rigid crystal the flowing sap of an expiring literature.

III.

It is a great misfortune for a poet to know his business too well; his poetry then shows the man of business, and not the poet. I wish I could admire Pope's works of imagination, but I cannot. In vain I read the testimony of his contemporaries, and even that of the moderns, and repeat to myself that in his time

---

[1] Johnson, *The Lives of the English Poets;* Alexander Pope, iii. 111.
[2] *Ibid.* iii. 105.

he was the prince of poets; that his Epistle from *Eloisa to Abelard* was received with a cry of enthusiasm; that a man could not then imagine a finer expression of true passion; that to this very day it is learned by heart, like the speech of Hippolyte in the *Phèdre* of Racine; that Johnson, the great literary critic, ranked it amongst "the happiest productions of the human mind;" that Lord Byron himself preferred it to the celebrated ode of Sappho. I read it again and am bored: this is not as it ought to be; but, in spite of myself, I yawn, and I open the original letters of Eloisa to find the cause of my weariness.

Doubtless poor Eloisa is a barbarian, nay worse a literary barbarian; she puts down learned quotations, arguments, tries to imitate Cicero, to arrange her periods; she could not do otherwise, writing a dead language, with an acquired style; perhaps the reader would do as much if he were obliged to write to his mistress in Latin.[1] But how does true feeling pierce through the scholastic form! "Thou art the only one who can sadden me, console me, make me joyful. . . . I should be happier and prouder to be called thy mistress than to be the lawful wife of an emperor. . . . Never, God knows, have I wished for anything else in thee but thee. It is thee alone whom I desire; nothing that thou couldst give; not marriage, not dowry: I never

[1] Rev. W. Elwin, in his edition of Pope's Works, ii. 224, says: "The authenticity of the Latin letters has usually been taken for granted, but I have a strong belief that they are a forgery. . . . It is far more likely that they are the fabrication of an unconcerned romancer, who speaks in the name of others with a latitude which people, not entirely degraded, would never adopt towards themselves. The suspicion is strengthened when the second party to the correspondence, the chief philosopher of his generation, exhibits the same exceptional depravity of taste."—TR.

dreamt of doing my own pleasure or my own will, thou
knowest it, but thine." Then come passionate words,
genuine love words,[1] then the unrestrained words of a
penitent, who says and dares everything, because she
wishes to be cured, to show her wound to her confessor,
even her most shameful wound; perhaps also because in
extreme agony, as in child-birth, modesty vanishes. All
this is very crude, very rude; Pope has more wit than
she, and how he endues her with it! In his hands she
becomes an academician, and her letter is a repertory
of literary effects. Portraits and descriptions; she
paints to Abelard the nunnery and the landscape:

> " In these lone walls (their days eternal bound),
> These moss-grown domes with spiry turrets crowned,
> Where awful arches make a noon-day night,
> And the dim windows shed a solemn light. . . .
> The wandering streams that shine between the hills,
> The grots that echo to the tinkling rills,
> The dying gales that pant upon the trees,
> The lakes that quiver to the curling breeze." [2]

Declamation and commonplace: she sends Abelard
discourses on love and the liberty which it demands,
on the cloister and the peaceful life which it affords, on
writing and the advantages of the post.[3] Antitheses

---

[1] "Vale, unice."
[2] Pope's Works, ed. Elwin; *Eloisa to Abelard*, ii. 245, *l.* 141-160.
[3] *Eloisa to Abelard*, ii. 240, *l.* 51-58:
> " Heav'n first taught letters for some wretch's aid,
> Some banished lover, or some captive maid;
> They live, they speak, they breathe what love inspires,
> Warm from the soul, and faithful to its fires,
> The virgin's wish without her fears impart,
> Excuse the blush, and pour out all the heart,
> Speed the soft intercourse from soul to soul,
> And waft a sigh from Indus to the Pole."

and contrasts, she forwards them to Abelard by the dozen; a contrast between the convent illuminated by his presence and desolate by his absence, between the tranquillity of the pure nun and the anxiety of the sinful nun, between the dream of human happiness and the dream of divine happiness. In fine, it is a *bravura*, with contrasts of *forte* and *piano*, variations and change of key. Eloisa makes the most of her theme, and sets herself to crowd into it all the powers and effects of her voice. Admire the *crescendo*, the shakes by which she ends her brilliant *morceaux;* to transport the hearer at the close of the portrait of the innocent nun, she says :

> " How happy is the blameless vestal's lot !
> The world forgetting, by the world forgot :
> Eternal sunshine of the spotless mind !
> Each prayer accepted and each wish resigned ;
> Labour and rest, that equal periods keep ;
> ' Obedient slumbers that can wake and weep ; '
> Desires composed, affections ever even ;
> Tears that delight, and sighs that waft to heav'n.
> Grace shines around her with serenest beams,
> And whisp'ring angels prompt her golden dreams.
> For her, th' unfading rose of Eden blooms,
> And wings of seraphs shed divine perfumes,
> For her the spouse prepares the bridal ring,
> For her white virgins hymeneals sing,
> To sounds of heavenly harps she dies away,
> And melts in visions of eternal day." [1]

Observe the noise of the big drum; I mean the grand contrivances, for so may be called all that a person says who wishes to rave and cannot; for instance, speaking

[1] *Eloisa to Abelard*, ii. 249, *l.* 207-222.

to rocks and walls, praying the absent Abelard to come, fancying him present, apostrophising grace and virtue :

> O grace serene !   O virtue heavenly fair !
> Divine oblivion of low-thoughted care !
> Fresh-blooming hope, gay daughter of the sky !
> And faith, our early immortality !
> Enter, each mild, each amicable guest ;
> Receive, and wrap me in eternal rest ! " [1]

Hearing the dead speaking to her, telling the angels :

> " I come ! I come !   Prepare your roseate bow'rs,
> Celestial palms, and ever-blooming flow'rs." [2]

This is the final symphony with modulations of the celestial organ.   I presume that Abelard cried " Bravo " when he heard it.

But this is nothing in comparison with the art exhibited by her in every phrase.   She puts ornaments into every line.   Imagine an Italian singer trilling every word.   O what pretty sounds ! how nimbly and brilliantly they roll along, how clear, and always exquisite ! it is impossible to reproduce them in another tongue.   Now it is a happy image, filling up a whole phrase ; now a series of verses, full of symmetrical contrasts ; two ordinary words set in relief by strange conjunction ; an imitative rhythm completing the impression of the mind by the emotion of the senses ; the most elegant comparisons and the most picturesque epithets ; the closest style and the most ornate.   Except truth, nothing is wanting.   Eloisa is worse than a singer, she is an author : we look at the back of her epistle to Abelard to see if she has not written on it " For Press."

[1] *Eloisa to Abelard*, ii. 254, *l.* 297-302.   [2] *Ibid.* 255, *l.* 317.

Pope has somewhere given a receipt for making an epic poem : take a storm, a dream, five or six battles, three sacrifices, funeral games, a dozen gods in two divisions ; shake together until there rises the froth of a lofty style. We have just seen the receipt for making a love-letter. This kind of poetry resembles cookery ; neither heart nor genius is necessary to produce it, but a light hand, an attentive eye, and a cultivated taste.

It seems that this kind of talent is made for light verses. It is factitious, and so are the manners of society. To make pretty speeches, to prattle with ladies, to speak elegantly of their chocolate or their fan, to jeer at fools, to criticise the last tragedy, to be good at insipid compliments or epigrams,—this, it seems, is the natural employment of a mind such as this, but slightly impassioned, very vain, a perfect master of style, as careful of his verses as a dandy of his coat. Pope wrote the *Rape of the Lock* and the *Dunciad ;* his contemporaries went into ecstasies about the charm of his badinage and the precision of his raillery, and believed that he had surpassed Boileau's *Lutrin* and *Satires.*

That may well be ; at all events the praise would be scanty. In Boileau there are, as a rule, two kinds of verse, as was said by a man of wit ;[1] most of which seem to be those of a sharp schoolboy in the third class, the rest those of a good schoolboy in the upper division. Boileau wrote the second verse before the first : this is why once out of four times his first verse only serves to stop a gap. Doubtless Pope had a more brilliant and adroit mechanism ; but this facility of hand does not suffice to make a poet, even a poet of the boudoir.

[1] M. Guillaume Guizot.

There, as elsewhere, we need genuine passion, or at least
genuine taste. When we wish to paint the pretty no-
things of conversation and the world, we must at least
like them. We can only paint well what we love.[1]
Is there no charming grace in the prattle and frivolity
of a pretty woman? Painters, like Watteau, have
spent their lives in feasting on them. A lock of hair
raised by the wind, a pretty arm peeping from underneath a great deal of lace, a stooping figure making the
bright folds of a petticoat sparkle, and the arch, half-
engaging, half-mocking smile of the pouting mouth,—
these are enough to transport an artist. Certainly he
will be aware of the influence of the toilet, as much so
as the lady herself, and will never scold her for passing
three hours at her glass; there is poetry in elegance.
He enjoys it as a picture; delights in the refinements
of worldly life, the grand quiet lines of the lofty, wain-
scoted drawing-room, the soft reflection of the high
mirrors and glittering porcelain, the careless gaiety of
the little sculptured Loves, locked in embrace above
the mantelpiece, the silvery sound of these soft voices,
buzzing scandal round the tea-table. Pope hardly if
at all rejoices in them; he is satirical and English
amidst this amiable luxury, introduced from France.
Although he is the most worldly of English poets, he is
not enough so: nor is the society around him. Lady
Mary Wortley Montague, who was in her time "the
pink of fashion," and who is compared to Madame de
Sévigné, has such a serious mind, such a decided style,
such a precise judgment, and such a harsh sarcasm,
that we would take her for a man. In reality the

[1] Goethe sings—"Liebe sei vor allen Dingen,
    Unser Thema, wenn wir singen."

English, even Lord Chesterfield and Horace Walpole,
never mastered the true tone of the *salon*. Pope is
like them; his voice is out of tune, and then suddenly
becomes biting. Every instant a harsh mockery blots
out the graceful images which he began to awaken.
Consider *The Rape of the Lock* as a whole; it is a
buffoonery in a noble style. Lord Petre had cut off a
lock of hair of a fashionable beauty, Mrs. Arabella
Fermor; out of this trifle the problem is to make an
epic, with invocations, apostrophes, the intervention of
supernatural beings, and the rest of poetic mechanism;
the solemnity of style contrasts with the littleness of
the events; we laugh at these bickerings as at insects
quarrelling. Such has always been the case in England; whenever Englishmen wish to represent social
life, it is with a superficial and assumed politeness;
at the bottom of their admiration there is scorn.
Their insipid compliments conceal a mental reservation;
let us observe them well, and we will see that they look
upon a pretty, well-dressed, and coquettish woman as a
pink doll, fit to amuse people for half-an-hour by her
outward show. Pope dedicates his poem to Mrs.
Arabella Fermor with every kind of compliment. The
truth is, he is not polite; a Frenchwoman would have
sent him back his book, and advised him to learn
manners; for one commendation of her beauty she
would find ten sarcasms upon her frivolity. Is it very
pleasant to have it said : " You have the prettiest eyes
in the world, but you live in the pursuit of trifles ? "
Yet to this all his homage is reduced.[1] His complimentary emphasis, his declaration that the " ravish'd

---

[1] See his *Epistle of the Characters of Women.* According to Pope,
this character is composed of love of pleasure and love of power.

hair . . . adds new glory to the shining sphere," [1] all his stock of phrases is but a parade of gallantry which betrays indelicacy and coarseness. Will she

> " Stain her honour, or her new brocade,
> Forget her pray'rs or miss a masquerade,
> Or lose her heart, or necklace at a ball ? " [2]

No Frenchman of the eighteenth century would have imagined such a compliment. At most, that bearish Rousseau, that former lackey and Geneva moralist, might have delivered this disagreeable thrust. In England it was not found too rude. Mrs. Arabella Fermor was so pleased with the poem, that she gave away copies of it. Clearly she was not hard to please, for she had heard much worse compliments. If we read in Swift the literal transcript of a fashionable conversation, we shall see that a woman of fashion of that time could endure much before she was angry.

But the strangest thing is, that this trifling is, for Frenchmen at least, no badinage at all. It is not at all like lightness or gaiety. Dorat, Gresset, would have been stupefied and shocked by it. We remain cold under its most brilliant hits. Now and then at most a crack of the whip arouses us, but not to laughter. These caricatures seem strange to us, but do not amuse. The wit is no wit: all is calculated, combined, artificially prepared; we expect flashes of lightning, but at the last moment they do not descend. Thus Lord Petre to " implore propitious heaven, and every power,"

> " To Love an altar built
> Of twelve vast French romances, neatly gilt.

[1] *Rape of the Lock*, c. v. 181, *l*. 141.   [2] *Ibid.* c. ii. 156, *l*. 107.

There lay three garters, half a pair of gloves,
And all the trophies of his former loves ;
With tender billets-doux he lights the pyre,
And breathes three am'rous sighs to raise the fire." [1]

We remain disappointed, not seeing the comicality of
the description.   We go on conscientiously, and in the
picture of Melancholy and her palace find figures much
stranger :

" Here sighs a jar, and there a goose-pye talks ;
Men proved with child, as pow'rful fancy works,
And maids turned bottles, call aloud for corks." [2]

We say to ourselves now that we are in China ; that so
far from Paris and Voltaire we must be surprised at
nothing, that these folk have ears different from ours,
and that a Pekin mandarin vastly relishes kettle-music.
Finally, we comprehend that, even in this correct age
and this artificial poetry, the old style of imagination
exists ; that it is nourished as before, by oddities and
contrasts ; and that taste, in spite of all culture, will
never become acclimatised ; that incongruities, far from
shocking, delight it ; that it is insensible to French
sweetness and refinements ; that it needs a succession
of expressive figures, unexpected and grinning, to pass
before it ; that it prefers this coarse carnival to delicate
insinuations ; that Pope belongs to his country, in spite
of his classical polish and his studied elegances, and
that his unpleasant and vigorous fancy is akin to that
of Swift.

We are now prepared and can enter upon his second
poem, *The Dunciad*.   We need much self-command not
to throw down this masterpiece as insipid, and even

[1] *Rape of the Lock*, c. ii. 153, *l*. 37-42.   [2] *Ibid*. c. iv. 169, *l*. 52.

disgusting. Rarely has so much talent been spent to
produce greater tedium. Pope wished to be avenged
on his literary enemies, and sang of Dulness, the sublime
goddess of literature, " daughter of Chaos and eternal
Night, . . . gross as her sire, and as her mother grave," [1]
queen of hungry authors, who chooses for her son and
favourite, first Theobald and afterwards Cibber. There
he is, a king, and to celebrate his accession she institutes
public games in imitation of the ancients; first a race
of booksellers, trying to seize a poet; then the struggle
of the authors, who first vie with each other in braying,
and then dash into the Fleet-ditch filth; then the strife
of critics, who have to undergo the reading of two
voluminous authors, without falling asleep.[2] Strange
parodies, to be sure, and in truth not very striking.
Who is not deafened by these hackneyed and bald
allegories, Dulness, poppies, mists, and Sleep? What
if I entered into details, and described the poetess
offered for a prize, " with cow-like udders, and with ox-
like eyes;" if I related the plunges of the authors,
floundering in the Fleet-ditch, the vilest sewer in the
town; if I transcribed all the extraordinary verses in
which

> " First he relates, how sinking to the chin,
> Smit with his mien, the mud-nymphs suck'd him in:
> How young Lutetia, softer than the down,
> Nigrina black, and Merdamante brown,
> Vied for his love in jetty bow'rs below." . . .[3]

I must stop. Swift alone might have seemed capable
of writing some passages, for instance that on the fall
of Curl. We might have excused it in Swift; the ex-

[1] Pope's Works. *The Dunciad*, bk. i.   [2] *Ibid.* bk. ii.   [3] *Ibid*

tremity of despair, the rage of misanthropy, the approach
of madness, might have carried him to such excess.
But Pope, who lived calm and admired in his villa, and
who was only urged by literary rancour! He can have
had no nerves! How could a poet have dragged his
talent wantonly through such images, and so constrained
his ingeniously woven verses to receive such dirt?
Picture a pretty drawing-room basket, destined only to
contain flowers and fancy-work, sent down to the
kitchen to be turned into a receptacle for filth.   In
fact, all the filth of literary life is here; and heaven
knows what it then was! In no age were hack-writers
so beggarly and so vile. Poor fellows, like Richard
Savage, who slept during one winter in the open air on
the cinders of a glass manufactory, lived on what he received for a dedication, knew the inside of a prison, rarely
dined, and drank at the expense of his friends; pamphleteers like Tutchin, who was soundly whipped;
plagiarists like Ward, exposed in the pillory and pelted
with rotten eggs and apples; courtesans like Eliza
Heywood, notorious by the shamelessness of their public
confessions; bought journalists, hired slanderers, vendors
of scandal and insults, half rogues, complete roysterers,
and all the literary vermin which haunted the gambling-
houses, the stews, the gin-cellars, and at a signal from a
bookseller stung honest folk for a crownpiece.   These
villanies, this foul linen, the greasy coat six years old,
the musty pudding, and the rest, are to be found in Pope
as in Hogarth, with English coarseness and precision.
This is their error, they are realists, even under the
classical wig; they do not disguise what is ugly and
mean; they describe that ugliness and meanness with
their exact outlines and distinguishing marks; they do

not clothe them in a fine cloak of general ideas; they do
not cover them with the pretty innuendoes of society.
This is the reason why their satires are so harsh.
Pope does not flog the dunces, he knocks them down;
his poem is hard and malicious; it is so much so,
that it becomes clumsy: to add to the punishment of
dunces, he begins at the ˙deluge, writes historical
passages, represents at length the past, present, and
future empire of˙ Dulness, the library of Alexandria
burned by Omar, learning extinguished by the invasion
of the barbarians and by the superstition of the middle-
age, the empire of stupidity which extends over
England and will swallow it up.   What paving-stones
to crush flies !

> " See skulking Truth to her old cavern fled,
> Mountains of casuistry heap'd o'er her head !
> Philosophy, that leaned on Heav'n before,
> Shrinks to her second cause, and is no more.
> Physic of Metaphysic begs defence,
> And Metaphysic calls for aid on sense ! . . .
> Religion blushing veils her sacred fires,
> And unawares Morality expires.
> Nor public flame, nor private, dares to shine ;
> Nor human spark is left, nor glimpse divine !
> Lo ! thy dread empire, Chaos ! is restored ;
> Light dies before thy uncreating word :
> Thy hand, great anarch ! lets the curtain fall ;
> And universal darkness buries all." [1]

The last scene ends with noise, cymbals and trombones,
crackers and fireworks.   As for me, I carry away from
this celebrated entertainment only the remembrance of
a hubbub.   Unwittingly I have counted the lights, I

[1] *The Dunciad,* the end.

know the machinery, I have touched the toilsome stage-property of apparitions and allegories. I bid farewell to the scene-painter, the machinist, the manager of literary effects, and go elsewhere to find the poet.

IV.

However a poet exists in Pope, and to discover him we have only to read him by fragments; if the whole is, as a rule, wearisome or shocking, the details are admirable. It is so at the close of every literary age. Pliny the younger, and Seneca, so affected and so stiff, are charming in small bits; each of their phrases, taken by itself, is a masterpiece; each verse in Pope is a masterpiece when taken alone. At this time, and after a hundred years of culture, there is no movement, no object, no action, which poets cannot describe. Every aspect of nature was observed; a sunrise, a landscape reflected in the water,[1] a breeze amid the foliage, and so forth. Ask Pope to paint in verse an eel, a perch, or a trout; he has the exact phrase ready; we might glean from him the contents of a " Gradus." He gives the features so exactly, that at once we think we see the thing; he gives the expression so copiously, that our imagination, however obtuse, will end by seeing it. He marks everything in the flight of a pheasant:

" See ! from the brake the whirring pheasant springs
And mounts exulting on triumphant wings. . . .

[1] Pope's Works, i. 352 ; *Windsor Forest, l.* 211.
   " Oft in her glass the musing shepherd spies
      The headlong mountains and the downward skies, '
      The wat'ry landscape of the pendant woods,
      And absent trees that tremble in the floods."

Ah ! what avail his glossy, varying dyes,
His purple crest, and scarlet-circled eyes,
The vivid green his shining plumes unfold,
His painted wings, and breast that flames with gold ? " [1]

He possesses the richest store of words to depict the sylphs which flutter round his heroine, Belinda :

" But now secure the painted vessel glides,
The sunbeams trembling on the floating tides :
While melting music steals upon the sky,
And softened sounds along the waters die ;
Smooth flow the waves, the zephyrs gently play, . . .
The lucid squadrons round the sails repair :
Soft o'er the shrouds the aerial whispers breathe,
That seemed but zephyrs to the train beneath.
Some to the sun their insect-wings unfold,
Waft on the breeze, or sink in clouds of gold ;
Transparent forms, too fine for mortal sight, ·
Their fluid bodies half dissolved in light.
Loose to the wind their airy garment flew,
Thin glitt'ring textures of the filmy dew,
Dipped in the richest tincture of the skies,
Where light disports in ever-mingling dyes ;
While ev'ry beam new transient colours flings,
Colours that change whene'er they wave their wings." [2]

Doubtless these are not Shakespeare's sylphs ; but side by side with a natural and living rose, we may still look with pleasure on a flower of diamonds, as they come from the hand of the jeweller, a masterpiece of art and patience, whose facets make the light glitter, and cast a shower of sparkles over the filagree foliage in which they are embedded. A score of times in a poem of

[1] Pope's Works, i. 347 ; *Windsor Forest, l.* 111–118.
[2] *Ibid.* ii. 154 ; *The Rape of the Lock,* c. 2, *l.* 47–68.

Pope's we stop to look with wonder on some of these literary adornments. He feels so well in what the strong point of his talent lies, that he abuses it; he delights to show his skill. What can be staler than a card party, or more repellent to poetry than the queen of spades or the king of hearts? Yet, doubtless for a wager, he has recorded in the *Rape of the Lock* a game of ombre; we follow it, hear it, recognise the dresses:

> " Behold four kings in majesty revered,
> With hoary whiskers and a forky beard;
> And four fair queens whose hands sustain a flower,
> Th' expressive emblem of their softer power;
> Four knaves in garb succinct, a trusty band;
> Caps on their heads and halberts in their hand;
> And parti-coloured troops, a shining train,
> Drawn forth to combat on the velvet plain." [1]

We see the trumps, the cuts, the tricks, and instantly afterwards the coffee, the china, the spoons, the fiery spirits (to wit, spirits of wine); we have here in advance the modes and periphrases of Delille. The celebrated verses in which Delille at once employs and describes imitative harmony, are translated from Pope.[2] It is an expiring poetry, but poetry still: an ornament to put on a mantelpiece is an inferior work of art, but still it is a work of art.

To descriptive talent Pope unites oratorical talent. This art, proper to the classical age, is the art of expressing ordinary general ideas. For a hundred and fifty years men of both the thinking countries, England

---

[1] Pope's Works, ii. 160, *The Rape of the Lock*, c. 3, 160, *l.* 37–44.
[2] " Peins-moi légèrement l'amant léger de Flore,
Qu'un doux ruisseau murmure en vers plus doux encore."

and France, employed herein all their study. They seized those universal and limited truths, which, being situated between lofty philosophical abstractions and petty sensible details, are the subject-matter of eloquence and rhetoric, and form what we now-a-days call commonplaces. They arranged them in compartments; methodically developed them; made them obvious by grouping and symmetry; disposed them in regular processions, which with dignity and majesty advance well disciplined, and in a body. The influence of this oratorical reason became so great, that it was imposed on poetry itself. Buffon ends by saying, in praise of certain verses, that they are as fine as fine prose. In fact, poetry at this time became a more affected prose subjected to rhyme. It was only a higher kind of conversation and more select discourse. It is powerless when it is necessary to paint or represent an action, when the need is to see and make visible living passions, large genuine emotions, men of flesh and blood; it results only in college epics like the *Henriade*, freezing odes and tragedies like those of Voltaire and Jean-Baptiste Rousseau, or those of Addison, Thomson, Dr. Johnson, and the rest. It makes them up of dissertations, because it is capable of nothing else but dissertations. Here henceforth is its domain; and its final task is the didactic poem, which is a dissertation in verse. Pope excelled in it, and his most perfect poems are those made up of precepts and arguments. Artifice in these is less shocking than elsewhere. A poem—I am wrong, essays like his upon *Criticism*, on *Man* and the *Government of Providence*, on the *Knowledge and Characters of Men*, deserve to be written after reflection; they are a study, and almost a scientific monograph. We may, we even ought, to weigh all the

words, and verify all the connections : art and attention
are not superfluous, but necessary ; the question concerns
exact precepts and close arguments.   In this Pope is incomparable.   I do not think that there is in the world
a versified prose like his ; that of Boileau is not to be
compared to it.   Not that its ideas are very worthy of
attention ; we have worn them out, they interest us no
longer.   The *Essay on Criticism* resembles Boileau's
Epîtres and *L'Art Poétique*, excellent works, no longer
read but in classes at school.   It is a collection of very
wise precepts, whose only fault is their being too true.
To say that good taste is rare ; that we ought to reflect
and learn before deciding ; that the rules of art are drawn
from nature ; that pride, ignorance, prejudice, partiality,
envy, pervert our judgment ; that a critic should be
sincere, modest, polished, kindly,—all these truths might
then be discoveries, but they are so no longer.   I suppose that in the time of Pope, Dryden, and Boileau, men
had special need of setting their ideas in order, and of
seeing them very distinctly in very clear phrases.   Now
that this need is satisfied, it has disappeared : we demand
ideas, not arrangement of ideas ; the pigeon-holes are
manufactured, fill them.   Pope was obliged to do it
once in the *Essay on Man*, which is a sort of *Vicaire
Savoyard*,[1] less original than the other.   He shows that
God made all for the best, that man is limited in his
capacity and ought not to judge God, that our passions
and imperfections serve for the general good and for
the ends of Providence, that happiness lies in virtue
and submission to the divine will.   We recognise here
a sort of deism and optimism, of which there was much

---

[1] A tale of J. J. Rousseau, in which he tries to depict a philosophical
clergyman.—TR.

at that time, borrowed, like those of Rousseau, from the *Théodicée* of Leibnitz,[1] but tempered, toned down, and arranged for the use of respectable people. The conception is not very lofty: this curtailed deity, making his appearance at the beginning of the eighteenth century, is but a residuum: religion having disappeared, he remained at the bottom of the crucible; and the reasoners of the time, having no metaphysical inventiveness, kept him in their system to stop a gap. In this state and at this place this deity resembles classic verse. He has an imposing appearance, is comprehended easily, is stripped of power, is the product of cold argumentative reason, and leaves the people who attend to him, very much at ease; on all these accounts he is akin to an Alexandrine. This poor conception is all the more wretched in Pope because it does not belong to him, for he is only accidentally a philosopher; and to find matter for his poem, three or four systems, deformed and attenuated, are amalgamated in his work. He boasts of having tempered them one with the other, and having "steered between the extremes."[2] The truth is, that he did not understand them, and that he jumbles incongruous ideas at every step. There is a passage in which, to obtain an effect of style, he becomes a pantheist; moreover he is bombastic, and assumes the supercilious, imperious tone of a young doctor of theology. I find no individual invention except in his *Moral Essays;* in them is a theory of dominant passion which is worth reading. After all, he went farther than Boileau, for instance, in the knowledge of man. Psychology is indigenous in England; we meet it there through-

---

[1] The *Théodicée* was written in French, and published in 1710.—TR.

[2] These words are taken from the *Design of an Essay on Man.*

out, even in the least creative minds. It gives rise to the novel, dispossesses philosophy, produces the essay, appears in the newspapers, fills current literature, like those indigenous plants which multiply on every soil.

But if the ideas are mediocre, the art of expressing them is truly marvellous : marvellous is the word. " I chose verse," says Pope in his *Design of an Essay on Man*, " because I found I could express them (ideas) more shortly this way than in prose itself." In fact, every word is effective : every passage must be read slowly ; every epithet is an epitome ; a more condensed style was never written ; and, on the other hand, no one laboured more skilfully in introducing philosophical formulas into the current conversation of society. His maxims have become proverbs. I open his *Essay on Man* at random, and fall upon the beginning of his second book. An orator, an author of the school of Buffon, would be transported with admiration to see so many literary treasures collected in so small a space :

> " Know then thyself, presume not God to scan
> The proper study of mankind is man.
> Placed on this isthmus of a middle state,
> A being darkly wise, and rudely great :
> With too much knowledge for the sceptic side,
> With too much weakness for the stoic's pride,
> He hangs between ; in doubt to act, or rest ;
> In doubt to deem himself a God or beast ;
> In doubt his mind or body to prefer ;
> Born but to die, and reas'ning but to err ;
> Alike in ignorance, his reason such,
> Whether he thinks too little or too much ;
> Chaos of thought and passion, all confused ;
> Still by himself abused or disabused ;

Created half to rise, and half to fall;
Great lord of all things, yet a prey to all;
Sole judge of truth in endless error hurled,
The glory, jest, and riddle of the world." [1]

The first verse epitomises the whole of the preceding Epistle, and the second epitomises the present Epistle; it is, as it were, a kind of staircase leading from one temple to another, regularly composed of symmetrical steps, so aptly disposed that from the first step we see at a glance the whole building we have left, and from the second the whole edifice we are about to visit. Have we ever seen a finer entrance, or one more conformable to the rules which bid us unite our ideas, recall them when developed, pre-announce them when not yet developed? But this is not enough. After this brief announcement, which premises that he is about to treat of human nature, a longer announcement is necessary, to paint beforehand, with the greatest possible splendour, this human nature of which he is about to treat. This is the proper oratorical exordium, like those which Bossuet places at the beginning of his funeral orations; a sort of elaborate portico to receive the audience on their entrance, and prepare them for the magnificence of the temple. The antitheses follow each other in couples like a succession of columns; thirteen couples form a suite; and the last is raised above the rest by a word, which concentrates and combines all. In other hands this prolongation of the same form would become tedious; in Pope's it interests us, so much variety is there in the arrangement and the adornments. In one place the antithesis is comprised in a single line, in another it occupies two; now it is in the substantives,

---

[1] Pope's Works, ii.; *An Essay on Man*, Ep. ii. 375, *l.* 1-18.

now in the adjectives and verbs; now only in the ideas, now it penetrates the sound and position of the words. In vain we see it reappear; we are not wearied, because each time it adds somewhat to our idea, and shows us the object in a new light. This object itself may be abstract, obscure, unpleasant, opposed to poetry; the style spreads over it its own light; noble images borrowed from the grand and simple spectacles of nature, illustrate and adorn it. For there is a classical architecture of ideas as well as of stones: the first, like the second, is a friend to clearness and regularity, majesty and calm; like the second, it was invented in Greece, transmitted through Rome to France, through France to England, and slightly altered in its passage. Of all the masters who have practised it in England, Pope is the most skilled.

After all is there anything in the lines just quoted but decoration? Translate them literally into prose, and of all those beauties there remains not one. If the reader dissects Pope's arguments, he will hardly be moved by them; he would instinctively think of Pascal's *Pensées*, and remark upon the astonishing difference between a versifier and a man. A good epitome, a good bit of style, well worked out, well written, he would say, and nothing further. Clearly the beauty of the verses arose from the difficulty overcome, the well-chosen sounds, the symmetrical rhythms; this was all, and it was not much. A great writer is a man who, having passions, knows his dictionary and grammar; Pope thoroughly knew his dictionary and his grammar, but stopped there.

People will say that this merit is small, and that I do not inspire them with a desire to read Pope's verses. True; at least I do not counsel them to read many

I would add, however, by way of excuse, that there is a kind in which he succeeds, that his descriptive and oratorical talents find in portraiture matter which suits them, and that in this he frequently approaches La Bruyère; that several of his portraits, those of Addison, Lord Hervey, Lord Wharton, the Duchess of Marlborough, are medals worthy of finding a place in the cabinets of the curious, and of remaining in the archives of the human race; that when he chisels one of these heads, the comprehensive images, the unlooked-for connections of words, the sustained and multiplied contrasts, the perpetual and extraordinary conciseness, the incessant and increasing impulse of all the strokes of eloquence brought to bear upon the same spot, stamp upon the memory an impress which we never forget. It is better to repudiate these partial apologies, and frankly to avow that, on the whole, this great poet, the glory of his age, is wearisome—wearisome to us. " A woman of forty," says Stendhal, " is only beautiful to those who have loved her in their youth." The poor muse in question is not forty years old for us; she is a hundred and forty. Let us remember, when we wish to judge her fairly, the time when we made French verses like our Latin verse. Taste became transformed an age ago, for the human mind has wheeled round; with the prospect the perspective has changed; we must take this change of place into account. Now-a-days we demand new ideas and bare sentiments; we care no longer for the clothing, we want the thing. Exordium, transitions, peculiarities of style, elegances of expression, the whole literary wardrobe, is sent to the old-clothes shop; we only keep what is indispensable; we trouble ourselves no more about adornment

but about truth. The men of the preceding century
were quite different. This was seen when Pope
translated the *Iliad;* it was the *Iliad* written in the
style of the *Henriade:* by virtue of this travesty the
public admired it. They would not have admired it
in the simple Greek guise; they only consented to see
it in powder and ribbons. It was the costume of the
time, and it was very necessary to put it on. Dr.
Johnson in his commercial and academical style affirms
even that the demand for elegance had increased so
much, that pure nature could no longer be borne.

Good society and men of letters made a little world
by themselves, which had been formed and refined
after the manner and ideas of France. They adopted
a correct and noble style at the same time as fashion
and fine manners. They held by this style as by
their coat; it was a matter of propriety or ceremony; .
there was an accepted and unalterable pattern; they
could not change it without indecency or ridicule; to
write, not according to the rules, especially in verse,
effusively and naturally, would have been like showing
oneself in the drawing-room in slippers and a dressing-
gown. Their pleasure in reading verse was to try
whether the pattern had been exactly followed, originality was only permitted in details; a man might
adjust here a lace, there some embroidered stripe,
but he was bound scrupulously to preserve the conventional form, to brush everything minutely, and never to
appear without new gold lace and glossy broadcloth.
The attention was only bestowed on refinements; a
more elaborate braid, a more brilliant velvet, a feather
more gracefully arranged; to this were boldness and
experiment reduced; the smallest incorrectness, the

slightest incongruity, would have offended their eyes; they perfected the infinitely little. Men of letters acted like these coquettes, for whom the superb goddesses of Michael Angelo and Rubens are but milk-maids, but who utter a cry of pleasure at the sight of a ribbon at twenty francs a yard. A division, a dis-placing of verses, a metaphor delighted them, and this was all which could still charm them. They went on day by day embroidering, bedizening, narrowing the bright classic robe, until at last the human mind, feeling fettered, tore it, cast it away, and began to move. Now that this robe is on the ground the critics pick it up, hang it up in their museum of ancient curiosities, so that everybody can see it, shake it, and try to conjec-ture from it the feelings of the fine lords and of the fine speakers who wore it.

V.

It is not everything to have a beautiful dress, strongly sewn and fashionable; a man must be able to get into it easily. Reviewing the whole train of the English poets of the eighteenth century, we perceive that they do not easily get into the classical dress. This gold-embroidered jacket, which fits a Frenchman so well, hardly suits their figure; from time to time a too powerful, awkward movement makes rents in the sleeves and elsewhere. For instance, Matthew Prior seems at first sight to have all the qualities necessary to wear the jacket well; he has been an ambassador to the French court, and writes pretty French *impromptus;* he turns off with facility little jesting poems on a dinner, a lady; he is gallant, a man of society, a pleasant story-teller, epicurean, even sceptical like the

courtiers of Charles II., that is to say, as far as and
including political roguery; in short, he is an accomplished man of the world, as times went, with a correct
and flowing style, having at command a light and a
noble verse, and pulling, according to the rules of
Bossu and Boileau, the string of mythological puppets.
With all this, we find him neither gay enough nor
refined enough. Bolingbroke called him wooden-faced,
stubborn, and said there was something Dutch in him.
His manners smacked very strongly of those of Rochester,
and the well-clad scamps whom the Restoration be-
queathed to the Revolution. He took the first woman
at hand, shut himself up with her for several days,
drank hard, fell asleep, and let her make off with his
money and clothes. Amongst other drabs, ugly enough
and always dirty, he finished by keeping Elizabeth Cox,
and all but married her; fortunately he died just in
time. His style was like his manners. When he
tried to imitate La Fontaine's *Hans Carvel,* he made it
dull, and lengthened it; he could not be piquant, but
he was biting; his obscenities have a cynical harshness;
his raillery is a satire; and in one of his poems *To a
Young Gentleman in Love,* the lash becomes a knock-
down blow. On the other hand, he was not a common
roysterer. Of his two principal poems, one on *Solomon*
paraphrases and treats of the remark of Ecclesiastes,
"All is vanity." From this picture we see forthwith
that we are in a biblical land : such an idea would not
then have occurred to a boon companion of the Duke
of Orleans, Regent of France. Solomon relates how he
in vain "proposed his doubts to the lettered Rabbins,"
how he has been equally unfortunate in the hopes and
desires of love, the possession of power, and ends by

trusting to an " omniscient Master, omnipresent King."
Here we have English gloom and English conclusions.[1]
Moreover, under the rhetorical and uniform composition
of his verses, we perceive warmth and passion, rich painting, a sort of magnificence, and the profusion of an
overcharged imagination. The sap in England is always
stronger than in France; the sensations there are
deeper, and the thoughts more original. Prior's other
poem, very bold and philosophical, against conventional
truths and pedantries, is a droll discourse on the seat
of the soul, from which Voltaire has taken many ideas
and much foulness. The whole armoury of the sceptic
and materialist was built and furnished in England,
when the French took to it. Voltaire has only selected
and sharpened the arrows. This poem is also wholly
written in a prosaic style, with a harsh common sense
and a medical frankness, not to be terrified by the
foulest abominations.[2] *Candide* and the *Earl of
Chesterfield's Ears,* by Voltaire, are more brilliant but
not more genuine productions. On the whole, with
his coarseness, want of taste, prolixity, perspicacity,
passion, there is something in this man not in accordance with classical elegance. He goes beyond it or
does not attain it.

[1] Prior's Works, ed. Gilfillan, 1851 :
    " In the remotest wood and lonely grot,
        Certain to meet that worst of evils, *thought.*"
[2] *Alma*, canto ii. *l.* 937-978 :
    " Your nicer Hottentots think meet
        With guts and tripe to deck their feet ;
        With downcast looks on Totta's legs
        The ogling youth most humbly begs,
        She would not from his hopes remove
        At once his breakfast and his love. . . .
        Before you see, you smell your toast,
        And sweetest she who stinks the most."

This dissonance increases, and attentive eyes soon discover under the regular cloak a kind of energetic and precise imagination, ready to break through it. In this age lived Gay, a sort of La Fontaine, as near La Fontaine as an ·Englishman can be, that is, not very near, but at least a kind and amiable good fellow, very sincere, very frank, strangely thoughtless, born to be duped, and a young man to the last. Swift said of him that he ought never to have lived more than twenty-two years. " In wit a man, simplicity a child," wrote Pope. He lived, like La Fontaine, at the expense of the great, travelled as much as he could at their charge, lost his money in South-Sea speculations, tried to get a place at court, wrote fables full of humanity to form the heart of the Duke of Cumberland,[1] and ended as a beloved parasite and the domestic poet of the Duke and Duchess of Queensberry. He had little of the grave in his character, and neither many scruples nor manners. It was his sad lot, he said, " that he could get nothing from the court, whether he wrote for or against it." And he wrote his own epitaph :

> " Life is a jest ; and all things show it,
> I thought so once ; but now I know it." [2]

This laughing careless poet, to revenge himself on the minister, wrote the *Beggars' Opera*, the fiercest and dirtiest of caricatures.[3] In this Opera they cut the throat of men in place of scratching them ; babes handle the knife like the rest. Yet Gay was a laugher, but in a style of his own, or rather in that of his

---

[1] The same duke who was afterwards nicknamed " the Butcher."
[2] *Poems on Several Occasions*, by Mr. John Gay, 1745, 2 vols. ii. 141.
[3] See vol. iii. ch. iii. p. 81.

country. Seeing " certain young men of insipid delicacy,"[1] Ambrose Philips, for instance, who wrote elegant
and tender pastorals, in the manner of Fontenelle, he
amused himself by parodying and contradicting them,
and in the *Shepherd's Week* introduced real rural
manners into the metre and form of the visionary
poetry : " Thou wilt not find my shepherdesses idly
piping on oaten reeds, but milking the kine, tying up
the sheaves, or if the hogs are astray, driving them to
their styes. My shepherd . . . sleepeth not under
myrtle shades, but under a hedge, nor doth he vigilantly
defend his flocks from wolves, because there are none."[2]
Fancy a shepherd of Theocritus or Virgil, compelled to
put on hobnailed shoes and the dress of a Devonshire
cowherd ; such an oddity would amuse us by the
contrast of his person and his garments. So here *The
Magician, The Shepherd's Struggle,* are travestied in a
modern guise. Listen to the song of the first shepherd,
" Lobbin Clout :"

> " Leek to the Welch, to Dutchmen butter's dear,
>   Of Irish swains potatoe is the chear ;
>   Oat for their feasts, the Scotish shepherds grind,
>   Sweet turnips are the food of Blouzelind.
>   While she loves turnips, butter I'll despise,
>   Nor leeks, nor oatmeal, nor potatoe prize."[3]

The other shepherd answers in the same metre ; and
the two continue, verse after verse, in the ancient
manner, but now amidst turnips, strong beer, fat pigs,
bespattered at will by modern country vulgarities and

---

[1] *Poems on Several Occasions ;* The Proeme to *The Shepherd's Week,*
i. 64.   [2] *Ibid.* i. 66.
[3] Gay's Poems, *The Shepherd's Week ;* first pastoral, *The Squabble,*
p. 80.

the dirt of a northern climate.   Van Ostade and Teniers love these vulgar and clownish idyls; and in Gay, as well as with them, unvarnished and sensual drollery has its sway.   The people of the north, who are great eaters, always liked country fairs.   The vagaries of toss-pots and gossips, the grotesque outburst of the vulgar and animal mind, put them into good humour.   A man must be a genuine man of the world or an artist, a French-man or an Italian, to be disgusted with them.   They are the product of the country, as well as meat and beer: let us try, in order that we may enjoy them, to forget wine, delicate fruits, to give ourselves blunted senses, to become in imagination compatriots of such men.   We have become used to the pictures of these drunken boobies, whom Louis XIV. called "baboons," to these red-faced cooks who clean fish, and to the like scenes.   Let us get used to Gay; to his poem *Trivia, or the Art of Walking the Streets of London;* to his advice as to dirty gutters, and shoes "with firm, well-hammer'd soles;" his description of the amours of the goddess Cloacina and a scavenger, whence sprang the little shoe-blacks.   He is a lover of the real, has a precise imagina-tion, does not see objects wholesale and from a general point of view, but singly, with all their outlines and sur-roundings, whatever they may be, beautiful or ugly, dirty or clean.   The other literary men act likewise, even the chief classical writers, including Pope.   There is in Pope a minute description, with high-coloured words, local details, in which comprehensive and characteristic features are stamped with such a liberal and sure hand, that we would take the author for a modern realist, and would find in the work an historical document.[1]

---

[1] *Epistle to Mrs. Blount,* "on her leaving the town."

As to Swift, he is the bitterest positivist, and more so
in poetry than in prose. Let us read his eclogue on
Strephon and Chloe, if we would know how far men
can debase the noble poetic drapery. They make a
dishclout of it, or dress clodhoppers in it; the Roman
toga and Greek chlamys do not suit these barbarians'
shoulders. They are like those knights of the middle-
ages, who, when they had taken Constantinople, muffled
themselves for a joke, in long Byzantine robes, and
went riding through the streets in these disguises,
dragging their embroidery in the gutter.

These men will do well, like the knights, to return
to their manor, to the country, the mud of their ditches,
and the dunghill of their farm-yards. The less man
is fitted for social life, the more he is fitted for solitary
life. He enjoys the country the more for enjoying
the world less. Englishmen have always been more
feudal and more fond of the country than Frenchmen.
Under Louis XIV. and Louis XV. the worst misfortune
for a nobleman was to go to his estate in the country
and grow rusty there; away from the smiles of the
king and the fine conversation of Versailles, there was
nothing left but to yawn and die. In England, in
spite of artificial civilisation and the charms of polite
society, the love of the chase and of bodily exercise,
political interests and the necessities of elections
brought the nobles back to their estates. And there
their natural instincts returned. A sad and impassioned
man, naturally self-dependent, converses with objects;
a grand grey sky, whereon the autumn mists slumber,
a sudden burst of sunshine lighting up a moist field,
depress or excite him; inanimate things seem to him
instinct with life; and the faint light, which in the morn-

ing reddens the fringe of heaven, moves him as much as
the smile of a young girl at her first ball. Thus is
genuine descriptive poetry born. It appears in Dryden,
in Pope himself, even in the writers of elegant pastorals,
and shines forth in Thomson's *Seasons*. This poet, the
son of a clergyman, and very poor, lived, like most of
the literary men of the time, on donations and literary
subscriptions, on sinecures and political pensions; for
lack of money he did not marry; wrote tragedies, because
tragedies brought in plenty of money; and ended by
settling in a country house, lying in bed till mid-day,
indolent, contemplative, but a simple and honest man,
affectionate and beloved. He saw and loved the country
in its smallest details, not outwardly only, as Saint Lam-
bert,[1] his imitator; he made it his joy, his amusement,
his habitual occupation; a gardener at heart, delighted
to see the spring arrive, happy to be able to add another
field to his garden. He paints all the little things,
without being ashamed, for they interest him, and takes
pleasure in "the smell of the dairy." We hear him
speak of the "insect armies," and "when the envenomed
leaf begins to curl,"[2] and of the birds which, foreseeing
the approaching rain, "streak their wings with oil, to
throw the lucid moisture trickling off."[3] He perceives
objects so clearly that he makes them visible: we
recognise the English landscape, green and moist, half
drowned in floating vapours, blotted here and there by
violet clouds, which burst in showers at the horizon,
which they darken, but where the light is delicately

---

[1] A French pastoral writer (1717-1803), who wrote, in imitation of
Thomson, *Les Saisons.*—TR.

[2] Poetical Works of J. Thomson, ed. R. Bell, 1855, 2 vols.; ii.
Spring. 18.   [3] *Ibid.* 19.

dimmed by the fog, and the clear heavens show at
intervals very bright and pure :

> " Th' effusive South
> Warms the wide air, and o'er the void of heaven
> Breathes the big clouds with vernal showers distent.[1] . .
> Thus all day long the full-distended clouds
> Indulge their genial stores, and well-showered earth
> Is deep enriched with vegetable life ;
> Till in the western sky, the downward sun
> Looks out, effulgent, from amid the flush
> Of broken clouds, gay-shifting to his beam.
> The rapid radiance instantaneous strikes
> The illumined mountain ; through the forest streams ;
> Shakes on the floods ; and in a yellow mist,
> Far smoking o'er the interminable plain,
> In twinkling myriads lights the dewy gems.
> Moist, bright, and green, the landscape laughs around." [2]

This is emphatic, but it is also opulent. In this air
and this vegetation, in this imagination and this style,
there is a heaping up, and, as it were, an impasto of
effaced or sparkling tints ; they are here the glistening
and lustrous robe of nature and art. We must see
them in Rubens—he is the painter and poet of the
teeming and humid clime ; but we discover it also in
others ; and in this magnificence of Thomson, in this
exaggerated, luxuriant, grand colouring, we find occa-
sionally the rich palette of Rubens.

VI.

All this suits ill the classical embroidery. Thomson's
visible imitations of Virgil, his episodes inserted to fill

---

[1] Poetical Works of Thomson, *Spring*, ii. 19.   [2] *Ibid.* 20.

up space, his invocations to spring, to the muse, to
philosophy, all these pedantic relics and conventionalisms, produce incongruity. But the contrast is
much more marked in another way. The worldly
artificial life such as Louis XIV. had made fashionable,
began to weary Europe. It was found meagre and
hollow; people grew tired of always acting, submitting
to etiquette. They felt that gallantry is not love, nor
madrigals poetry, nor amusement happiness. They
perceived that man is not an elegant doll, or a dandy
the masterpiece of nature, and that there is a world
beyond the drawing-room. A Genevese plebeian (J. J.
Rousseau), a Protestant and a recluse, whom religion,
education, poverty, and genius had led more quickly
and further than others, spoke out the public secret
aloud; and it was thought that he had discovered or re-
discovered the country, conscience, religion, the rights of
man, and natural sentiments. Then appeared a new
personality, the idol and model of his time, the man of
feeling, who, by his grave character and liking for nature,
contrasted with the man at court. Doubtless the man
of feeling has not escaped the influence of the places he
has frequented. He is refined and insipid, melting at
the sight of the young lambs nibbling the newly grown
grass, blessing the little birds, who give a concert to
celebrate their happiness. He is emphatic and wordy,
writes tirades about sentiment, inveighs against the
age, apostrophises virtue, reason, truth, and the abstract
divinities, which are engraved in delicate outline on
frontispieces. In spite of himself, he continues a
man of the drawing-room and the academy; after
uttering sweet things to the ladies, he utters them to
nature, and declaims in polished periods about the

Deity. But after all, it is through him that the revolt against classical customs begins; and in this respect, he is more advanced in Germanic England than in Latin France. Thirty years before Rousseau, Thomson had expressed all Rousseau's sentiments, almost in the same style. Like him, he painted the country with sympathy and enthusiasm. Like him, he contrasted the golden age of primitive simplicity with modern miseries and corruption. Like him, he exalted deep love, conjugal tenderness, the union of souls and perfect esteem animated by desire, paternal affection, and all domestic joys. Like him, he combated contemporary frivolity, and compared the ancient republics with modern States:

> " Proofs of a people, whose heroic aims
> Soared far above the little selfish sphere
> Of doubting modern life." [1]

Like Rousseau, he praised gravity, patriotism, liberty, virtue; rose from the spectacle of nature to the contemplation of God, and showed to man glimpses of immortal life beyond the tomb. Like him, in short, he marred the sincerity of his emotion and the truth of his poetry by sentimental vapidities, by pastoral billing and cooing, and by such an abundance of epithets, personified abstractions, pompous invocations and oratorical tirades, that we perceive in him beforehand the false and ornamental style of Thomas,[2] David,[3] and the first French Revolution.

[1] Poetical Works of Thomson, *Liberty*, part i. 102.

[2] Anthony Léonard Thomas (1732-1785) wrote memoirs and essays on the character of celebrated men in highly oratorical and pompous style.—Tr.

[3] See the paintings of David, called *Les Fêtes de la Révolution*.

Other authors follow in the same track. The literature of that period might be called the library of the man of feeling. First there was Richardson, the puritanic printer, with his Sir Charles Grandison,[1] a man of principles, an accomplished model of a gentleman, a professor of decorum and morality, with a soul into the bargain. There is Sterne too, a refined and sickly blackguard, who, amidst his buffooneries and oddities, pauses to weep over an ass or an imaginary prisoner.[2] There is, in particular, Henry Mackenzie, " the Man of Feeling," whose timid, delicate hero weeps five or six times a day ; who grows consumptive through sensibility, dares not broach his love till at the point of death, and dies in broaching it. Naturally, praise induces satire ; and in the opposite camp we see Fielding, a valiant roysterer, and Sheridan, a brilliant but naughty fellow, the one with Blifil, the other with Joseph Surface, two hypocrites, especially the second, not coarse, red-faced, and smelling of the vestry, like Tartuffe, but worldly, well-clad, a fine talker, loftily serious, sad and gentle from excess of tenderness, who, with his hand on his heart and a tear in his eye, showers on the public his sentences and periods whilst he soils his brother's reputation and debauches his neighbour's wife. When a man of feeling has been thus created, he soon has an epic made for him. A Scotsman, a man of wit, of too much wit, having published on his own account an unsuccessful rhapsody, wished to recover his expenses, visited the mountains of his country, gathered picturesque images, collected fragments of legends, plastered over the whole an abundance of eloquence and rhetoric, and created a Celtic Homer, Ossian, who with Oscar, Malvina,

[1] See vol. iii. p. 285.   [2] See vol. iii. p. 308.

and his whole troop, made the tour of Europe, and, about 1830, ended by furnishing baptismal names for French *grisettes* and *perruquiers*. Macpherson displayed to the world an imitation of primitive manners, not over-true, for the extreme rudeness of barbarians would have shocked the people, but yet well enough preserved or portrayed to contrast with modern civilisation, and persuade the public that they were looking upon pure nature. A keen sympathy with Scottish landscape, so grand, so cold, so gloomy, rain on the hills, the birch trembling to the wind, the mist of heaven and the vague musing of the soul, so that every dreamer found there the emotions of his solitary walks and his philosophic sadness ; chivalric exploits and magnanimity, heroes who set out alone to engage an army, faithful virgins dying on the tomb of their betrothed ; an impassioned, coloured style, affecting to be abrupt, yet polished ; able to charm a disciple of Rousseau by its warmth and elegance : here was some-thing to transport the young enthusiasts of the time ; civilised barbarians, scholarly lovers of nature, dreaming of the delights of savage life, whilst they shook off the powder which the hairdresser had left on their coats.

Yet this is not the course of the main current of poetry ; it runs in the direction of sentimental reflection : the greatest number of poems, and those most sought after, are emotional dissertations. In fact, a man of feeling breaks out in excessive declamations. When he sees a cloud, he dreams of human nature and constructs a phrase. Hence at this time among poets, swarm the melting philosophers and the tearful academicians ; Gray, the morose hermit of Cambridge, and Akenside, a noble thinker, both learned imitators of lofty Greek poetry; Beattie, a metaphysical moralist, with a young girl's nerves and an old maid's hobbies; the amiable and affectionate Goldsmith who wrote the *Vicar of Wakefield*, the most charming of Protestant pastorals; poor Collins, a young enthusiast, who was disgusted with life, would read nothing but the Bible, went mad, was shut up in an asylum, and in his intervals of liberty wandered in Chichester cathedral, accompanying the music with sobs and groans; Glover, Watts, Shenstone, Smart, and others. The titles of their works sufficiently indicate their character. One writes a poem on *The Pleasures of Imagination*, another odes on the *Passions* and on *Liberty*; one an *Elegy written in a Country Churchyard* and a *Hymn to Adversity*, another a poem on a *Deserted Village*, and on the character of surrounding civilisations (Goldsmith's *Traveller*); one a sort of epic on *Thermopylæ*, and another the moral history of a young *Minstrel*. They were nearly all grave, spiritual men, impassioned for noble ideas, with Christian aspirations or convictions, given to meditating on man, inclined to melancholy, to description, invocation, lovers of abstraction and allegory, who, to attain greatness, willingly mounted on stilts. One of the least strict and most noted of them was Young, the author of *Night Thoughts*, a clergyman and a courtier, who, having vainly attempted to enter Parliament, then to become a bishop, married, lost his wife and children, and made use of his misfortunes to write meditations on *Life, Death, Immortality, Time, Friendship, The Christian Triumph, Virtue's Apology, A Moral Survey of the Nocturnal Heavens*, and many other similar pieces. Doubtless there are brilliant flashes of imagination in his poems; seriousness and elevation are not wanting; we can even see that

he aims at them ; but we discover much more quickly
that he makes the most of his grief, and strikes attitudes.
He exaggerates and declaims, studies effect and style,
confuses Greek and Christian ideas.   Fancy an unhappy
father, who says :

> " *Silence* and *Darkness !*   Solemn sisters !   Twins
>   From ancient *Night* !   I to *Day's* soft-ey'd sister pay my
>   court, ...[1]
>   (Endymion's rival !) and her aid implore ;
>   Now first implor'd in succour to the *Muse*."[2]

And a few pages further on he invokes heaven and
earth, when mentioning the resurrection of the Saviour.
And yet the sentiment is fresh and sincere.   Is it not
one of the greatest of modern ideas to put Christian
philosophy into verse ?   Young and his contemporaries
say beforehand that which Chateaubriand and Lamartine
were to discover.   The true, the futile, all is here forty
years earlier than in France.   The angels and the other
celestial machinery long figured in England before
appearing in Chateaubriand's *Génie du Christianisme*
and the *Martyrs*.   Atala and Chactas are of the same
family as Malvina and Fingal.   If Lamartine read
Gray's odes and Akenside's reflections, he would find
there the melancholy sweetness, the exquisite art, the fine
arguments, and half the ideas of his own poetry.   And
nevertheless, near as they were to a literary renovation,
Englishmen did not yet attain it.   In vain the foundation
was changed, the form remained.   They did not shake
off the classical drapery ; they write too well, they dare
not be natural.   They have always a patent stock of fine

---

[1] Young's *Night Thoughts*.   Night the First : On Life, Death, and
Immortality.   [2] *Ibid*. Night the Third : Narcissa.

suitable words, poetical elegances, where each of them thought himself bound to go and pick out his phrases. It boots them nothing to be impassioned or realistic; like Shenstone, to dare to describe a *Schoolmistress*, and the very part on which she whips a young rascal; their simplicity is conscious, their frankness archaic, their emotion formal, their tears academical. Ever, at the moment of writing, an august model starts up, a sort of schoolmaster, weighing on each with his full weight, with all the weight which a hundred and twenty years of literature can give his precepts. Their prose is always the slave of the period: Dr. Johnson, who was at once the La Harpe and the Boileau of his age, explains and imposes on all the studied, balanced, irreproachable phrase; and classical ascendency is still so strong that it domineers over nascent history, the only kind of English literature which was then European and original. Hume, Robertson, and Gibbon were almost French in their taste, language, education, conception of man. They relate like men of the world, cultivated and well-informed, with charm and clearness, in a polished, rhythmic, sustained style. They show a liberal spirit, an unvaried moderation, an impartial reason. They banish from history all coarseness and tediousness. They write without fanaticism or prejudice. But, at the same time, they attenuate human nature; comprehend neither barbarism nor loftiness; paint revolutions and passions, as people might do who had seen nothing but decked drawing-rooms and dusted libraries; they judge enthusiasts with the coldness of chaplains or the smile of a sceptic; they blot out the salient features which distinguish human physiognomies; they cover all the harsh points of truth with a brilliant and uniform varnish. At last there started up an unfortunate Scotch peasant (Burns) rebelling against the world, and in love, with the yearnings, lusts, greatness, and irrationality of modern genius. Now and then, behind his plough, he lighted on genuine verses, verses such as Heine and Alfred de Musset have written in our own days. In those few words, combined after a new fashion, there was a revolution. Two hundred new verses sufficed. The human mind turned on its hinges, and so did civil society. When Roland, being made a minister, presented himself before Louis XVI. in a simple dress-coat and shoes without buckles, the master of the ceremonies raised his hands to heaven, thinking that all was lost. In reality, all was changed.

BOOK IV.

MODERN LIFE.

—✦—

CHAPTER I.

Ideas and Productions.

I.

On the eve of the nineteenth century the great modern revolution began in Europe. The thinking public and the human mind changed, and whilst these changes took place a new literature sprang up.

The preceding age had done its work. Perfect prose and classical style put within reach of the most backward and the dullest minds the notions of literature and the discoveries of science. Moderate monarchies and regular administrations had permitted the middle class to develop itself under the pompous aristocracy of the court, as useful plants may be seen shooting up beneath trees which serve for show and ornament. They multiply, grow, rise to the height of their rivals, envelop them in their luxuriant growth, and obscure them by their dense clusters. A new world, a world of citizens and plebeians, henceforth occupies the ground, attracts the gaze, imposes its form on manners, stamps its image on minds. Towards the close of the century a sudden

concourse of extraordinary events brings it all at once
to the light, and sets it on an eminence unknown to
any previous age. With the grand applications of
science, democracy appears. The steam-engine and
spinning-jenny create in England towns of from three
hundred and fifty thousand to five hundred thousand
souls. The population is doubled in fifty years, and
agriculture becomes so perfect, that, in spite of this
enormous increase of mouths to be fed, one-sixth of the
inhabitants provide from the same soil food for the rest;
imports increase threefold, and even more ; the tonnage
of vessels increases sixfold, the exports sixfold and
more.[1] Comfort, leisure, instruction, reading, travel,
whatever had been the privilege of a few, became the
common property of the many. The rising tide of
wealth raised the best of the poor to comfort, and the
best of the well-to-do to opulence. The rising tide
of civilisation raised the mass of the people to the rudi-
ments of education, and the mass of citizens to complete
education. In 1709 appeared the first daily newspaper,[2] as big as a man's hand, which the editor did not
know how to fill, and which, added to all the other
papers, did not circulate to the extent of three thousand
numbers in the year. In 1844 the Stamp Office showed
that 71 million newspapers had been printed during the
past year, many as large as volumes, and containing
as much matter. Artisans and townsfolk, enfranchised, enriched, having gained a competence, left the
low depths where they had been buried in their narrow
parsimony, ignorance, and routine ; they made their

---

[1] See Alison, *History of Europe ;* Porter, *Progress of the Nation.*

[2] In the *Fourth Estate,* by F. Knight Hunt, 2 vols. 1840, it is said
(i. 175) that the first daily and morning paper, *The Daily Courant,*
appeared in 1709.—Tr.

appearance on the stage now, doffed their workman's and supernumerary's dress, assumed the leading parts by a sudden irruption or a continuous progress, by dint of revolutions, with a prodigality of labour and genius, amidst vast wars, successively or simultaneously in America, France, the whole of Europe, founding or destroying states, inventing or restoring sciences, conquering or acquiring political rights. They grew noble through their great deeds, became the rivals, equals, conquerors of their masters ; they need no longer imitate them, being heroes in their turn : like them, they can point to their crusades; like them, they have gained the right of having a poetry; and like them, they will have a poetry.

In France, the land of precocious equality and completed revolutions, we must observe this new character —the plebeian bent on getting on; Augereau, son of a greengrocer; Marceau, son of a lawyer; Murat, son of an innkeeper; Ney, son of a cooper ; Hoche, formerly a sergeant, who in his tent, by night, read Condillac's *Traité des Sensations ;* and chief of all, that spare young man, with lank hair, hollow cheeks, eaten up with ambition, his heart full of romantic fancies and grand rough-hewn ideas, who, a lieutenant for seven years, read twice through the whole stock of a bookseller at Valence, who about this time (1792) in Italy, though suffering from itch, had just destroyed five armies with a troop of barefooted heroes, and gave his government an account of his victories with all his faults of spelling and of French.   He became master, proclaimed himself the representative of the Revolution, declared, " that a career is open to talent," and impelled others along with him in his enterprises.   They follow him, because there is glory, and above all, advancement, to be won. " Two officers," says Stendhal, " commanded a battery at Talavera; a ball laid low the captain. ' So!' said the lieutenant, ' François is dead, I shall be captain.' ' Not yet,' said François, who was only stunned, and got on his feet again." These two men were neither enemies nor wicked; on the contrary, they were companions and comrades; but the lieutenant wanted to rise a step. Such was the sentiment which provided men for the exploits and carnage of the Empire, which caused the Revolution of 1830, and which now, in this vast stifling democracy, compels men to vie with each other in intrigues and labour, genius and baseness, to get out of their primitive condition, and raise themselves to the summit, of which the possession is given up to their rivalry or promised to their toil. The dominant character now-a-days is no longer the man of the drawing-room, whose position in society is settled and whose fortune is made; elegant and careless, with no employment but to amuse himself and to please; who loves to converse, who is gallant, who passes his life in conversation with finely dressed ladies, amidst the duties of society and the pleasures of the world: it is the man in a black coat, who works alone in his room or rushes about in a cab to make friends and protectors; often envious, feeling himself always above or below his station in life, sometimes resigned, never satisfied, but fertile in invention, not sparing his labour, finding the picture of his blemishes and his strength in the drama of Victor Hugo and the novels of Balzac.[1]

This man has also other and greater cares. With

---

[1] To realise the contrast, compare *Gil Blas* and *Ruy Blas*, Marivaux', *Paysan Parvenu* and Stendhal's Julien Sorel (in *Rouge et Noir*).

the state of human society, the form of the human mind has changed. It changed by a natural and irresistible development, like a flower growing into fruit, like fruit turning to seed. The mind renews the evolution which it had already performed in Alexandria, not as then in a deleterious atmosphere, amidst the universal degradation of enslaved men, in the increasing decadence of a disorganised society, amidst the anguish of despair and the mists of a dream; but lapt in a purifying atmosphere, amidst the visible progress of an improving society and the general ennobling of lofty and free men, amidst the proudest hopes, in the wholesome clearness of experimental sciences. The oratorical age which declined, as it declined in Athens and Rome, grouped all ideas in beautiful commodious compartments, whose subdivisions instantaneously led the gaze towards the object which they define, so that thenceforth the intellect could enter upon the loftiest conceptions, and seize the aggregate which it had not yet embraced. Isolated nations, French, English, Italians, Germans, drew near and became known to each other through the upheaving of the first French Revolution and the wars of the Empire, as formerly races divided from one another, Greeks, Syrians, Egyptians, Gauls, by the conquests of Alexaʼ der and the domination of Rome : so that henceforth each civilisation, expanded by the collision with neighbouring civilisations, can pass beyond its national limits, and multiply its ideas by the commixture of the ideas of others. History and criticism spring up as under the Ptolemies ; and from all sides, throughout the universe, in all directions, they were engaged in resuscitating and explaining literatures, religions, manners, societies,

philosophies : so that thenceforth the intellect, enfranchised by the spectacle of past civilisations, can
escape from the prejudices of its century, as it has
escaped from the prejudices of its country. A new
race, hitherto torpid, gave the signal : Germany communicated to the whole of Europe the impetus to a
revolution of ideas, as France to a revolution of manners. These simple folk who smoked and warmed
themselves by a stove, and seemed only fit to produce
learned editions, became suddenly the promoters and
leaders of human thought. No race has such a comprehensive mind ; none is so well adapted for lofty
speculation. We see it in their language, so abstract,
that away from the Rhine it seems an unintelligible
jargon. And yet thanks to this language, they
attained to superior ideas. For the specialty of
this revolution, as of the Alexandrian revolution, was
that the human mind became more capable of abstraction. They made, on a large scale, the same step
as the mathematicians when they pass from arithmetic.
to algebra, and from ordinary calculation to the
computation of the infinite. They perceived, that
beyond the limited truths of the oratorical age,
there were deeper unfoldings ; they passed beyond
Descartes and Locke, as the Alexandrians went beyond
Plato and Aristotle : they understood that a great
operative architect, or round and square atoms, were not
causes ; that fluids, molecules, and monads were not
forces ; that a spiritual soul or a physiological secretion
would not account for thought. They sought religious
sentiment beyond dogmas, poetic beauty beyond rules,
critical truths beyond myths. They desired to grasp
natural and moral powers as they are, and independ-

ently of the fictitious supports to which their predecessors had attached them. All these supports, souls and atoms, all these fictions, fluids, and monads, all these conventions, rules of the beautiful and of religious symbols, all rigid classifications of things natural, human and divine, faded away and vanished. Thenceforth they were nothing but figures; they were only kept as an aid to the memory, and as auxiliaries of the mind; they served only provisionally, and as starting-points. Through a common movement along the whole line of human thought, causes draw back into an abstract region, where philosophy had not been to search them out for eighteen centuries. Then appeared the disease of the age, the restlessness of Werther and Faust, very like that which in a similar moment agitated men eighteen centuries ago; I mean, discontent with the present, the vague desire of a higher beauty and an ideal happiness, the painful aspiration for the infinite. Man suffered through doubt, yet he doubted; he tried to seize again his beliefs, they melted in his hand; he would settle and rest in the doctrines and the satisfactions which sufficed for his predecessors, and he does not find them sufficient. He launches, like Faust, into anxious researches through science and history, and judges them vain, dubious, good for men like Wagner,[1] learned pedants and bibliomaniacs. It is the "beyond" he sighs for; he forebodes it through the formulas of science, the texts and confessions of the churches, through the amusements of the world, the intoxication of love. A sublime truth exists behind coarse experience and transmitted catechisms; a grand happiness exists beyond the pleasures of society and family

---

[1] The disciple of Faust.

joys. Whether men are sceptical, resigned, or mystics, they have all caught a glimpse of or imagined it, from Goethe to Beethoven, from Schiller to Heine; they have risen towards it in order to stir up the whole swarm of their grand dreams; they will not be consoled for falling away from it; they have mused upon it, even during their deepest fall; they have instinctively dwelt, like their predecessors the Alexandrians and Christians, in that splendid invisible world in which, in ideal peace, slumber the creative essences and powers; and the vehement aspiration of their heart has drawn from their sphere the elementary spirits, "film of flame, who flit and wave in eddying motion! birth and the grave, an infinite ocean, a web ever growing, a life ever glowing, ply at Time's whizzing loom, and weave the vesture of God."[1]

Thus rises the modern man, impelled by two sentiments, one democratic, the other philosophic. From the shallows of his poverty and ignorance he exerts himself to rise, lifting the weight of established society and admitted dogmas, disposed either to reform or to destroy them, and at once generous and rebellious. These two currents from France and Germany at this moment swept into England. The dykes there were so strong, they could hardly force their way, entering more slowly than elsewhere, but entering nevertheless. They made for themselves a new channel between the ancient barriers, and widened without bursting them, by a peaceful and slow transformation which continues till this day.

[1] Goethe's *Faust.* sc. 1.

II.

The new spirit broke out first in a Scottish peasant, Robert Burns: in fact, the man and the circumstances were suitable; scarcely ever was seen together more of misery and talent. He was born January 1759, amid the hoar frost of a Scottish winter, in a cottage of clay built by his father, a poor farmer of Ayrshire; a sad condition, a sad country, a sad lot. A part of the gable fell in a few days after his birth, and his mother was obliged to seek refuge with her child, in the middle of a storm, in a neighbour's house. It is hard to be born in Scotland; it is so cold there, that in Glasgow on a fine day in July, whilst the sun was shining, I did not feel my overcoat too warm. The soil is wretched; there are many bare hills, where the harvest often fails. Burns' father, no longer young, having little more than his arms to depend upon, having taken his farm at too high a rent, burdened with seven children, lived parsimoniously, or rather fasting, in solitude, to avoid temptations to expense. "For several years butchers' meat was a thing unknown in the house." Robert went barefoot and bareheaded; at "the age of thirteen he assisted in thrashing the crop of corn, and at fifteen he was the principal labourer on the farm." The family did all the labour; they kept no servant, male or female. They had not much to eat, but they worked hard. "This kind of life —the cheerless gloom of a hermit, with the unceasing toil of a galley slave—brought me to my sixteenth year," Burns says. His shoulders were bent, melancholy seized him; "almost every evening he was constantly afflicted with a dull headache, which at a future period of his life was exchanged for a palpitation.

of the heart, and a threatening of fainting and suffocation in his bed in the night-time." "The anguish of mind which we felt," says his brother, "was very great." The father grew old; his gray head, careworn brow, temples "wearing thin and bare," his tall bent figure, bore witness to the grief and toil which had spent him. The factor wrote him insolent and threatening letters which "set all the family in tears." There was a respite when the father changed his farm, but a lawsuit sprang up between him and the proprietor: "After three years' tossing and whirling in the vortex of litigation, my father was just saved from the horrors of a gaol by consumption, which after two years' promises kindly stepped in." In order to snatch something from the claws of the lawyers, the two sons were obliged to step in as creditors for arrears of wages. With this little sum they took another farm. Robert had seven pounds a year for his labour; for several years his whole expenses did not exceed this wretched pittance; he had resolved to succeed by dint of abstinence and toil: "I read farming books, I calculated crops, I attended markets; ... but the first year, from unfortunately buying bad seed, the second from a late harvest, we lost half our crops." Troubles came apace; poverty always engenders them. The mastermason Armour, whose daughter was Burns' sweetheart, was said to contemplate prosecuting him, to obtain a guarantee for the support of his expected progeny, though he refused to accept him as a son-in-law. Jean Armour abandoned him; he could not give his name to her child. He was obliged to hide; he had been publicly admonished by the church. He said: "Even in the hour of social mirth, my gaiety is the madness

of an intoxicated criminal under the hands of the
executioner." He resolved to leave the country; he
agreed with Dr. Charles Douglas for thirty pounds a
year to be bookkeeper or overseer on his estate in
Jamaica; for want of money to pay the passage, he
was about to "indent himself," that is, become bound
as apprentice, when the success of a volume of poetry
he had published put a score of guineas into his hands,
and for a time brought him brighter days. Such was
his life up to the age of twenty-seven, and that which
succeeded was little better.

Let us fancy in this condition a man of genius, a
true poet, capable of the most delicate emotions and the
loftiest aspirations, wishing to rise, to rise to the summit,
of which he deemed himself capable and worthy.[1]

Ambition had early made itself heard in him: "I
had felt early some stirrings of ambition, but they were
the blind groping of Homer's Cyclops round the walls
of his cave. . . . The only two openings by which I
could enter the temple of fortune were the gate of
niggardly economy, or the path of little chicaning
bargain-making. The first is so contracted an aperture,
I never could squeeze myself into it; the last I always
hated—there was contamination in the very entrance."[2]
Low occupations depress the soul even more than the
body; man perishes in them—is obliged to perish; of
necessity there remains of him nothing but a machine:
for in the kind of action in which all is monotonous,
in which throughout the very long day the arms lift
the same flail and drive the same plough, if thought

---

[1] Most of these details are taken from the *Life and Works of
Burns*, by R. Chambers, 1851, 4 vols.

[2] Chambers' *Life of Burns*, i. 14.

does not take this uniform movement, the work is ill
done. The poet must take care not to be turned aside
by his poetry; to do as Burns did, "think only of his
work whilst he was at it." He must think of it always,
in the evening unyoking his cattle, on Sunday putting
on his new coat, counting on his fingers the eggs and
poultry, thinking of the kinds of dung, finding a means
of using only one pair of shoes, and of selling his hay
at a penny a truss more. He will not succeed if he
has not the patient dulness of a labourer, and the crafty
vigilance of a petty shopkeeper. How could poor
Burns succeed? He was out of place from his birth,
and tried his utmost to raise himself above his condition.[1] At the farm at Lochlea, during meal-times, the
only moments of relaxation, parents, brothers, and
sisters, ate with a spoon in one hand and a book in the
other. Burns, at the school of Hugh Rodger, a teacher
of mensuration, and later at a club of young men at
Tarbolton, strove to exercise himself in general questions,
and debated *pro* and *con* in order to see both sides of
every idea. He carried a book in his pocket to study
in spare moments in the fields; he wore out thus
two copies of Mackenzie's *Man of Feeling.* "The
collection of songs was my *vade mecum.* I pored
over them driving my cart, or walking to labour, song
by song, verse by verse, carefully noting the true,
tender, sublime, or fustian." He maintained a correspondence with several of his companions in the same
rank of life in order to form his style, kept a commonplace book, entered in it ideas on man, religion, the
greatest subjects, criticising his first productions. Burns
says, "Never did a heart pant more ardently than mine

---

[1] My great constituent elements are pride and passion.

to be distinguished." He thus divined what he did
not learn, rose of himself to the level of the most
highly cultivated; in a while, at Edinburgh, he was to
read through and through respected doctors, Blair himself; he was to see that Blair had attainments, but no
depth.   At this time he studied minutely and lovingly
the old Scotch ballads; and by night in his cold little
room, by day whilst whistling at the plough, he
invented forms and ideas.   We must think of this in
order to measure his efforts, to understand his miseries
and his revolt.   We must think that the man in whom
these great ideas are stirring, threshed the corn, cleaned
his cows, went out to dig peats, waded in the muddy
snow, and dreaded to come home and find the bailiffs
prepared to carry him off to prison.   We must think
also, that with the ideas of a thinker he had the delicacies and reveries of a poet.   Once, having cast his
eyes on an engraving representing a dead soldier, and
his wife beside him, his child and dog lying in the snow,
suddenly, involuntarily, he burst into tears.   He writes :

There is scarcely any earthly object gives me more—I do
not know if I should call it pleasure—but something which
exalts me, something which enraptures me—than to walk in the
sheltered side of a wood, or high plantation, in a cloudy winter
day, and hear the stormy wind howling among the trees and
raving over the plain.[1] . . . I listened to the birds and frequently turned out of my path, lest I should disturb their
little songs or frighten them to another station.

The slavery of mechanical toil and perpetual economy
crushed this ,swarm of grand or graceful dreams
as soon as they began to soar.   Burns was moreover

---

[1] Extract from Burns' commonplace-book ; Chambers' *Life*, i. 79.

proud, so proud, that afterwards in the world, amongst the great, "an honest contempt for whatever bore the appearance of meanness and servility" made him "fall into the opposite error of hardness of manner." He had also the consciousness of his own merits. "*Pauvre inconnu* as I then was, I had pretty nearly as high an opinion of myself and of my works as I have at. this moment, when the public has decided in their favour."[1] Who can wonder that we find at every step in his poems the bitter protests of an oppressed and rebellious plebeian ?

We find such recriminations against all society, against State and Church. Burns has a harsh tone, often the very phrases of Rousseau, and wished to be a "vigorous savage," quit civilised life, the dependence and humiliations which it imposes on the wretched.

"It is mortifying to see a fellow, whose abilities would scarcely have made an eight-penny taylor, and whose heart is not worth three farthings, meet with attention and notice that. are withheld from the son of ꝛenius and poverty."[2] It is hard to

> " See yonder poor, o'erlabour'd wight,
>   So abject, mean, and vile,
>   Who begs a brother of the earth
>   To give him leave to toil ;
>   And see his lordly fellow-worm
>   The poor petition spurn,
>   Unmindful, though a weeping wife
>   And helpless offspring mourn."[3]

---

[1] Chambers' *Life*, i. 231. Burns had a right to think so : when he arrived at night in an inn, the very servants woke their fellow-labourers to come and hear him talk.

[2] Chambers' *Life and Works of Robert Burns*, ii. 68.

[3] *Man was made to Mourn*, a dirge.

Burns says also:

> " While winds frae off Ben-Lomond blaw,
> And bar the doors wi' driving snaw, . . .
> I grudge a wee the great folks' gift,
> That live so bien an' snug :
> I tent less, and want less
> Their roomy fire-side ;
> But hanker and canker
> To see their cursed pride.
>
> It's hardly in a body's power
> To keep, at times, frae being sour,
> To see how things are shar'd ;
> How best o' chiels are whiles in want,
> While coofs on countless thousands rant,
> And ken na how to wair 't." [1]

But " a man's a man for a' that," and the peasant is as good as the lord. There are men noble by nature, and they alone are noble ; the coat is the business of the tailor, titles a matter for the Herald's office. " The rank is but the guinea's stamp, the man's the gowd for a' that."

Against men who reverse this natural equality Burns is pitiless ; the least thing puts him out of temper. Read his " Address of Beelzebub, to the Right Honourable the Earl of Breadalbane, President of the Right Honourable and Honourable the Highland Society, which met on the 23d of May last at the Shakspeare, Covent Garden, to concert ways and means to frustrate the designs of five hundred Highlanders, who, as the society were informed by Mr. Mackenzie of Applecross, were so audacious, as to attempt an escape from their lawful lords and masters, whose property they were, by

---

[1] *First Epistle to Davie, a brother poet.*

emigrating from the lands of Mr. M'Donald of Glengarry
to the wilds of Canada, in search of that fantastic thing
—liberty !" Rarely was an insult more prolonged and
more biting, and the threat is not far behind. He
warns Scotch members like a revolutionist, to withdraw
"that curst restriction on aquavitae," "get auld Scotland back her kettle :"

> "An', Lord, if ance they pit her till't,
> Her tartan petticoat she'll kilt,
> An' durk an' pistol at her belt,
> She'll tak the streets,
> An' rin her whittle to the hilt
> I' the first she meets !" [1]

In vain he writes, that

> "In politics if thou wouldst mix
> And mean thy fortunes be ;
> Bear this in mind, be deaf and blind,
> Let great folks hear and see." [2]

Not alone did he see and hear, but he also spoke, and
that aloud. He congratulates the French, on having
repulsed conservative Europe, in arms against them.
He celebrates the Tree of Liberty, planted "where ance
the Bastile stood :"

> "Upo' this tree there grows sic fruit,
> Its virtues a' can tell, man ;
> It raises man aboon the brute,
> It makes him ken himsel', man.
> Gif ance the peasant taste a bit,
> He's greater than a Lord, man. . . .

---

[1] *Earnest Cry and Prayer to the Scotch Representatives.*
[2] *The Creed of Poverty ;* Chambers' *Life,* iv. 86.

> King Loui' thought to cut it down,
> When it was unco sma', man.
> For this the watchman cracked his crown,
> Cut off his head and a', man." [1]

A strange gaiety, savage and nervous, and which, in better style, resembles that of the *Ca ira.*

Burns is hardly more tender to the church. At that time the strait puritanical garment began to give way. Already the learned world of Edinburgh had Frenchified, widened, adapted it to the fashions of society, decked it with ornaments, not very brilliant, it is true, but select. In the lower strata of society dogma became less rigid, and approached by degrees the looseness of Arminius and Socinus. John Goldie, a merchant, had quite recently discussed the authority of Scripture.[2] John Taylor had denied original sin. Burns' father, pious as he was, inclined to liberal and humane doctrines, and detracted from the province of faith to add to that of reason. Burns, after his wont, pushed things to an extreme, thought himself a deist, saw in the Saviour only an inspired man, reduced religion to an inner and poetic sentiment, and attacked with his railleries the paid and patented orthodox people. Since Voltaire, no literary man in religious matters was more bitter or more jocose. According to him, ministers are shopkeepers trying to cheat each other out of their customers, decrying at the top of their voice the shop next door, puffing their drugs in numberless advertisements, and here and there setting up fairs to push the trade. These "holy fairs" are gatherings of the pious, where the sacrament is administered. One after another the clergymen preach

---

[1] *The Tree of Liberty.*   [2] 1780.

and thunder, in particular a Rev. Mr. Moodie, who raves
and fumes to throw light on points of faith—a terrible
figure :

> " Should Hornie, as in ancient days,
>   'Mong sons o' God present him,
> The vera sight o' Moodie's face
>   To's ain het hame had sent him
>   Wi' fright that day.
>
> Hear how he clears the points o' faith
> Wi' rattlin' an' wi' thumpin' !
> Now meekly calm, now wild in wrath,
> He's stampin' an' he's jumpin' !
> His lengthen'd chin, his turn'd-up snout,
> His eldritch squeel and gestures,
> Oh ! how they fire the heart devout,
> Like cantharidian plasters,
>   On sic a day ! " [1]

The minister grows hoarse ; now " Smith opens out his
cauld harangues," then two more ministers speak. At last
the audience rest, " the Change-house fills," and people
begin to eat ; each brings cakes and cheese from his bag ;
the young folks have their arms round their lasses' waists.
That was an attitude to listen in !   There is a great
noise in the inn ; the cans rattle on the board ; whisky
flows, and provides arguments to the tipplers commenting on the sermons.   They demolish carnal reason, and
exalt free faith.   Arguments and stamping, shouts of
sellers and drinkers, all mingle together.   It is a " holy
fair :"

> " But now the Lord's ain trumpet touts,
>   Till a' the hills are rairin',
> An' echoes back return the shouts ;
>   Black Russell is na sparin' ;

[1] *The Holy Fair.*

His piercing words, like Highlan' swords,
Divide the joints and marrow.
His talk o' hell, where devils dwell,
Our vera sauls does harrow
        Wi' fright that day.

A vast unbottom'd boundless pit,
Fill'd fu' o' lowin' brunstane,
Wha's raging flame, an scorchin' heat,
Wad melt the hardest whunstane.
The half-asleep start up wi' fear,
An' think they hear it roarin',
When presently it does appear
'Twas but some neebor snorin'
        Asleep that day. . . .

How monie hearts this day converts
O' sinners and o' lasses !
Their hearts o' stane, gin night, are gane,
As saft as ony flesh is.
There's some are fou o' love divine,
There's some are fou o' brandy." [1]
Etc. etc.

The young men meet the girls, and the devil does a
better business than God. A fine ceremony and
morality! Let us cherish it carefully, and our wise
theology too, which damns men.

As for that poor dog common sense, which bites so
hard, let us send him across seas; let him go " and
bark in France." For where shall we find better men
than our " unco guid "—Holy Willie for instance ? He
feels himself predestinated, full of never-failing grace;
therefore all who resist him resist God, and are fit only
to be punished; may He " blast their name, who bring

---

[1] *The Holy Fair.*

thy elders to disgrace, and public shame."[1] Burns
says also:

> " An honest man may like a glass,
> An honest man may like a lass,
> But mean revenge an' malice fause
> He'll still disdain ;
> An then cry zeal for gospel laws
> Like some we ken. . . .
> . . . I rather would be
> An atheist clean,
> Than under gospel colours hid be
> Just for a screen." [2]

There is a beauty, an honesty, a happiness outside the
conventionalities and hypocrisy, beyond correct preachings and proper drawing-rooms, unconnected with
gentlemen in white ties and reverends in new bands.

In 1785 Burns wrote his masterpiece, the *Jolly
Beggars*, like the *Gueux* of Béranger ; but how much
more picturesque, varied, and powerful ! It is the end
of autumn, the gray leaves float on the gusts of the
wind ; a joyous band of vagabonds, happy devils, come
for a junketing at the change-house of Poosie Nansie :

> " Wi' quaffing and laughing
> They ranted and they sang ;
> Wi' jumping and thumping
> The very girdle rang."

First, by the fire, in old red rags, is a soldier, and his
old woman is with him ; the jolly old girl has drunk
freely ; he kisses her, and she again pokes out her greedy
lips ; the coarse loud kisses smack like " a cadger's

---

[1] *Holy Willie's Prayer.*   [2] *Epistle to the Rev. John M'Math.*

whip." "Then staggering and swaggering, he roar'd
this ditty up :"

> " I lastly was with Curtis, among the floating batt'ries,
>   And there I left for witness an arm and a limb ;
>   Yet let my country need me, with Elliot to head me,
>   I'd clatter on my stumps at the sound of a drum. . . .
>   He ended ; and the kebars sheuk,
>   Aboon the chorus' roar ;
>   While frighted rattons backward leuk,
>   And seek the benmost bore."

Now it is the "doxy's" turn :

> " I once was a maid, tho' I cannot tell when,
>   And still my delight is in proper young men. . . .
>   Some one of a troop of dragoons was my daddie,
>   No wonder I'm fond of a sodger laddie.
>   The first of my loves was a swaggering blade,
>   To rattle the thundering drum was his trade. . . .
>   The sword I forsook for the sake of the church. . . .
>   Full soon I grew sick of my sanctified sot,
>   The regiment at large for a husband I got,
>   From the gilded spontoon to the fife I was ready,
>   I asked no more but a sodger laddie.
>   But the peace it reduc'd me to beg in despair,
>   Till I met my old boy at a Cunningham fair ;
>   His rags regimental they flutter'd so gaudy,
>   My heart it rejoic'd at a sodger laddie. . . .
>   But whilst with both hands I can hold the glass steady,
>   Here's to thee, my hero, my sodger laddie."

This is certainly a free and easy style, and the poet is
not mealy-mouthed. His other characters are in the
same taste, a Merry Andrew, a raucle carlin (a stout
beldame), a " pigmy-scraper wi' his fiddle," a travelling

tinker,—all in rags, brawlers and gipsies, who fight, bang, and kiss each other, and make the glasses ring with the noise of their good humour:

> " They toomed their pocks, and pawned their duds,
>   They scarcely left to co'er their fuds,
>   To quench their lowin' drouth."

And their chorus rolls about like thunder, shaking the rafters and walls.

> " A fig for those by law protected !
>   Liberty's a glorious feast !
> Courts for cowards were erected,
>   Churches built to please the priest !
>
> What is title ?   What is treasure ?
>   What is reputation's care ?
> If we lead a life of pleasure,
>   'Tis no matter how or where !
>
> With the ready trick and fable,
>   Round we wander all the day ;
> And at night, in barn or stable,
>   Hug our doxies on the hay.
>
> Life is all a variorum,
>   We regard not how it goes ;
> Let them cant about decorum,
>   Who have characters to lose.
>
> Here's to budgets, bags and wallets !
>   Here's to all the wandering train !
> Here's our ragged brats and callets !
>   One and all cry out—Amen."

Has any man better spoken the language of rebels and levellers ?   There is here, however, something else than tne instinct of destruction and an appeal to the senses ; there is hatred of cant and return to nature. Burns sings :

> " Morality, thou deadly bane,
> Thy tens o' thousands thou hast slain ;
> Vain is his hope, whose stay and trust is
> In moral mercy, truth and justice ! " [1]

Mercy ! this grand word renews all. Now, as formerly, eighteen centuries ago, men rose above legal formulas and prescriptions ; now, as formerly, under Virgil and Marcus Aurelius, refined sensibility and wide sympathies embraced beings who seemed for ever out of the pale of society and law. Burns pities, and that sincerely, a wounded hare, a mouse whose nest was upturned by his plough, a mountain daisy. Is there such a very great difference between man, beast, or plant ? A mouse stores up, calculates, suffers like a man :

> " I doubt na, whiles, but thou may thieve ;
> What then ? poor beastie, thou maun live."

We even no longer wish to curse the fallen angels, the grand malefactors, Satan and his troop. Like the " randie, gangrel bodies, who in Poosie Nancy's held the splore," they have their good points, and perhaps after all are not so bad as people say :

> " Hear me, auld Hangie, for a wee,
> An' let poor damned bodies be ;
> I'm sure sma' pleasure it can gie,
> E'en to a deil,
> To skelp an' scaud poor dogs like me,
> An' hear us squeel ! . . .

---

[1] *A Dedication to Gavin Hamilton.*

Then you, ye auld, snic-drawing dog!
Ye came to Paradise incog.,
An' played on man a cursed brogue,
 (Black be your fa' !)
An' gied the infant warld a shog,
 'Maist ruin'd a'. . . .

But, fare you weel, auld Nickie-ben!
O wad ye tak a thought an' men'!
Ye aiblins might—I dinna ken—
 Still hae a stake—
I'm wae to think upo' yon den,
 Ev'n for your sake." [1]

We see that he speaks to the devil as to an unfortunate comrade, a disagreeable fellow, but fallen into trouble. Let us take another step, and we will see in a contemporary, Goethe, that Mephistopheles himself is not overmuch damned; his god, the modern god, tolerates him and tells him he has never hated such as he. For wide conciliating nature assembles in her company, on equal terms, the ministers of destruction and life. In this deep change the ideal changes; citizen and orderly life, strict Puritan duty, do not exhaust all the powers of man. Burns cries out in favour of instinct and enjoyment, so as to seem epicurean. He has genuine gaiety, a glow of jocularity; laughter commends itself to him; he praises it as well as the good suppers of good comrades, where wine is plentiful, pleasantry abounds, ideas pour forth, poetry sparkles, and causes a carnival of beautiful figures and good-humoured people to move about in the human brain.

He always was in love.[2] He made love the great

---

[1] *Address to the Deil.*
[2] He himself says : " I have been all along a miserable dupe to Love."

end of existence, to such a degree that at the club which he founded with the young men of Tarbolton, every member was obliged " to be the declared lover of one or more fair ones." From the age of fifteen this was his main business. He had for companion in his harvest toil a sweet and lovable girl, a year younger than himself : " In short, she, altogether unwittingly to herself, initiated me in that delicious passion, which, in spite of acid disappointment, gin-horse prudence, and book-worm philosophy, I hold to be the first of human joys, our dearest blessing here below." [1] He sat beside her with a joy which he did not understand, to " pick out from her little hand the cruel nettle-stings and thistles." He had many other less innocent fancies ; it seems to me that by his very nature he was in love with all women : as soon as he saw a pretty one, he grew lively ; his commonplace-book and his songs show that he set off in pursuit after every butterfly, golden or not, which seemed about to settle. Moreover he did not confine himself to Platonic reveries ; he was as free of action as of words ; broad jests crop up freely in his verses. He calls himself an unregenerate heathen, and he is right. He has even written obscene verses ; and Lord Byron refers to a quantity of his letters, of course unpublished, than which worse could not be imagined :[2] it was the excess of the sap which overflowed in him, and soiled the bark. Doubtless he did not boast about these excesses, he rather repented of them ; but as to the uprising and blooming of the free poetic life in the open air, he found no fault with it. He thought that

His brother Gilbert said : "He was constantly the victim of some fair enslaver."   [1] Chambers' *Life of Burns,* i. 12.
   [2] Byron's Works, ed. Moore, 17 vols., ii. 302, *Journal,* Dec. 13, 1813.

love, with the charming dreams it brings, poetry, pleasure, and the rest, are beautiful things, suitable to human instincts, and therefore to the designs of God. In short, in contrast with morose Puritanism, he approved joy and spoke well of happiness.[1]

Not that he was a mere epicurean; on the contrary, he could be religious. When, after the death of his father, he prayed aloud in the evening, he drew tears from those present; and his *Cottar's Saturday Night* is the most heartfelt of virtuous idyls. I even believe he was fundamentally religious. He advised his " pupil as he tenders his own peace, to keep up a regular warm intercourse with the Deity." What he made fun of was official worship; but as for religion, the language of the soul, he was greatly attached to it. Often before Dugald Stewart at Edinburgh, he disapproved of the sceptical jokes which he heard at the supper table. He thought he had " every evidence for the reality of a life beyond the stinted bourne of our present existence;" and many a time, side by side with a jocose satire, we find in his writings stanzas full of humble repentance, confiding fervour, or Christian resignation. These, if you will, are a poet's contradictions, but they are also a poet's divinations; under these apparent variations there rises a new ideal; old narrow moralities are to give place to the wide sympathy of the modern man, who loves the beautiful wherever it meets him, and who, refusing to mutilate human nature, is at once Pagan and Christian.

This originality and divining instinct exist in his style as in his ideas. The specialty of the age in which we live, and which he inaugurated, is to blot out

---

[1] See a passage from Burns' commonplace-book in Chambers' *Life of Burns*, i. 93.

rigid distinctions of class, catechism, and style; academic, moral, or social conventions are falling away, and we claim in society a mastery for individual merit, in morality for inborn generosity, in literature for genuine feeling. Burns was the first to enter on this track, and he often pursues it to the end. When he wrote verses, it was not on calculation or in obedience to fashion: "My passions, when once lighted up, raged like so many devils, till they got vent in rhyme; and then the conning over my verses, like a spell, soothed all into quiet."[1] He hummed them to old Scotch airs which he passionately loved, as he drove his plough, and which, he says, as soon as he sang them, brought ideas and rhymes to his lips. That, indeed, was natural poetry; not forced in a hothouse, but born of the soil between the furrows, side by side with music, amidst the gloom and beauty of the climate, like the violet heather of the moors and the hillside. We can understand that it gave vigour to his tongue. For the first time this man spoke as men speak, or rather as they think, without premeditation, with a mixture of all styles, familiar and terrible, hiding an emotion under a joke, tender and jeering in the same place, apt to place side by side tap-room trivialities and the high language of poetry,[2] so indifferent was he to rules, content to exhibit his feeling as it came to him, and as he felt it. At last, after so many years, we escape from measured declamation, we hear a man's voice! and what is better still, we forget the voice in the emotion which it expresses, we feel this emotion reflected in ourselves,

[1] Chambers' *Life*, i. 38.
[2] See *Tam o' Shanter, Address to the Deil, The Jolly Beggars, A Man's a Man for a' that, Green Grow the Rashes*, etc.

we enter into relations with a soul. Then form seems to fade away and disappear: I think that this is the great feature of modern poetry; seven or eight times has Burns reached it.

He has done more; he has made his way, as we say now-a-days. On the publication of his first volume he became suddenly famous. Coming to Edinburgh, he was feasted, caressed, admitted on a footing of equality in the best drawing-rooms, amongst the great and the learned, loved of a woman who was almost a lady. For one season he was sought after, and he behaved worthily amidst these rich and noble people. He was respected, and even loved. A subscription brought him a second edition and five hundred pounds. He also at last had won his position, like the great French plebeians, amongst whom Rousseau was the first. Unfortunately he brought thither, like them, the vices of his condition and of his genius. A man does not rise with impunity, nor, above all, desire to rise with impunity: we also have our vices, and suffering vanity is the first of them. "Never did a heart pant more ardently than mine to be distinguished," said Burns. This grievous pride marred his talent, and threw him into follies. He laboured to attain a fine epistolary style, and brought ridicule on himself by imitating in his letters the men of the academy and the court. He wrote to his lady-loves with choice phrases, full of periods as pedantic as those of Dr. Johnson. Certainly we dare hardly quote them, the emphasis is so grotesque.[1] At other times he committed to his common-

---

[1] "O Clarinda, shall we not meet in a state, some yet unknown state of being, where the lavish hand of plenty shall minister to the highest wish of benevolence, and where the chill north-wind of prudence shall never blow over the flowery fields of enjoyment?"

place-book literary expressions that occurred to him, and six months afterwards sent them to his correspondents as extemporary effusions and natural improvisations. Even in his verses, often enough, he fell into a grand conventional style; [1] brought into play sighs, ardours, flames, even the big classical and mythological machinery. Béranger, who thought or called himself the poet of the people, did the same. A plebeian must have much courage to venture on always remaining himself, and never slipping on the court dress. Thus Burns, a Scottish villager, avoided, in speaking, all Scotch village expressions : he was pleased to show himself as well-bred as fashionable folks. It was forcibly and by surprise that his genius drew him away from the proprieties : twice out of three times his feeling was marred by his pretentiousness.

His success lasted one winter, after which the wide incurable wound of plebeianism made itself felt,—I mean that he was obliged to work for his living. With the money gained by the second edition of his poems he took a little farm. It was a bad bargain ; and, moreover, we can imagine that he had not the money-grubbing character necessary. He says : " I might write you on farming, on building, on marketing ; but my poor distracted mind is so torn, so jaded, so racked, and bedeviled with the task of the superlatively damned obligation to make one guinea do the business of three, that I detest, abhor, and swoon at the very word business." Soon he left his farm, with empty pockets, to fill at Dumfries the small post of exciseman, which

---

[1] *Epistle to James Smith :*

" O Life, how pleasant is thy morning,
Young Fancy's rays the hills adorning,
Cold-pausing Caution's lesson spurning ! "

was worth, in all, £90 a year.   In this fine employment
he branded leather, gauged casks, tested the make of
candles, issued licences for the transit of spirits.   From
his dunghills he passed to office work and grocery:
what a life for such a man!   He would have been
unhappy, even if independent and rich.   These great
innovators, these poets, are all alike.   What makes
them poets is the violent afflux of sensations.   They
have a nervous mechanism more sensitive than ours;
the objects which leave us cool, transport them suddenly
beyond themselves.   At the least shock their brain is
set going, after which they once more fall flat, loathe
existence, sit morose amidst the memories of their
faults and their lost pleasures.   Burns said : " My
worst enemy is *moi-même*. . . . There are just two
creatures I would envy: a horse in his wild state
traversing the forests of Asia, or an oyster on some of
the desert shores of Europe.   The one has not a wish
without enjoyment, the other has neither wish nor
fear."   He was always in extremes, at the height of
exaltation or in the depth of depression·; in the morning, ready to weep; in the evening at table or under
the table; enamoured of Jean Armour, then on her
refusal engaged to another, then returning to Jean, then
quitting her, then taking her back, amidst much scandal,
many blots on his character, still more disgust.   In
such heads ideas are like cannon balls : the man, hurled
onwards, bursts through everything, shatters himself,
begins again the next day, but in a contrary direction,
and ends by finding nothing left in him, but ruins within
and without.   Burns had never been prudent, and was
so less than ever, after his success at Edinburgh.   He
had enjoyed too much; he henceforth felt too acutely

the painful sting of modern man, namely the disproportion between the desire for certain things and the power of obtaining them. Debauch had all but spoiled his fine imagination, which had before been " the chief source of his happiness ;" and he confessed that, instead of tender reveries, he had now nothing but sensual desires. He had been kept drinking till six in the morning ; he was very often drunk at Dumfries, not that the whisky was very good, but it makes thoughts to whirl about in the head ; and hence poets, like the poor, are fond of it. Once at Mr. Riddell's he made himself so tipsy that he insulted the lady of the house; next day he sent her an apology which was not accepted, and, out of spite, wrote rhymes against her : a lamentable excess, betraying an unseated mind. At thirty-seven he was worn out. One night, having drunk too much, he sat down and went to sleep in the street. It was January, and he caught rheumatic fever. His family wanted to call in a doctor. " What business has a physician to waste his time on me ? " he said ; " I am a poor pigeon not worth plucking." He was horribly thin, could not sleep, and could not stand on his legs. " As to my individual self, I am tranquil. But Burns' poor widow and half a dozen of his dear little ones, there I am as weak as a woman's tear." He was even afraid he should not die in peace, and had the bitterness of being obliged to beg. Here is a letter he wrote to a friend : " A rascal of a haberdasher, taking into his head that I am dying, has commenced a process against me, and will infallibly put my emaciated body into jail. Will you be so good as to accommodate me, and that by return of post, with ten pounds ? O James ! did you know the pride of my heart, you would

feel doubly for me! Alas, I am not used to beg!"[1]
He died a few days afterwards, at thirty-eight. His
wife was lying-in of her fifth child at the time of her
husband's funeral.

III.

A sad life, most often the life of the men in advance
of their age; it is not wholesome to go too quick.
Burns was so much in advance, that it took forty years
to catch him. At this time in England, the conservatives and the believers took the lead before sceptics
and revolutionists. The constitution was liberal, and
seemed to be a guarantee of rights; the church was
popular, and seemed to be the support of morality.
Practical capacity and speculative incapacity turned the
mind aside from the propounded innovations, and bound
them down to the established order. The people found
themselves well off in their great feudal house, widened
and accommodated to modern needs; they thought it
beautiful, they were proud of it; and national instinct,
like public opinion, declared against the innovators who
would throw it down to build it up again. Suddenly a
violent shock changed this instinct into a passion, and
this opinion into fanaticism. The French Revolution,
at first admired as a sister, had shown itself a fury and a
monster. Pitt declared in Parliament, "that one of
the leading features of this (French) Government was
the extinction of religion and the destruction of property."[2] Amidst universal applause, the whole thinking and influential class rose to stamp out this party of

[1] Chambers' *Life ;* Letter to Mr. Js. Burnes, iv. 205.
[2] *The Speeches of William Pitt*, 2d ed. 3 vols. 1808, ii. 17, Jan.
21, 1794.

robbers, united brigands, atheists on principle; and
Jacobinism, sprung from blood to sit in purple, was
persecuted even in its child and champion " Buonaparte,
who is now the sole organ of all that was formerly
dangerous and pestiferous in the revolution."[1]   Under
this national rage liberal ideas dwindled; the most illustrious friends of Fox — Burke, Windham, Spencer —
abandoned him: out of a hundred and sixty partisans in
the House of Commons, only fifty remained to him. The
great Whig party seemed to be disappearing; and in
1799, the strongest minority that could be collected
against the Government was twenty-nine. Yet English
Jacobinism was taken by the throat and held down:

"The *Habeas Corpus* Act was repeatedly suspended. . . .
Writers who propounded doctrines adverse to monarchy and
aristocracy, were proscribed and punished without mercy. It
was hardly safe for a republican to avow his political creed over
his beefsteak and his bottle of port at a chophouse. . . . Men
of cultivated mind and polished manners were (in Scotland),
for offences which at Westminster would have been treated as
mere misdemeanours sent to herd with felons at Botany Bay."[2]

But the intolerance of the nation aggravated that of
the Government. If any one had dared to avow democratic sentiments, he would have been insulted. The
papers represented the innovators as wretches and
public enemies. The mob in Birmingham burned the
houses of Priestley and the Unitarians. And in the
end Priestley was obliged to leave England.

New theories could not arise in this society armed
against new theories. Yet the revolution made its

[1] *The Speeches of William Pitt*, iii. 152, Feb. 17, 1800.
[2] Macaulay's Works, vii.; *Life of William Pitt*, 396.

entrance; it entered disguised, and through an indirect way, so as not to be recognised. It was not social ideas, as in France, that were transformed, nor philosophical ideas as in Germany, but literary ideas; the great rising tide of the modern mind, which elsewhere overturned the whole edifice of human conditions and speculations, succeeded here only at first in changing style and taste. It was a slight change, at least apparently, but on the whole of equal value with the others; for this renovation in the manner of writing is a renovation in the manner of thinking: the one led to all the rest, as a central pivot being set in motion causes all the indented wheels to move also.

Wherein consists this reform of style? Before defining it, I prefer to exhibit it; and for that purpose, we must study the character and life of a man who was the first to use it, without any system—William Cowper: for his talent is but the picture of his character, and his poems but the echo of his life. He was a delicate, timid child, of a tremulous sensibility, passionately tender, who, having lost his mother at six, was almost at once subjected to the fagging and brutality of a public school. These, in England, are peculiar: a boy of about fifteen singled him out as a proper object upon whom he might practise the cruelty of his temper; and the poor little fellow, ceaselessly ill-treated, " conceived," he says, " such a dread of his (tormentor's) figure, . . . that I well remember being afraid to lift my eyes upon him higher than his knees; and that I knew him better by his shoe-buckles than by any other part of his dress."[1] At the age of nine melancholy seized him, not the sweet reverie which we call by that name, but the profound

---

[1] *The Works of W. Cowper*, ed. Southey, 8 vols. 1843.

dejection, gloomy and continual despair, the horrible malady of the nerves and the soul, which leads to suicide, Puritanism, and madness. " Day and night I was upon the rack, lying down in horror, and rising up in despair."[1]

The evil changed form, diminished, but did not leave him. As he had only a small fortune, though born of a high family, he accepted, without reflection, the offer of his uncle, who wished to give him a place as clerk of the journals of the House of Lords ; but he had to undergo an examination, and his nerves were unstrung at the very idea of having to speak in public. For six months he tried to prepare himself ; but he read without understanding. His continual misery brought on at last a nervous fever. Cowper writes of himself : " The feelings of a man when he arrives at the place of execution, are probably much like mine, every time I set my foot in the office, which was every day, for more than a half year together.[2] In this situation, such a fit of passion has sometimes seized me, when alone in my chambers, that I have cried out aloud, and cursed the hour of my birth ; lifting up my eyes to heaven not as a suppliant, but in the hellish spirit of rancorous reproach and blasphemy against my Maker."[3] The day of examination came on : he hoped he was going mad, so that he might escape from it ; and as his reason held out, he thought even of " self-murder." At last, " in a horrible dismay of soul," insanity came, and he was placed in an asylum, whilst " his conscience was scaring him, and the avenger of blood pursuing him "[4] to the extent even of thinking himself damned, like

---

[1] *The Works of W. Cowper*, ed. Southey, i. 18.
[2] *Ibid.* 79.   [3] *Ibid.* 81.   [4] *Ibid.* 97.

Bunyan and the first Puritans.   After several months
his reason returned, but it bore traces of the strange
lands where it had journeyed alone.   He remained sad,
like a man who thought himself in disfavour with God,
and felt himself incapable of an active life.   However,
a clergyman, Mr. Unwin, and his wife. very pious and
very regular people, had taken charge of him.   He tried
to busy himself mechanically, for instance, in making
rabbit-hutches, in gardening, and in taming hares.   He
employed the rest of the day like a Methodist, in reading Scripture or sermons, in singing hymns with his
friends, and speaking of spiritual matters.   This way
of living, the wholesome country air, the maternal tenderness of Mrs. Unwin and Lady Austen, brought him
a few gleams of light.   They loved him so generously,
and he was so lovable !   Affectionate, full of freedom
and innocent raillery, with a natural and charming imagination, a graceful fancy, an exquisite delicacy, and so
unhappy !   He was one of those to whom women devote
themselves, whom they love maternally, first from compassion, then by attraction, because they find in them
alone the consideration, the minute and tender attentions,
the delicate observances which men's rude nature cannot
give them, and which their more sensitive nature nevertheless craves.   These sweet moments, however, did not
last.   He says : " My mind has always a melancholy
cast, and is like some pools I have seen, which, though
filled with a black and putrid water, will nevertheless
in a bright day reflect the sunbeams from their surface."
He smiled as well as he could, but with effort ; it was
the smile of a sick man who knows himself incurable,
and tries to forget it for an instant, at least to make
others forget it : " Indeed, I wonder that a sportive

thought should ever knock at the door of my intellects, and still more that it should gain admittance.   It is as if harlequin should intrude himself into the gloomy chamber where a corpse is deposited in state.   His antic gesticulations would be unseasonable at any rate, but more specially so if they should distort the features of the mournful attendants into laughter.   But the mind, long wearied with the sameness of a dull, dreary prospect, will gladly fix his eyes on anything that may make a little variety in its contemplations, though it were but a kitten playing with her tail."[1]   In reality, he had too delicate and too pure a heart: pious, irreproachable, austere, he thought himself unworthy of going to church, or even of praying to God.   He says also: "As for happiness, he that once had communion with his Maker must be more frantic than ever I was yet, if he can dream of finding it at a distance from Him."[2]   And elsewhere: "The heart of a Christian, mourning and yet rejoicing, (is) pierced with thorns, yet wreathed about with roses.   I have the thorn without the rose.   My brier is a wintry one; the flowers are withered, but the thorn remains."   On his deathbed, when the clergyman told him to confide in the love of the Redeemer, who desired to save all men, he uttered a passionate cry, begging him not to give him such consolations.   He thought himself lost, and had thought so all his life.   One by one, under this terror all his faculties gave way.   Poor charming soul, perishing like a frail flower transplanted from a warm land to the snow: the world's temperature was too rough for it;

---

[1] *The Works of W. Cowper*, ed. Southey; Letter to the Rey. John Newton, July 12, 1780.

[2] *Ibid.* Letter to Rev. J. Newton, August 5, 1786.

and the moral law, which should have supported it, tore it with its thorns.

Such a man does not write for the pleasure of making a noise. He made verses as he painted or worked at his bench to occupy himself, to distract his mind. His soul was too full; he need not go far for subjects. Picture this pensive figure, silently wandering and gazing along the banks of the Ouse. He gazes and dreams. A buxom peasant girl, with a basket on her arm; a distant cart slowly rumbling on behind horses in a sweat; a sparkling spring, which polishes the blue pebbles,—this is enough to fill him with sensations and thoughts. He returned, sat in his little summer-house, as large as a sedan-chair, the window of which opened out upon a neighbour's orchard, and the door on a garden full of pinks, roses, and honeysuckle. In this nest he laboured. In the evening, beside his friend, whose needles were working for him, he read, or listened to the drowsy sounds without. Rhymes are born in such a life as this. It sufficed for him, and for their birth. He did not need a more violent career: less harmonious or monotonous, it would have upset him; impressions small to us were great to him; and in a room, a garden, he found a world. In his eyes the smallest objects were poetical. It is evening; winter; the postman comes :

> " The herald of a noisy world,
> With spattered boots, strapp'd waist, and frozen locks;
> News from all nations lumbering at his back.
> True to his charge, the close-packed load behind,
> Yet careless what he brings, his one concern
> Is to conduct it to the destined inn;
> And, having dropped the expected bag, pass on.

> He whistles as he goes, light-hearted wretch,
> Cold and yet cheerful : messenger of grief
> Perhaps to thousands, and of joy to some."[1]

At last we have the precious "close-packed load;" we open it; we wish to hear the many noisy voices it brings from London and the universe :

> " Now stir the fire, and close the shutters fast,
> Let fall the curtains, wheel the sofa round,
> And while the bubbling and loud-hissing urn
> Throws up a steamy column, and the cups,
> That cheer but not inebriate, wait on each,
> So let us welcome peaceful evening in."[2]

Then he unfolds the whole contents of the newspaper—politics, news, even advertisements—not as a mere realist, like so many writers of to-day, but as a poet; that is, as a man who discovers a beauty and harmony in the coals of a sparkling fire, or the movement of fingers over a piece of wool-work; for such is the poet's strange distinction. Objects not only spring up in his mind more powerful and more precise than they were of themselves, and before entering there; but also, once conceived, they are purified, ennobled, coloured, like gross vapours, which, being transfigured by distance and light, change into silky clouds, lined with purple and gold. For him there is a charm in the rolling folds of the vapour sent up by the tea-urn, sweetness in the concord of guests assembled around the same table in the same house. This one expression, " News from India," causes him to see India itself, " with her plumed and jewelled turban."[3] The mere notion of " excise " sets before his eyes " ten thousand casks, for ever dribbling out their

---

[1] *The Task*, iv.; *The Winter Evening.*   [2] *Ibid.*   [3] *Ibid.*

base contents, touched by the Midas finger of the State, (which) bleed gold for ministers to sport away."[1] Strictly speaking, nature is to him like a gallery of splendid and various pictures, which to us ordinary folk are always covered up with cloths. At most, now and then, a rent suffers us to imagine the beauties hid behind the uninteresting curtains; but the poet raises these curtains, one and all, and sees a picture where we see but a covering. Such is the new truth which Cowper's poems brought to light. We know from him that we need no longer go to Greece, Rome, to the palaces, heroes, and academicians, in search of poetic objects. They are quite near us. If we see them not, it is because we do not know how to look for them; the fault is in our eyes, not in the things. We may find poetry, if we wish, at our fireside, and amongst the beds of our kitchen-garden.[2]

Is the kitchen-garden indeed poetical? To-day, perhaps; but to-morrow, if my imagination is barren, I shall see there nothing but carrots and other kitchen stuff. It is my feelings which are poetical, which I must respect, as the most precious flower of beauty. Hence a new style. We need no longer, after the old oratorical fashion, box up a subject in a regular plan, divide it into symmetrical portions, arrange ideas into files, like the pieces on a draught-board. Cowper takes the first subject that comes to hand—one which Lady Austen gave him at hap-hazard—the *Sofa*, and speaks about it for a couple of pages; then he goes whither

---

[1] *The Task*, iv.; *The Winter Evening.*

[2] Crabbe may also be considered one of the masters and renovators of poetry, but his style is too classical, and he has been rightly nicknamed "a Pope in worsted stockings."

the bent of his mind leads him, describing a winter
evening, a number of interiors and landscapes, mingling
here and there all kinds of moral reflections, stories,
dissertations, opinions, confidences, like a man who
thinks aloud before the most intimate and beloved of
his friends.   Let us look at his great poem, the *Task*.
" The best didactic poems," says Southey, " when compared with the *Task*, are like formal gardens in comparison with woodland scenery."   If we enter into details, the
contrast is greater still.   He does not seem to dream
that he is being listened to ; he only speaks to himself.
He does not dwell on his ideas, as the classical writers
do, to set them in relief, and make them stand out by
repetitions and antitheses ; he marks his sensation, and
that is all.   We follow this sensation in him as it gradually springs up ; we see it rising from a former one, swelling, falling, remounting, as we see vapour issuing from a
spring, and insensibly rising, unrolling, and developing
its shifting forms.   Thought, which in others was
congealed and rigid, becomes here mobile and fluent ;
the rectilinear verse grows flexible ; the noble vocabulary widens its scope to let in vulgar words of
conversation and life.   At length poetry has again
become lifelike ; we no longer listen to words, but we
feel emotions ; it is no longer an author, but a man
who speaks.   His whole life is there, perfect, beneath
its black lines, without falsehood or concoction ; his
whole effort is bent on removing falsehood and concoction.   When he describes his little river, his dear Ouse,
" slow winding through a level plain of spacious meads,
with cattle sprinkled o'er,"[1] he sees it with his inner
eye ; and each word, cæsura, sound, answers to a change

[1] *The Task,* i. ;. *The Sofa.*

of that inner vision. It is so in all his verses; they are full of personal emotions, genuinely felt, never altered or disguised; on the contrary, fully expressed, with their transient shades and fluctuations; in a word, as they are, that is, in the process of production and destruction, not all complete, motionless, and fixed, as the old style represented them. Herein consists the great revolution of the modern style. The mind, outstripping the known rules of rhetoric and eloquence, penetrates into profound psychology, and no longer employs words except to mark emotions.

IV.

Now[1] appeared the English romantic school, closely resembling the French in its doctrines, origin, and alliances, in the truths which it discovered, the exaggerations it committed, and the scandal it excited. The followers of that school formed a sect, a sect of "dissenters in poetry," who spoke out aloud, kept themselves close together, and repelled settled minds by the audacity and novelty of their theories. For their foundation were attributed to them the anti-social principles and the sickly sensibility of Rousseau; in short, a sterile and misanthropical dissatisfaction with the present institutions of society. Southey, one of their leaders, began by being a Socinian and Jacobin; and one of his first poems, *Wat Tyler*, cited the glory of the past Jacquerie in support of the present revolution. Another, Coleridge, a poor fellow, who had served as a dragoon, his brain stuffed with incoherent reading and humanitarian dreams, thought of founding

[1] 1793-1794.

in America a communist republic, purged of kings and priests; then, having turned Unitarian, steeped himself at Göttingen in heretical and mystical theories on the Logos and the absolute. Wordsworth himself, the third and most moderate, had begun with enthusiastic verses against kings:

> "Great God, . . . grant that every sceptred child of clay,
> Who cries presumptuous, ' Here the flood shall stay,'
> May in its progress see thy guiding hand,
> And cease the acknowledged purpose to withstand;
> Or, swept in anger from the insulted shore,
> Sink with his servile bands, to rise no more!"[1]

But these rages and aspirations did not last long; and at the end of a few years, the three, brought back into the pale of Church and State, became, Coleridge, a Pittite journalist, Wordsworth, a distributor of stamps, and Southey, poet-laureate; all zealous converts, decided Anglicans, and intolerant Conservatives. In point of taste, however, they had advanced, not retired. They had violently broken with tradition, and leaped over all classical culture to take their models from the Renaissance and the middle-age. One of their friends, Charles Lamb, like Saint-Beuve, had discovered and restored the sixteenth century. The most unpolished dramatists, like Marlowe, seemed to these men admirable; and they sought in the collections of Percy and Warton, in the old national ballads and ancient poetry of foreign lands, the fresh and primitive accent which had been wanting in classical literature, and whose presence seemed to them to be a sign of truth and

---

[1] Wordsworth's Works, new edition, 1870, 6 vols.; *Descriptive Sketches during a Pedestrian Tour*, i. 42.

beauty. Above every other reform, they laboured to
destroy the grand aristocratical and oratorical style,
such as it sprang from methodical analyses and court
polish. They proposed to adapt to poetry the ordinary
language of conversation, such as is spoken in the
middle and lower classes, and to replace studied
phrases and a lofty vocabulary by natural tones and
plebeian words. In place of the classical mould, they
tried stanzas, sonnets, ballads, blank verse, with the
roughness and subdivisions of the primitive poets. They
adopted or arranged the metres and diction of the
thirteenth and sixteenth centuries. Charles Lamb
wrote an archaic tragedy, *John Woodvil*, which we
might fancy to have been written during Elizabeth's
reign. Others, like Southey, and Coleridge, in particular, manufactured totally new rhythms, as happy at
times, and at times also as unfortunate, as those of
Victor Hugo : for instance, a verse in which accents,
and not syllables, were counted ;[1] a singular medley of
confused attempts, manifest abortions, and original
inventions. The plebeian having doffed the aristocratical costume, sought another; borrowed one piece of
his dress from the knights or the barbarians, another
from peasants or journalists, not too critical of incongruities, pretentious and satisfied with his motley and
badly sewn cloak, till at last, after many attempts and
many rents, he ended by knowing himself, and selecting
the dress that fitted him.

In this confusion of labours two great ideas stand
out : the first producing historical poetry, the second
philosophical ; the one especially manifest in Southey

---

[1] In English poetry as since modified, no one dreams of limiting
the number of syllables, even in blank verse.—Tr.

and Walter Scott, the other in Wordsworth and
Shelley; both European, and displayed with equal brilliancy in France by Hugo, Lamartine, and Musset;
with greater brilliancy in Germany by Goethe, Schiller,
Rückert, and Heine; both so profound, that none of
their representatives, except Goethe, divined their
scope; and hardly now, after more than half a century,
can we define their nature, so as to forecast their
results.

The first consists in saying, or rather foreboding,
that our ideal is not the ideal; it is only one ideal,
but there are others. The barbarian, the feudal man,
the cavalier of the Renaissance, the Mussulman, the
Indian, each age and each race has conceived its
beauty, which was a beauty. Let us enjoy it, and for
this purpose put ourselves entirely in the place of
the discoverers; for it will not suffice to depict, as
the previous novelists and dramatists have done, modern
and national manners under old and foreign names;
let us paint the sentiments of other ages and other
races with their own features, however different these
features may be from our own, and however unpleasing
to our taste. Let us show our hero as he was, grotesque or not, with his true costume and speech : let him
be fierce and superstitious if he was so; let us dash the
barbarian with blood, and load the Covenanter with his
bundle of biblical texts. Then one by one on the
literary stage men saw the vanished or distant civilisations return; first the middle age and the Renaissance;
then Arabia, Hindostan, and Persia; then the classical
age, and the eighteenth century itself; and the historic
taste becomes so eager, that from literature the contagion spread to other arts. The theatre changed its

conventional costumes and decorations into true ones.
Architecture built Roman villas in our northern climates,
and feudal towers amidst our modern security.   Painters
travelled to imitate local colouring, and studied to
reproduce moral colouring.   Every man became a
tourist and an archæologist; the human mind quitting its individual sentiments to adopt all sentiments
really felt, and finally all possible sentiments, found its
pattern in the great Goethe, who by his *Tasso, Iphigenia,
Divan,* his second part of *Faust,* became a citizen of all
nations and a contemporary of all ages, seemed to live
at pleasure at every point of time and place, and gave
an idea of universal mind.   Yet this literature, as it
approached perfection, approached its limit, and was
only developed in order to die.   Men did comprehend
at last that attempted resurrections are always incomplete, that every imitation is only an imitation, that
the modern accent infallibly penetrates the words
which we place in the mouths of ancient characters,
that every picture of manners must be indigenous and
contemporaneous, and that archaic literature is essentially untrue.   People saw at last that it is in the
writers of the past that we must seek the portraiture
of the past; that there are no Greek tragedies but the
Greek tragedies; that the concocted novel must give
place to authentic memoirs, as the fabricated ballad to
the spontaneous; in other words, that historical literature must vanish and become transformed into criticism
and history, that is, into exposition and commentary of
documents.

How shall we select in this multitude of travellers and historians, disguised as poets?   They abound
like swarms of insects, hatched on a summer's day

amidst a rank vegetation; they buzz and glitter, and the mind is lost in their sparkle and hum. Which shall I quote? Thomas Moore, the gayest and most French of all, a witty railer,[1] too graceful and *recherché*, writing descriptive odes on the Bermudas, sentimental Irish melodies, a poetic Egyptian tale,[2] a romantic poem on Persia and India;[3] Lamb, a restorer of the old drama; Coleridge, a thinker and dreamer, a poet and critic, who in *Christabel* and the *Ancient Mariner* reopened the vein of the supernatural and the fantastic; Campbell, who, having begun with a didactic poem on the *Pleasures of Hope*, entered the new school without giving up his noble and half-classical style, and wrote American and Celtic poems, only slightly Celtic and American; in the first rank, Southey, a clever man, who, after several mistakes in his youth, became the professed defender of aristocracy and cant, an indefatigable reader, an inexhaustible writer, crammed with erudition, gifted in imagination, famed like Victor Hugo for the freshness of his innovations, the combative tone of his prefaces, the splendours of his picturesque curiosity, having spanned the universe and all history with his poetic shows, and embraced in the endless web of his verse, Joan of Arc, Wat Tyler, Roderick the Goth, Madoc, Thalaba, Kehama, Celtic and Mexican traditions, Arabic and Indian legends, successively a Catholic, a Mussulman, a Brahmin, but only in verse; in reality, a prudent and respectable Protestant. The above-mentioned authors have to be taken as examples merely—there are dozens behind; and I think that, of all fine visible or imaginable sceneries, of all great real or legendary events, at all times, in the four

[1] See *The Fudge Family*.   [2] *The Epicurean*.   [3] *Lalla Rookh*.

quarters of the world, not one has escaped them. The
diorama they show us is very brilliant; unfortunately
we perceive that it is manufactured. If we would
have its fellow picture, let us imagine ourselves at the
opera. The decorations are splendid, we see them
coming down from above, that is, from the ceiling,
thrice in an act; lofty Gothic cathedrals, whose rose-
windows glow in the rays of the setting sun, whilst
processions wind round the pillars, and the lights flicker
over the elaborate copes and the gold embroidery of
the priestly vestments; mosques and minarets, moving
caravans creeping afar over the yellow sand, whose
lances and canopies, ranged in line, fringe the immacu-
late whiteness of the horizon; Indian paradises, where
the heaped roses swarm in myriads, where fountains
mingle their plumes of pearls, where the lotus spreads
its large leaves, where thorny plants raise their many
thousand purple calices around the apes and croco-
diles which are worshipped as divinities, and crawl in
the thickets. Meantime the dancing-girls lay their
hands on their heart with deep and delicate emotion,
the tenor sing that they are ready to die, tyrants roll
forth their deep bass voice, the orchestra struggles
hard, accompanying the variations of sentiment with
the gentle sounds of flutes, the lugubrious clamours of
the trombones, the angelic melodies of the harps; till
at last, when the heroine sets her foot on the throat of
the traitor, it breaks out triumphantly with its thousand
vibrant voices harmonised into a single strain. A fine
spectacle! we depart mazed, deafened; the senses give
way under this inundation of splendours; but as we
return home, we ask ourselves what we have learnt,
felt—whether we have, in truth, felt anything. After

all, there is little here but decoration and scenery; the sentiments are factitious; they are operatic sentiments : the authors are only clever men, libretti-makers, manufacturers of painted canvas; they have talent without genius; they draw their ideas not from the heart, but from the head. Such is the impression left by *Lalla Rookh*, *Thalaba*, *Roderick the last of the Goths*, *The Curse of Kehama*, and the rest of these poems. They are great decorative machines suited to the fashion. The mark of genius is the discovery of some wide unexplored region in human nature, and this mark fails them; they prove only much cleverness and knowledge. After all, I prefer to see the East in Orientals from the East, rather than in Orientals in England; in Vyasa or Firdousi, rather than in Southey[1] and Moore. These poems may be descriptive or historical; they are less so than the texts, notes, emendations, and justifications which their authors carefully print at the foot of the page.

Beyond all general causes which have fettered this literature, there is a national one : the mind of these men is not sufficiently flexible, and too moral. Their imitation is only literal. They know past times and distant lands only as antiquaries and travellers. When they mention a custom, they put their authorities in a foot-note; they do not present themselves before the public without testimonials; they establish by weighty certificates that they have not committed an error in topography or costume. Moore, like Southey, named his authorities; Sir John Malcolm, Sir William Ouseley, Mr. Carey, and others, who returned from the

---

[1] See also *The History of the Caliph Vathek*, a fantastic but powerfully written tale, by W. Beckford, published first in French in 1784.

East, and had lived there, state that his descriptions
are wonderfully faithful, that they thought that Moore
had travelled in the East.   In this respect their minuteness is ridiculous ;[1] and their notes, lavished without
stint, show that their matter-of-fact public required to
ascertain whether their poetical commodities were
genuine produce.   But that broader truth, which lies
in penetrating into the feelings of characters, escaped
them ; these feelings are too strange and immoral.
When Moore tried to translate and recast Anacreon, he
was told that his poetry was fit for " the stews."[2]   To
write an Indian poem, we must be pantheistical at heart,
a little mad, and pretty generally visionary ; to write a
Greek poem, we must be polytheistic at heart, fundamentally pagan, and a naturalist by profession.   This
is the reason that Heine spoke so fitly of India, and
Goethe of Greece.   A genuine historian is not sure
that his own civilisation is perfect, and lives as gladly
out of his country as in it.   Judge whether Englishmen can succeed in this style.   In their eyes, there is
only one rational civilisation, which is their own ; every
other morality is inferior, every other religion is extravagant.   With such narrowness, how can they reproduce
these other moralities and religions ? .   Sympathy alone
can restore extinguished or foreign manners, and sympathy here is forbidden.   Under this narrow rule, historical poetry, which itself is hardly likely to live,
languishes as though suffocated under a leaden cover.

One of them, a novelist, critic, historian, and poet,
the favourite of his age, read over the whole of Europe,
was compared and almost equalled to Shakspeare, had

---

[1] See the notes of Southey, worse than those of Chateaubriand in
the *Martyrs*.   [2] *Edinburgh Review.*

more popularity than Voltaire, made dressmakers and duchesses weep, and earned about two hundred thousand pounds.   Murray, the publisher, wrote to him : " I believe I might swear that I never experienced such unmixed pleasure as the reading of this exquisite work (first series of *Tales of my Landlord*) has afforded me. . . . Lord Holland said, when I asked his opinion : ' Opinion ! we did not one of us go to bed last night —nothing slept but my gout.'"[1]   In France, fourteen hundred thousand volumes of these novels were sold, and they continue to sell.   The author, born in Edinburgh, was the son of a Writer to the Signet, learned in feudal law and ecclesiastical history, himself an advocate, a sheriff, and always fond of antiquities, especially national antiquities ; so that by his family, education, by his own instincts, he found the materials for his works and the stimulus for his talent.   His past recollections were impressed on him at the age of three, in a farm-house, where he had been taken to try the effect of bracing air on his little shrunken leg.   He was wrapt naked in the warm skin of a sheep just killed, and he crept about in this attire, which passed for a specific.   He continued to limp, and became a reader.   From his infancy he listened to the stories which he afterwards gave to the public,—that of the battle of Culloden, of the cruelties practised on the Highlanders, the wars and sufferings of the Covenanters.   At three he used to sing out the ballad of Hardyknute so loudly, that he prevented the village minister, a man gifted with a very fine voice, from being heard, and even from hearing himself.   As soon as he had heard " a Border-raid

---

[1] Lockhart, *Life of Sir Walter Scott*, 10 vols., 2d ed., 1839, ii. ch. xxxvii. p. 170.

ballad," he knew it by heart. But in other things he
was indolent, studied by fits and starts, and did not
readily learn dry hard facts ; yet for poetry, old songs,
and ballads, the flow of his genius was precocious, swift,
and invincible. The day on which he first opened,
" under a platanus tree," the volumes in which Percy had
collected the fragments of ancient poetry, he forgot
dinner, " notwithstanding the sharp appetite of thirteen,"
and thenceforth he overwhelmed with these old rhymes
not only his schoolfellows, but every one else who would
listen to him. After he had become a clerk to his father,
he crammed into his desk all the works of imagination
which he could find. " The whole Jemmy and Jenny
Jessamy tribe I abhorred," he said, " and it required
the art of Burney, or the feeling of Mackenzie, to fix my
attention upon a domestic tale. But all that was
adventurous and romantic, . . . that touched upon
knight-errantry, I devoured."[1] Having fallen ill, he was
kept a long time in bed, forbidden to speak, with no other
pleasure than to read the poets, novelists, historians, and
geographers, illustrating the battle-descriptions by setting in line and disposing little pebbles, which represented the soldiers. Once cured, and able to walk well,
he turned his walks to the same purpose, and developed
a passion for the country, especially the historical regions.
He said :

" But show me an old castle or a field of battle, and I was at
home at once, filled it with its combatants in their proper costume, and overwhelmed my hearers by the enthusiasm of my
description. In crossing Magus Moor, near St. Andrews, the
spirit moved me to give a picture of the assassination of the
Archbishop of St. Andrews to some fellow-travellers with whom

[1] Lockhart's *Life of Sir W. Scott ;* Autobiography, i. 62.

I was accidentally associated, and one of them, though well acquainted with the story, protested my narrative had frightened away his night's sleep."[1]

Amidst other excursions, in search after knowledge, he travelled once every year during seven years in the wild district of Liddesdale, exploring every stream and every ruin, sleeping in the shepherds' huts, gleaning legends and ballads. We can judge from this of his antiquarian tastes and habits. He read provincial charters, the wretched middle-age Latin verses, the parish registers, even contracts and wills. The first time he was able to lay his hand on one of the great "old Border war-horns," he blew it all along his route. Rusty mail and dirty parchment attracted him, filled his head with recollections and poetry. In truth, he had a feudal mind, and always wished to be the founder of a distinct branch of an historical family. · Literary glory was only secondary; his talent was to him only as an instrument. He spent the vast sums which his prose and verse had won, in building a castle in imitation of· the ancient knights, "with a tall tower at either end, . . . sundry zigzagged gables, . . . a myriad of indentations and parapets, and machicollated eaves; most fantastic waterspouts; labelled windows, not a few of them painted glass; . . . stones carved with heraldries innumerable;"[2] apartments filled with sideboards and carved chests, adorned with "cuirasses, helmets, swords of every order, from the claymore and rapier to some German executioner's swords." For long years he held open house there, so to speak, and did to every stranger the "honours of Scotland," trying to revive the old

---

[1] Lockhart's *Life of Sir W. Scott*, Autobiography, i. 72.
[2] *Ibid.* vii.; Abbotsford in 1825

feudal life, with all its customs and its display; dispensing liberal and joyous hospitality to all comers, above all to relatives, friends, and neighbours; singing ballads and sounding pibrochs amidst the clinking of glasses; holding gay hunting-parties, where the yeomen and gentlemen rode side by side; and encouraging lively dances, where the lord was not ashamed to give his hand to the miller's daughter. He himself, frank of speech, happy, amidst his forty guests, kept up the conversation with a profusion of stories, lavished from his vast memory and imagination, conducted his guests over his domain, extended at large cost, amidst new plantations whose future shade was to shelter his posterity; and he thought with a poet's smile of the distant generations who would acknowledge for their ancestor Sir Walter Scott, first baronet of Abbotsford.

The Lady of the Lake, Marmion, The Lord of the Isles, The Fair Maid of Perth, Old Mortality, Ivanhoe, Quentin Durward, who does not know these names by heart? From Walter Scott we learned history. And yet is this history? All these pictures of a distant age are false. Costumes, scenery, externals alone are exact; actions, speech, sentiments, all the rest is civilised, embellished, arranged in modern guise. We might suspect it when looking at the character and life of the author; for what does he desire, and what do the guests, eager to hear him, demand? Is he a lover of truth as it is, foul and fierce; an inquisitive explorer, indifferent to contemporary applause, bent alone on defining the transformations of living nature? By no means. He is in history, as he is at Abbotsford, bent on arranging points of view and Gothic halls. The moon will come in well there between the towers; here

is a nicely placed breastplate, the ray of light which it
throws back is pleasant to see on these old hangings;
suppose we took out the feudal garments from the wardrobe and invited the guests to a masquerade? The entertainment would be a fine one, in accordance with their
reminiscences and their aristocratic principles. English
lords, fresh from a bitter war against French democracy,
ought to enter zealously into this commemoration of
their ancestors. Moreover, there are ladies and young
girls, and we must arrange the show, so as not to shock
their severe morality and their delicate feelings, make
them weep becomingly; not put on the stage over-
strong passions, which they would not understand; on
the contrary, select heroines to resemble them, always
touching, but above all correct; young gentlemen,
Evandale, Morton, Ivanhoe, irreproachably brought up,
tender and grave, even slightly melancholic (it is the
latest fashion), and worthy to lead them to the altar.
Is there a man more suited than the author to compose
such a spectacle? He is a good Protestant, a good
husband, a good father, very moral, so decided a Tory
that he carries off as a relic a glass from which the
king has just drunk. In addition, he has neither
talent nor leisure to reach the depths of his characters.
He devotes himself to the exterior; he sees and
describes forms and externals much more at length
than inward feelings. Again, he treats his mind like
a coal-mine, serviceable for quick working, and for the
greatest possible gain: a volume in a month, sometimes in a fortnight even, and this volume is worth
one thousand pounds. How should he discover, or
how dare exhibit, the structure of barbarous souls?
This structure is too difficult to discover, and too little

pleasing to show.   Every two centuries, amongst men,
the proportion of images and ideas, the mainspring of
passions, the degree of reflection, the species of inclinations, change.   Who, without a long preliminary
training, now understands and relishes Dante, Rabelais,
and Rubens?   And how, for instance, could these
great Catholic and mystical dreams, these vast temeri-
ties, or these impurities of carnal art, find entrance into
the head of this gentlemanly citizen?   Walter Scott
pauses on the threshold of the soul, and in the
vestibule of history, selects in the Renaissance and
the Middle-age only the fit and agreeable, blots out
plain spoken words, licentious sensuality, bestial ferocity.   After all, his characters, to whatever age he
transports them, are his neighbours, " cannie" farmers,
vain lairds, gloved gentlemen, young marriageable ladies,
all more or less commonplace, that is, steady; by their
education and character at a great distance from the
voluptuous fools of the Restoration, or the heroic
brutes and fierce beasts of the Middle-age.   As he has
the greatest supply of rich costumes, and the most inexhaustible talent for scenic effect, he makes all his people
get on very pleasantly, and composes tales which, in
truth, have only the merit of fashion, though that
fashion may last a hundred years yet.

   That which he himself acted lasted for a shorter time.
To sustain his princely hospitality and his feudal
magnificence, he went into partnership with his
printers; lord of the manor in public and merchant in
private, he gave them his signature, without keeping
a check over the use they made of it.[1]   Bankruptcy

   [1] If Constable's *Memorials* (3 vols. 1873) had been published when
M. Taine wrote this portion of his work he perhaps would have seen

followed; at the age of fifty-five he was ruined, and
one hundred and seventeen thousand pounds in debt.
With admirable courage and uprightness he refused all
favour, accepting nothing but time, set to work on the
very day, wrote untiringly, in four years paid seventy
thousand pounds, exhausted his brain so as to become
paralytic, and to perish in the attempt. Neither in
his conduct nor his literature did his feudal tastes
succeed, and his manorial splendour was as fragile as
his Gothic imaginations. He had relied on imitation,
and we live by truth only; his glory is to be found
elsewhere; there was something solid in his mind as
well as in his writings. Beneath the lover of the
Middle-age we find, first the "pawky" Scotchman, an
attentive observer, whose sharpness became more intense by his familiarity with law; a good-natured man,
easy and cheerful, as beseems the national character,
so different from the English. One of his walking
companions (Shortreed) said: "Eh me, sic an endless
fund o' humour and drollery as he had wi' him!
Never ten yards but we were either laughing or
roaring and singing. Wherever we stopped, how
brawlie he suited himsel' to everybody! He aye did
as the lave did; never made himsel' the great man,
or took ony airs in the company."[1] Grown older and
graver, he was none the less amiable, the most agreeable
of hosts, so that one of his guests, a farmer, I think,
said to his wife, when home, after having been at Abbotsford, "Ailie, my woman, I'm ready for my bed . . . I

reason to alter this opinion, because it is clear that, so far from Sir
Walter's printer and publisher ruining him, they, if not ruined by Sir
Walter, were only equal sharers with him in the imprudences that led
to the disaster.—Tr.

[1] Lockhart's *Life*, i. ch. vii. 269.

wish I could sleep for a towmont, for there's only ae thing in this warld worth living for, and that's the Abbotsford hunt!"[1]

In addition to a mind of this kind, he had all-discerning eyes, an all-retentive memory, a ceaseless studiousness which comprehended the whole of Scotland, and all classes of people; and we see his true talent arise, so agreeable, so abundant and so easy, made up of minute observation and gentle raillery, recalling at once Teniers and Addison. Doubtless he wrote badly, at times in the worst possible manner:[2] it is clear that he dictated, hardly re-read his writing, and readily fell into a pasty and emphatic style,—a style very common in the present times, and which we read day after day in prospectuses and newspapers. What is worse, he is terribly long and diffuse; his conversations and descriptions are interminable; he is determined, at all events, to fill three volumes. But he has given to Scotland a citizenship of literature—I mean to the whole of Scotland: scenery, monuments, houses, cottages, characters of every age and condition, from the baron to the fisherman, from the advocate to the beggar, from the lady to the fishwife. When we mention merely his name they crowd forward; who does not see them coming from every niche of memory? The Baron of Bradwardine, Dominie Sampson, Meg Merrilies, the antiquary, Edie Ochiltree, Jeanie Deans and her father,—innkeepers, shopkeepers, old wives, an entire people.

---

[1] Lockhart's *Life*, vi. ch. xlix. 252.

[2] See the opening of *Ivanhoe*: "Such being our chief scene, the date of our story refers to a period towards the end of the reign of Richard I., when his return from his long captivity had become an event rather wished than hoped for by his despairing subjects, who were in the meantime subjected to every species of subordinate oppression." It is impossible to write in a heavier style.

What Scotch features are absent? Saving, patient, "cannie," and of course "pawky;" the poverty of the soil and the difficulty of existence has compelled them to be so: this is the specialty of the race. The same tenacity which they introduced into everyday affairs they have introduced into mental concerns,—studious readers and perusers of antiquities and controversies, poets also; legends spring up readily in a romantic land, amidst time-honoured wars and brigandism. In a land thus prepared, and in this gloomy clime, Presbyterianism sunk its sharp roots. Such was the real and modern world, lit up by the far-setting sun of chivalry, as Sir Walter Scott found it; like a painter who, passing from great show-pictures, finds interest and beauty in the ordinary houses of a paltry provincial town, or in a farm surrounded by beds of beetroots and turnips. A continuous archness throws its smile over these interior and *genre* pictures, so local and minute, and which, like the Flemish, indicate the rise of well-to-do citizens. Most of these good folk are comic. Our author makes fun of them, brings out their little deceits, parsimony, fooleries, vulgarity, and the hundred thousand ridiculous habits people always contract in a narrow sphere of life. A barber, in *The Antiquary*, moves heaven and earth about his wigs; if the French Revolution takes root everywhere, it was because the magistrates gave up this ornament. He cries out in a lamentable voice: "Haud a care, haud a care, Monkbarns! God's sake, haud a care!—Sir Arthur's drowned already, and an ye fa' over the cleugh too, there will be but ae wig left in the parish, and that's the minister's."[1]   Mark how the author smiles, and

[1] Sir Walter Scott's Works, 48 vols., 1829; *The Antiquary*, ch. viii.

without malice : the barber's candid selfishness is the effect of the man's calling, and does not repel us. Walter Scott is never bitter; he loves men from the bottom of his heart, excuses or tolerates them; does not chastise vices, but unmasks them, and that not rudely. His greatest pleasure is to pursue at length, not indeed a vice, but a hobby; the mania for odds and ends in an antiquary, the archæological vanity of the Baron of Bradwardine, the aristocratic drivel of the Dowager Lady Bellenden,——that is, the amusing exaggeration of an allowable taste; and this without anger, because, on the whole, these ridiculous people are estimable, and even generous. Even in rogues like Dirk Hatteraick, in cut-throats like Bothwell, he allows some goodness. In no one, not even in Major Dalgetty, a professional murderer, a result of the thirty years' war, is the odious unveiled by the ridiculous. In this critical refinement and this benevolent philosophy, he resembles Addison.

He resembles him again by the purity and endurance of his moral principles. His amanuensis, Mr. Laidlaw, told him that he was doing great good by his attractive and noble tales, and that young people would no longer wish to look in the literary rubbish of the circulating libraries. When Walter Scott heard this, his eyes filled with tears : " On his deathbed he said to his son-in-law : ' Lockhart, I may have but a minute to speak to you. My dear, be a good man——be virtuous, be religious——be a good man. Nothing else will give you any comfort when you come to lie here.' " [1] This was almost his last word. By this fundamental honesty and this broad humanity, he was the Homer of modern

[1] Lockhart's *Life*, x. 217.

citizen life. Around and after him, the novel of manners, separated from the historical romance, has produced
a whole literature, and preserved the character which he
stamped upon it. Miss Austen, Miss Bronté, Mrs.
Gaskell, George Eliot, Bulwer, Thackeray, Dickens, and
many others, paint, especially or entirely in his style,
contemporary life, as it is, unembellished, in all ranks,
often amongst the people, more frequently still amongst
the middle class. And the causes which made the
historical novel come to naught, in Scott and others,
made the novel of manners, by the same authors, succeed.
These men were too minute copyists and too decided
moralists, incapable of the great divinations and the
wide sympathies which unlock the door of history;
their imagination was too literal, and their judgment too
unwavering. It is precisely by these faculties that they
created a new species of novel, which multiplies to this
day in thousands of offshoots, with such abundance, that
men of talent in this branch of literature may be counted
by hundreds, and that we can only compare them, for
their original and national spirit, to the great age of Dutch
painting. Realistic and moral, these are their two features. They are far removed from the great imagination
which creates and transforms, as it appeared in the Renaissance or in the seventeenth century, in the heroic or
noble ages. They renounce free invention; they narrow
themselves to scrupulous exactness; they paint with infinite detail costumes and places, changing nothing; they
mark little shades of language; they are not disgusted by
vulgarities or platitudes. Their information is authentic
and precise. In short, they write like citizens for
fellow-citizens, that is, for well-ordered people, members
of a profession, whose imagination does not soar high,

and sees things through a magnifying glass, unable
to relish anything in the way of a picture except interiors and make-believes.   Ask a cook which picture
she prefers in the Museum, and she will point to a
kitchen, in which the stewpans are so well painted that
a man is tempted to put soup and bread in them.   Yet
beyond this inclination, which is now European, Englishmen have a special craving, which with them is national
and dates from the preceding century ; they desire that
the novel, like all other things, should contribute to
their great work,—the amelioration of man and society.
They ask from it the glorification of virtue, and the
chastisement of vice.   They send it into all the corners
of civil society, and all the events of private history, in
search of examples and expedients, to learn thence the
means of remedying abuses, succouring miseries, avoid-
ing temptations.   They make of it an instrument of
inquiry, education, and morality.   A singular work,
which has not its equal in all history, because in all
history there has been no society like it, and which—of
moderate attraction for lovers of the beautiful, admirable
to lovers of the useful—offers, in the countless variety
of its painting, and the invariable stability of its spirit,
the picture of the only democracy which knows how to
restrain, govern, and reform itself.

V.

Side by side with this development there was another, and with history philosophy entered into literature,
in order to widen and modify it.   It was manifest
throughout, on the threshold as in the centre.   On the
threshold it had planted æsthetics : every poet, becoming
theoretic, defined before producing the beautiful, laid

down principles in his preface, and originated only after a preconceived system.   But the ascendency of metaphysics was much more visible yet in the middle of the work than on its threshold; for not only did it prescribe the form of poetry, but it furnished it with its elements.   What is man, and what has he come into the world to do?   What is this far-off greatness to which he aspires?   Is there a haven which he may reach, and a hidden hand to conduct him thither?   These are the questions which poets, transformed into thinkers, agreed to agitate; and Goethe, here as elsewhere the father and promoter of all lofty modern ideas, at once sceptical, pantheistic, and mystic, wrote in *Faust* the epic of the age and the history of the human mind. Need I say that in Schiller, Heine, Beethoven, Victor Hugo, Lamartine, and de Musset, the poet, in his individual person, always speaks the words of the universal man?   The characters which they have created, from *Faust* to *Ruy Blas*, only served them to exhibit some grand metaphysical and social idea; and twenty times this too great idea, bursting its narrow envelope, broke out beyond all human likelihood and all poetic form, to display itself to the eyes of the spectators.   Such was the domination of the philosophical spirit, that, after doing violence to literature, or rendering it rigid, it imposed on music humanitarian ideas, inflicted on painting symbolical designs, penetrated current speech, and marred style by an overflow of abstractions and formulas, from which all our efforts now fail to liberate us.   As an overstrong child, which at its birth injures its mother, so it has contorted the noble forms which had endeavoured to contain it, and dragged literature through an agony of struggles and sufferings.

This philosophical spirit was not born in England, and from Germany to England the passage was very long. For a considerable time it appeared dangerous or ridiculous. One of the reviews stated even, that Germany was a large country peopled by hussars and classical scholars; that if folks go there, they will see at Heidelberg a very large tun, and could feast on excellent Rhine wine and Westphalian ham, but that their authors were very heavy and awkward, and that a sentimental German resembles a tall and stout butcher crying over a killed calf. If at length German literature found entrance, first by the attraction of extravagant dramas and fantastic ballads, then by the sympathy of the two nations, which, allied against French policy and civilisation, acknowledged their cousinship in speech, religion, and blood, German metaphysics did not enter, unable to overturn the barrier which a positive mind and a national religion opposed to it. It tried to pass, with Coleridge for instance, a philosophical theologian and dreamy poet, who toiled to widen conventional dogma, and who, at the close of his life, having become a sort of oracle, endeavoured, in the pale of the Church, to unfold and unveil before a few faithful disciples the Christianity of the future. It did not make head; the English mind was too positive, the theologians too enslaved. It was constrained to transform itself and become Anglican, or to deform itself and become revolutionary; and to produce a Wordsworth, a Byron, a Shelley, instead of a Schiller and Goethe.

The first, Wordsworth, a new Cowper, with less talent and more ideas than the other, was essentially a man of inner feelings, that is, engrossed by the concerns of the soul. Such men ask what they have come to do

in this world, and why life has been given to them ;
if they are right or wrong, and if the secret movements
of their heart are conformable to the supreme law, without taking into account the visible causes of their conduct.   Such, for men of this kind, is the master conception which renders them serious, meditative, and as
a rule gloomy.[1]   They live with eyes turned inwards,
not to mark and classify their ideas, like physiologists,
but as moralists, to approve or blame their feelings.
Thus understood, life becomes a grave business, of uncertain issue, on which we must incessantly and
scrupulously reflect.   Thus understood, the world
changes its aspect ; it is no longer a machine of wheels
working into each other, as the philosopher says, nor a
splendid blooming plant, as the artist feels,—it is the
work of a moral being, displayed as a spectacle to moral
beings.

Figure such a man facing life and the world ; he sees
them, and takes part in it, apparently like any one else ;
but how different is he in reality !   His great thought
pursues him ; and when he beholds a tree, it is to
meditate on human destiny.   He finds or lends a sense
to the least objects : a soldier marching to the sound
of the drum makes him reflect on heroic sacrifice, the
support of societies ; a train of clouds lying heavily on
the verge of a gloomy sky, endues him with that
melancholy calm, so suited to nourish moral life.   There
is nothing which does not recall him to his duty and
admonish him of his origin.   Near or far, like a great
mountain in a landscape, his philosophy will appear
behind all his ideas and images.   If he is restless, im-

---

[1] The Jansenists, the Puritans, and the Methodists are the extremes
of this class.

passioned, sick with scruples, it will appear to him
amidst storm and lightning, as it did to the genuine
Puritans, to Cowper, Pascal, Carlyle. It will appear to
him in a greyish kind of fog, imposing and calm, if he
enjoys, like Wordsworth, a calm mind and a quiet
life. Wordsworth was a wise and happy man, a thinker
and a dreamer, who read and walked. He was from
the first in tolerably easy circumstances, and had a
small fortune. Happily married, amidst the favours
of government and the respect of the public, he lived
peacefully on the margin of a beautiful lake, in sight
of noble mountains, in the pleasant retirement of an
elegant house, amidst the admiration and attentions of
distinguished and chosen friends, engrossed by contemplations which no storm came to distract, and by poetry
which was produced without any hindrance. In this
deep calm he listens to his own thoughts; the peace
was so great, within him and around him, that he could
perceive the imperceptible. " To me, the meanest flower
that blows, can give Thoughts that do often lie too deep
for tears." He saw a grandeur, a beauty, a teaching in
the trivial events which weave the woof of our most
commonplace days. He needed not, for the sake of
emotion, either splendid sights or unusual actions.
The dazzling glare of lamps, the pomp of the theatre,
would have shocked him; his eyes were too delicate,
accustomed to quiet and uniform tints. He was a
poet of the twilight. Moral existence in commonplace
existence, such was his object—the object of his choice.
His paintings are cameos with a grey ground, which
have a meaning; designedly he suppresses all which
might please the senses, in order to speak solely to the
heart.

Out of this character sprang a theory,—his theory of art, altogether spiritualistic, which, after repelling classical habits, ended by rallying Protestant sympathies, and won for him as many partisans as it had raised enemies.[1]   Since the only important thing is moral life, let us devote ourselves solely to nourishing it.   The reader must be moved, genuinely, with profit to his soul ; the rest is indifferent : let us, then, show him objects moving in themselves, without dreaming of clothing them in a beautiful style.   Let us strip ourselves of conventional language and poetic diction.   Let us neglect noble words, scholastic and courtly epithets, and all the pomp of factitious splendour, which the classical writers thought themselves bound to assume, and justified in imposing.   In poetry, as elsewhere, the grand question is, not ornament, but truth.   Let us leave show, and seek effect.   Let us speak in a bare style, as like as possible to prose, to ordinary conversation, even to rustic conversation, and let us choose our subjects at hand, in humble life.   Let us take for our characters an idiot boy, a shivering old peasant woman, a hawker, a servant stopping in the street.   It is the truth of sentiment, not the dignity of the folks, which makes the beauty of a subject ; it is the truth of sentiment, not dignity of the words, which makes the beauty of poetry.   What matters that it is a villager who weeps, if these tears enable me to see the maternal sentiment ?   What matters that my verse is a line of rhymed prose, if this line displays a noble emotion ? Men read that they may carry away emotion, not phrases ; they come to us to look for moral culture, not pretty ways of speaking.   And thereupon Wordsworth,

[1] See the preface of his second edition of *Lyrical Ballads.*

classifying his poems according to the different faculties
of men and the different ages of life, undertakes to
lead us through all compartments and degrees of inner
education, to the convictions and sentiments which he
has himself attained.

All this is very well, but on condition that the
reader is in Wordsworth's position; that is, essentially
a philosophical moralist, and an excessively sensitive
man.   When I shall have emptied my head of all
worldly thoughts, and looked up at the clouds for ten
years to refine my soul, I shall love this poetry.
Meanwhile the web of imperceptible threads by which
Wordsworth endeavours to bind together all sentiments
and embrace all nature, breaks in my fingers; it is too
fragile; it is a woof of woven spider-web, spun by a
metaphysical imagination, and tearing as soon as a hand
of flesh and blood tries to touch it.   Half of his pieces
are childish, almost foolish;[1] dull events described in a
dull style, one platitude after another, and that on
principle.   All the poets in the world would not reconcile us to so much tedium.   Certainly a cat playing
with three dry leaves may furnish a philosophical
reflection, and figure forth a wise man sporting with
the fallen leaves of life; but eighty lines on such a
subject make us yawn—much worse, smile.   At this
rate we will find a lesson in an old tooth-brush, which
still continues in use.   Doubtless, also, the ways of
Providence are not to be fathomed, and a selfish and
brutal artisan like Peter Bell may be converted by
the beautiful conduct of an ass full of fidelity and
unselfishness; but this sentimental prettiness quickly
grows insipid, and the style, by its factitious simplicity,

---

[1] *Peter Bell; The White Doe; The Kitten and Falling Leaves,* etc.

renders it still more insipid. We are not over-pleased to see a grave man seriously imitate the language of nurses, and we murmur to ourselves that, with so many emotions, he must wet so many handker-chiefs. We will acknowledge, if you like, that your sentiments are interesting; yet there is no need to trot them all out before us.

We imagine we hear him say: "Yesterday I read Walton's *Complete Angler;* let us write a sonnet about it. On Easter Sunday I was in a valley in Westmoreland; another sonnet. Two days ago I put too many questions to my little boy and caused him to tell a lie; a poem. I am going to travel on the Continent and through Scotland; poems about all the incidents, monuments, adventures of the journey."

You must consider your emotions very precious, that you put them all under glass! There are only three or four events in each of our lives worthy of being related; our powerful sensations deserve to be exhibited, because they recapitulate our whole exist-ence; but not the little effects of the little agitations which pass through us, and the imperceptible oscillations of our everyday condition. Else I might end by explaining in rhyme that yesterday my dog broke his leg, and that this morning my wife put on her stockings inside out. The specialty of the artist is to cast great ideas in moulds as great; Wordsworth's moulds are of bad common clay, cracked, unable to hold the noble metal which they ought to contain.

But the metal is really noble; and besides several very beautiful sonnets, there is now and then a work, amongst others his largest, *The Excursion,* in which we forget the poverty of the getting up to admire the purity

and elevation of the thought. In truth, the author
hardly puts himself to the trouble of imagining; he walks
along and converses with a pious Scotch pedlar: this is
the whole of the story. The poets of this school
always walk, look at nature and think of human destiny;
it is their permanent attitude. He converses, then, with
the pedlar, a meditative character, who has been educated by a long experience of men and things, who
speaks very well (too well!) of the soul and of God, and
relates to him the history of a good woman who died of
grief in her cottage; then he meets a solitary, a sort of
sceptical Hamlet—morose, made gloomy by the death
of his family, and the disappointments suffered during
his long journeyings; then a clergyman, who took them
to the village churchyard, and described to them the
life of several interesting people who are buried there.
Observe that, just in proportion as reflections and moral
discussions arise, and as scenery and moral descriptions
spread before us in hundreds, so also dissertations
entwine their long thorny hedgerows, and metaphysical
thistles multiply in every corner. In short, the poem is
as grave and dull as a sermon. And yet, in spite of this
ecclesiastical air and the tirades against Voltaire and his
age,[1] we feel ourselves impressed as by a discourse of
Théodore Jouffroy. After all, Wordsworth is convinced;
he has spent his life meditating on these kinds of ideas,
they are the poetry of his religion, race, climate; he is
imbued with them; his pictures, stories, interpretations
of visible nature and human life tend only to put the

[1] This dull product of a scoffer's pen
  Impure conceits discharging from a heart
  Hardened by impious pride!
Wordsworth's Works, 7 vols. 1849; *The Excursion,* book 2; *The Solitary.*

mind in a grave disposition which is proper to the inner man.   I enter here as in the valley of Port Royal : a solitary nook, stagnant waters, gloomy woods, ruins, gravestones, and above all the idea of responsible man, and the obscure beyond, to which we involuntarily move.   I forget the careless French fashions, the custom of not disturbing the even tenor of life.   There is an imposing seriousness, an austere beauty in this sincere reflection; we begin to feel respect, we stop and are moved.   This book is like a Protestant temple, august, though bare and monotonous.   The poet sets forth the great interests of the soul :

> " On Man, on Nature, and on Human Life,
>   Musing in solitude, I oft perceive
>   Fair trains of imagery before me rise,
>   Accompanied by feelings of delight
>   Pure, or with no unpleasing sadness mixed ;
>   And I am conscious of affecting thoughts
>   And dear remembrances, whose presence soothes
>   Or elevates the Mind, intent to weigh
>   The good and evil of our mortal state.
>   —To these emotions, whencesoe'er they come,
>   Whether from breath of outward circumstance,
>   Or from the Soul—an impulse to herself,—
>   I would give utterance in numerous verse.
>   Of Truth, of Grandeur, Beauty, Love, and Hope,
>   And melancholy Fear subdued by Faith ;
>   Of blessed consolations in distress ;
>   Of moral strength, and intellectual Power ;
>   Of joy in widest commonalty spread ;
>   Of the individual Mind that keeps her own
>   Inviolate retirement, subject there
>   To Conscience only, and the law supreme
>   Of that Intelligence which governs all—
>   I sing." [1]

---

[1] Wordsworth's Works, 7 vols. 1849. vii. : *The Excursion*, Preface, 11.

This intelligence, the only holy part of man, is holy in all stages; for this, Wordsworth selects as his characters a pedlar, a parson, villagers; in his eyes rank, education, habits, all the worldly envelope of a man, is without interest; what constitutes our worth is the integrity of our conscience; science itself is only profound when it penetrates moral life; for this life fails nowhere:

> "To every Form of being is assigned . . .
> An *active* principle :—howe'er removed
> From sense and observation, it subsists
> In all things, in all natures ; in the stars
> Of azure heaven, the unenduring clouds,
> In flower and tree, in every pebbly stone
> That paves the brooks, the stationary rocks,
> The moving waters, and the invisible air.
> Whate'er exists hath properties that spread
> Beyond itself, communicating good,
> A simple blessing, or with evil mixed ;
> Spirit that knows no insulated spot,
> No chasm, no solitude ; from link to link
> It circulates, the Soul of all the worlds." [1]

Reject, then, with disdain this arid science :

> "Where Knowledge, ill begun in cold remarks
> On outward things, with formal inference ends ;
> Or, if the mind turn inward, she recoils,
> At once—or, not recoiling, is perplexed— [2]
> Lost in a gloom of uninspired research. . . .
>   Viewing all objects unremittingly
>   In disconnexion dead and spiritless ;

---

[1] Wordsworth's Works, 7 vols. 1849, vii. book 9 ; *Discourse of the Wanderer*, opening verses, 315.

[2] *Ibid.* vii. ; *The Excursion*, book 4 ; *Despondency Corrected*, 137.

> And still dividing, and dividing still,
> Breaks down all grandeur." [1]

Beyond the vanities of science and the pride of the world, there is the soul, whereby all are equal, and the broad and inner Christian life opens at once its gates to all who would enter :

> "The sun is fixed,
> And the infinite magnificence of heaven
> Fixed within reach of every human eye.
> The sleepless Ocean murmurs for all ears,
> The vernal field infuses fresh delight
> Into all hearts. . . .
> The primal duties shine aloft like stars,
> The charities that soothe and heal and bless
> Are scattered at the feet of man—like flowers."

So, at the end of all agitation and all search appears the great truth, which is the abstract of the rest :

> "Life, I repeat, is energy of love
> Divine or human ; exercised in pain,
> In strife and tribulation ; and ordained,
> If so approved and sanctified, to pass,
> Through shades and silent rest to endless joy." [2]

The verses sustain these serious thoughts by their grave harmony, as a motet accompanies meditation or prayer. They resemble the grand and monotonous music of the organ, which in the eventide, at the close of the service, rolls slowly in the twilight of arches and pillars.

When a certain phase of human intelligence comes

---

[1] Wordsworth's Works, 7 vols. 1849, vii. ; *The Excursion*, book 4 ; *Despondency Corrected*, 149.

[2] *Ibid.* last lines of book 5, *The Pastor*, 20.

to light, it does so from all sides; there is no part
where it does not appear, no instincts which it does
not renew.　It enters simultaneously the two opposite camps, and seems to undo with one hand what
it has made with the other.　If it is, as it was
formerly, the oratorical style, we find it at the same
time in the service of cynical misanthropy, and in that
of decorous humanity, in Swift and in Addison.　If it
is, as now, the philosophical spirit, it produces at once
conservative harangues and socialistic utopias, Wordsworth and Shelley.[1]　The latter, one of the greatest
poets of the age, son of a rich baronet, beautiful as an
angel, of extraordinary precocity, gentle, generous,
tender, overflowing with all the gifts of heart, mind,
birth, and fortune, marred his life, as it were, wantonly,
by allowing his conduct to be guided by an enthusiastic
imagination which he should have kept for his verses.
From his birth he had "the vision" of sublime beauty
and happiness; and the contemplation of an ideal
world set him in arms against the real.　Having refused at Eton to be a fag of the big boys, he was
treated by boys and masters with a revolting cruelty;
suffered himself to be made a martyr, refused to obey,
and, falling back into forbidden studies, began to form
the most immoderate and most poetical dreams.　He
judged society by the oppression which he under-
went, and man by the generosity which he felt in
himself; thought that man was good, and society bad,
and that it was only necessary to suppress established
institutions to make earth "a paradise."　He became a
republican, a communist, preached fraternity, love, even
abstinence from flesh, and as a means the abolition of

[1] See also the novels of Godwin, *Caleb Williams*, and others.

kings, priests, and God.[1]   We can fancy the indignation
which such ideas roused in a society so obstinately
attached to established order—so intolerant, in which,
above the conservative and religious instincts, Cant
spoke like a master.   Shelley was expelled from the
university; his father refused to see him; the Lord
Chancellor, by a decree, took from him, as being
unworthy, the custody of his two children; finally, he
was obliged to quit England.   I forgot to say that at
eighteen he married a young girl of inferior rank, that
they separated, that she committed suicide, that he
undermined his health by his excitement and suffering,[2]
and that to the end of his life he was nervous or ill.
Is not this the life of a genuine poet?   Eyes fixed
on the splendid apparitions with which he peopled
space, he went through the world not seeing the high
road, stumbling over the stones of the roadside.   He
possessed not that knowledge of life which most poets
share in common with novelists.   Seldom has a mind
been seen in which thought soared in loftier regions,
and more removed from actual things.   When he tried
to create characters and events—in *Queen Mab*, in
Alastor, in *The Revolt of Islam*, in *Prometheus*—he only
produced unsubstantial phantoms.   Once only, in the
Cenci, did he inspire a living figure (Beatrice) worthy
of Webster or old Ford; but in some sort this was in
spite of himself, and because in it the sentiments were
so unheard of and so strained that they suited super-
human conceptions.   Elsewhere his world is throughout

---

[1] *Queen Mab*, and notes.   At Oxford Shelley issued a kind of thesis,
calling it "On the Necessity of Atheism."

[2] Some time before his death, when he was twenty-nine, he said,
"If I die now, I shall have lived as long as my father."

beyond our own. The laws of life are suspended or transformed. We move in Shelley's world between heaven and earth, in abstraction, dreamland, symbolism: the beings float in it like those fantastic figures which we see in the clouds, and which alternately undulate and change form capriciously, in their robes of snow and gold.

For souls thus constituted, the great consolation is nature. They are too finely sensitive to find amusement in the spectacle and picture of human passions. Shelley instinctively avoided that spectacle; the sight re-opened his own wounds. He was happier in the woods, at the sea-side, in contemplation of grand landscapes. The rocks, clouds, and meadows, which to ordinary eyes seem dull and insensible, are, to a wide sympathy, living and divine existences, which are an agreeable change from men. No virgin smile is so charming as that of the dawn, nor any joy more triumphant than that of the ocean when its waves swell and shimmer, as far as the eye can reach, under the lavish splendour of heaven. At this sight the heart rises unwittingly to the sentiment of ancient legends, and the poet perceives in the inexhaustible bloom of things the peaceful soul of the great mother by whom everything grows and is supported. Shelley spent most of his life in the open air, especially in his boat; first on the Thames, then on the Lake of Geneva, then on the Arno, and in the Italian waters. He loved desert and solitary places, where man enjoys the pleasure of believing infinite what he sees, infinite as his soul. And such was this wide ocean, and this shore more barren than its waves. This love was a deep Teutonic instinct, which, allied to pagan emotions, produced his

poetry, pantheistic and yet full of thought, almost Greek
and yet English, in which fancy plays like a foolish,
dreamy child, with the splendid skein of forms and
colours. A cloud, a plant, a sunrise,—these are his
characters : they were those of the primitive poets,
when they took the lightning for a bird of fire, and the
clouds for the flocks of heaven. But what a secret
ardour beyond these splendid images, and how we feel
the heat of the furnace beyond the coloured phantoms,
which it sets afloat over the horizon ![1] Has any one
since Shakspeare and Spenser lighted on such tender
and such grand ecstasies ? Has any one painted so
magnificently the cloud which watches by night in the
sky, enveloping in its net the swarm of golden bees,
the stars :

> " The sanguine sunrise, with his meteor eyes,
>   And his burning plumes outspread,
>   Leaps on the back of my sailing rack,
>   When the morning star shines dead . . .[2]
>   That orbed maiden with white fire laden,
>   Whom mortals call the moon,
>   Glides glimmering o'er my fleece-like floor,
>   By the midnight breezes strewn." [3]

Read again those verses on the garden, in which the
sensitive plant dreams. Alas! they are the dreams of
the poet, and the happy visions which floated in his
virgin heart up to the moment when it opened out and
withered. I will pause in time; I will not proceed,
as he did, beyond the recollections of his spring-time:

[1] See in Shelley's Works, 1853, *The Witch of Atlas, The Cloud, To
a Sky-lark*, the end of *The Revolt of Islam, Alastor*, and the whole of
Prometheus.

[2] *The Cloud*, c. iii. 502.   [3] *Ibid.* c. iv. 503.

" The snowdrop, and then the violet,
Arose from the ground with warm rain wet,
And their breath was mixed with fresh odour, sent
From the turf, like the voice and the instrument.

Then the pied wind-flowers and the tulip tall,
And narcissi, the fairest among them all,
Who gaze on their eyes in the stream's recess,
Till they die of their own dear loveliness.

And the Naiad-like lily of the vale,
Whom youth makes so fair and passion so pale,
That the light of its tremulous bells is seen
Through their pavilions of tender green;

And the hyacinth purple, and white, and blue,
Which flung from its bells a sweat peal anew
Of music so delicate, soft, and intense,
It was felt like an odour within the sense;

And the rose like a nymph to the bath addrest,
Which unveiled the depth of her glowing breast,
Till, fold after fold, to the fainting air
The soul of her beauty and love lay bare;

And the wand-like lily, which lifted up,
As a Mænad, its moonlight-coloured cup,
Till the fiery star, which is its eye,
Gazed through the clear dew on the tender sky . . .

And on the stream whose inconstant bosom
Was prankt, under boughs of embowering blossom,
With golden and green light, slanting through
Their heaven of many a tangled hue,

Broad water-lilies lay tremulously,
And starry river-buds glimmered by,
And around them the soft stream did glide and dance
With a motion of sweet sound and radiance.

And the sinuous paths of lawn and of moss,
Which led through the garden along and across,
Some open at once to the sun and the breeze,
Some lost among bowers of blossoming trees,

Were all paved with daisies and delicate bells,
As fair as the fabulous asphodels,
And flowerets which drooping as day drooped too,
Fell into pavilions, white, purple, and blue,
To roof the glow-worm from the evening dew." [1]

Everything lives here, everything breathes and yearns for something. This poem, the story of a plant, is also the story of a soul—Shelley's soul, the sensitive. Is it not natural to confound them? Is there not a community of nature amongst all the dwellers in this world? Verily there is a soul in everything; in the universe is a soul; be the existence what it will, uncultured or rational, defined or vague, ever beyond its sensible form shines a secret essence and something divine, which we catch sight of by sublime illuminations, never reaching or penetrating it. It is this presentiment and yearning which sustains all modern poetry,— now in Christian meditations, as with Campbell and Wordsworth, now in pagan visions, as with Keats and Shelley. They hear the great heart of nature beat; they wish to reach it; they try all spiritual and sensible approaches, through Judea and through Greece, by consecrated doctrines and by proscribed dogmas. In this splendid and fruitless effort the greatest become exhausted and die. Their poetry, which they drag with them over these sublime tracks, is torn to pieces. One alone, Byron, attains the summit; and of all these

[1] Shelley's Works, 1853, *The Sensitive Plant*, 490.

grand poetic draperies, which float like banners, and seem to summon men to the conquest of supreme truth, we see now but tatters scattered by the wayside.

Yet these men did their work. Under their multiplied efforts, and by their unconscious working together, the idea of the beautiful is changed, and other ideas change by contagion. Conservatives contribute to it as well as revolutionaries, and the new spirit breathes through the poems which bless and those which curse Church and State. We learn from Wordsworth and Byron, by profound Protestantism [1] and confirmed scepticism, that in this sacred cant-defended establishment there is matter for reform or for revolt; that we may discover moral merits other than those which the law tickets and opinion accepts; that beyond conventional confessions there are truths; that beyond respected social conditions there are grandeurs; that beyond regular positions there are virtues; that greatness is in the heart and the genius; and all the rest, actions and beliefs, are subaltern. We have just seen that beyond literary conventionalities there is a poetry, and consequently we are disposed to feel that beyond religious dogmas there may be a faith, and beyond social institutions a justice. The old edifice totters, and the Revolution enters, not by a sudden inundation, as in France, but by slow infiltration. The wall built up against it by public intolerance cracks and opens: the war waged against Jacobinism, republican and imperial, ends in victory; and henceforth we may regard opposing ideas, not as opposing enemies, but as ideas. We regard them,

---

[1] Our life is turned out of her course, whenever man is made an offering, a sacrifice, a tool, or implement, a passive thing employed as a brute mean."—Wordsworth, *The Excursion.*

and, accommodating them to the different countries, we import them. Roman Catholics are enfranchised, rotten boroughs abolished, the electoral franchise lowered; unjust taxes, which kept up the price of corn, are repealed; ecclesiastical tithes changed into rent-charges; the terrible laws protecting property are modified, the assessment of taxes brought more and more on the rich classes; old institutions, formerly established for the advantage of a race, and in this race of a class, are only maintained when for the advantage of all classes; privileges become functions; and in this triumph of the middle class, which shapes opinion and assumes the ascendency, the aristocracy, passing from sinecures to services, seems now legitimate only as a national nursery, kept up to furnish public men. At the same time narrow orthodoxy is enlarged. Zoology, astronomy, geology, botany, anthropology, all the sciences of observation, so much cultivated and so popular, forcibly introduce their dissolvent discoveries. Criticism comes in from Germany, re-handles the bible, re-writes the history of dogma, attacks dogma itself. Meanwhile poor Scottish philosophy is dried up. Amidst the agitations of sects, endeavouring to transform each other, and rising Unitarianism, we hear at the gates of the sacred ark the continental philosophy roaring like a tide. Now already it has reached literature: for fifty years all great writers have plunged into it,— Sydney Smith, by his sarcasms against the numbness of the clergy, and the oppression of the Catholics; Arnold, by his protests against the religious monoply of the clergy, and the ecclesiastical monopoly of the Anglicans; Macaulay, by his history and panegyric of the liberal revolution; Thackeray, by attacking the nobles, in the interests of the middle class; Dickens, by attacking dignitaries and wealthy men, in the interests of the lowly and poor; Currer Bell and Mrs. Browning, by defending the initiative and independence of women; Stanley and Jowett, by introducing the German exegesis, and by giving precision to biblical criticism; Carlyle, by importing German metaphysics in an English form; Stuart Mill, by importing French positivism in an English form; Tennyson himself, by extending over the beauties of all lands and all ages the protection of his amiable dilettantism and his poetical sympathies,—each according to his power and his difference of position; all retained within reach of the shore by their practical prejudices, all strengthened against falling by their moral prejudices; all bent, some with more of eagerness, others with more of distrust, in welcoming or giving entrance to the growing tide of modern democracy and philosophy in State and Church, without doing damage, and gradually, so as to destroy nothing, and to make everything bear fruit.

END OF VOL. III.

5